A New Star-Rating System & Other Exciting News from Frommer's!

In our continuing effort to publish the savviest, most up-to-date, and most appealing travel guides available, we've added some great new features.

Frommer's guides now include a new **star-rating system.** Every hotel, restaurant, and attraction is rated from 0 to 3 stars to help you set priorities and organize your time.

We've also added **seven brand-new features** that point you to the great deals, in-the-know advice, and unique experiences that separate travelers from tourists. Throughout the guide, look for:

Finds	Special finds—those places only insiders know about
Fun Fact	Fun facts—details that make travelers more informed and their trips more fun
Kids	Best bets for kids—advice for the whole family
Moments	Special moments—those experiences that memories are made of
Overrated	Places or experiences not worth your time or money
Tips	Insider tips—some great ways to save time and money
Value	Great values—where to get the best deals

We've also added a **"What's New"** section in every guide—a timely crash course in what's hot and what's not in every destination we cover.

Here's what the critics say about Frommer's:

"Amazingly easy to use. Very portable, very complete."

—*Booklist*

"Detailed, accurate, and easy-to-read information for all price ranges."

—*Glamour Magazine*

"Hotel information is close to encyclopedic."

—*Des Moines Sunday Register*

"Frommer's Guides have a way of giving you a real feel for a place."

—*Knight Ridder Newspapers*

Frommer's®

Amsterdam
12th Edition

by George McDonald

WILEY

Wiley Publishing, Inc.

About the Author

George McDonald is a former deputy editor of and currently contributing writer for *Holland Herald,* the in-flight magazine for KLM Royal Dutch Airlines. He has written extensively about Amsterdam and the Netherlands for international magazines and travel books such as *Frommer's Belgium, Holland & Luxembourg; Frommer's Europe;* and *Frommer's Europe from $70 a Day.*

Published by:

Wiley Publishing, Inc.

909 Third Ave.
New York, NY 10022

ISBN 0-7645-6737-3
ISSN 0899-3181

Editor: John Vorwald
Production Editor: Suzanna R. Thompson
Cartographer: Elizabeth Puhl
Photo Editor: Richard Fox
Production by Wiley Indianapolis Composition Services

Front cover photo: People sitting at the Playerswacht Cafe
Back cover photo: Bunches of tulips for sale

For information on our other products and services or to obtain technical support, please contact our Customer Care Department within the U.S. at 800-762-2974, outside the U.S. at 317-572-3993 or fax 317-572-4002.

Wiley also publishes its books in a variety of electronic formats. Some content that appears in print may not be available in electronic formats.

Manufactured in the United States of America

5 4 3 2 1

Contents

List of Maps

An Invitation to the Reader

In researching this book, we discovered many wonderful places—hotels, restaurants, shops, and more. We're sure you'll find others. Please tell us about them, so we can share the information with your fellow travelers in upcoming editions. If you were disappointed with a recommendation, we'd love to know that, too. Please write to:

Frommer's Amsterdam, 12th Edition
Wiley Publishing, Inc. • 909 Third Ave. • New York, NY 10022

An Additional Note

Please be advised that travel information is subject to change at any time—and this is especially true of prices. We therefore suggest that you write or call ahead for confirmation when making your travel plans. The authors, editors, and publisher cannot be held responsible for the experiences of readers while traveling. Your safety is important to us, however, so we encourage you to stay alert and be aware of your surroundings. Keep a close eye on cameras, purses, and wallets, all favorite targets of thieves and pickpockets.

New! Frommer's Star Ratings & Icons

Every hotel, restaurant, and attraction listing in this guide has been ranked for quality, value, service, amenities, and special features using a star-rating scale. In country, state, and regional guides, we also rate towns and regions to help you narrow down your choices and budget your time accordingly. Hotels and restaurants in the Very Expensive and Expensive categories are rated on a scale of one (highly recommended) to three stars (exceptional). Those in the Moderate and Inexpensive categories rate from zero (recommended) to two stars (very highly recommended). Attractions, towns, and regions are rated according to the following scale: zero stars (recommended), one star (highly recommended), two stars (very highly recommended), and three stars (must-see).

In addition to the rating system, we also use seven icons to highlight insider information, useful tips, special bargains, hidden gems, memorable experiences, kid-friendly venues, places to avoid, and other useful information:

| Finds | Fun Fact | Kids | Moments | Overrated | Tips | Value |

The following abbreviations are used for credit cards:

AE American Express	DISC Discover	V Visa
DC Diners Club	MC MasterCard	

FROMMERS.COM

Now that you have the guidebook to a great trip, visit our website at **www.frommers.com** for travel information on nearly 2,500 destinations. With features updated regularly, we give you instant access to the most current trip-planning information available. At Frommers.com, you'll also find the best prices on airfares, accommodations, and car rentals—and you can even book travel online through our travel booking partners. At Frommers.com, you'll also find the following:

- Online updates to our most popular guidebooks
- Vacation sweepstakes and contest giveaways
- Newsletter highlighting the hottest travel trends
- Online travel message boards with featured travel discussions

What's New in Amsterdam

Having been in the van of a national economy that did better than most in Europe during the 1990s, Amsterdam entered the general slowdown of 2001 and 2002 with some healthy wind still filling its sails. You see this in a continuing upgrading of hotel facilities, more classy (and costly) restaurants, and an expansion in attraction options.

ACCOMMODATIONS The city's still top-heavy when it comes to hotels, with too many luxury-class lodgings and not enough genuinely good places lower down the price scale. Here are a couple of good tips in the latter category—places that aren't new but that have done something new to set themselves apart from the crowd.

Just off Damrak, but maybe too close to the Red Light District for some people's taste (then again, for others, maybe not close enough), the **Winston,** Warmoesstraat 129 (✆ **020/623-1380**), has lifted itself out of the grunge-hostel class and converted itself into something of an arty establishment. You might even hear some (pretty fanciful) comparisons being made with New York's Chelsea. The overhaul has substance as well as style, and the standard of the guest rooms has benefited, too.

Way out east, not far from the Tropical Museum, the **Hotel Arena,** 's-Gravesandestraat 51 (✆ **020/850-2410**), has done something similar, minus the pop-art scribbling but with greater polish. This, too, used to be a hostel (and before that an orphanage),

and the rambling spaces where once were the 19th- and 20th-century dormitories now house stylish doubles and twins.

In recent years, a lot of Amsterdam's most character-rich high-end hotels have been swallowed up by international chains, and while that hasn't automatically diminished their unique character, it has shaved off a little of the cachet.

Though part of a mini-chain itself, the boutique hotel **Blakes Amsterdam,** Keizersgracht 384 (✆ **020/530-2010**), has gone some way toward compensating for this. A splendid location on one of the city's most prestigious canals hasn't hurt any, but the Blakes really is its own best advocate. See chapter 4 for more details.

DINING There are many—count me among them—who regret exceedingly the demise in 2001 of the superb restaurant Kort that graced a prime canalside site just off Prinsengracht. **Moko,** Amstelveld 12 (✆ **020/626-1199**), its replacement in the same great location, lacks Kort's all-round superiority, but makes up for this to a considerable extent with an adventurous, South Seas–influenced menu and an experimental style that (after 10pm) mixes music from a live deejay with dining.

Amsterdam's redeveloping waterfront is gradually taking on more importance on other fronts, too. In the dining-out category, that includes **Wilhelmina-Dok,** Nordwal 1 (✆ **020/632-3701**), on the north side of the IJ channel. It has a great outdoor terrace that's sheltered from waterfront breezes, and a cozy interior, that together with some fine, plain cooking, more than justifies the short ferryboat jaunt across the IJ.

You'll likely find it easier by now to get a table at **De Kas,** Kamerlingh Onneslaan 3 (**020/462-4562**), in Amsterdam South than it was when this cool restaurant in a converted greenhouse first opened its doors in 2001. It scored an instant, blisteringly hot reputation and had a waiting list for reservations that was months long. All that fuss, and a see-and-be-seen house-style, make it worth a traipse out to its green-field site near the Amstel Station. See chapter 5 for more details.

WHAT TO SEE & DO   There's bad news for visitors who come to Amsterdam to admire some of the best of both Dutch and world art. Most of the city's (and the nation's) premier cultural collection, the **Rijksmuseum,** Stadhouderskade 42 (© **020/670-7047**), is closed for renovation, for 5 long years beginning in late 2003. As a consolation, one wing remains open to display important paintings by the 17th-century Dutch Masters.

At the opposite end of Museumplein, the modern art **Stedelijk Museum,** Paulus Potterstraat 13 (© **020/573-2737**), closes its doors completely, for renovation and new construction, for more than 2 years beginning at the start of 2003. Plans are in place to put some of the museum's collection on view at other city venues.

The **Heineken Experience,** Stadhouderskade 78 (© **020/523-9666**), in the city's former Heineken brewing plant, used to be an unpretentious attraction that gave you a low-key insight into the company and its beer, and that donated the modest admission to charity. Now, after a major redevelopment, it charges (and keeps) a hefty admission for exposing you to an all-arms, multimedia marketing assault aimed at fixing the magic word "Heineken" deep in your psyche. It's not very Dutch to do this kind of thing, but some of the exhibits and hands-on experiences are kind of fun, and most visitors appear to love it.

Another Amsterdam institution that has livened up its act is **Madame Tussaud's,** Dam 20 (© **020/622-9949**), which has reopened after an 11-week face-lift costing 4 million euros. Some of the waxen faces that have been lifted are among the most famous in the world in general and in Holland in particular, both historically and from the present day. After all this artificial excitement, it makes for a sober change to visit the **Verzetsmuseum (Resistance Museum),** Plantage Kerklaan 61 (© **020/620-2535**), which tells the tales of Amsterdam's dark days of occupation, collaboration, deportation of its Jewish community to death camps, and heroic resistance during World War II. It could easily have been a gloomy trip down this particular memory lane, were it not for the brilliant ingenuity that the Dutch Resistance brought to bear on the problem of combating the Nazis. See chapter 6 for more details.

The Best of Amsterdam

Easygoing, liberal Amsterdam has never entirely shed its reputation as a hippie haven, even with an economy that has moved far beyond this cliché. It's surprising how many people still think of the city as caught in some rose-tinted time warp of free love, free drugs, free everything. The heady heyday of the '60s and '70s—if it ever existed to the extent legend and the soft-focus afterglow of memory would have us believe—has given way to new millennium realities.

Prosperity has settled like a North Sea mist around the graceful cityscape of canals and 17th-century town houses. A tour of the burgeoning suburban business zones provides evidence enough of the new priorities. The city government has worked assiduously to transform Amsterdam from a hippie haven to a cosmopolitan international business center, and there seems little doubt it is succeeding.

Fortunately, it has not been completely successful. Amsterdam is still "different." Its citizens, bubbling along happily in their multiracial melting pot, are not so easily poured into the restrictive molds of trade and industry. Not only do free thinking and anything goes still have their place, they are the watchwords by which Amsterdam lives its collective life. Don't kid yourself, though. All this free living is fueled by the wealth a successful economy generates, not by the combustion of semi-legal exotic plants.

A side effect of the city's concern with economics and image is that youthful backpackers who don't wash much, stay in cheap hostels, and think smoking hash is the high point of the city's cultural life, are no longer quite as welcome as they once were. When they come back in 10 years with a salary that allows them to stay at a good hotel, buy tickets for the Concertgebouw and the Muziektheater, eat in a Japanese restaurant, and pick up a diamond or two, why then, everything will be different.

Still, all is far from lost: You can smoke hash all the livelong day if that's what you want. More important, you can enjoy Amsterdam, its culture, history, and beauty, without stretching the limits of your credit cards.

Amsterdam has been drawn to a human scale. Few skyscrapers mar the clarity of the sky and the populace mostly walks or bikes from place to place. The historic center recalls Amsterdam's Golden Age as the command post of a vast trading network and colonial empire, when wealthy merchants constructed gabled residences along neatly laid-out canals. A delicious irony is that the placid old structures also host brothels, smoke shops, and some extravagant nightlife. The city's inhabitants, proud of their pragmatic, live-and-let-live attitude, have decided to control what they cannot effectively outlaw. They permit licensed prostitution in the Red Light District—as much a tourist attraction as the Rijksmuseum or the Stedelijk Museum—and the sale of hashish and marijuana in designated "coffeeshops."

But don't think most Amsterdammers drift around town trailing clouds of marijuana smoke. They are too busy zipping around on bikes, rollerblading through Vondelpark, browsing arrays of ethnic dishes, or simply watching the parade of street life from a sidewalk cafe. A new generation of entrepreneurs has revitalized old neighborhoods like the Jordaan, turning some of the distinctive houses into offbeat stores and bustling cafes, hotels, and restaurants.

Amsterdam doesn't merely have style, but content too. The city will quickly capture you in its spell, especially at night, when many of the more than 1,200 bridges spanning the 160 canals are lit with tiny lights that give them a fairy-tale appearance; or on a morning when the cityscape slowly emerges from a dispersing mist to reveal its treasures. Besides the many canals and bridges, Amsterdam offers up such delights as the Van Gogh Museum, the Rembrandthuis Museum, the Waterlooplein flea market, the floating flower market, antiquarian bookstores, brown cafes (the Dutch equivalent of a neighborhood bar) and tasting houses, and chic cafes and nightclubs.

Perhaps Amsterdam's greatest asset is its inhabitants. Many speak English fluently and virtually all are friendly to visitors. Plop yourself down amid the nicotine-stained walls of a brown cafe to enjoy a beer or a *jenever* (gin), and you'll soon find yourself chatting with an amiable Amsterdammer.

Between dips into artistic and historical treasures, be sure to take time out to absorb the freewheeling spirit of Europe's most vibrant city.

1 Frommer's Favorite Amsterdam Experiences

- **Cruising Amsterdam's Canals:** Save yourself inches of shoe leather by hopping aboard a glass-topped canal boat for a cruise through Amsterdam's beautiful canals, from where you get the best possible view of all those gabled Golden Age merchants' houses. Just ignore anyone who tells you it's a tourist trap—it *is* a tourist trap, I suppose, but it got that way by being justifiably popular. See p. 163.

- **Viewing Old Masters at the Rijksmuseum:** Unfortunately for visitors during a fair part of the upcoming 5 years or so, most of the Rijksmuseum will be closed for refurbishment. If you are one of the lucky ones to get there before the renovation begins (late 2003), you'll likely have to jostle with a crowd for an ideal viewing position in front of Rembrandt's *The Night Watch*. There's more space elsewhere among the 200-plus rooms that display an ocean of paintings by Dutch and other European masters (along with enough other assorted treasures to make you feel like you've been ingesting culture from a firehose). See p. 135.

- **Visiting with Vincent:** At the Van Gogh Museum, where the world's largest collection of Vincent's works is housed in perpetuity, you can trace the artistic and psychological development of this great, unfortunate painter. See p. 138.

- **Remembering Anne Frank:** The clear and haunting words of a young girl trying to survive and to grow up in unimaginable circumstances have moved millions since they were first published in the aftermath of World War II. They speak both for her and, in a way, for all those whose voices were never heard. It's a melancholy but unforgettable experience to spend a reflective moment in the Anne Frankhuis, amid the stark surroundings of Anne's hideaway from the Nazi terror. See p. 139.

Amsterdam Orientation

North Sea

BEVERWIJK

IJMUIDEN

Volendam

Monnickendam   Marken

ZAANSTAD

Noordzee Kanaal

Zandvoort

HAARLEM

AMSTERDAM

IJsselmeer

Schiphol Airport

AMSTELVEEN

BUSSUM

Amsterdamse Bos

Aalsmeer

Westeinder-plassen

Kager-plassen

Amstel

HILVERSUM

Loosdrechtse-plassen

Amsterdam-Rijnkanaal

Leiden

UTRECHT

The Hague

GOUDA

IJssel

Delft

Lek

ROTTERDAM

0   5 mi
0   5 km

Airport ✈   Railroad ———

- **Treating Your Ears to the Concertgebouw:** Take in a classical music concert at one of the world's most acoustically perfect halls, home to the famed Royal Concertgebouw Orchestra and prime stop for visiting philharmonias (the musicians are sometimes pretty good, too). See p. 215.

- **Going Tiptoe Through the Tulips:** Join in with four centuries of Dutch tradition and go overboard for a flower that, though its homeland is among the mountain-fringed plains of Turkey and Iran, has become synonymous with Holland. In spring you'll find them everywhere, but sharp promotion (and at least a seed of truth) has it that the best place to pick up a bunch of tulips from Amsterdam is from the floating Flower Market on the Singel. See p. 159 and p. 210.

- **Hunting for Antiques:** Five hundred and more years of Amsterdam history, including a guaranteed piece of the city's 17th-century Golden Age, is there for the wrapping in the Spiegelgracht antiques quarter. And all you need to acquire it is a fistful of euros or some flexible plastic. See chapter 8.

- **Shopping for a Steal at a Street Market:** You'll have to get up pretty early and be pretty slick to hoodwink a Dutch street trader and score a genuine kill at the Waterlooplein flea market or the Albert Cuyp street market. But bargains have been sighted at both, and local color is guaranteed. See chapter 8.

- **Biking the City:** If you want to look like an Amsterdammer, you have to get up on the saddle of a bike that's so battered, ancient, and worn that no self-respecting bicycle thief would waste a second

of their valuable time trying to steal it (ah, but they will). Then, you go charging like Custer at the Little Bighorn into the ruckus of trams, cars, buses, and other bikes. An alternative is to rent a bike and join the flow of one of Amsterdam's classic experiences—but go carefully. See chapter 7.

- **Riding a Canal Bike:** Amsterdam natives—and even some long-term expats who ought to know better but who are trying to pass themselves off as Amsterdam natives—scoff long and loud at this. Let them. Pedal yourself through the water for an hour or two on your own private tourboat and at your own speed, to view the canals in style (not much style, I'll admit). See p. 166.

- **Skating the Canals:** When the canals freeze over—and sadly it doesn't happen every winter—you'll find few Amsterdammers to argue with the proposition that God is a Dutchman. The chance to go around on the ice is one of the few things that can pry the locals off of their bikes. Strap on a pair of long-bladed *Noren* skates and join them on their favorite winter outdoor activity. See p. 170.

- **Shuttling Across the Harbor on the IJ Ferry:** The short passage by ferryboat back and forth across the IJ channel between Centraal Station and Amsterdam Noord (North) is a great little cruise and provides a good view of the harbor. What's more, the ferries on the shortest routes are free. See p. 57.

- **Crossing Bridges When you Come to Them:** Amsterdam has more bridges and more canals than Venice, a city that Italians are proud to call "the Amsterdam of the South." Find out what makes Italians so humble by crossing as many of the 1,200 bridges over the untroubled waters of Amsterdam's canals as you can reasonably fit in. The views are great. See chapter 6.

• **Living the "Americain" Dream:** Join *tout* Amsterdam for coffee, tea, and *gâteau* in the stunning Art Nouveau ambience of the American Hotel's Café Americain. The service has improved somewhat since a post-war Dutch writer described the waiters as "unemployed knife throwers." See p. 119.

• **Beaching About Zandvoort:** Come rain, hail, or shine (and, often enough, come all three on the same day), Amsterdam rides the train for the short hop out to Amsterdam's brassy but not classy sea coast resort and lets the bracing North Sea air blow away all that hash and marijuana smoke. See chapter 10.

• **Popping a Herring:** Chasing herring is what got this city started, and Amsterdam folk are still in hot pursuit. They like their herring fresh and raw from a neighborhood fish stall. Now, raw herring is something of an acquired taste. But the only way to acquire the taste for it is to try, and the only way to eat it in the approved Dutch manner is whole, holding the fish by its tail, with your face to that wide Holland sky. See chapter 5.

• **Dining Out on a *Rijsttafel* (Rice Table):** The concept of "Dutch cuisine" is generally considered to be a contradiction in terms. Luckily, Dutch colonialists in Holland's former possession, Indonesia, were inventive enough to supply an alternative. Consisting of anything from 10 to 30 little Indonesian dishes, some of them as fiery as a Space Shuttle launch, a

rijsttafel is a great introduction to Indonesian cuisine and a substantial meal in its own right. See p. 100.

• **Sinking a *Jenever* (Dutch Gin):** Spend a leisurely evening absorbing the atmosphere, and sundry beverages of an alcoholic nature, in a brown cafe, the traditional Amsterdam watering hole. These old bars—centuries old in many cases—have seen plenty in their time, and still have space for more. Your first sip of *jenever* must be from a glass that's a "look, no hands" effort, leaning over the bar. See p. 107.

• **Walking on the Wild Side:** Stroll through the neighborhood known as De Wallen, to examine the quaint gabled architecture along its narrow 16th-century canals, peruse the shelves of its antiquarian and secondhand bookstores, and observe the everyday life of the inhabitants as they walk the dog, ride their bikes to the shops, take the kids to school. Oh, yes, and since this is the Red Light District, you might also notice certain minimally attired ladies watching the world go by through their red-fringed windows. See p. 161.

• **Boosting Ajax:** Should you somehow manage to wangle a ticket (saying you're a pal of the Queen *might* help), you can shout yourself hoarse for Amsterdam's soccer hotshots, Ajax, one of the all-time great clubs of world football, at their high-tech stadium, the Amsterdam ArenA, in the southeastern suburbs. See chapter 6.

• **Visiting a "Coffeeshop":** Yes it's true—smoking marijuana is officially tolerated in Amsterdam's very special "smoking coffeeshops." These places aren't your neighborhood cafes, and they're not for everyone, but they're an established part of Amsterdam's alternative tradition. You'll be able to buy and smoke marijuana inside, and no law-enforcement agency is going to hassle you. See chapter 9.

2 Best Hotel Bets

For the full details on these hotels, see chapter 4.

- **Best Value:** Taking all factors into account—price, location, facilities, hospitality, Dutchness, and that indefinable something that makes a stay memorable—the **Estheréa,** Singel 303–309 (© **020/624-5146**), is the best value in town. See p. 81.
- **Best Location:** Just off Leidseplein, the city's most lively square, close to theaters, cinemas, the casino, heaps of shops and restaurants, canal boats, street performers, trams, and general gusto, you find the **Crowne Plaza Amsterdam-American,** Leidsekade 97 (© **020/556-3000**). It's a great location all on its own, and its Art Deco Café Americain is a city institution. See p. 84.
- **Best for Canalside Luxury:** No fewer than 24 old canal houses along the Prinsengracht were converted to create the **Hotel Pulitzer Amsterdam,** Prinsengracht 315–331 (© **020/523-5235**)—which would ordinarily be considered a serious loss, except that the Pulitzer is a genuine prizewinner. See p. 79.
- **Best for Tradition: Die Port van Cleve,** Nieuwezijds Voorburgwal 176–180 (© **020/624-4860**), is one of the city's oldest hotels, but has entirely modernized rooms, so you can celebrate the 17th-century in 21st-century comfort. See p. 72.
- **Best for Families:** The **Crowne Plaza Amsterdam City Centre,** Nieuwezijds Voorburgwal 5 (© **020/620-0500**), provides reliable accommodations and service in a family-friendly environment close to Centraal Station and the main transport links. You also get an indoor swimming pool. See p. 69.
- **Best for Business Travelers:** The **NH Barbizon Palace,** Prins Hendrikkade 59–72 (© **020/556-4564**), is modern, luxurious, stylish, and efficient, and has an excellent location—opposite Centraal Station—and a full range of business facilities. See p. 74.
- **Best for Prestige:** Prestige isn't everything, of course, but the opulent **Amstel Inter-Continental Amsterdam,** Professor Tulpplein 1 (© **020/622-6060**), has it in abundance and offers much more, including one of the city's best restaurants and a superb location beside the River Amstel. This is the first choice of visiting celebrities, so don't be surprised if you see some famous faces. See p. 93.
- **Best Unknown Hotel:** A combination of location, decor, personal service, enthusiastic owners, and general all-round quality wins the small and little-known **Seven Bridges,** Reguliersgracht 31 (© **020/623-1329**), this accolade. See p. 82.
- **Best Budget Hotel:** Many cheap hotels in Amsterdam leave a lot to be desired. Not so the **Museumzicht,** Jan Luykenstraat 22 (© **020/671-2954**), a plain, clean, and friendly hotel in a superb location across from the Rijksmuseum. See p. 92.

- **Best American Welcome:** T. Boddy, American owner of the **Amsterdam Wiechmann,** Prinsengracht 328–332 (② **020/626-3321**), got his introduction to Europe courtesy of Uncle Sam during World War II. He's still enjoying the fruits of victory at his command post on the Prinsengracht, and extends a warm welcome to visiting compatriots. See p. 80.

3 Best Dining Bets

For the full details on these restaurants, see chapter 5.

- **Best for Opulence:** Royalty eat at **La Rive,** in the Amstel Inter-Continental Amstel Hotel, Professor Tulpplein 1 (② **020/622-6060**), as do movie stars, rock stars, opera stars, tennis stars, and even ordinary folks with well-padded pocketbooks. It's luxuriously opulent, the location is great, and the food is outstanding. See p. 129.

- **Best Value:** It breaks my heart to write this, because I know it will only make it harder to find a seat at **De Prins,** Prinsengracht 124 (② **020/624-9382**). But duty calls. When you eat in this handsome, friendly, cozy, warm—in a Dutch word, *gezellig*—brown cafe–restaurant, you'll wonder why you paid twice as much for food half as good in that other place the evening before. See p. 117.

- **Best Decor: Café Americain,** in the Crowne Plaza Amsterdam-American Hotel, Leidsekade 97 (② **020/556-3232**), really ought to be on UNESCO's World Cultural Heritage list. We're talking Americain the beautiful; the Dutch Art Nouveau and Art Deco elegance includes magnificent chandeliers and velvet upholstery. In the past, *tout* Amsterdam liked to be seen here (and some of it still does), but now it's mostly for tourists. Don't let that worry you, though: It's still great. See p. 119.

- **Best Alfresco Dining: Moko,** Amstelveld 12 (② **020/626-1199**), has a terrace beside the Prinsengracht, set back from the water (and the traffic) and shaded by trees. But even the setting pales in comparison to the food. See p. 115.

- **Best Romantic Meal:** Ignore all those whose lips curl into a sneer at such a suggestion—*"Why, the very idea!"*—and clamber aboard an **Amsterdam Dinner Cruise,** run by Holland International (② **020/622-7788**). I won't go so far as to say you'll never eat better, but you have the music, the candlelight, the canals, and maybe the moon over the water, too. See p. 130.

- **Best Ambience:** Short of smuggling french fries into a performance, you can't eat closer to the Concertgebouw than at **Bodega Keyzer,** Van Baerlestraat 96 (② **020/671-1441**). Keyzer has some great stories, some great customers, some great looks, and some great food. See p. 125.

- **Best Grand Cafe:** It's not just because of its balcony overlooking Rembrandtplein, or its youthful palm court orchestra, or its breezy Caribbean atmosphere that somehow mixes happily with its continental look, or even just because of its excellent food, that **Royal Café de Kroon,** Rembrandtplein 17 (② **020/625-2011**), is the best grand cafe in town. It's because of all these things, and because it really is rather grand. See p. 122.

- **Best Traditional Dutch:** It sounds contradictory to say that **D'Vijff Vlieghen** ("The Five Flies"),

Spuistraat 294–302 (© 020/530-4060), is a tad touristy and still traditional Dutch, but somehow it manages to be both. See p. 107.

- **Best American:** Well, Tex-Mex anyway. **Rose's Cantina,** Reguliersdwarsstraat 38–40 (© 020/625-9797), is more of a popular institution than a truly great eatery, though the food can be quite good. You'll probably have to wait a while for a table, during which time Rose's deploys its secret weapon—marvelous margaritas—which is why it's sometimes hard to say how the food tastes. See p. 110.

- **Best Steak:** They've been selling and counting steaks at **De Poort,** Nieuwezijds Voorburgwal 176–180 (© 020/624-0047), for well over a century. Maybe you'll be the lucky one who gets number 7,000,000. See p. 108.

- **Best Vegetarian: Bolhoed,** Prinsengracht 60–62 (© 020/626-1803), takes this title for its *joie de vivre,* romantic atmosphere, and excellent and imaginative vegetarian cooking. See p. 113.

- **Best Fast Getaway:** You wouldn't expect that a restaurant on a train station platform would be a good place to eat, but **1e Klas,** Platform 2, Centraal Station (© 020/627-3306), is just about worth missing your train for. It offers plenty of good choices and standards that go far enough above the usual run of train station buffets. See p. 112.

- **Best Sandwich:** The only problem with **Sal Meijer,** Scheldestraat 45 (© 020/673-1313), is that it's a bit removed from the action. You can have them deliver, but their delicious authentic kosher sandwiches are well worth a tram ride. See p. 120.

- **Best Indonesian:** Amsterdammers seem to think they own Indonesian food (though not as much as denizens of The Hague do), and everyone has his or her own favorite place. With so many Indonesian restaurants in the city, it's hard to pick just one. Still, **Kantjil en de Tijger,** Spuistraat 291 (© 020/620-0994), has a restrained, refined character and consistently good food. See p. 109.

- **Best Brunch:** At **Café Luxembourg,** Spuistraat 22–24 (© 020/620-6264), you can read the international newspapers provided for you while drinking coffee that actually tastes like coffee and munching your way through an extensive range of breakfast plates, sandwiches, and snacks. See p. 111.

- **Best Business Lunch:** If it's a casual affair, many Amsterdam businesspeople will be perfectly happy with a snack from a seafood stall, but if you aim to impress, try the **Mangerie de Kersentuin,** in the Garden Hotel, Dijsselhofplantsoen 7 (© 020/570-5600). The cuisine is the perfect counterpart to the elegant, refined, yet unstuffy surroundings. See p. 130.

- **Best View:** The big picture windows at the **Excelsior,** in the Hôtel de l'Europe, Nieuwe Doelenstraat 2–8 (© 020/531-1777), provide an unsurpassed view of the Amstel River and Muntplein. See p. 103.

- **Best Kids' Spot:** For small diners with big appetites, there can be no better experience than the **KinderKookKafé,** Oudezijds Achterburgwal 193 (© 020/625-3527), where kids even get to cook their own meals (carefully supervised). See p. 118.

- **Best Pretheater Dinner:** A lot depends on what theater you're going to, of course, as proximity can be a virtue in itself. If you are bound for opera or dance at the Muziektheater, make it **Breitner,**

Amstel 212 (© **020/627-7879**), which has lots of practice at getting theatergoers fed and watered in style without adding to the stress factor. See p. 113.

• **Best Late-Night Dinner:** You can't help feeling a little sorry for the staff at **De Knijp,** Van Baerlestraat 134 (© **020/671-4248**), when you saunter in round about midnight. They've been going hard for hours, but are ready, willing, and just about able to do it one more time. See p. 128.

2

Planning Your Trip
to Amsterdam

Amsterdam isn't hard to get to grips with even if you arrive there cold (in the preparedness sense). The local tourist organization, **VVV Amsterdam,** prides itself on being able to answer any conceivable travel question that any conceivable traveler might have, excepting only those that are illegal or of doubtful moral worth (this being Amsterdam both of these concepts have a lot of built-in elasticity). The city is foreign, of course, but not impossibly so, one reason being that so many Dutch speak English.

Of course, any trip to a foreign destination can become an ordeal if not at least minimally planned. Although in the last couple of years the dollar has moved up strongly against the euro, that might change, and the Netherlands remains an expensive country, which for most travelers adds financial force to the wisdom of planning.

To really put your best foot forward, you want to know how much the important things will cost; how you're going to get there; what documents, clothing, and other travel necessities you should bring along; and when you should go to best take advantage of special events in the city. In this chapter you'll find the information you need to help you plan your trip before you leave home.

1 Visitor Information

TOURIST OFFICES
Before leaving for the Netherlands, you can obtain information on the country and its travel facilities by contacting the **Netherlands Board of Tourism (NBT),** which maintains offices in countries around the world. Their Internet address is **www.go holland.com**, and the e-mail address is info@goholland.com. In the **United States,** you can reach them at: 355 Lexington Ave., 21st Floor, New York, NY 10017 (© **212/370-7360;** fax 212/370-9507); c/o Northwest Airlines, 11101 Aviation Blvd., Suite 200, Los Angeles, CA 90045 (© **310/ 348-9339;** fax 310/348-9344); 225 N. Michigan Ave., Suite 1854,

Chicago, IL 60601 (© **312/819-1636;** fax 312/819-1740).

For **Britain** and **Ireland,** NBT has a mailing address only: PO Box 30783, London WC2B 6DH (© **020/7539-7950;** fax 020/7539-7953; www.visitholland.com/uk; information@nbt.org.uk); in **Canada:** 25 Adelaide St. East, Suite 710, Toronto, ON M5C 1Y2 (© **416/ 363-1577;** fax 416/363-1470; info@ goholland.com).

You can also contact the umbrella organization in the Netherlands for the country's many local VVV tourist information organizations (see Visitor Information under "Orientation," in chapter 3): **Netherlands Board of**

Amsterdam on the Web

The official site from the Netherlands Board of Tourism, **www.go holland.com**, is awkwardly designed (expanding your browser to its full size helps), but it does have useful advice. The most comprehensive site is VVV Amsterdam's **www.visitamsterdam.nl**. For a tighter focus on places to see and be seen, try **www.amsterdamhotspots.nl**. If you're interested in an American expat's experiences in the city, go to **www.homepage-amsterdam.com**. You'll love the clear images at **www.channels.nl**, one of the best virtual tours on the Net; you can direct your own tour and chat with others about Amsterdam.

Good eating out info is available from **www.dinner-in-amsterdam. nl** and **www.specialbite.nl**.

Tourism (NBT), Vlietweg 15, Postbus 458, 2260 MG Leidschendam (*ℭ* **070/371-5705;** fax 070/320-1654; www.holland.com; info@nbt.nl).

2 Entry Requirements & Customs

DOCUMENTS

Citizens of the United States, Canada, Australia, and New Zealand need only a valid passport for a visit to the Netherlands for stays of less than 3 months. Citizens of the United Kingdom and Ireland, like all other citizens of the European Union (EU), need only an identity card—but as neither country has an official identity card it makes sense to carry the passport. If you are a citizen of another country, be sure to check the travel regulations before you leave.

If you are planning to stay longer than 3 months in the Netherlands, contact the **Bureau Vreemdelingen-politie** (Foreigner Police Office) at Johan Huizingalaan 757 (*ℭ* **020/ 559-6300**) in Amsterdam for further information.

No health and vaccination certificates are required, and drivers need only produce a valid driver's license from their home country.

Safeguard your passport in an inconspicuous, inaccessible place like a money belt and keep a copy of the critical pages with your passport number in a separate place. If you lose your passport, visit the nearest consulate of your native country as soon as possible for a replacement.

CUSTOMS
WHAT YOU CAN BRING INTO THE NETHERLANDS

Visitors 17 years and older arriving from countries that are not members of the European Union may bring in duty-free 200 cigarettes or 100 cigarillos or 50 cigars or 250 grams of tobacco, 1 liter of liquor or 2 liters of wine, and 50 milliliters of perfume. Import of most other goods is unlimited, so long as import duty is paid and does not exceed a value of 250€. Forbidden products include firearms, counterfeit goods, banned narcotic substances, protected animals and plants, and products made from these.

Duty-free shopping was abolished in all EU countries in 1999. Therefore, standard allowances do not apply to goods bought in another EU country and brought into the Netherlands.

Destination: Amsterdam—Red Alert Checklist

- Have you booked your tickets yet for classical music at the Concert-gebouw and opera and dance at the Muziektheater (see "The Per-forming Arts," in chapter 9)?
- If you purchased traveler's checks, have you recorded the check num-bers, and stored the documentation separately from the checks?
- Did you pack your camera and an extra set of camera batteries, and purchase enough film? Don't worry if you didn't because all of these items are easily available in Amsterdam—but they might cost more than at home. If you packed film in your checked baggage, did you invest in protective pouches to shield film from airport x-rays?
- Do you have a safe, accessible place to store money?
- Did you bring your ID cards that could entitle you to discounts such as AAA and AARP cards, student IDs, and so on?
- Did you bring emergency drug prescriptions and extra glasses and/or contact lenses?
- Do you have your credit card PINs?
- If you have an E-ticket, do you have documentation?
- Do you have the address and phone number of your country's con-sulate in Amsterdam and/or its embassy in The Hague with you (see "Fast Facts: Amsterdam," in chapter 3)?
- Did you pack that umbrella? You *might not* need it, but you likely will.

There are no limitations on the amount of foreign currency you can bring into the country.

At your port of entry you enter either the EU Citizens or Non-EU Citizens section at Passport Control, and then one of two Customs clear-ance aisles, red or green, depending on whether or not you have "goods to declare."

If you're carrying valuables with you, take the receipts along. When you return home, these receipts will be proof that you owned such items before your trip to Amsterdam, and thus will protect you against any unwarranted duty charges. Also, keep receipts for current foreign pur-chases together and accessible to show Customs officials when returning home.

WHAT YOU CAN TAKE HOME

Returning **U.S. citizens** who have been away for at least 48 hours are allowed to bring back, once every 30 days, $400 worth of merchandise duty-free. You'll be charged a flat rate of 4% duty on the next $1,000 worth of purchases. Be sure to have your receipts handy. On mailed gifts, the duty-free limit is $100. You cannot bring fresh foodstuffs into the United States; tinned foods, however, are allowed. For more information, con-tact the **U.S. Customs Service,** 1300 Pennsylvania Ave. NW, Washington, DC 20229 (© **877/287-8867**) and request the free pamphlet *Know Before You Go*. It's also available on the Web at www.customs.gov. (Click on "Trav-eler Information," then "Know Before You Go.")

For a clear summary of **Canadian** rules, write for the booklet *I Declare,* issued by the **Canada Customs and Revenue Agency** (© 800/461-9999 in Canada, or 204/983-3500; www.ccra-adrc.gc.ca). Canada allows its citizens a C$750 exemption, and you're allowed to bring back duty-free one carton of cigarettes, 1 can of tobacco, 40 imperial ounces of liquor, and 50 cigars. In addition, you're allowed to mail gifts to Canada valued at less than C$60 a day, provided they're unsolicited and don't contain alcohol or tobacco (write on the package "Unsolicited gift, under $60 value"). All valuables should be declared on the Y-38 form before departure from Canada, including serial numbers of valuables you already own, such as expensive foreign cameras. *Note:* The $750 exemption can only be used once a year and only after an absence of 7 days.

Citizens of the U.K. who are returning from a European Union (EU) country will go through a separate Customs Exit (called the "Blue Exit") especially for EU travelers. In essence, there is no limit on what you can bring back from an EU country, as long as the items are for personal use (this includes gifts), and you have already paid the necessary duty and tax. However, customs law sets out guidance levels. If you bring in more than these levels, you may be asked to prove that the goods are for your own use. Guidance levels on goods bought in the EU for your own use are 800 cigarettes, 200 cigars, 1kg smoking tobacco, 10 liters of spirits, 90 liters of wine (of this not more than 60 liters can be sparkling wine), and 110 liters of beer. For more information, contact

HM Customs & Excise, Passenger Enquiry Point, 2nd Floor Wayfarer House, Great South West Road, Feltham, Middlesex, TW14 8NP (© **0181/910-3744;** from outside the U.K. 44/181-910-3744), or consult their website at www.passport.gov.uk.

The duty-free allowance in **Australia** is A$400 or, for those under 18, A$200. Upon returning to Australia, citizens can bring in 250 cigarettes or 250 grams of loose tobacco and 1,125 milliliters of alcohol. If you're returning with valuable goods you already own, such as foreign-made cameras, you should file form B263. A helpful brochure, available from Australian consulates or Customs offices, is *Know Before You Go.* For more information, contact **Australian Customs Services,** GPO Box 8, Sydney NSW 2001 (© **02/6275-6666** in Australia; 202/797-3189 in the U.S.), or go to **www.customs.gov.au**.

The duty-free allowance for **New Zealand** is NZ$700. Citizens over 17 can bring in 200 cigarettes, or 50 cigars, or 250 grams of tobacco (or a mixture of all three if their combined weight doesn't exceed 250g); plus 4.5 liters of wine and beer, or 1.125 liters of liquor. New Zealand currency does not carry import or export restrictions. Fill out a certificate of export, listing the valuables you are taking out of the country; that way, you can bring them back without paying duty. Most questions are answered in a free pamphlet available at New Zealand consulates and Customs offices: *New Zealand Customs Guide for Travellers, Notice no. 4.* For more information, contact **New Zealand Customs,** 50 Anzac Ave., P.O. Box 29, Auckland (© **09/359-6655**).

3 Money

CURRENCY

The **euro** (€) is the currency in the Netherlands. There are 100 euro cents to each euro. Eight euro **coins** are in circulation: .01€, .02€, .05€, .10€, .20€, .50€, 1€, and 2€. The seven

What Things Cost in Amsterdam	U.S. $	U.K. £
Taxi from the airport to the city center	35.00	22.45
Tram from Centraal Station to Leidseplein	1.40	0.90
Local telephone call	0.25	0.15
Double room at the NH Grand Hotel Krasnapolsky (expensive)	290.00–340.00	185.90–217.95
Double room at the Tulip Inn Dam Square Hotel (moderate)	225.00–250.00	144.25–160.25
Double room at the Prinsenhof Hotel (inexpensive)	60.00–80.00	38.45–51.30
Dinner for one, without wine, at the Excelsior Restaurant (expensive)	75.00	48.10
Dinner for one, without wine, at Café-Restaurant Amsterdam (moderate)	40.00	25.65
Dinner for one, without wine, at Nam Kee (inexpensive)	20.00	12.80
Glass of beer	2.50	1.60
Coca-Cola	2.00	1.30
Cup of coffee	2.00	1.30
Roll of ASA 100 color film, 36 exposures	10.00	6.40
Admission to the Van Gogh Museum	7.00	4.50
Movie ticket	8.00	5.15
Ticket to the Concertgebouw	12.50–100.00	8.00–64.00

euro **banknotes** are: 5€, 10€, 20€, 50€, 100€, 200€, and 500€. The price conversions in this book are based on an exchange rate of 1€ = US$1. Bear in mind that exchange rates fluctuate daily.

Note: At this writing, the dollar/euro rate was close enough to parity to make the simple mental math of US$1 = 1€ worthwhile for a comparison of prices between dollars and euros. But the rate was changing fast (to the dollar's disadvantage) and the further it moves away from parity the more significant will be any inaccuracy where large amounts are concerned. The dollar/euro rate is sure to fluctuate, but so long as it remains close to 1 for 1, it makes calculation simple for American visitors.

The euro is based on the decimal system, but the Netherlands uses the continental numbering system in which a comma replaces the decimal point. Consequently, you will not see prices written in the familiar format of 1.95, 3.50, 5.00, and so on, but as 1,95; 3,50; 5,00; and so on. The continental numbering system also places a point where we would place a comma, so that bigger numbers will be seen as 1.250,55; 2.327,95; instead of as 1,250.55; 2,327.95; and so on. Just remember to reverse the system you're used to: comma in place of point; point in place of comma.

It's a good idea to exchange at least some money—just enough to cover airport incidentals and transportation to your hotel—before you leave home, so you can avoid the less-favorable rates you'll get at airport currency exchange desks. Check with your local American Express or Thomas Cook office or your bank. American Express cardholders can order foreign currency over the phone at ℂ **800/807-6233.**

For details on **currency exchange,** see "Fast Facts: Amsterdam," in chapter 3.

ATMS

ATMs, which you find all over the city, are linked to a network that most likely includes your bank at home. **Cirrus** (ℂ 800/424-7787; www. mastercard.com) and **PLUS** (ℂ 800/ 843-7587; www.visa.com) are the two most popular networks in the United States; call or check online for ATM locations at your destination. Be sure you know your four-digit PIN before you leave home and be sure to find out your daily withdrawal limit before you depart. You can also get cash advances on your credit card at an ATM. Keep in mind that credit card companies try to protect themselves from theft by limiting the funds someone can withdraw away from home. It's therefore best to call your credit card company before you leave and let them know where you're going and how much you plan to spend. You'll get the best exchange rate if you withdraw money from an ATM, but keep in mind that many banks impose a fee every time a card is used at an ATM in a different city or bank. On top of this, the bank from which you withdraw cash may charge its own fee.

You can withdraw euros from bank automated teller machines (ATMs) at many locations in the city (see "Fast Facts: Amsterdam," in chapter 3, for more details). You find ATMs at Schiphol Airport, Centraal Station and other main train stations, and throughout the city.

TRAVELER'S CHECKS

Traveler's checks are something of an anachronism from the days before the ATM (automated teller machine) made cash accessible at any time. Traveler's checks used to be the only sound alternative to traveling with dangerously large amounts of cash. They were as reliable as currency, but, unlike cash, could be replaced if lost or stolen.

These days, traveler's checks seem less necessary because most cities have 24-hour ATMs that allow you to withdraw small amounts of cash as needed. However, you're likely to be charged an ATM withdrawal fee if the bank is not your own, so if you're withdrawing money every day, you might be better off with traveler's checks—provided that you don't mind showing identification every time you want to cash one.

You can get traveler's checks at almost any bank. **American Express** offers denominations of $20, $50, $100, $500, and (for cardholders only) $1,000. You'll pay a service charge ranging from 1% to 4%. You can also get American Express traveler's checks over the phone by calling ℂ **800/221-7282;** Amex gold and platinum cardholders who use this number are exempt from the 1% fee. AAA members can obtain checks without a fee at most AAA offices.

Visa offers traveler's checks at Citibank locations nationwide, as well as at several other banks. The service charge ranges between 1.5% and 2%; checks come in denominations of $20, $50, $100, $500, and $1,000. Call ℂ **800/732-1322** for information. **MasterCard** also offers traveler's checks. Call ℂ **800/223-9920** for a location near you.

CREDIT CARDS

Credit cards are invaluable when traveling. They are a safe way to carry money and provide a convenient record of all your expenses. You can also withdraw cash advances from your credit cards at any bank (though you'll start paying hefty interest on the advance the moment you receive the cash.) At most banks, you don't even need to go to a teller; you can get a cash advance at the ATM if you know your PIN. If you've forgotten yours, or didn't even know you had one, call the number on the back of your credit card and ask the bank to send it to you. It usually takes 5 to 7 business days, though some banks will provide the number over the phone if you tell them your mother's maiden name or pass some other security clearance. Keep in mind, though, that your credit card company will likely charge a commission (1% or 2%) on every foreign purchase you make.

Visa and **MasterCard** (also known as **EuroCard** in Europe) are the most widely used cards in the Netherlands. **American Express** is often accepted, mostly in the middle- and upper-bracket category. **Diners Club** is not as commonly accepted as American Express. Credit cards are not so commonly accepted in Holland as in the United States and Britain. Many restaurants and shops, and some hotels, don't accept them at all, and others add a 5% surcharge for card payment. You can use these cards to withdraw cash from many ATMs (see above).

WHAT TO DO IF YOUR WALLET GETS STOLEN

Be sure to block charges against your account the minute you discover a card has been lost or stolen. Then be sure to file a police report.

Almost every credit card company has an emergency 800-number to call if your card is stolen. They may be able to wire you a cash advance off your credit card immediately, and in many places, they can deliver an emergency credit card in a day or two. The issuing bank's toll-free number is usually on the back of your credit card—though of course, if your card has been stolen, that won't help you unless you recorded the number elsewhere.

Citicorp Visa's U.S. emergency number is (C) **800/336-8472.** American Express cardholders and traveler's check holders should call (C) **800/221-7282.** MasterCard holders should call (C) **800/307-7309.** Otherwise, call the toll-free number directory at (C) **800/555-1212.**

Should your credit card be lost or stolen while you're in Holland, contact: **American Express** ((C) 020/504-8666); **Diners Club** ((C) 020/654-5500); **MasterCard** ((C) 030/283-5555); **Visa** ((C) 0800/022-4176).

Odds are that if your wallet is gone, the police won't be able to recover it for you. However, it's still worth informing the authorities. Your credit-card company or insurer may require a police report number or record of the theft.

If you choose to carry traveler's checks, be sure to keep a record of their serial numbers separate from your checks. You'll get a refund faster if you know the numbers.

If you need emergency cash over the weekend when all banks and American Express offices are closed, you can have money wired to you from **Western Union** ((C) **800/325-6000;** www.westernunion.com). You must present valid ID to pick up the cash at the Western Union office. However, in most countries, you can pick up a money transfer even if you don't have valid identification, as long as you can answer a test question provided by the sender. Be sure to let the sender know in advance that you don't have ID. If you need to use a test question instead of ID, the sender must take cash to his or her local Western Union office, rather than transferring the money over the phone or online.

4 When to Go

In-season in Amsterdam means from mid-April to mid-October. The peak of the tourist season is July and August, when the weather is at its finest. Weather, however, is never really extreme at any time of year; and if you're one of the growing numbers who favor shoulder- or off-season travel, you'll find the city every bit as attractive during these months. Not only are airlines, hotels, and restaurants cheaper and less crowded during this time (with more relaxed and personalized service), but there are also some very appealing events going on. As an example, the bulb fields near Amsterdam are bursting with color from mid-April to mid-May.

The cultural season is in full swing between September and May in Amsterdam, along with The Hague, Rotterdam, Utrecht, and other nearby towns and cities.

THE WEATHER

In Amsterdam, if you don't like the weather wait for a minute. The summertime temperature doesn't often rise above 75°F (24°C), making for a pleasant, balmy, urban climate. July and August are the best months for in-line skating in the Vondelpark, soaking up some rays on cafe terraces, eating at an outside restaurant terrace in the evening, and going topless on the beach at Zandvoort. September usually

has a few weeks of fine late-summer weather; and there are even sunny spells in winter, when brilliant, crisp weather alternates with clouded skies.

Although the temperature rarely dips below freezing in winter, remember that Amsterdam and much of Holland is below sea level, making fog, mist, and dampness your too-frequent companions. This damp chill often seems to cut through to your very bones, so you'll want to layer yourself in Gore-Tex or something similar in the colder months. There are, however, plenty of bright but cold days in winter, and if the temperature falls far enough, canals, rivers, and lakes freeze to become sparkling highways for skaters through the city and surrounding countryside. Throughout the year, you can also expect some rain. The average annual rainfall is 25 inches. Most of it falls November through January, though substantial showers can occur year-round.

Some pointers on being prepared for Amsterdam's often unpredictable weather: First, invest in a fold-up umbrella and hope you never have to use it; likewise, carry a raincoat (with a wool liner for winter). Second, pack a sweater or two (even in July) and be prepared to layer your clothing at any time of year. Don't worry: You're allowed to leave some space for T-shirts, skimpy tops, and sneakers.

Amsterdam's Average Monthly Temperature & Days of Rain

	Jan	Feb	Mar	Apr	May	June	July	Aug	Sept	Oct	Nov	Dec
Temp. (°F)	36	36	41	46	54	59	62	62	58	51	44	38
Temp. (°C)	2	2	5	8	12	15	17	17	14	11	7	3
Days of rain	21	17	19	20	19	17	20	20	19	20	22	23

THE BEST TIMES TO GO

High season is the spring tulip season (early Apr to mid-May) and the school vacations in July and August. The city is very busy at both times, which

means that hotel rooms are hard to find and bargains don't exist at all (but who wants to tiptoe through the tulips in Nov, or sit on a sidewalk cafe terrace in a snowstorm?). If you're planning to travel at these times, you should book several months in advance. Summer is also the best time for cycling, which is an essential Dutch experience; try a canal bike if you're squeamish about going on the roads.

In winter, room rates are generally cheaper, and cafes and restaurants are less crowded and more genuine in feel. You won't find such a big line to get into the Anne Frank House (though you'll still find a line); you'll be able to stand longer in front of Rembrandt's *The Night Watch* and your favorite van Gogh; and you might get a chance to go skating on the canals. You also get a better view of those canals, because the trees that border them shed their screen of leaves in the winter; and as an added bonus, the lights from all those canal-side windows, whose curtains are never closed, glow with Japanese-lantern charm on the inky surface.

There's no worst of times to visit Amsterdam: It's a year-round stimulation of the brain's pleasure center.

HOLIDAYS

A Dutch holiday can add a festive note to your trip, particularly if it involves a parade or special observance somewhere in the country. But expect banks, shops, and most museums to be closed, and public transportation to operate on Sunday schedules for the following holidays: **New Year's Day** (Jan 1); **Good Friday, Easter Sunday, Easter Monday; Ascension Day** (Thurs, 40 days after Easter); **Queen's Day** (Queen Beatrix's official birthday, Apr 30); **Pentecost Sunday** (7th Sun after Easter) and **Pentecost Monday;** and **Christmas Day** (Dec 25) and **December 26.**

In addition, there are two World War II "Remembrance Days," neither of which is an official holiday, though some establishments close: May 4 honors all those who died in the war; May 5 celebrates the Liberation.

AMSTERDAM CALENDAR OF EVENTS

One of the biggest and most eagerly awaited winter events in Holland is the **Elfstedentocht (Eleven Cities Race),** in which skaters compete over a 201km (125-mile) course through the Friesland province north of Amsterdam. The first race was run in 1909, and it has been run only 13 times since. Perhaps the weather and ice conditions will allow the race to be held when you are visiting. If so, it's well worth going out of your way to see—and even to take part in. Contact **Provincial VVV Friesland** (© 0900/202-4060).
The following listing includes events outside Amsterdam but still relatively close by.

January

New Year, throughout the center, but mostly at the Dam and Nieuwmarkt. This celebration is wild, and not always so wonderful. Many of Amsterdam's youthful spirits celebrate the New Year with firecrackers, which they cheerfully—you could even say drunkenly—throw at the feet of passersby. This keeps hospital emergency departments busy. January 1.

Concert and Theater Season is in full swing at venues throughout the city, such as the Concertgebouw, Muziektheater, and Stadsschouwburg, but also at lots of smaller places. Contact **VVV Amsterdam** (© 0900/400-4040) or **Amsterdam Uit Buro** (© 0900/019-1040). September to May.

Rotterdam International Film Festival. Contact **Stichting Film Festival Rotterdam** (© 010/411-8080; fax 010/413-5132). January 22 to February 2, 2003; similar dates in 2004.

February

Carnival. Amsterdammers' chance to show that they can party just as wildly as their southern compatriots at *their* carnivals in Maastricht and Den Bosch. An objective observer (one who's still sober) would have to report that the Amsterdammers fail miserably, mainly because the southerners are the true Dutch experts on the art of carnival. Contact **VVV Amsterdam** (© **0900/ 400-4040**). Early February.

March

Windmill Days, Zaanse Schans. All four working windmills are open to the public at this re-created old village and open-air museum in the Zanstreek, just north of Amsterdam (see "The Zaanstreek," in chapter 10). Contact **VVV Zaanstreek/ Waterland** (© **075/616-2221**). March to October.

HISWA, RAI. The name might look like some strange hieroglyphic, but this refers to the annual Amsterdam Boat Show at the RAI Convention Center. Holland is big on boats, and here you'll see just how big. Contact **RAI** (© **020/549- 1212**). March 3 to 10, 2001; similar dates in 2002.

Stille Omgang. This silent procession along Kalverstraat is walked by Catholics every year to celebrate the "Miracle of the Host," which occurred in 1345 (see "Amsterdam's Origins," in Appendix A, for the full story). The procession begins at the Royal Palace on the Dam and goes from midnight to 2:30am. Contact the **Gezelschap voor de Stille Omgang** (©020/524-5415). Sunday closest to March 15.

Opening of Keukenhof Flower Gardens, Lisse. The greatest flower show on earth blooms with a spectacular display of tulips and narcissi, daffodils and hyacinths, bluebells, crocuses, lilies, amaryllis, and many other flowers at this 70-acre garden in the heart of the bulb country. There's said to be nearly eight million flowers, but who's counting? Contact **Keukenhof Gardens**

(© **025/246-5555**). Late March to mid-May.

April

National Museum Weekend. A weekend during which most museums in Amsterdam and 440 throughout the Netherlands offer free and reduced admission and have special exhibitions. Contact **Stichting Museumjaarkaart** (© **0900/404-0910**). April 12 and 13, 2003; similar dates in 2004.

Bloemencorso (Flower Parade). Floats keyed to a different floral theme each year parade from Noordwijk to Haarlem. Contact **VVV Noorwijk** (© **071/361- 9321**). April 26, 2003; late April Saturday in 2004.

Koninginnedag (Queen's Day). This nationwide holiday for the House of Orange is vigorously celebrated in Amsterdam, with the city center so jam-packed with people that it's virtually impossible to move. A street market all over the city features masses of stalls, run by everyone from individual kids selling old toys to professional market folk in town to make a killing. Orange ribbons, orange hair, and orange-painted faces are everywhere, as are Dutch flags. Street music and theater combine with probably too much drinking, but Koninginnedag remains a good-natured if boisterous affair. *Tip:* Wear something orange, even if it's only orange suspenders or an orange ribbon in your hair. Contact **VVV Amsterdam** (© **0900/400- 4040**). Gay and lesbian celebrations center on the city's main gay areas and the Homomonument (see "Other Monuments & Sights," in chapter 6). There are stage performances, from belly-dancing to drag, stalls publicizing various gay and lesbian organizations, and food and drink. April 30.

May

Herdenkingsdag (Memorial Day). Countrywide observance honoring the victims of World War II, principally marked by 2 minutes of silence at 8pm. Be on the street at 8pm. Contact **VVV Amsterdam** (📞 **0900/400-4040**). May 4.

Bevrijdingsdag (Liberation Day), throughout the city. A slightly less frenetic version of Koninginnedag (see "April," above), recalling the country's liberation from Nazi occupation at the end of World War II. Canadian troops made it into the city first, so Canadian flags are popular accessories. More street markets, music, and theater. Contact **VVV Amsterdam** (📞 **0900/400-4040**). Gay and lesbian participation includes stage performances, from belly-dancing to drag, stalls publicizing various gay and lesbian organizations, and food and drink. May 5.

Oosterpark Festival. A multicultural festival of song and dance held at the Oosterpark in multiracial district Amsterdam Oost (East). Contact **VVV Amsterdam** (📞 **0900/ 400-4040**). First week of May.

National Windmill Day, throughout Holland. Around two-thirds of the country's almost 1,000 windmills spin their sails and are open to the public, including Amsterdam's six. Contact **Vereniging de Hollandse Molen** (📞 **020/623-8703**). Second Saturday in May.

National Cycling Day, throughout Holland. On this day, Dutch people get on their bikes and pedal. So what else is new? Contact **VVV Amsterdam** (📞 **0900/400-4040**) for special events and routes in the city. Second Saturday in May.

Drum Rhythm Festival, Westergasfabriek. Feel the rhythm in your soul at this annual festival that attracts some good acts. Contact **Westergasfabriek** (📞 **020/581- 0425**). Mid-May.

Floating Amsterdam. Transforms the lower reaches of the Amstel River into an outdoor theater. Performances are held near the Muziektheater. Contact **VVV Amsterdam** (📞 **0900/400-4040**) or **Amsterdam Uit Buro** (📞 **0900/ 019-1040**). Last 2 weeks in May.

Vlaggetjesdag (Flag Day), Scheveningen and IJmuiden. Fishin ports open the herring season with a highly competitive race to bring the first herring back for Queen Beatrix. Dutchflags fly everywhere. Contact **VVV Scheveningen** (📞 **0900/340- 3505**) and **VVV IJmuiden** (📞 **025/ 551-5611**). End of May.

Open Ateliers, the Jordaan. Could be subtitled "Artists Working in Garrets," as around 50 Jordaan artists throw open the doors of their studios to an awestruck public. This is a biennial event. Contact **Open Ateliers Jordaan** (📞 **020/638- 1885**). End of May, 2003.

June

Holland Festival, Amsterdam, The Hague, Rotterdam, and Utrecht. Each year, these four cities join forces to present a cultural buffet of music, opera, theater, film, and dance. The schedule includes all the major Dutch companies and visiting companies and soloists from around the world. Although it would seem that a festival taking place in four cities at one time would be impossible to enjoy, Holland is a very compact nation, and the event's organizers skillfully rotate performers among auditoriums in the four cities. Even for tourists, it's possible to see much of the festival's offerings. Don't wait until the last minute to plan for this event, however; it becomes more popular every year. Contact **Sticht-ing Holland Festival** (℡ 020/627-6566). Throughout June.

Frisian Eleven Cities Bike Race, Bolsward, Friesland. A biking version of Friesland's famous Elfstedentocht Ice-Skating Race (see introduction to the "Calendar of Events," above), based on enthusiasm and the idea that roads and bikes are more reliable than frozen canals and skates. Contact **Provincial VVV Friesland** (℡ 0900/202-4060). June 9, 2003; May 31, 2004.

Echo Grachtenloop (Echo Canal Run). You can either watch or join in as thousands of footloose people run along the city-center canals. The routes are 5km, 10km, and 18km (3, 6, and 11 miles). Contact **De Echo** (℡ 020/585-9222). First Sunday in June.

Kunst RAI. An annual arts fair at the RAI Congress Center, in which many Dutch art galleries participate. The theme is the art of a different country each year. Contact the **RAI** (℡ 020/549-1212). First half of June.

Amsterdam Roots Festival. Various venues. This festival features music and dance from all over the world. Workshops, films, and exhibits are also offered. Contact **Stichting Melkweg** (℡ 020/624-1777). Early to mid-June.

Open Garden Days, Herengracht, Keizersgracht, and Prinsengracht. If you wonder what the gardens behind the gables of all those fancy canalside houses look like, this is your chance to find out. A number of the best are open to the public for a few days each June. Contact **Stichting De Amsterdamse Grachtentuin** (℡ 020/422-2379). Mid-June.

Vondelpark Open-Air Theater. Everything goes here: theater, all kinds of music (including full-scale concerts by the famed Concertgebouw Orchestra) and dance, even operetta. Contact **Vondelpark Open-Air Theater** (℡ 020/673-1499). June to end of August.

Over Het IJ Festival. Opposite Centraal Station, on the other side of the IJ channel. Avant-garde theater, music, and dance performed beside the water on an old wharf. Contact **Over Het IJ Festival** (℡ 020/673-1499). End of June to end of July.

July

Arts Adventure, venues throughout the city. An extension of the cultural program through the previously dormant summer months—when most tourists visit the city. It includes more offbeat and informal events across the full range of the arts than would be the case with the main (Sept–June) cultural program of opera, ballet, and classical music. Contact **VVV Amsterdam** (℡ 0900/400-4040) or **Amsterdam Uit Buro** (℡ 0900/019-1040). July and August.

Tourist Market, Hoorn. Colorful crafts collections are on display in the streets of this pretty harbor town on the IJsselmeer, north of Amsterdam. Contact **VVV Hoorn** (℡ 0900/403-1055). Every Wednesday from July to mid-August.

North Sea Jazz Festival, The Hague. One of the world's leading gatherings of top international jazz (and blues) musicians unfolds over 3 concert-packed days at the city's giant Nederlands Congresgebouw. Last-minute tickets are scarce, so book as far ahead as you can. Contact **North Sea Jazz Festival**

(✆ **015/215-7756;** www.northsea jazz.nl). July 11 to 13, 2003; July 9 to 11, 2004.

Skûtsjesilen, the Frisian Lakes. Sailing races with traditional Frisian sailing ships, called *skûtsjes*. Contact **Provincial VVV Friesland** (✆ **0900/202-4060**). Mid-July.

August

Gay Pride Festival. This is a big event in Europe's most gay-friendly city. A crowd of 150,000 people turns out to watch the highlight Boat Parade's display of 100 or so outrageously decorated boats cruising on the canals. In addition, there are street discos and open-air theater performances, a sports program, and a film festival. (The entire festival's future is in the balance, and subject to the City Council not revoking its permission on "public order" grounds.) Contact **Gay Business Amsterdam** (✆/fax **020/620-8807**). Assuming the event goes ahead, dates are July 31 to August 3, 2003, with the Boat Parade August 2; and August 5 to 8, 2004, with the Boat Parade August 7.

Prinsengracht Concert, Prinsengracht Canal. Classical music floats up from a boat moored outside the Pulitzer Hotel on an evening in August. Contact **Hotel Pulitzer Amsterdam** (✆ **020/523-5235**). Third week in August.

Holland Festival of Early Music, Utrecht. Marvelous concerts of music from the Middle Ages through the Romantic era. Contact **Organisatie Oude Muziek** (✆ **030/236-2236**). August 29 to September 7, 2003; August 27 to September 5, 2004.

Uitmarkt, Dam and other venues. Amsterdam previews the soon-to-open cultural season with this great open market of information and free performances at impromptu outdoor venues and theaters and concert halls. Both professional and amateur groups take part in the shows, which run the gamut of music, opera, dance, theater, and cabaret. Contact **Amsterdam Uitmarkt** (✆ **020/626-2656**). Last weekend in August.

International Fireworks Festival. On the Pier and Boulevard of Scheveningen. Contact **VVV Scheveningen** (✆ **0900/340-3505**). Late August.

September

World Port Days. Events and festivities around Rotterdam's harbor. Contact **VVV Rotterdam** (✆ **0900/403-4065**). Early September.

Jordaan Festival. This loosely organized festival in the trendy Jordaan neighborhood features food, games, fun, and lots of drinking and music in the street and in many cafes in the area. Contact **Stichting Jordaan Festival** (✆ **020/624-6908**). Early September.

Bloemencorso, Aalsmeer to Amsterdam. Every year for nearly half a century, Amsterdam has been the final destination for the Flower Parade that originates in Aalsmeer. The parade features a large number of floats that carry a variety of in-season flowers (so don't expect to see tulips). The parade follows an established route and ends at the Dam. Contact **Stichting Bloemencorso** (✆ **029/793-9393**). First Saturday in September.

Open Monumentendag, all over the country. A chance to see historical buildings and monuments that are usually not open to the public—and to get in free as well. Contact **Vereniging Open Monumentendag** (✆ **020/470-1170**). Second Saturday in September.

State Opening of Parliament. Queen Beatrix rides in a splendid gold coach to the Ridderzaal (Knights' Hall) in The Hague to open the legislative session. Contact **VVV Den Haag** (℅ **0900/ 340-5051**). Third Tuesday in September.

October

Leidens Ontzet (Relief of Leiden), Leiden. Procession and festivities commemorating the raising of the 1574 Spanish siege that came close to starving the town into submission. *Haring en witte brood* (herring and white bread) are distributed. Contact **VVV Leiden** (℅ **0900/222-2333**). October 3 (Oct 4 when the 3rd is a Sun).

Herfstflora, Naarden. Splendid display of autumn flowers at this old fortress town in Het Gooi, east of Amsterdam. Contact **VVV Naarden** (℅ **035/694-2836**). Early October.

November

Leather Pride is a growing happening of parties and other events for gays and lesbians from around the world. Contact **Leather Pride Nederland** (℅ and fax **020/422-3737**). First weekend of November.

International Flower Show. Largest exhibit of autumn-blooming flowers, in Aalsmeer. Contact **KMPT** (℅ **029/734-4033**). Early November.

Sinterklaas Arrives. Holland's equivalent of Santa Claus (St. Nicholas) launches the Christmas season when he arrives in the city by boat at the Centraal Station pier. Accompanied by black-painted assistants, called *Zwarte Piet* (Black Peter), who hand out sweets to kids along the way, he goes in stately procession through Amsterdam before being given the keys to the city by the mayor at the Dam. Contact **VVV Amsterdam** (℅ **0900/ 400-4040**). Third Saturday of November.

Crossing Border Festival, Amsterdam. Literature, pop music, and cinema are combined in this international festival. Contact **VVV Amsterdam** (℅ **0900/400-4040**). Mid-November.

Spiegelkwartier Open House, Spiegel Quarter. Amsterdam's famous art and antiques quarter throws open its doors to all for 2 days—of course, you won't be locked out at other times either. Late November or early December.

December

Sinterklaas, throughout Holland. Saint Nicholas's Eve is the traditional day in Holland for exchanging Christmas gifts. Join some Dutch friends or a Dutch family if possible. December 5.

5 Insurance, Health & Safety

TRAVEL INSURANCE AT A GLANCE

Check your existing insurance policies before you buy travel insurance to cover trip cancellation, lost luggage, medical expenses, or car-rental insurance. You're likely to have partial or complete coverage. But if you need some, ask your travel agent about a comprehensive package. The cost of travel insurance varies widely, depending on the cost and length of your trip, your age and overall health, and the type of trip you're taking. Insurance for extreme sports or adventure travel, for example, will cost more than coverage for a cruise. Some insurers provide packages for specialty vacations, such as skiing or backpacking. More dangerous activities may be excluded from basic policies.

And keep in mind that in the aftermath of the terrorist attacks of September 11, 2001, a number of airlines, cruise lines, and tour operators are no longer covered by insurers. *The bottom line:* Always, always check the fine print before you sign on; more and more policies have built-in exclusions and restrictions that may leave you out in the cold if something does go awry.

For information, contact one of the following popular insurers:

- **Access America** (© 800/284-8300); www.accessamerica.com)
- **Travel Guard International** (© 800/826-1300; www.travel guard.com)
- **Travel Insured International** (© 800/243-3174; www.travel insured.com)
- **Travelex Insurance Services** (© 800/228-9792; www.travelex-insurance.com)

TRIP-CANCELLATION INSURANCE (TCI)

There are three major types of trip-cancellation insurance—one, in the event that you pre-pay a cruise or tour that gets canceled, and you can't get your money back; a second when you or someone in your family gets sick or dies, and you can't travel (but beware that you may not be covered for a pre-existing condition); and a third, when bad weather makes travel impossible. Some insurers provide coverage for events like jury duty; natural disasters close to home, like floods or fire; even the loss of a job. A few have added provisions for cancellations due to terrorist activities. Always check the fine print before signing on, and don't buy trip-cancellation insurance from the tour operator that may be responsible for the cancellation; buy it only from a reputable travel insurance agency. Don't overbuy. You won't be reimbursed for more than the cost of your trip.

MEDICAL INSURANCE

Most health insurance policies cover you if you get sick away from home—but check, particularly if you're insured by an HMO. With the exception of certain HMOs and Medicare/Medicaid, your medical insurance should cover medical treatment—even hospital care—overseas. However, most out-of-country hospitals make you pay your bills up front, and send you a refund after you've returned home and filed the necessary paperwork. Members of **Blue Cross/Blue Shield** can now use their cards at select hospitals in most major cities worldwide (© **800/810-BLUE** or www.bluecares.com for a list of hospitals).

Some credit cards (American Express and certain gold and platinum Visas and MasterCards, for example) offer automatic flight insurance against death or dismemberment in case of an airplane crash if you charged the cost of your ticket.

If you require additional insurance, try one of the following companies:

- **MEDEX International,** 9515 Deereco Rd., Timonium, MD 21093-5375 (© **888/MEDEX-00** or 410/453-6300; fax 410/453-6301; www.medexassist.com)
- **Travel Assistance International** (© **800/821-2828;** www.travel-assistance.com), 9200 Keystone Crossing, Suite 300, Indianapolis, IN 46240 (for general information on services, call the company's Worldwide Assistance Services, Inc., at © **800/777-8710**).
- Only for diving destinations: **The Divers Alert Network** (DAN) (© **800/446-2671** or 919/684-8181; www.diversalertnetwork. org).

The cost of travel medical insurance varies widely. Check your existing policies before you buy additional coverage. Also, check to see if your medical insurance covers you for emergency medical evacuation: If you have to buy a one-way same-day ticket home and forfeit your nonrefundable round-trip ticket, you may be out big bucks.

LOST-LUGGAGE INSURANCE

On domestic flights, checked baggage is covered up to $2,500 per ticketed passenger. On international flights (including U.S. portions of international trips), baggage is limited to approximately $9.05 per pound, up to approximately $635 per checked bag. If you plan to check items more valuable than the standard liability, you may purchase "excess valuation" coverage from the airline, up to $5,000. Be sure to take any valuables or irreplaceable items with you in your carry-on luggage. If you file a lost luggage claim, be prepared to answer detailed questions about the contents of your baggage, and be sure to file a claim immediately, as most airlines enforce a 21-day deadline. Before you leave home, compile an inventory of all packed items and a rough estimate of the total value to ensure you're properly compensated if your luggage is lost. You will only be reimbursed for what you lost, no more. Once you've filed a complaint, persist in securing your reimbursement; there are no laws governing the length of time it takes for a carrier to reimburse you. If you arrive at a destination without your bags, ask the airline to forward them to your hotel or to your next destination; they will usually comply. If your bag is delayed or lost, the airline may reimburse you for reasonable expenses, such as a toothbrush or a set of clothes, but the airline is under no legal obligation to do so.

Lost luggage may also be covered by your homeowner's or renter's policy.

Many platinum and gold credit cards cover you as well. If you choose to purchase additional lost-luggage insurance, be sure not to buy more than you need. Buy in advance from the insurer or a trusted agent (prices will be much higher at the airport).

CAR-RENTAL INSURANCE (LOSS/DAMAGE WAIVER OR COLLISION DAMAGE WAIVER)

If you hold a private auto insurance policy, you probably are covered in the United States, but not abroad, for loss or damage to the car, and liability in case a passenger is injured. The credit card you used to rent the card also may provide some coverage.

Car-rental insurance probably does not cover liability if you caused the accident. Check your own auto insurance policy, the rental company policy, and your credit card coverage for the extent of coverage: Is your destination covered? Are other drivers covered? How much liability is covered if a passenger is injured? (If you rely on your credit card for coverage, you may want to bring a second credit card with you, as damages may be charged to your card and you may find yourself stranded with no money.)

Car-rental insurance costs about $20 a day.

THE HEALTHY TRAVELER
WHAT TO DO IF YOU GET SICK AWAY FROM HOME

If you worry about getting sick away from home, consider purchasing **medical travel insurance** and carry your ID card in your purse or wallet. In most cases, your existing health plan will provide the coverage you need. See the section on insurance earlier in this chapter for more information.

If you suffer from a chronic illness, consult your doctor before your departure. For conditions like epilepsy, diabetes, or heart problems, wear a **Medic Alert Identification Tag** (© 800/825-3785; www.medicalert. org), which will immediately alert doctors to your condition and give them access to your records through Medic Alert's 24-hour hot line.

Pack **prescription medications** in your carry-on luggage, and carry prescription medications in their original containers. Also bring along copies of your prescriptions in case you lose your pills or run out. Carry the generic name of prescription medicines, in case a local pharmacist is unfamiliar with the brand name.

And don't forget sunglasses and an extra pair of contact lenses or prescription glasses.

Contact the **International Association for Medical Assistance to Travelers (IAMAT)** (© 716/754-4883 or 416/652-0137; www.sentex.net/~iamat) for tips on travel and health concerns in the countries you're visiting, and lists of local, English-speaking doctors. The United States **Centers for Disease Control and Prevention** (© 800/311-3435; www.cdc.gov) provides up-to-date information on necessary vaccines and health hazards by region or country (Their booklet, *Health Information for International Travel,* is $25 by mail; on the Internet, it's free). Any foreign consulate can provide a list of area doctors who speak English. If you get sick, consider asking your hotel concierge to recommend a local doctor—even his or her own. You can also try the emergency room at a local hospital; many have walk-in clinics for emergency cases that are not life threatening. You may not get immediate attention, but you won't pay the high price of an emergency room visit (usually a minimum of $300 just for signing your name).

You will encounter few health problems when traveling in the Netherlands. The tap water is safe to drink, the milk is pasteurized, and health services are good. If a medical emergency arises, your hotel staff can usually put you in touch with a reliable doctor. If not, contact the **Central Medical Service** (© 020/592-3434).

THE SAFE TRAVELER

In Amsterdam, if it isn't bolted to the floor somebody will try to steal it—and even if it is bolted to the floor somebody will try to steal it. Be wary of pickpockets on trams, buses, and Metro trains, and in train and Metro stations. Constant public announcements at Centraal Station and Schiphol Airport warn about pickpockets, and signs on the trams say in a multitude of languages ATTENTION: PICKPOCKETS. Drivers occasionally recognize members of the fraternity (and sorority) who board their vehicle and will put out an announcement for passengers to watch out—with everyone now on high alert the thieves usually slink off at the next stop. Pickpockets and other thieves often wait until you are occupied or distracted—or act to occupy or distract you—before making their move. Consider wearing a money belt. Women should wear their purse crossed over their shoulder so that it hangs in front, with the clasp or zipper facing in. Backpacks worn on the back are an open invitation to thieves, so either don't wear them like this or don't put anything valuable in them.

Violence is not unknown to Amsterdam, but it's not at all a violent city (save for an occasional incident of foreign drug dealers whacking each other, which, unless innocents are caught in the crossfire, usually merits a single-sentence news story on p. 21 of the local paper). Drug-related crime is prevalent, most of it nonviolent, relatively minor, and opportunistic, such as the rampant stealing of bikes and the pickpocketing referred to above. Mugging and armed robbery do happen, though incidents are not common.

There are some risky areas, especially in and around the Red Light District. Be wary of walking alone after dark through narrow alleyways and along empty stretches of canal. Stick to populated thoroughfares whenever possible. Don't use ATMs at night in quiet areas. It's wise to stay out of Vondelpark at night, but there are cafes on the edge of the park that are busy until closing time.

The rules about not walking alone in poorly lit and unpopulated areas at night apply especially to women. Although Amsterdam is generally safe, incidents of harassment do occur, and rape is not unknown. Public transportation is usually busy even late at night, so you generally won't have to worry about being alone in a tram or Metro train. Sit close to the driver, where this is possible, if you feel nervous. Many local women go around by bike at night.

Amsterdam has some weird folks who may lock onto you for one reason or another. If you can't shrug them off, go into a cafe or hotel and either wait until they leave or call a taxi to take you away. More common are beggars. The generous Dutch welfare system ensures that few, if any, locals need to resort to panhandling. Those who do this might be drug addicts, illegal immigrants, young visitors trying to make their money last longer, lazy ne'er-do-wells—and some genuine hardship and hard-luck cases. If you are prepared to give money to these people, keep some coins (or bills!) handy rather than have to go rummaging through your billfold or purse, which might get grabbed by the intended recipient of your generosity.

Note: Listing some of the possible dangers together like this can give a false impression of the threat of crime in Amsterdam. There is no need to be afraid to do the things you want to do. Amsterdammers certainly aren't. Just remember to exercise the usual rules of caution and observation that apply in any big city. Stay alert. Be aware of your immediate surroundings. Report any crime committed against you to the police.

6 Tips for Travelers with Special Needs

TRAVELERS WITH DISABILITIES

Most disabilities shouldn't stop anyone from traveling. There are more options and resources out there than ever before.

The old center of Amsterdam— filled with narrow cobbled streets, steep humpback bridges, zillions of little barrier pillars called *Amsterdammetjes,* and bicycles parked all over the place—can be hard going. But many hotels and restaurants provide easy access for people with disabilities, and some display the international wheelchair symbol in their brochures and advertising. It's always a good idea to call ahead to find out just what the situation is before you book; in particular, bear in mind that many older hotels have no elevator and have steep, narrow stairways. Many, but not all, museums and other sights are wheelchair accessible, wholly or partly, and some have adapted toilets. Always call ahead to check on accessibility at sights you wish to visit.

The Netherlands Board of Tourism issues a *Holland for the Handicapped* brochure. Schiphol Airport has a service to help travelers with disabilities through the airport. Not all trams in Amsterdam are easily accessible for wheelchairs, but the new trams being introduced on some routes have low central doors that are accessible. The Metro system is fully accessible, but that's not as good as it sounds because few Metro stations are near places where visitors want to go. Taxis are also difficult, but new mini-van taxis are an improvement. Or, call ahead to book with **Boonstra Taxis** (© 020/613-4134), which has wheelchair-accessible cabs. There's comprehensive assistance for travelers on **Netherlands Railways** (© 030/235-5555) trains and in stations. If you give them a day's notice of your journey by visiting a station or calling ahead they can arrange for assistance along the way.

AGENCIES/OPERATORS

- **Flying Wheels Travel** (© 800/535-6790; www.flyingwheels travel.com) offers escorted tours and cruises that emphasize sports and private tours in minivans with lifts.
- **Access Adventures** (© 716/889-9096), a Rochester, New York–based agency, offers customized itineraries for a variety of travelers with disabilities.
- **Accessible Journeys** (© 800/TINGLES or 610/521-0339; www.disabilitytravel.com) caters specifically to slow walkers and wheelchair travelers and their families and friends.

ORGANIZATIONS

- **The Moss Rehab Hospital** (© 215/456-9603; www.moss resourcenet.org) provides friendly, helpful phone assistance through its **Travel Information Service.**
- **The Society for Accessible Travel and Hospitality** (© 212/447-7284; fax 212-725-8253; www.sath.org) offers a wealth of travel resources for all types of disabilities and informed recommendations on destinations, access guides, travel agents, tour operators, vehicle rentals, and companion services. Annual membership costs $45 for adults; $30 for seniors and students.
- **The American Foundation for the Blind** (© 800/232-5463; www.afb.org) provides information on traveling with Seeing Eye dogs.

- **The Royal Association for Disability and Rehabilitation (RADAR),** Unit 12, City Forum, 250 City Rd., London EC1V 8AF (© 020/7250-3222), publishes three holiday "fact packs" for £2 each or £5 for all three. The first one provides general information, including planning and booking a holiday, insurance, and finances; the second outlines transportation available when going abroad and equipment for rent; the third covers specialized accommodations.

PUBLICATIONS

- **Mobility International USA** (© 541/343-1284; www.miusa.org) publishes *A World of Options,* a 658-page book of resources, covering everything from biking trips to scuba outfitters, and a biannual newsletter, *Over the Rainbow.* Annual membership is $35.
- **Twin Peaks Press** (© 360/694-2462) publishes travel-related books for travelers with special needs.
- *Open World for Disability and Mature Travel* magazine, published by the Society for Accessible Travel and Hospitality (see above), is full of good resources and information. A year's subscription is $13 ($21 outside the U.S.).

GAY & LESBIAN TRAVELERS

In Amsterdam, you can get information, or just meet people, by visiting **COC,** Rozenstraat 14 (© 020/626-3087; www.cocamsterdam.nl), the Amsterdam branch of the Dutch lesbian and gay organization. On the premises there is a daytime cafe serving coffee and quiches, a meeting space for special interest groups, weekend discos (mainly men on Fri, women on Sat), and a special ethnic evening called Strange Fruit on Sundays. The **Gay and Lesbian Switchboard** (© 020/623-6565;

www.switchboard.nl), open daily from 10am to 10pm, can provide you with all kinds of information and advice.

You shouldn't have much trouble finding information about gay and lesbian bars and clubs because they are well publicized. Also see "Gay & Lesbian Bars" under "The Bar Scene" in chapter 9. The free biweekly listings magazine *Shark,* amusingly subtitled "Underwater Amsterdam," is a great source of cultural information, in particular for the off-beat and alternative scenes, and comes with a centerfold pullout, titled *Queer Fish,* which has excellent lesbian and gay listings. *Gay News Amsterdam* and *Gay & Night,* competing bilingual monthly magazines in both Dutch and English, are available free in gay establishments around the city but lack extensive listings information.

The **International Gay & Lesbian Travel Association** (IGLTA) (© **800/ 448-8550** or 954/776-2626; fax 954/ 776-3303; www.iglta.org) links travelers up with gay-friendly hoteliers, tour operators, and airline and cruise-line representatives. It offers monthly newsletters, marketing mailings, and a membership directory that's updated once a year. Membership is $200 yearly, plus a $100 administration fee for new members.

AGENCIES/OPERATORS
- **Above and Beyond Tours** (© **800/397-2681;** www.above beyondtours.com) offers gay and lesbian tours worldwide and is the exclusive gay and lesbian tour operator for United Airlines.
- **Now, Voyager** (© **800/255- 6951;** www.nowvoyager.com) is a San Francisco–based gay-owned and -operated travel service.
- **Olivia Cruises & Resorts** (© **800/631-6277** or 510/655- 0364; http://oliviatravel.com) charters entire resorts and ships

for exclusive lesbian vacations all over the world.

PUBLICATIONS
- *Frommer's Gay & Lesbian Europe* is an excellent travel resource.
- *Out and About* (© **800/929- 2268** or 415/644-8044; www.out andabout.com) offers guidebooks and a newsletter 10 times a year packed with solid information on the global gay and lesbian scene.
- *Spartacus International Gay Guide* and *Odysseus* are good, annual English-language guidebook focused on gay men, with some information for lesbians. You can get them from most gay and lesbian bookstores, or order them from **Giovanni's Room** bookstore, 1145 Pine St., Philadelphia, PA 19107 (© **215/ 923-2960;** www.giovannisroom. com).
- *Gay Travel A to Z: The World of Gay & Lesbian Travel Options at Your Fingertips,* by Marianne Ferrari (Ferrari Publications), is a very good gay and lesbian guidebook series.

SENIOR TRAVEL
Mention the fact that you're a senior when you first make your travel reservations. All major airlines and many hotels offer discounts for seniors. Major airlines also offer coupons for domestic travel for seniors over sixty. Typically, a book of four coupons costs less than $700, which means you can fly anywhere in the continental U.S. for under $350 round-trip. In most cities, people over the age of 60 qualify for reduced admission to theaters, museums, and other attractions, as well as discounted fares on public transportation.

Sightseeing attractions and entertainments in the Netherlands often offer senior discounts, but some of these places offer these reductions only to Dutch citizens, on production of an appropriate ID. Be sure to ask when you buy your ticket.

In Amsterdam, the **VVV tourist offices** can furnish addresses and telephone numbers for church and social organizations whose activities are slanted toward the upper age brackets. They can also advise you of municipal social agencies for help with specific problems.

Members of **AARP** (formerly known as the American Association of Retired Persons), 601 E St. NW, Washington, DC 20049 (© **800/ 424-3410** or 202/434-2277; www. aarp.org), get discounts on hotels, airfares, and car rentals. AARP offers members a wide range of benefits, including *Modern Maturity* magazine and a monthly newsletter. Anyone over 50 can join.

The **Alliance for Retired Americans,** 8403 Colesville Rd., Suite 1200, Silver Spring, MD 20910 (© **301/ 578-8422;** www.retiredamericans. org), offers a newsletter six times a year and discounts on hotel and auto rentals; annual dues are $13 per person or couple. *Note:* Members of the former National Council of Senior Citizens receive automatic membership in the Alliance.

AGENCIES/OPERATORS

- **Grand Circle Travel** (© **800/ 221-2610** or 617/350-7500; www.gct.com) offers package deals for the 50-plus market, mostly of the tour-bus variety, with free trips thrown in for those who organize groups of 10 or more.
- **Elderhostel** (© **877/426-8056;** www.elderhostel.org) arranges study programs for those aged 55 and over (and a spouse or companion of any age) in the United States and in more than 80 countries around the world. Most

courses last five to seven days in the United States (2–4 weeks abroad), and many include airfare, accommodations in university dormitories or modest inns, meals, and tuition.

- **Interhostel** (© **800/733-9753;** www.learn.unh.edu/interhostel), organized by the University of New Hampshire, also offers educational travel for seniors. On these escorted tours, the days are packed with seminars, lectures, and field trips, with sightseeing led by academic experts. **Interhostel** takes travelers 50 and over (with companions over 40), and offers one- and two-week trips, mostly international.

PUBLICATIONS

- *The Book of Deals* is a collection of more than 1,000 senior discounts on airlines, lodging, tours, and attractions around the country; it's available for $9.95 by calling © **800/460-6676**.
- *101 Tips for the Mature Traveler* is available from Grand Circle Travel (© **800/221-2610** or 617/ 350-7500; fax 617/346-6700).
- *The 50+ Traveler's Guidebook* (St. Martin's Press).
- *Unbelievably Good Deals and Great Adventures That You Absolutely Can't Get Unless You're Over 50* (Contemporary Publishing Co.).

FAMILY TRAVEL

The family vacation is a rite of passage for many households, one that in a split second can devolve into a *National Lampoon* farce. But as any veteran family vacationer will assure you, a family trip can be among the most pleasurable and rewarding times of your life.

Arrange ahead of time for such necessities as a crib, bottle warmer, and car seat (in the Netherlands, small children are not allowed to ride in the front seat). For information on babysitters, see "Fast Facts: Amsterdam," in chapter 3.

AGENCIES/OPERATORS

Familyhostel (© **800/733-9753;** www.learn.unh.edu/familyhostel) takes the whole family on moderately priced domestic and international learning vacations. All trip details are handled by the program staff, and lectures, field trips, and sightseeing are guided by a team of academics. For kids ages 8 to 15 accompanied by their parents and/or grandparents.

PUBLICATIONS

How to Take Great Trips with Your Kids (The Harvard Common Press) is full of good general advice that can apply to travel anywhere.

WEBSITES

- **Family Travel Network** (www. familytravelnetwork.com) offers travel tips and reviews of family-friendly destinations, vacation deals, and thoughtful features such as "What to Do When Your Kids Are Afraid to Travel" and "Kid-Style Camping."
- **Travel with Your Children** (www.travelwithyourkids.com) is a comprehensive site offering sound advice for traveling with children.
- **The Busy Person's Guide to Travel with Children** (http://wz.com/travel/TravelingWith Children.html) offers a "45-second newsletter" where experts weigh in on the best websites and resources for tips for traveling with children.

WOMEN TRAVELERS
AGENCIES/OPERATORS

- **Women Welcome Women World Wide (5W)** (© **203/259-7832** in the U.S.; www.womenwelcome women.org.uk) works to foster international friendships by enabling women of different countries to visit one another (men can come along on the trips; they just can't join the club). It's a big, active organization, with more than 3,000 members from all walks of life in some 70 countries.
- **The Women's Travel Club** (© **800/480-4448;** www.womens travelclub.com) was designed by a woman in search of female travel companions because her husband preferred work to travel. Now the group organizes 25 to 30 tours a year, with an emphasis on foreign culture, scenery, and safety.

PUBLICATIONS

- The Virago ***Women's Travel Guide*** series is excellent but covers only three cities to date: London, San Francisco, and Amsterdam.
- ***Safety and Security for Women Who Travel,*** by Sheila Swan Laufer and Peter Laufer (Travelers' Tales, Inc.), offers common-sense advice and tips on safe travel.

WEBSITE

Journeywoman (www.journey woman.com) is a lively travel resource just for women.

SINGLE TRAVELERS

Many people prefer traveling alone. Unfortunately, the solo traveler is often forced to pay a punishing "single supplement" charged by many resorts, cruise lines, and tours for the privilege of sleeping alone.

Many reputable tour companies offer single-only trips. Among the 2002 bicycle and walking tours offered by **Experience Plus!** (© **800/ 685-4565;** fax 970-493-0377; www. xplus.com) are a single-only cycling trip from Venice to Florence and a bike tour of Costa Rica. **Backroads** (© **800/462-2848;** www.backroads. com) offers more than 260 active trips to some 60 destinations worldwide, including Bali, Belize, and Ireland.

OPERATORS/ROOMMATE FINDERS

- **Travel Companion Exchange (TCE)** (© 631/454-0880; www.travelcompanions.com) is one of the nation's oldest roommate finders for single travelers. Register with them and find a travel mate who will split the cost of the room with you and be around as little, or as often, as you like during the day.
- **Travel Buddies Singles Travel Club** (© 800/998-9099; www.travelbuddiesworldwide.com) runs small, intimate, single-friendly group trips and will match you with a roommate free of charge and save you the cost of single supplements.
- **TravelChums** (© 212/799-6464; www.travelchums.com) is an Internet-only travel-companion matching service hosted by respected New York–based Shaw Guides travel service.

- **The Single Gourmet Club** (© 212/980-8788; fax 212/980-3138; www.singlegourmetny.com), is the charter club of an international social, dining, and travel club for singles of all ages, with offices in 21 cities in the USA and Canada. Membership costs $75 for the first year; $40 to renew.

PUBLICATIONS

- *Traveling Solo: Advice and Ideas for More Than 250 Great Vacations,* by Eleanor Berman (Globe Pequot), gives advice on traveling alone, whether on your own or on a group tour.
- *Outdoor Singles Network* (P.O. Box 781, Haines, AK 99827; http://kcd.com/ci/osn) is a quarterly newsletter for outdoor-loving singles, ages 19 to 90. The network will help you find a travel companion, pen pal, or soulmate. Subscriptions are $55, and your own personal ad is printed free in the next issue. Current issues are $15.

7 Getting There

BY PLANE
FROM THE U.S. Partner airlines **KLM Royal Dutch Airlines** (© 800/374-7747; www.klm.com) and **Northwest Airlines** (© 800/447-4747; www.nwa.com), together offer direct flights and easy connections from most U.S. cities to Amsterdam's Schiphol Airport. These include service twice daily from New York; daily from Chicago, Los Angeles, and Houston; and two to six times a week from Atlanta, Baltimore, Boston, Detroit, Memphis, Minneapolis/St. Paul, San Francisco, Orlando, and Washington, D.C.

Other airlines fly direct from the United States to Amsterdam. **United Airlines** (© 800/241-6522; www.ual.com) flies nonstop from

Washington Dulles. **Delta Airlines** (© 800/241-4141; www.delta-air.com) has daily nonstop service from Atlanta and New York. **Martinair** (© 800/627-8462; www.martinairusa.com) has nonstop flights year-round from Miami, Orlando, Tampa, and Denver, and from May to September from Newark, Los Angeles, and Oakland.

FROM CANADA KLM/Northwest (© 800/361-5073; www.klm.com; www.nwa.com) has daily nonstop flights from Toronto, and several flights a week from Calgary, Montreal, Ottawa, Winnipeg, and Vancouver.

Air Canada (© 800/555-1212; www.aircanada.ca) flies daily from Toronto to Amsterdam.

FROM THE U.K. London and many smaller British cities have daily flights by **British Airways** (© 0845/773-3377 www.britishairways.com), **KLM UK** (© 0870/507-4074; www.klmuk.com), and **British Midland** (© 0870/607-0555; www.british midland.co.uk).

Easy Jet, from London (Gatwick and Luton), Liverpool, Edinburgh, Glasgow, and Belfast to Amsterdam: UK (© 0870/600-0000); Holland (© 023/568-4880; www.easyjet.com).

FROM IRELAND Aer Lingus (© 01/886-8888; www.aerlingus.ie) flies daily from Dublin.

FROM AUSTRALIA KLM (© 1300/303-747; www.klm.com) flies from Sydney to Amsterdam 3 days a week. **Qantas** (© 800/227-4500; www.qantas.com.au) flies twice a week.

FROM NEW ZEALAND KLM (© 09/309-1782; www.klm.com) flies from Auckland to Amsterdam.

NEW AIR TRAVEL SECURITY MEASURES

In the wake of the terrorist attacks of September 11, 2001, the airline industry began implementing sweeping security measures in airports. Expect a lengthy check-in process and extensive delays. Although regulations vary from airline to airline, you can expedite the process by taking the following steps:

- **Arrive early.** Arrive at the airport at least 2 hours before your scheduled flight.
- **Try not to drive your car to the airport.** Parking and curbside access to the terminal may be limited. Call ahead and check.
- **Don't count on curbside check-in.** Some airlines and airports have

---

Tips **What You Can Carry On—And What You Can't**

The Transportation Security Administration (TSA), the government agency that now handles all aspects of airport security, has devised new restrictions for carry-on baggage, not only to expedite the screening process but to prevent potential weapons from passing through airport security. Passengers are now limited to bringing just one carry-on bag and one personal item onto the aircraft (previous regulations allowed two carry-on bags and one personal item, like a briefcase or a purse). For more information, go to the TSA's website, www.tsa.gov. The agency has released an updated list of items passengers are not allowed to carry onto an aircraft:

Not permitted: knives and box cutters, corkscrews, straight razors, metal scissors, golf clubs, baseball bats, pool cues, hockey sticks, ski poles, ice picks.

Permitted: nail clippers, nail files, tweezers, eyelash curlers, safety razors (including disposable razors), syringes (with documented proof of medical need), walking canes and umbrellas (must be inspected first).

The airline you fly may have **additional restrictions** on items you can and cannot carry on board. Call ahead to avoid problems.

Tips All About E-Ticketing

Only yesterday **electronic tickets (E-tickets)** were the fast and easy ticket-free alternative to paper tickets. E-tickets allowed passengers to avoid long lines at airport check-in, all the while saving the airlines money on postage and labor. With the increased security measures in airports, however, an E-ticket no longer guarantees an accelerated check-in. You often can't go straight to the boarding gate, even if you have no bags to check. You'll probably need to show your printed E-ticket receipt or confirmation of purchase, as well as a photo ID, and sometimes even the credit card with which you purchased your E-ticket. That said, buying an E-ticket is still a fast, convenient way to book a flight; instead of having to wait for a paper ticket to come through the mail, you can book your fare by phone or on the computer, and the airline will immediately confirm by fax or e-mail. In addition, airlines often offer frequent-flier miles as incentive for electronic bookings.

stopped curbside check-in altogether, whereas others offer it on a limited basis. For up-to-date information on specific regulations and implementations, check with the individual airline.

- **Be sure to carry plenty of documentation.** A government-issued photo ID (federal, state, or local) is now required. You may need to show this at various checkpoints. With an E-ticket, you may be required to have with you printed confirmation of purchase, and perhaps even the credit card with which you bought your ticket (see "All About E-Ticketing," below). This varies from airline to airline, so call ahead to make sure you have the proper documentation. And be sure that your ID is **up-to-date:** an expired driver's license, for example, may keep you from boarding the plane altogether.

- **Know what you can carry on— and what you can't.** Travelers in the United States are now limited to one carry-on bag, plus one personal bag (such as a purse or a briefcase). The FAA has also

issued a list of newly restricted carry-on items; see the box "What You Can Carry On—and What You Can't."

- **Prepare to be searched.** Expect spot-checks. Electronic items, such as a laptop or cellphone, should be readied for additional screening. Limit the metal items you wear on your person.

- **It's no joke.** When a check-in agent asks if someone other than you packed your bag, don't decide that this is the time to be funny. The agents will not hesitate to call an alarm.

- **No ticket, no gate access.** Only ticketed passengers will be allowed beyond the screener checkpoints, except for those people with specific medical or parental needs.

FLYING FOR LESS: TIPS FOR GETTING THE BEST AIRFARE

Passengers within the same airplane cabin are rarely paying the same fare. Business travelers who need to purchase tickets at the last minute, change their itinerary at a moment's notice, or get home for the weekend pay the premium rate. Passengers who can book their ticket long in advance, who can stay over Saturday night, or who are willing to travel on a Tuesday, Wednesday, or Thursday after 7pm, will pay a fraction of the full fare. On many flights, even the shortest hops, the full fare is close to $1,000 or more, while a 7- or 14-day advance purchase ticket may cost less than half that amount. Here are a few other easy ways to save.

• Airlines periodically lower prices on their most popular routes. Check the travel section of your Sunday newspaper for advertised discounts or call the airlines directly and ask if any **promotional rates** or special fares are available. You'll almost never see a sale during the peak summer vacation months of July and August, or during the Thanksgiving or Christmas seasons; but in periods of low-volume travel, you should pay no more than $400 for a domestic cross-country flight. If your schedule is flexible, say so, and ask if you can secure a cheaper fare by staying an extra day, by flying midweek, or by flying at less-trafficked hours. If you already hold a ticket when a sale breaks, it may even pay to exchange your ticket, which usually incurs a $100 to $150 charge.

Note: The lowest-priced fares are often nonrefundable, require advance purchase of 1 to 3 weeks and a certain length of stay, and carry penalties for changing dates of travel.

• **Consolidators,** also known as bucket shops, are a good place to find low fares. Consolidators buy seats in bulk from the airlines and then sell them back to the public at prices usually below even the airlines' discounted rates. Their

small ads usually run in Sunday newspaper travel sections. And before you pay, request a confirmation number from the consolidator and then call the airline to confirm your seat. Be aware that bucket shop tickets are usually nonrefundable or rigged with stiff cancellation penalties, often as high as 50% to 75% of the ticket price. Protect yourself by paying with a credit card rather than cash. Keep in mind that if there's an airline sale going on, or if it's high season, you can often get the same or better rates by contacting the airlines directly, so do some comparison shopping before you buy. Also check out the name of the airline; you may not want to fly on some obscure Third World airline, even if you're saving $10. And check whether you're flying on a charter or a scheduled airline; the latter is more expensive but more reliable.

• **Council Travel** (✆ 800/226-8624; www.counciltravel.com) and **STA Travel** (✆ 800/781-4040; www.statravel.com) cater especially to young travelers, but their bargain-basement prices are available to people of all ages. **The TravelHub** (✆ 888/AIR-FARE; www.travelhub.com) represents nearly 1,000 travel agencies, many of whom offer consolidator and discount fares. Other reliable consolidators include **1-800-FLY-CHEAP** (www.1800flycheap. com); **TFI Tours International** (✆ 800/745-8000 or 212/736-1140; www.lowestprice.com), which serves as a clearinghouse for unused seats; or "rebators" such as **Travel Avenue** (✆ 800/333-3335; www.travelavenue.com) and the **Smart Traveller** (✆ 800/448-3338 in the U.S., or 305/448-3338), which rebate part of their commissions to you.

- Search **the Internet** for cheap fares. Great last-minute deals are available through free weekly e-mail services provided directly by the airlines.
- Look into **courier flights**—though they are usually not available on domestic flights. These companies hire couriers to hand-deliver packages or mail, and use your luggage allowance for themselves; in return, you get a deeply discounted ticket—for example, $300 round-trip to Europe in winter. Flights often become available at the last minute, so check in often. **Halbart Express** has offices in New York (© **718/656-8189**), Los Angeles (© **310/417-9790**), and Miami (© **305/593-0260**). **Jupiter Air** (www.jupiter air.com) has offices in New York (© **718/656-6050**), Los Angeles (© **310/670-5123**), and San Francisco (© **650/697-1773**).
- Join a travel club such as **Moment's Notice** (© **718/234-6295;** www.moments-notice.com) or **Sears Discount Travel Club** (© **800/433-9383,** or 800/255-1487 to join; www.travelers advantage.com), which supply unsold tickets at discounted prices. You pay an annual membership fee to get the club's hot line num-ber. Of course, you're limited to what's available, so you have to be flexible.
- Join **frequent-flier clubs.** It's best to accrue miles on one program, so you can rack up free flights and achieve elite status faster. But it makes sense to open as many accounts as possible, no matter how seldom you fly a particular airline. It's free, and you'll get the best choice of seats, faster response to phone inquiries, and prompter service if your luggage is stolen, your flight is canceled or delayed, or if you want to change your seat.

BY BOAT

DFDS Seaways (U.K.: © **08705/ 000-333;** www.dfdsseaways.co.uk. Netherlands: © **025/553-4546;** www. dfdsseaways.nl), has daily car-ferry service from Newcastle in northeast England to IJmuiden on the North Sea coast west of Amsterdam; the overnight journey time is 14 hours. At press time, the fare for a foot passenger, one-way, was £51. From IJmuiden, you can either go by train to Amsterdam Centraal Station, or by jetfoil with Fast Flying Ferries to a pier behind Centraal Station (see "Hot Jets," in chapter 10).

P&O North Sea Ferries (© **01482/377-177** in the U.K.; © **018/125-5555** in the Netherlands; www.ponsf.com), has daily car-ferry service between Hull in northeast England and Rotterdam Europoort; the overnight journey time is 14 hours. At press time, the fare for a foot passenger, one-way, was £53 ($82). Ferry company buses shuttle between the Rotterdam Europoort terminal and Rotterdam Centraal Station, from where there are frequent trains to Amsterdam.

Stena Line (U.K.: © **01233/647-047.** Netherlands: © **017/438-9333.** www.stenaline.com) has a daily overnight freight-ferry service that carries some private vehicles (no passengers without vehicles) between Harwich in southeast England and Hoek van Holland (Hook of Holland) near Rotterdam; journey time is 8 hours, 30 minutes. At press time, the fare for a foot passenger, one-way, was £24.

BY TRAIN

Rail service to Amsterdam from other cities in the Netherlands and elsewhere in Europe is frequent and fast. International and Inter City express trains arrive at Centraal Station from Brussels and Paris, and from several German cities and from more distant locations in eastern Europe, Spain,

Austria, Switzerland, and Italy. There's also the Amsterdam/Brussels Inter-City train, and connections can be made in Brussels to the North Express, the Oostende-Vienna Express, the Oostende-Moscow Express, and the Trans-Europe Express. **Nederlandse Spoorwegen** (Netherlands Railways; www.ns.nl) trains arrive in Amsterdam from towns and cities all over Holland. Schedule and fare information on travel in Holland is available by calling ℂ **0900/9292,** and for international trains, call ℂ **0900/9296.**

The distinctive burgundy-colored **Thalys** (www.thalys.com) high-speed train, with a top speed of 300kmph (186 mph), connecting Paris, Brussels, Amsterdam, and (via Brussels) Cologne, has cut travel times from Amsterdam to Paris to 4¼ hours, and to Brussels to 2¼ hours—figures that will be reduced to closer to 3¼ hours and 1¾ hours respectively when the high-speed rail lines in Holland are operational. For Thalys information and reservations in France, call ℂ **08/3635-3536;** in Belgium, ℂ **0800/95-777;** in Germany, ℂ **0221/19419;** and in Holland, ℂ **0900/9296.** Tickets are also available from main train stations and travel agents. One-way weekday first-class (Comfort 1) fares from Paris to Amsterdam in late 2000 were about $120; tourist class (Comfort 2) one-way tickets were about $80; on weekends the respective one-way fares were $75 and $68. Four Thalys trains run between Paris and Amsterdam every day via Brussels.

Britain is connected to the Continent via the Channel Tunnel. On the **Eurostar** (www.eurostar.com) high-speed train (top speed 258kmph/160 mph), the travel time between London Waterloo Station and Brussels Midi Station (the closest connecting point for Amsterdam) is 3¼ hours. On weekends the respective one-way fares were £140 and £100. Departures from London to Brussels are approximately every 2 hours at peak times. For Eurostar reservations, call ℂ **0345/303-030** in Britain, and ℂ **020/423-4444** in Holland.

The **Eurailpass** allows unlimited first-class travel throughout the rail systems of many European countries, including the Netherlands, at a cost of $554 for 15 days, $718 for 21 days, $890 for 1 month, $1,260 for 2 months, and $1,588 for 3 months. The **Eurail Youth Pass** allows unlimited second-class travel to those under 26 years of age at a cost of $388 for 15 days, $499 for 21 days, $623 for 1 month, $882 for 2 months, and $1,089 for 3 months. Other deals are available as well. Both the Eurailpass and the Eurail Youth Pass should be purchased before leaving the United States (they're more expensive if you buy in Europe) and are available through **Rail Europe** (ℂ **800/438-7245;** www.raileurope.com), and through travel agents.

BY BUS

Eurolines (www.eurolines.com) coach service operates between London Victoria Bus Station and Amsterdam Amstel Station (via ferry), with four departures daily in the summer. Travel time is just over 12 hours. For reservations, contact Eurolines (ℂ **0990/808-080** in Britain or 020/560-8788 in Holland).

BY CAR

Holland is crisscrossed by a network of major international highways. European expressways E19, E35, E231, and E22 converge on Amsterdam from France and Belgium to the south and from Germany to the north and east. These roads also have Dutch designations; as you approach the city they are, respectively: A4, A2, A1, and A7. Amsterdam's ring road is A10. Distances between destinations are relatively short, traffic is invariably heavy but road conditions are otherwise excellent, service stations are plentiful, and highways are plainly signposted.

If you want to drive from Britain to Amsterdam, you can use the fast and efficient **Le Shuttle** auto transporter through the Channel Tunnel from Folkestone to Calais (a 35-min. trip), and drive up from there. Le Shuttle has departures every 15 minutes at peak times, every 30 minutes at times of average demand, and every hour at night. In late 1998, fares ranged from £120 to £190 ($190–$290) per car, depending on the day, time, and other variables. The cheapest transits are usually midweek between 2 and 5am. For information, call ✆ **0990/353-535** for Le Shuttle reservations in Britain, ✆ **03/21-00-61-00** in France, ✆ **020/504-0540** in Holland. Reserving in advance makes sense at the busiest times, but the system is so fast, frequent, and simple that you may prefer to retain travel flexibility by just showing up, buying your ticket, waiting in line for a short while, and then driving aboard.

Driving tip one: The main drawback of driving into Amsterdam lies in the monumental traffic jam you're likely to encounter coming into the city. What's more, to reduce traffic congestion, the authorities have introduced tough measures on parking charges and parking violations. If you must drive into the city, do yourself a favor and park the car in a garage, then walk or use public transportation within the city (see "Getting Around," in chapter 3).

Driving tip two: When passing other cars on a Dutch *snelweg* (expressway), watch out for those all-too-common, brain-free tailgaters who race up behind you, brake hard from 161kmph (100 mph) or more, and then sit right on your trunk trying to force you out of their way, often flashing their lights at you by way of adding drama to the scene. The only thing to do is ignore them as best you can, continue with your own maneuver, and move across when it's safe to do so.

8 Escorted Tours & Package Deals

Before you start your search for the lowest airfare, you may want to consider booking your flight as part of a travel package such as an escorted tour or a package tour. What you lose in adventure, you'll gain in time and money saved when you book accommodations, and maybe even food and entertainment, along with your flight.

PACKAGE TOURS FOR INDEPENDENT TRAVELERS
Package tours are not the same thing as escorted tours. With a package tour, you travel independently but pay a group rate. Packages usually include airfare, a choice of hotels, and car rentals, and packagers often offers several options at different prices. In many cases, a package that includes airfare, hotel, and transportation to

and from the airport will cost you less than just the hotel alone would have, had you booked it yourself. That's because packages are sold in bulk to tour operators—who resell them to the public at a cost that drastically undercuts standard rates.

RECOMMENDED PACKAGE TOUR OPERATORS
One good source of package deals is the airlines themselves. Most major airlines offer air/land packages, including **American Airlines Vacations** (✆ 800/321-2121; http://aav1.aavacations.com), **Delta Vacations** (✆ 800/221-6666; www.deltavacations.com), and **US Airways Vacations** (✆ 800/455-0123 or 800/422-3861; www.usairwaysvacations.com), **Continental Airlines**

Vacations (© 800/301-3800; www.
coolvacations.com), and **United Vacations** (© 888/854-3899; www.united
vacations.com).

Online Vacation Mall (© 800/
839-9851; www.onlinevacationmall.
com) allows you to search for and
book packages offered by a number of
tour operators and airlines. The
United States Tour Operators Association's website (www.ustoa.com)
has a search engine that allows you to
look for operators that offer packages
to a specific destination. Travel packages are also listed in the travel section
of your local Sunday newspaper. **Liberty Travel** (© 888/271-1584;
www.libertytravel.com), one of the
biggest packagers in the Northeast,
often runs full-page ads in Sunday
papers. Or check ads in the national
travel magazines such as *Arthur Frommer's Budget Travel Magazine, Travel &
Leisure, National Geographic Traveler,*
and *Condé Nast Traveler.*

QUESTIONS TO ASK IF YOU BOOK A PACKAGE TOUR

- What are the **accommodations
choices** available and are there
price differences? Once you find
out, look them up in a Frommer's
guidebook. Most countries rate
their hotels, so ask about the rating of the hotel in question. Or
get this information from the government tourist office or its website.
- What **type of room** will you be
staying in? Don't take whatever is
thrown your way. Request a nonsmoking room, a quiet room, a
room with a view, or whatever you
fancy.
- Look for **hidden expenses.** Ask
whether airport departure fees and
taxes are included in the total cost.

ESCORTED TOURS (TRIPS WITH GUIDES)

Escorted Tours are structured group
tours, with a group leader. The price

usually includes everything from airfare to hotels, meals, tours, admission
costs, and local transportation.

QUESTIONS TO ASK IF YOU BOOK AN ESCORTED TOUR

- What is the **cancellation policy?**
Do they require a deposit? Can
they cancel the trip if they don't
get enough people? Do you get a
refund if they cancel? If *you* cancel?
How late can you cancel if you are
unable to go? When do you pay in
full? *Note:* If you choose an
escorted tour, think strongly about
purchasing trip-cancellation insurance from an independent agency,
especially if the tour operator asks
you to pay up front. See the section on "Insurance, Health &
Safety," above.
- How busy is the **schedule?** How
much sightseeing is planned each
day? Is ample time allowed for
relaxing or wandering solo?
- What is the **size** of the group?
Generally, the smaller the group,
the more flexible the itinerary, and
the less time you'll spend waiting
for people to get on and off the
bus. Tour operators may be evasive
about this, because they may not
know the exact size of the group
until everyone has made reservations; but they should be able to
give you a rough estimate. Some
tours have a minimum group size
and may cancel the tour if they
don't book enough people.
- What is included in the **price?**
You may have to pay for transportation to and from the airport.
A box lunch may be included in
an excursion, but drinks might
cost extra. Beer might be
included, but wine might not.
Can you opt out of certain activities, or does the bus leave once a
day, with no exceptions? Are all
your meals planned in advance?
Can you choose your entree at
dinner? Are tips included?

- What are the **names of the hotels** where you'll be staying? Once you've gotten the names, look them up in a Frommer's guidebook. Foreign countries rate their hotels, so ask about the rating of the hotel in question. This information is usually available for free from government tourist offices and their websites.
- What **type of room** will you be staying in? Don't take whatever is thrown your way. Request a nonsmoking room, a quiet room, a room with a view, or whatever your fancy.
- What are the **demographics** of the group with whom you'll be traveling? What is the age range? What is the gender breakdown? Is this mostly a trip for couples?
- If you plan to be traveling alone, what is the **single supplement?** Will they find you a roommate at your request?

9 Tips on Accommodations

TIPS FOR SAVING ON YOUR HOTEL ROOM

The **rack rate** is the maximum rate that a hotel charges for a room. It's the rate you'd get if you walked in off the street and asked for a room for the night. Hardly anybody pays these prices, however, and there are many ways around them.

- **Don't be afraid to bargain.** Most rack rates include commissions of 10% to 25% for travel agents, which some hotels may be willing to reduce if you make your own reservations and haggle a bit. Always ask whether a room less expensive than the first one quoted is available, or whether any special rates apply to you. You may qualify for corporate, student, military, senior, or other discounts. Be sure to mention membership in AAA, AARP, frequent-flier programs, or trade unions, which may entitle you to special deals as well. Find out the hotel policy on children—do kids stay free in the room or is there a special rate?
- **Rely on a qualified professional.** Certain hotels give travel agents discounts in exchange for steering business their way, so if you're shy about bargaining, an agent may be better equipped to negotiate discounts for you.
- **Dial direct.** When booking a room in a chain hotel, compare the rates offered by the hotel's local line with that of the toll-free number. Also check with an agent and online. A hotel makes nothing on a room that stays empty, so the local hotel reservation desk may be willing to offer a special rate unavailable elsewhere.
- **Remember the law of supply and demand.** Resort hotels are most crowded and therefore most expensive on weekends, so discounts are usually available for midweek stays. Business hotels in downtown locations are busiest during the week, so you can expect big discounts over the weekend. Avoid high-season stays whenever you can: planning your vacation just a week before or after official peak season can mean big savings.
- **Look into group or long-stay discounts.** If you come as part of a large group, you should be able to negotiate a bargain rate, since the hotel can then guarantee occupancy in a number of rooms. Likewise, if you're planning a long stay (at least 5 days), you might qualify for a discount. As a general

rule, expect one night free after a seven-night stay.

- **Avoid excess charges.** When you book a room, ask whether the hotel charges for parking. Many hotels charge a fee just for dialing out on the phone in your room. Find out whether your hotel imposes a surcharge on local and long-distance calls. A pay phone, however inconvenient, may save you money, although many calling cards charge a fee when you use them on pay phones. Finally, ask about local taxes and service charges, which could increase the cost of a room by 25% or more.

- **Watch for coupons and advertised discounts.** Scan ads in your local Sunday newspaper travel section, an excellent source for up-to-the-minute hotel deals.

- **Consider a suite.** If you are traveling with your family or another couple, you can pack more people into a suite (which usually comes with a sofa bed), and thereby reduce your per-person rate. Remember that some places charge for extra guests.

- **Book an efficiency.** A room with a kitchenette allows you to shop for groceries and cook your own meals. This is a big moneysaver, especially for families on long stays.

- Join hotel **frequent-visitor clubs,** even if you don't use them much.

You'll be more likely to get upgrades and other perks.

- Many hotels offer **frequent-flier points.** Don't forget to ask for yours when you check in.

- **Investigate reservations services.** These outfits usually work as consolidators, buying up or reserving rooms in bulk, and then dealing them out to customers at a profit. You can get 10% to 50% off; but remember, these discounts apply to inflated rack rates that savvy travelers rarely end up paying. You may get a decent rate, but always call the hotel as well to see if you can do better.

Among the more reputable reservations services, offering both telephone and online bookings, are: **Accommodations Express** (© **800/950-4685;** www.accommodationsexpress.com); **Hotel Reservations Network** (© **800/715-7666;** www.hoteldiscounts.com or www.180096HOTEL.com); **Quikbook** (© **800/789-9887,** includes fax on demand service; www.quikbook.com). Online, try booking your hotel through **Arthur Frommer's Budget Travel** (www.frommers.com). **Microsoft Expedia** (www.expedia.com) features a "Travel Agent" that will also direct you to affordable lodgings.

3

Getting to Know Amsterdam

Amsterdam Center is small enough that its residents think of it as a village, but it can be one confusing village until you get the hang of it. It's easy to think you are headed in one direction along the canal ring, only to discover that you are going completely the other way. Those concentric rings of major canals are the city's defining characteristic, along with several important squares that act as focal points.

This chapter explains how the city is laid out, introduces you to its neighborhoods, tells you how to get around, and squeezes in a bunch of other useful stuff besides.

1 Orientation

ARRIVING
BY PLANE
An airliner descending into **Amsterdam Airport Schiphol** (℗ **0900/0141;** www.schiphol.nl), 18km (11 miles) from the city, has to descend a little further than would be the case for most any other airport on earth, because the runway is 4.5m (15 ft.) below sea level on the floor of what was once a lake. Schiphol (pronounced *skhip*-ol) is the main airport in the Netherlands, handling just about all of the country's international arrivals and departures. It's easy to figure out why frequent travelers regularly vote Schiphol one of the world's favorite airports, for its ease of use and its massive duty-free shopping center.

After you deplane, moving walkways take you to the Arrivals Hall, where you pass through Passport Control, Customs, and Baggage Reclaim. Facilities like free luggage carts, currency exchange, ATMs, restaurants, bars, shops, babyrooms, restrooms, and showers are available. Beyond these, Schiphol Plaza combines train station access, the Airport Hotel, a shopping mall (sporting that most essential Dutch service—a flower store), bars and restaurants, restrooms, baggage lockers, airport and tourist information desks, car-rental and hotel reservation desks, check-in for scheduled domestic flights (also available are charter and air-taxi aircraft, including helicopters), and more, all in a single location. Bus, shuttle, and taxi stops are just outside.

For tourist information and to make hotel reservations, go to the **Holland Tourist Information (HTi)** desk in Schiphol Plaza (℗ **0900/400-4040**), open daily from 7am to 10pm.

The airport has multistory **parking garages** within walking distance of Schiphol Plaza and a network of short- and long-term parking lots linked by frequent shuttle to the passenger terminal.

GETTING TO AMSTERDAM   The Dutch Railways' Schiphollijn (Schiphol Line) **trains** for Amsterdam's Centraal Station (with stops at De Lelylaan and De Vlugtlaan stations in west Amsterdam) depart from Schiphol Station, downstairs from Schiphol Plaza. Frequency ranges from four trains an hour at peak times to one an hour at night. The fare is 2.95€ one-way; the trip takes around 20 minutes.

An alternative route serves both Amsterdam Zuid/World Trade Center station and RAI station (beside the big RAI Convention center). Be sure to check which one is best for your hotel (including any tram or bus interchange). If you're staying at a hotel near Leidseplein, Rembrandtplein, in the Museum Quarter, or in Amsterdam South, this route may be a better bet for you than Centraal Station. The fare is 2.95€ one-way; the trip takes around 15 minutes. From Amsterdam Zuid/World Trade Center, take tram no. 5 for Leidseplein and the Museum Quarter; from RAI, take tram no. 4 for Rembrandtplein.

The **KLM Hotel Bus** shuttles between the airport and Amsterdam, serving 16 top hotels directly and many more that are close to these stops. The fare is 8€ one-way, 14€ round-trip. No reservations are needed and buses depart from in front of Schiphol Plaza every 20 minutes from 7am to 6pm and every 30 minutes from 6 to 9:30pm. Check at the KLM Hotel Desk for information. If you're not staying at one of the above hotels, the clerks can tell you which shuttle stop is closest to your chosen lodgings. In addition, many individual hotels near the airport and in town have their own shuttle service.

Bus no. 197 departs every half hour from in front of Schiphol Plaza for Amsterdam's downtown Marnixstraat bus station. The fare is 3.40€. This bus is a lot slower than both the train and the KLM Hotel Bus.

Taxis are expensive, but they're the preferred choice if your luggage is burdensome or if there are two or more people to share the cost. You find taxi stands at both ends of the sidewalk in front of Schiphol Plaza. Taxis from the airport are all metered. Expect to pay around 38€ to the Center. Remember, a service charge is already included in the fare.

BY TRAIN

Traveling by train in the Netherlands is convenient, with frequent service to many places around the country and modern, clean trains that run on time. Whether you arrive by Thalys high-speed train from Brussels or Paris, by ordinary international train, or by Netherlands Railways train from elsewhere in Holland, you'll likely find yourself deposited at Amsterdam's Centraal Station, built over 100 years ago on an artificial island in the IJ channel. The building, an ornate architectural wonder on its own, is the focus of much activity. It's at the hub of the city's concentric rings of canals and connecting main streets, and is the originating point for most of the city's trams, Metro trains, and buses.

For information on trains (and other public transportation) in Holland, call ℂ **0900/9292;** for international trains, call ℂ **0900/9296.**

An office of VVV Amsterdam tourist information is inside the station on platform 2 and another office is right in front of the station on Stationsplein; both offices have hotel reservation desks. Other facilities include a GWK Bureau de Change, where you can exchange traveler's checks, U.S. dollars, and other currencies (see "Currency Exchange" in "Fast Facts: Amsterdam," later in this chapter), ATMs, train info center, luggage lockers, restaurants and snack bars, newsstands, and other stores. The station is a departure point for Metro trains, trams (streetcars), buses, taxis, passenger ferries across the IJ waterway and around the harbor, water taxis, canal-boat tours, and the Museum Boat. There are usually street musicians performing a barrel organ.

A less welcoming aspect of the station is the pickpocket convention that's in full swing at all times. Messages broadcast in multiple languages warn people to be on their guard, but the artful dodgers still seem to do good business. Avoid becoming one of their victims by keeping your money and other valuables under wraps, especially among crowds. Then, as likely as not, there'll be a "heroin whore" or two, a platoon of panhandlers, and more than a whiff of pot smoke in the air.

An array of tram stops are on either side of the main station exit—virtually all of Amsterdam's hotels are within a 15-minute tram ride from Centraal Station. The Metro station is downstairs, just outside the main exit. City bus stops are to the left of the main exit, and the taxi stands are to the right. (You'll find details on public transportation within the city under "Getting Around," later in this chapter.) At the public transportation tickets and information office on Stationsplein, you can buy a *strippenkaart* or *dagkaart* for trams, Metros, and buses (see "Getting Around," later in this chapter).

BY BUS
International coaches—in particular those of **Eurolines** (*C* **020/560-8788; www.eurolines.com**)—arrive at the bus terminal opposite Amstel train station in the south of the city. From here you can go by train and Metro train to Centraal Station, and by tram no. 12 to the Museumplein area and to connecting points for trams to the Center.

BY CAR
European expressways E19, E35, E231, and E22 converge on Amsterdam from France and Belgium to the south and from Germany to the north and east. As you approach the city, you'll also notice that these roads also have Dutch national numbers, respectively A4, A2, A1, and A7. Amsterdam's ring road is designated A10.

In many European cities, the best advice is to drive to the city, park your car, and never touch it again till you leave. In Amsterdam, even better advice is not to bring it into the city in the first place (for a sufficiency of reasons why not, see the "By Car" section under "Getting Around," later in this chapter).

VISITOR INFORMATION
Few countries have a more organized approach to tourism or are more meticulous in their attention to detailed travel information than the Netherlands. Every province and municipality has its own tourist organization and even small towns and villages have efficient information offices with multilingual attendants on duty. These amazing tourist offices all have the tongue-twisting name **Vereniging voor Vreemdelingenverkeer (Association for Foreigner Travel).** Even the Dutch don't much like saying that every time so they call it simply the **VVV** (pronounced *vay-vay-vay*). All tourist information offices in the Netherlands, from big city and province-wide offices down to the tiniest village booth, are called VVV Whatever—VVV Amsterdam, VVV Delft, VVV Haarlem, VVV Leiden, and so on, and the blue-and-white, triangular VVV logo is a common sight around the country. VVV offices can book accommodations for you, help with travel arrangements, tell you what's on where, and . . . well, if there's anything they can't do, I have yet to discover it. To find the offices anywhere in the country, look for a blue-and-white roadside sign bearing the letters VVV.

Amsterdam's excellent but often overloaded tourist information organization, **VVV Amsterdam** (*C* **0900/400-4040;** fax 020/625-2869; www.visit amsterdam.nl), has an office inside Centraal Station, on platform 2, another just outside the station at Stationsplein 10, and a booth at Leidseplein 1 (tram: 1, 2, 5, 6, 7, 10), on the corner of Leidsestraat. All three locations are invariably extremely busy—don't visit a VVV office to purchase tickets for public transportation, unless you're also going there for something else that only the VVV can supply. Handle the VVV phone number with caution, as it costs a steep .55€ a minute, which is tolerable if you get an instant response and not so good if you have to hold. VVV Amsterdam's correspondence address is Postbus 3901, 1001 AS Amsterdam. The VVV can help you with almost any question about the city and reserves hotel rooms, books tours, sells special reduced-rate passes for attractions and public transportation, provides brochures and maps, and more. The offices are open daily from 9am to 5pm in the low season; the evening open hours gradually increase and then decrease back to the baseline time on a somewhat unpredictable schedule as the high season proceeds.

Be sure to pick up a copy of the VVV's *Day by Day/What's On in Amsterdam,* for 2€. This monthly magazine is full of details about the month's art exhibits, concerts, and theater performances, and lists restaurants, bars, dance clubs, and more. Or purchase a copy of the yellow **Visitors Guide,** like a miniature Yellow Pages, which has a wealth of addresses and phone numbers. The **Amsterdam Uit Buro (AUB) Ticketshop,** Leidseplein 26 (℗ **0900/0191;**

Your Passport to Amsterdam

A sound way to get the most out of your trip is to avail yourself of the **Amsterdam Pass.** The credit card–size pass is valid for 1 day for 26€, 2 days for 36€, and 3 days for 46€. It allows free travel on public transportation; free admission to more than 20 museums and attractions, including to the Rijksmuseum or the Van Gogh Museum (not both), and Stedelijk Museum, and discounted admission to more museums and attractions; a free canal boat cruise; discounted excursions, including reduced rates on the Museum Boat and the Canal Bus; and discounts in selected restaurants and stores. Total possible savings on the pass are in the region of 100€.

Before purchasing one, consider carefully whether you'll get your money's worth out of this pass. Remember, this is Holland, where the local fondness for the coin of the realm is proverbial and killer bargains are thin on the ground. You'll have to work yourself pretty hard to come out ahead on the cost of the pass, jumping on and off trams, buses and canal boats, and running into and out of museums that fall mostly into the solid-culture class.

Some of Amsterdam's most memorable experiences come from unprogrammed strolling, hanging out on cafe terraces, and visiting offbeat shops and attractions, and you might not have much time left for those. But if a diet of solid culture is what you're here for, and you're ready to work at achieving it, the pass should be a sound investment.

Only the person whose signature is on it can use the pass, which is available from Holland Tourist Information at Schiphol Airport and from VVV tourist information offices in the city.

www.aub.nl; tram: 1, 2, 5, 6, 7, 10), can give you information regarding cultural events and books tickets for almost every venue in town. The office is open Monday through Wednesday and Saturday from 10am to 6pm, Thursday from 10am to 9pm, and Sunday from noon to 6pm. Using their service instead of chasing down tickets on your own can save you precious hours. You can purchase tickets with a credit card by phone daily from 9am to 9pm, and online at any time. AUB publishes the free monthly magazine *Uitkrant* (it's in Dutch, but it isn't difficult to understand the listings information).

CITY LAYOUT

Amsterdammers will tell you it's easy to find your way around their city. However, when each resident offers you a different pet theory of how best to maintain your sense of direction, you begin to sense that the city's layout can be confusing. Some of the natives' theories actually do work. If you try to "think in circles," "follow the canals" (the one I use most), or "watch the way the trams go," you might be able to spend fewer minutes a day consulting a map or trying to figure out where you are and which way to walk to find the Rijksmuseum, a restaurant, or your hotel.

When you step out of Centraal Station's main entrance, you're facing south toward the Center. From here, the city is laid out around you along four concentric semicircles of canals: Singel, Herengracht, Keizersgracht, and Prinsengracht. It was along these canals that 16th- and 17th-century merchants built their elegant homes, most of which are still standing. The largest and most stately canal houses are along Herengracht. Connecting these canals are many smaller canals and streets, radiating out from the Center. The area inside the Singelgracht canal, which forms an outer rim to the canal zone, is the Old City.

A main street called Damrak leads from Centraal Station to the main central square called the Dam. In the 17th century, Damrak was a canal, its quays filled with small cargo boats and lined with ships' chandlers and mapmaker stores. Narrow side streets like Haringpakkerssteeg and Zoutsteeg recall the herring packers of yore (*haring* means "herring") and the place where ships used to unload salt (*zout* means "salt"). In the late 19th century, Damrak was lined with fancy stores and filled with elegant shoppers. Today, it is a brash thoroughfare bordered by souvenir stores and noisy cafes. Houses on the bank facing the canal boat dock stand in the water, Venice-style.

To the left of the Dam, where the original dam on the Amstel River was built and on which stands the Royal Palace, is the famous Red Light District, where government-licensed prostitutes sit behind windows, waiting for customers. A block to the right of Damrak is Nieuwendijk (it becomes Kalverstraat when it crosses the Dam), a pedestrians-only shopping street. If you follow Kalverstraat to the end, you're at Muntplein beside the old Mint Tower. Cross over Muntplein and continue in the same direction to reach Rembrandtplein, one of the city's main nightlife areas.

The other main nightlife area is Leidseplein, on the last concentric canal, Singelgracht (not to be confused with the first concentric canal, Singel). Leidseplein is at the end of Leidsestraat, a pedestrians-only shopping street that leads from Singel to Singelgracht.

The re-landscaped green Museumplein, where you find the city's three most famous museums—the Rijksmuseum, Van Gogh Museum, and Stedelijk Museum—is a 5-minute walk along Singelgracht from Leidseplein.

Human Statistics

The Old City, inside the arc of the Singelgracht canal, covers an area of 8 sq. km (3 sq. miles), containing 44,000 dwellings that house 80,000 people. Two-thirds of them are native Dutch, the remainder ethnic minorities and foreign residents. By 2020, half of the population is expected to be of immigrant stock, much of it Muslim. The residents share this central space with 8,000 historical monuments, more than 2,000 shops, 1,500 cafes and restaurants, and 210 hotels. Every working day 680,000 people pour into the center by public transportation, bike, and car.

One other area worth mentioning is the Jordaan (pronounced yor-*daan*), an old neighborhood that's now filled with inexpensive restaurants, offbeat stores, and small galleries. The Jordaan lies between Brouwersgracht, Prinsengracht, Looiersgracht, and Lijnbaansgrach. If you turn right off Damrak at any point between Centraal Station and the Dam, when you cross Prinsengracht you're in the Jordaan.

THE PRINCIPAL SQUARES   There are six major squares in Amsterdam that will be the "hubs" of your visit:

The Dam is the heart of the city and the site of the original dam across the Amstel River that gave the city its name. Encircling the square are the Royal Palace, the Nieuwe Kerk, and several department stores, hotels, and restaurants. On the square is the National Monument of World War II.

Leidseplein and the streets around it form Amsterdam's Times Square, glittering with restaurants, nightclubs, discos, performance centers, a casino, and movie theaters.

Rembrandtplein is another entertainment center, bustling with restaurants and cafes.

Museumplein and **Waterlooplein** are the cultural hubs, with the Rijksmuseum, Concertgebouw, Van Gogh Museum, and Stedelijk Museum on and around Museumplein, and the Muziektheater and a superb flea market at Waterlooplein.

Muntplein is essentially a busy transportation hub. It's easily recognizable for the Munttoren (Mint Tower), from 1620, one of the city's original fortress towers, which is topped by a distinctive crown ornament. Muntplein affords access to Kalverstraat, a popular shopping street, and to Rembrandtplein.

STREET MAPS   A map is essential. The maps in this book will help you understand Amsterdam's basic pattern of waterways and the relationships between the major squares or landmarks and the major connecting thoroughfares. Once you get the hang of the necklace pattern of the four major canals and become familiar with the names (or series of names) of each of the five principal roads that go through into the Center, all you need do as you walk along is keep track of whether you're walking toward or away from the Dam, the heart of the city, or simply circling around it.

The most detailed and helpful maps of Amsterdam are those published by Suurland-Falkplan. Their handy **Amsterdam Tourist Map,** small and easy to unfold, is available from news vendors for 2.50€. It shows every street and canal; gives tram routes and tram stops; pinpoints churches and many museums; locates address numbers; and identifies one-way streets, bridges, and canals. For more detailed coverage of the entire city and its suburbs, including a street name index, buy Suurland-Falkplan's **Stadsplattegrond Amsterdam** for 6€. The VVV tourist information offices have several other maps available, including the small but detailed **VVV Amsterdam** map, which costs 2€.

FINDING AN ADDRESS   Wherever possible in this book, I've attempted to locate the addresses given by adding the name of a nearby square, major thoroughfare, adjacent canal, or well-known sight. Street numbers along the canals ascend (as you look at the map) from left to right (west to east); on streets leading away from Centraal Station and out from the Center, they ascend from top to bottom (north to south).

Now, all you need to know is that, in Dutch, -*straat* means "street," -*gracht* means "canal," -*plein* means "square," and -*laan* means "avenue," all of which are used as suffixes attached directly to the name of the thoroughfare (for example, Princes' Canal becomes Prinsengracht).

NEIGHBORHOODS IN BRIEF

From the standpoint of tourism and for the purposes of locating the hotels and restaurants reviewed in this book, I've divided the city of Amsterdam into six major neighborhoods. Some of these neighborhoods could have been further subdivided and there are inevitable "border disputes" about where one area begins and another ends and in which one a particular establishment properly belongs.

The Old Center   This core area around the Dam and Centraal Station, and through the neighborhood known as De Wallen (The Walls), which contains the Red Light District, is the oldest part of the city. It includes the main downtown shopping areas and attractions such as the Royal Palace, the Amsterdam Historical Museum, Madame Tussaud's, and many of the canal-boat piers. There are plenty of reasons for wanting to lodge in the Center, right in the heart of things. And a few reasons for not: It's a busy part of town, filled with traffic, noise, and social whirl. If it's tranquillity you're after, most of the Center is not the place to find it.

The Canal Belt   The semicircular, multistrand "necklace" of waterways called the *Grachtengordel* in Dutch was built around the old Center during the city's 17th-century Golden Age. Its vista of elegant, gabled mansions fronting long, tree-lined canals forms the image that's most often associated

Amsterdam. It includes many hotels, both large and small, restaurants, sightseeing attractions such as the Anne Frankhuis and the canal-house museums, and antiques shops. It would be a shame to visit this watery city without staying in a hotel overlooking one of the canals, especially since canal-house hotels are generally in 300-year-old buildings. So if you really want to experience Amsterdam, splurge a bit, even if it's only for a night or two, and stay at one of the canal-house hotels.

Around Leidseplein   The city's most happening nightlife square and its immediate surroundings, cover such a small area that it could perhaps have been included under "The Canal Belt." But so distinctive is it that it demands to be picked out and highlighted on its own. In addition to performance venues, movie theaters, bars, and cafes, there are plenty of good hotels and restaurants in this oftentimes frenetically busy area.

Around Rembrandtplein   Like Leidseplein, but on a somewhat reduced scale, this square is the focus for a swatch of hotels, restaurants, cafes, and nightlife venues that's lively enough to justify picking it out from its surroundings.

The Jordaan This nest of small streets and canals lies west of the Center, beyond the major canals. Once a working-class neighborhood, it's become fashionable, like New York City's SoHo, with a growing number of upscale boutiques and restaurants. Still, its "indigenous" residents are alive and well and show no sign of succumbing to the gentrification going on around them. In its long history, the old Jordaan has seen plenty of trends and fashions come and go, and it will still be there whether the trendy boutiques and restaurants prosper or not. But there are only a couple of Jordaan hotel choices in this book (though some other hotels, along the rim of the Jordaan on Prinsengracht, are included in the "Canal Belt" neighborhood). The Jordaan is a great residential neighborhood but, sadly, it just doesn't have a lot of good hotel options.

Museumplein & Vondelpark Gracious and residential, this area surrounds the three major museums on Museumplein—the Rijksmuseum, the Van Gogh Museum, and the Stedelijk Museum—and hosts the Concertgebouw concert hall, many restaurants, Amsterdam's most elegant shopping streets (Pieter Cornelisz

Hooftstraat and Van Baerlestraat), and its best-known park. The U.S. Consulate is here, too. The area is filled with small hotels, few of them chain hotels, that in general offer better value for money than those in the Center and along the Canal Belt.

Amsterdam East A residential zone on the far bank of the Amstel River that's the location of sightseeing attractions like the Maritime and Tropical museums, and also of Artis, the local zoo. It's an area of Amsterdam that's rich in ethnic minority groups. The segment along the Amstel contains great views, a status-symbol hotel and restaurant, and a top performance venue.

Amsterdam South This prestigious modern residential area is the site of a number of hotels, particularly along Apollolaan, a broad avenue the locals call the Gold Coast for its rows of expensive houses.

Amsterdam West The district west of the Singelgracht canal covers a lot of ground but doesn't have much to recommend it in the way of sights and delights.

Amsterdam North On the north bank of the IJ channel, this district has been little more than a dormitory suburb up until now, but there are some signs that this is beginning to change and that dining and entertainment possibilities are opening up.

2 Getting Around

When you look at a map of Amsterdam, you may think the city is too large to explore on foot. This isn't true: It's possible to see almost every important sight on a 4-hour walk. Be sure to wear good walking shoes, as those charming cobbles get under your soles and on your nerves after a time, so leave your thin-soled shoes or boots at home.

If you're going around on foot, remember that cars have the right of way when turning. Don't step in front of one thinking it's going to stop for you. And

Amsterdam Neighborhoods

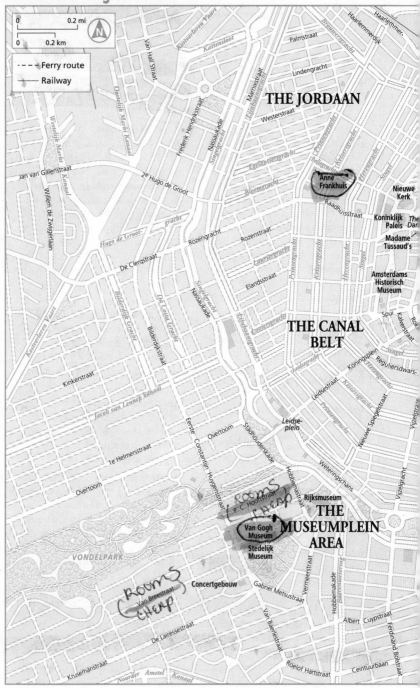

THE JORDAAN

THE CANAL BELT

THE MUSEUMPLEIN AREA

VONDELPARK

Anne Frankhuis

Nieuwe Kerk

Koninklijk Paleis

The Dam

Madame Tussaud's

Amsterdams Historisch Museum

Rijksmuseum

Van Gogh Museum

Stedelijk Museum

Concertgebouw

ROOMS CHEAP

ROOMS CHEAP

0   0.2 mi
0   0.2 km

- - - Ferry route
—— Railway

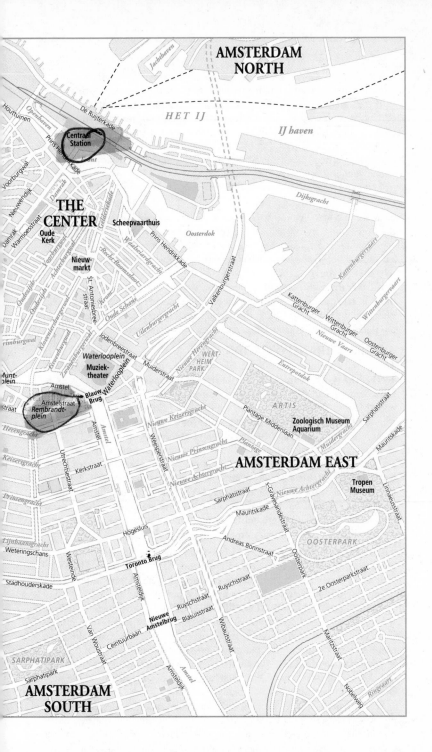

AMSTERDAM
NORTH

Jachthaven

De Ruijterkade

HET IJ

IJ haven

Houttuinen

Openhaven

Prins Hendrikkade

Centraal
Station

Voorburgwal

Damrak

THE
CENTER

Oude
Kerk

Nieuw-
markt

Scheepvaarthuis

Prins Hendrikkade

Oosterdok

Dijksgracht

Nieuwendijk

Warmoesstraat

Damrak

Voorburgwal

Achtergracht

St. Antoniesbree-
straat

Oude Schans

Rechte Boomssloot

Waddenardgracht

Kromme

Kattenburgervaart

Valkenburgerstraat

Kattenburger
Gracht

Wittenburger
Gracht

Nieuwe Vaart

Oostenburger
Gracht

Wittenburgervaart

Oudezijds

Oudezijds

Jodenbreestraat

Uilenburgergracht

rimburgwal

Groenburgwal

Zwanenburgwal

Waterlooplein

Muiderstraat

Nieuwe Herengracht

WERT-
HEIM
PARK

Entrepotdok

Munt-
plein

Muziek-
theater

Waterlooplein

ARTIS

Sarphatistraat

Amstel

Blauw
Brug

Plantage Middenlaan

Zoologisch Museum
Aquarium

Amstelstraat
Rembrandt-
plein

Amstel

Amstel

Nieuwe Keizersgracht

Weesperstraat

Nieuwe Prinsengracht

Plantage

Muidergracht

Mauritskade

Herengracht

Nieuwe Achtergracht

AMSTERDAM EAST

Keizersgracht

Kerkstraat

Utrechtsestraat

Tropen
Museum

Prinsengracht

Sarphatistraat

's-Gravesandestraat

Nieuwe Achtergracht

Linnaeusstraat

Lijnbaansgracht

Weteringschans

Hogesluis

Mauritskade

Andreas Bonnstraat

Oosterpark

OOSTERPARK

Stadhouderskade

Toronto Brug

Amsteldijk

Westeinde

Ruyschstraat

Ruyschstraat

2e Oosterparkstraat

Van Woustraat

Nieuwe
Amstelbrug

Ceintuurbaan

Blasiusstraat

Wibautstraat

Maritzstraat

SARPHATIPARK

Sarphatipark

Amstel

Amsteldijk

Nobelweg

Ringvaart

AMSTERDAM
SOUTH

> ⟮*Tips* **Urban Minefield**
>
> In such a beautiful city, with high gables in many and varied shapes and forms, there's a temptation to walk along gazing upward. Be careful. There's the possibility you'll walk straight into a canal, but that's a minor danger compared to the one underfoot. Many Amsterdammers have dogs, some of them the size of Shetland ponies. Signs on the sidewalk saying HOND IN DE GOOT (DOG IN THE GUTTER) are mostly ignored by both owner and dog. Take your eye off the ground for so much as an instant and you (and your footwear) might regret it.

be aware that many motorists consider road signs and red lights to be no more than interesting and occasionally useful suggestions. When crossing a street, watch out for trams, buses, and bikes, too. Look both ways before walking across a dedicated bike lane—some bikers get unreasonably irritated if you force them to crash into you.

Kids are irresistibly attracted to water, so watch out for them anywhere near the vast expanse of water in this city of 160 canals. Protective fencing rarely exists and the low metal railings that are supposed to keep cars from rolling into the water are ideally positioned for small feet to stumble over.

BY PUBLIC TRANSPORTATION

The central information and ticket sales point for Amsterdam's **Gemeente Vervoerbedrijf (GVB/Municipal Transportation Company)** is **GVB Tickets & Info,** Stationsplein (© **0900/9292;** www.gvb.nl), in front of Centraal Station, open Monday through Friday from 7am to 9pm, Saturday and Sunday from 8am to 9pm. You can buy some tickets here for less money than if you bought them from tram drivers and conductors and bus drivers.

Most tram and bus shelters and all Metro stations have maps that show the entire urban transit network. All stops have signs that list the main stops yet to be made by the trams or buses that can be boarded at that location. Detailed maps of the network are available from the GVB Tickets & Info office for .70€.

Daytime hours of operation for public transportation are from 6am (trams start at 7:30am on Sun) to around 12:30am. Night buses operate a limited service thereafter, with buses usually on an hourly schedule.

TICKETS & FARES   There are 11 fare zones in greater Amsterdam, but you likely won't travel often beyond the Center zone 5700 (Centrum). Make sure your ticket is validated for the number of zones you plan to travel through and for the duration of the ride takes (see below for how to validate).

Children 3 and under travel free; children 4 to 11 ride on reduced-rate tickets.

You can purchase tickets from VVV Amsterdam tourist information offices, the GVB Tickets & Info office (see above), tram drivers or conductors (on some trams there's an onboard ticket automat instead), bus drivers, train and Metro station ticket booths, and automats at train and Metro stations. Not every kind of ticket is available from each of these sources, and some tickets can be purchased also from post offices and some newsstands.

Several types of tickets are valid on trams, buses, and the Metro. The most popular type is a **strippenkaart (strip card),** for which the fare system is based on canceling one more of the ticket's strips than the number of zones you travel through—two strips for one zone, three strips for two zones, and so on. A strip card is good for any number of transfers on trams, buses, and Metro trains within 1 hour of the time stamped on it (this goes up in steps to a maximum 3½ hr. as the number of validated zones increases). More than one person can use a strip card, so long as it is stamped for each passenger. On buses, the driver stamps your card. An eight-strip card is 5.60€, a 15-strip card 5.90€, and a 45-strip card 17.40€.

An *enkeltje* (single ticket) is 1.40€ for one zone and 2.10€ for two zones; a *retourtje* (return ticket), valid twice on the same day, is 4.30€. A *dagkaart* (day card), which is valid also at night, is 5.20€. Also available are multiple-day cards valid from two to nine days, for 8.30€ to 25€.

Note: You need to use public transportation a lot to make the day and multi-day cards worthwhile. Should you plan to walk most of the time and take trams only around the Center, you're probably better off with a strip card.

If you are staying in town for a week or more, you might want to consider one of seven different *sterrabonnement* (star subscription) cards. These run from 8.90€ for a single-zone card for a week, to 175€ for a multiple-zone card for a month (and ten times the appropriate monthly rate for a year). It's best to ask about these—and other special tickets such as those for night buses, multiple trips, and groups of ten or more people—at the GVB Tickets & Info office (see above).

Validation: On trams, be sure to stamp your ticket in the yellow machines in the front, middle, and rear of the vehicle, or visit the conductor at the rear. To use the machine with a strip card, fold your card at the line and punch it in. Don't punch in each individual strip but count down the number of strips you need and punch in the last one; if you need more than one strip card to cover the required number, stamp the last strip on the old card and the last strip required on a new one. At Metro stations use the machines at platform entrances and on the platforms (you must have a valid ticket to be allowed on the Metro platforms). Make sure the machine actually did stamp your ticket, and with the correct date.

Most Amsterdam trams either have a conductor or operate on the honor system, but teams of roving inspectors do their best to keep everyone honest. The fine for riding without a ticket or not having one properly stamped is 30€, plus 2.10€ for a ticket, payable on the spot.

BY TRAM & BUS Half the fun of Amsterdam is walking along the canals. The other half is riding the smooth new blue-and-light-gray trams (and some surviving clackety old yellow ones) that roll through most major streets. There are 17 tram routes, 11 of which (1, 2, 4, 5, 9, 13, 16, 17, 24, and 25) begin and end at Centraal Station, so you know you can always get back to that central point if you get lost and have to start over again. The other tram routes are 3, 6, 7, 10, 12, and 14. To board a tram, push the *deur open* (door open) button on the outside of the car beside the door; you board trams that have conductors at the rear and the doors open automatically. Getting off, you also have to push a *deur open* button. Tram doors close automatically and they do it quite quickly, so don't hang around but do tread on the bottom step to prevent the door from closing.

An extensive bus network complements the trams. Many bus routes begin and end at Centraal Station. A minibus service, *De Opstapper,* is helping to solve one of Amsterdam's toughest public transportation problems: how to get access to the long and narrow canalside streets in the city center. White *Opstapper* (literally "step aboarder") minibuses go in both directions along Prinsengracht, between Centraal Station, the Amstel River, and Waterlooplein. A bus departs every 10 minutes from each terminus, Monday through Saturday from 7:30am to 6:30pm. There are no regular stops; just hold out your hand and the driver will stop, and then tell the driver when you want to get out again. You can use any valid public transportation ticket; with a *strippenkaart,* the full one-zone trip—which makes a great mini-sightseeing tour—requires two strips.

BY METRO   It can't compare to the labyrinthine systems of Paris, London, and New York, but Amsterdam does have its own Metro, with four lines—50, 51, 53, and 54—that run partly overground and bring people in from the suburbs. You may want to take them simply as a sightseeing excursion, though to be frank, few of the sights on the lines are worth going out of your way for. On these lines you validate your strip card on the platform before boarding. Due to open in 2004 (but almost sure to be delayed), the Noord/Zuid (North/South) Metro line will have greater utility for tourists, bisecting as it will the city from north to south, from Buikslotermeerplein in Amsterdam Noord, under the IJ to Centraal Station, Rokin, Ceintuurbaan, and Station Zuid/World Trade Center.

BY TRAIN   The railway network is not as useful within Amsterdam as the tram, bus, and Metro network. In addition to Centraal Station, which is the public transportation hub, there are seven stations in the city: Zuid/World Trade Center, RAI, and Amstel in the south; Lelylaan, De Vlugtlaan, and Sloterdijk in the west; and Muiderpoort in the east. Because the transportation network is tightly integrated, all train stations are also served by two or more of the other modes. The excellent Dutch railway network comes into its own for longer distances. It's by far the best way to get to Schiphol Airport, Haarlem, Amsterdam's North Sea coast resort Zandvoort, Hoorn on the IJsselmeer shore, and all other points in Holland.

BY TAXI   It used to be that you couldn't simply hail a cab from the street in Amsterdam, but nowadays they often stop if you do. Otherwise, call **Taxi Centrale** (© **0900/677-7777**) or find one of the taxi stands sprinkled around the city, generally near the luxury hotels or at major squares such as the Dam, Centraal Station, Spui, Rembrandtplein, Westermarkt, and Leidseplein. Taxis have rooftop signs and blue license tags, and are metered. Fares—which include the tip—begin at 2.20€ when the meter starts and run up at the rate of 1.80€ a kilometer, or 1.10€ a mile. Make sure the meter starts out at the correct rate, bearing in mind that the tariffs listed above are likely to increase somewhat during the lifetime of this book.

Most Amsterdam taxi drivers are smoothly functioning professional machines who seem to have been spat out of the same soulless mold. To a budget traveler, their fares are little short of a mugging—if short at all. And then they expect a tip. Don't use taxis unless your need is dire or you can split the cost between two or more travelers. On the plus side, the drivers generally won't rip you off; they don't need to.

ON THE WATER

With all the water Amsterdam has, it makes sense to use it for transportation. Although the options for canal transport are limited (with the exception of cruises and excursions), they do exist, and as an additional benefit they offer a unique and attractive view of the city. Given the ongoing redevelopment work in the old harbor areas, where new residential projects are sprouting like tulips in springtime, it seems likely that water transportation will be increasingly important in the future.

See also "Canal Tour-Boats," "Water Bikes," and "Powerboats," under "Organized Tours," in chapter 6.

BY FERRY   IJ ferries connect the Center with Amsterdam Noord (North), across the IJ channel. The short crossings are free, which makes them ideal mini-cruises for the cash-strapped, and they provide a good view of the harbor. Ferries depart from piers behind Centraal Station along De Ruyterkade. One route goes every 10 to 15 minutes between Pier 7 and Buiksloterweg on the north shore. A second route, employing new ferries introduced in 2002, goes every 20 to 30 minutes from Pier 8 to IJplein, a more easterly point on the north shore. Both services operate round the clock.

BY WATER BUS   Two different companies operate water buses that bring you to, or close to, many of the city's top museums, other attractions, sights, and shopping and entertainment districts. **Canal Bus** (© 020/623-9886) has three routes—Green Line, Red Line, and Blue Line—with a total of 11 stops that include: Centraal Station, Westermarkt, Leidseplein, Rijksmuseum (with an extension to the RAI Convention Center when big shows are on there), Waterlooplein, and East Amsterdam. Hours of operation are daily from 10am to 5pm, with two buses an hour at peak times. A day-pass, valid until noon next day and including a discount on museum admissions, is 14€ for adults, 10€ for children under 14 (children young enough to sit on an adult's lap go free). The **All Amsterdam Transport Pass,** valid on the Canal Bus, trams, buses and the Metro, is 17€ a day, and is available from GVB Tickets & Info, VVV tourist information offices, and the Canal Bus company. It's a good value if you make extensive use of its unlimited travel facility on both the Canal Bus and GVB public transportation.

The **Museumboot (Museum Boat)** (© 020/530-1090)—*boot* is pronounced just like boat—operates a circular scheduled service every 30 minutes in summer and every 45 minutes in winter from 9:30am to 5pm, from Prins Hendrikkade, in front of Centraal Station to Westermarkt, Leidseplein, Museum Quarter, Herengracht, Waterlooplein, and the Eastern Dock. A day ticket is 14€ for adults, 9€ for children 4 to 12, and free for children under 4, and entitles you to discounts of up to 50% on admission to some museums and attractions. Or, from 1pm, you can purchase a "stop-ticket" from the boatman at any of the seven stops (see "Catching the Museum Boat," in chapter 6, for more details).

BY WATER TAXI   Since you're in the city of canals, you might like to splurge on a water taxi. These launches do more or less the same thing as landlubber taxis, except that they do it on the canals and the Amstel River, and in the harbor. You can move faster than on land and you get your very own canal cruise. To order one, call **Watertaxi** (© 020/535-6363), or pick one up from the dock outside Central Station, close to the VVV office. For up to eight people the fare is 70€ for 30 minutes and 50€ for each subsequent half hour.

BY SWIMMING   Believe it or not, some folks (perhaps influenced by too many trips to the "coffeeshop") think this is a good way to get around the canals. It isn't. Swallow so much as one mouthful of that witch's brew and a close encounter with a hospital stomach pump will lie in your immediate future.

BIKES, MOPEDS & MORE
BY BIKE   Instead of renting a car, follow the Dutch example and ride a bike (*fiets*). Sunday, when the city is quiet, is a particularly good day to pedal through

the park and to practice riding on cobblestones and dodging trams before venturing forth into the fray of an Amsterdam rush hour. There are 600,000 bikes in the city, so you'll have plenty of company. Bike-rental rates are around 7€ a day or 30€ a week; a deposit is required.

Going by bike is mostly safe—or at any rate not as suicidal as it looks—thanks to a vast network of dedicated bike lanes. Bikes even have their own traffic lights. Amsterdam's battle-scarred bike-borne veterans of the traffic wars make it almost a point of principle to ignore every safety rule ever written and though they mostly live to tell the tale, don't think the same will necessarily apply for you (see "Biking in Amsterdam," below).

MacBike rents a range of bikes, including tandems and six-speed touring bikes. Outlets are at Mr. Visserplein 2 (② **020/620-0985;** tram: 9, 14); Marnixstraat 220 (② **020/626-6964;** tram: 10, 13, 14, 17); and 's-Gravesandestraat 49 (② **020/693-2104;** tram: 7, 10). **Bike City,** Bloemgracht 70 (② **020/626-3721;** tram: 13, 14, 17), near the Anne Frankhuis, rents bikes, provides maps and suggested routes both inside and outside the city, and will even store and maintain your own bike. **Damstraat Rent-a-Bike,** Damstraat 22–24 (② **020/625-5029;** tram: 4, 9, 14, 16, 24, 25), has a central

 Biking in Amsterdam

What are the rules of the road for biking in Amsterdam? Apparently, there are none. Bikers can go anywhere they want, whenever they want, however they want, and do whatever they want when they get there. Or so you would think from the antics of Amsterdam's massed legions of bikers. They're enough to throw a scare into a bunch of Hell's Angels. Particularly terrifying are the mothers with two kids, one on the front handlebars and the other in a kid's seat at the back, dicing with the trams at Leidseplein. Biking is one activity where you should disregard the maxim "When in Amsterdam, do as the Amsterdammers do"—you might easily end up dead, which could spoil your entire vacation.

It takes a while to get used to moving smoothly and safely through the whirl of trams, cars, buses, trucks, fellow bikers, and pedestrians, particularly if you're on a typically ancient and much-battered *stadfiets* (city bike), also known as an *omafiets* (grandmother bike)—the only kind that makes economic sense here, since anything fancier will attract a crowd of people wanting to steal it. It's better to develop your street smarts slowly. I know this sounds like wimpish advice—you might have mountain-biked from one end of the Rockies to another for all I know—but remember that not everyone on the *straat* is as sensible as you are.

The first rule of biking in Amsterdam: Don't argue with trams—they bite back, hard. The second rule: Cross tram lines perpendicularly so your wheels don't get caught in the grooves, which could pitch you out of the saddle. And the third rule: Don't crash into civilians (pedestrians). That's about it. Like everyone else, you'll likely end up making up the rest of the rules as you go along.

location near the Dam. Feminists both male and female might want to give their business to **Zijwind Fietsen,** a women's cooperative, at Ferdinand Bolstraat 168 (☎ **020/673-7026;** tram 25), though it's a bit out from the Center.

Warning: Always lock both your bike frame and one of the wheels to something solid and fixed, because theft is common.

BY MOPED   If you draw the line at pedaling, maybe a scooter would be more suitable. **Mokum Scooter Rental,** Willemsstraat 133 (☎ **020/422-0266;** tram: 3), rents these for 45€ for 24 hours, including a helmet, insurance, and two locks. Scooters travel in the bike lanes, which in theory gives them an added margin of safety.

BY OTHER MEANS   If you own a pair of rollerblades or even one of those dinky little scooter things, by all means bring them along. You can go around in the bike lanes while saving yourself some money and staying fit.

BY CAR

To drive in the Netherlands, you need only a valid passport, your driver's license, and, if you're bringing your own car, a valid registration and green card proving international insurance.

Don't rent a car to get around Amsterdam. You will regret both the expense and the hassle. The city is a jumble of one-way streets, narrow bridges, and no-parking zones. In addition, it's not uncommon to hear that an automobile, apparently left parked with the hand brake carelessly disengaged, has rolled through a flimsy foot-high railing and into a canal. Should you choose to park, you need either to feed the parking meter or to have a parking permit prominently displayed in your car. Your hotel can sell you this permit, but for short periods it's probably better just to use a meter (if you're lucky enough to find a free one). The city's feared **Dienst Parkeerbeheer (Parking Service Authority),** responsible for clamping and towing illegally parked cars, is well-staffed, hardworking, and efficient. If you don't keep your meter fed or if you park in an illegal space, you're almost sure to fall victim to the authority's search-and-destroy patrols. Their operations are swift and merciless, and the cost of transgression is high.

They don't merely write you a citation, they reinforce the ticket with a wheel-clamp (also known as a "Texas boot"), which costs 68€ to have removed, payable at one of four offices (see below). If the fine isn't paid within 24 hours, they tow your car to a car-pound at Daniël Goedkoopstraat 7 (Metro: Spaklerweg), open 24 hours a day, way out in the boonies of the southeastern Over Amstel district, and they charge you a whopping 154€ for every day it's out there. You can pay wheel-clamp fines at this office and at three other Servicepunten Stadstoezicht offices in the city: Beukenplein 50 (tram: 3, 7, 10); Jan Pieter Heijestraat 94 (tram: 1, 6, 7, 17); and Weesperstraat 105A (Metro: Weesperplein). The phone number for information (☎ **020/553-0333**) is the same for all four offices, and each one of the three city offices is open Monday through Friday from 8am to 6pm and Saturday from 8am to 3:30pm.

The rate for parking in the Center is 2.80€ an hour Monday through Saturday from 9am to midnight and Sunday from noon to midnight. You pay less for each hour if you pay for a block of hours at the same time: 17€ from 9am to 7pm; 11€ from 7pm to midnight; 25€ from 9am to midnight. One-day and 3-day street parking permits are available from many hotels for 15€ and 45€, respectively. You can purchase these permits from Parking Service Authority offices at Bakkerstraat 13; Ceintuurbaan 159; Nieuwezijds Kolk parking lot (off Nieuwezijds Voorburgwal); Kinkerstraat 17; and Cruquiuskade 25. Amsterdam

intends to further restrict traffic through the Center, so expect even more diffi-
culties.

To avoid these charges, or private parking lot rates, you can leave your car at
the free Park & Ride parking lots at some of the outer Metro and train stations
(directions are indicated with blue-and-white P&R signs on the way). Private
parking lots are dotted around town and cost from about 2€ to 4€ an hour and
10€ to 25€ a day in summer, depending on the location. The largest lots are at
Centraal Station, Damrak, under Waterlooplein, adjacent to Leidseplein, and at
Marnixstraat.

As if all the parking hassle isn't bad enough, anything left in your car is money
on the hoof for every junkie and ne'er-do-well in town. They can withdraw your
CD player, cellular phone, and camera faster than you can get cash from an
ATM. Cars with foreign license tags are especially tempting, since they are more
likely to have something interesting in the trunk.

Outside the city, driving is a different story and you may want to rent a car
to tour the nearby countryside. All the top international firms are here: **Avis,**
Nassaukade 380 (*©* **020/683-6061;** tram: 1, 6); **Budget,** Overtoom 121
(*©* **020/612-6066;** tram: 1, 6); **Europcar,** Overtoom 197 (*©* **020/683-2123;**
tram: 1, 6); and **Hertz,** Overtoom 333 (*©* **020/612-2441;** tram: 1, 6). Each of
these firms also has a desk at the airport. Rates begin at around 45€ a day for a
small car with unlimited mileage.

 FAST FACTS: **Amsterdam**

American Express The offices at Damrak 66 (*©* **020/504-7777;** tram: 4, 9,
14, 16, 24, 25) and Van Baerlestraat 39 (*©* **020/673-8550;** tram: 2, 3, 5, 12),
are open Monday through Friday from 9am to 5pm, and Saturday from
9am to noon. The Damrak office provides currency exchange and books
tours; the Van Baerlestraat office only books tours.

Airport See "Getting There," in chapter 2.

ATM Networks Among the centrally located automated teller machines
(ATMs) accessible by cards linked to the Cirrus and Plus networks, and the
major credit cards and charge cards, are those at **ABN-AMRO Bank,** Dam
2 (tram: 4, 9, 14, 16, 24, 25) and Leidsestraat 1 (tram: 1, 2, 5), at Leidseplein; **Rabobank,** Dam 16 (tram: 4, 9, 14, 16, 24, 25); and **Fortis Bank,** Singel 548 (tram: 4, 9, 14, 16, 24, 25), at the Flower Market.

Babysitters Many hotels can arrange babysitters. A reliable local organization is **Oppascentrale Kriterion** (*©* **020/624/5848**), which has vetted
babysitters over 18. Its rates are 5€ to 6€ an hour, with extra charges for
administration, Friday and Saturday evening bookings, and for hotels.

Business Hours **Banks** are open Monday through Friday from 9am to 4 or
5pm, and some to 7pm on Thursday. Open hours for **offices** are Monday
through Friday from 9 or 10am to 4 or 5pm. Regular **shopping** hours are
Monday from 10 or 11am to 6pm; Tuesday, Wednesday, and Friday from
9am to 6pm; Thursday from 9am to 9pm; Saturday from 9am to 5pm; and
some stores are open Sunday from noon to 5pm.

Car Rentals See "Getting Around," earlier in this chapter.

Climate See "When to Go," in chapter 2.

Convention Center **RAI Convention Center,** Europaplein (© 020/549-1212; Metro: RAI), in the south of the city. Events include the Home Interiors Fair, the Dutch Art and Antiques Fair, the Love & Marriage Fair, the Car Show, and (this being Holland) the Bike Show.

Currency See "Money," in chapter 2.

Currency Exchange The best options for changing money are the VVV tourist offices, banks, and, if you carry American Express traveler's checks, **American Express** (see above). Other fair-dealing options are **Thomas Cook,** Damrak 125 (© 020/620-3236; tram: 4, 9, 14, 16, 29, 24, 25), Dam 23–25 (© 020/625-0922; tram: 4, 9, 14, 16, 29, 24, 25), and Leidseplein 31A (© 020/626-7000; tram: 1, 2, 5, 6, 7, 10); and the **Grenswisselkantoor (GWK)** exchanges at Schiphol Airport (© 020/653-5121), Centraal Station (© 020/627-2731), and at some international border crossings and main train stations. These organizations can provide cash advances for holders of American Express, Diners Club, MasterCard, and Visa credit and charge cards. GWK can arrange money transfers through **Western Union.**

Hotels and bureaux de change (currency-exchange offices), which are open regular hours plus evenings and weekends, often charge a low commission (or none at all) but may give a low exchange rate—always know *exactly* how much you are going to get in your hand before agreeing to the transaction.

There are clusters of banks, such as ABN-AMRO, Rabobank, Fortis, and NMB, around the Dam, the Flower Market, and at Leidseplein.

Dentists Call the Central Medical Service (© 020/592-3434).

Doctors Call the Central Medical Service (© 020/592-3434).

Driving Rules See "Getting Around," earlier in this chapter.

Drugstores For such items as toothpaste, deodorant, and razor blades, go to a *drogerij* (drugstore), or a supermarket. See also "Pharmacies," below.

Electricity Before you weigh down your luggage with all your favorite appliances, note that the Netherlands runs on 220 volts electricity (North America uses 110 volts). So you need to take with you a small voltage transformer (available in drug and appliance stores and by mail order) that plugs into the round-holed European electrical outlet and converts the Dutch voltage from 220 volts down to 110 volts for any small appliance up to 1,500 watts. Don't try to plug an American appliance directly into a European outlet without a transformer; you may ruin your appliance and possibly even start a fire. Some American appliances (such as some electric shavers) are engineered to operate on either 110 volts or 220 volts, but even with these you usually need to buy a plug adapter for Dutch outlets.

Embassies & Consulates The **U.S. Consulate** in Amsterdam is at Museumplein 19 (© 020/575-5309; tram: 3, 5, 12, 16), open Monday through Friday from 8:30am to noon and 1:30 to 3:30pm; the U.S. Embassy in The Hague is at Lange Voorhout 102 (© 070/310-9209). The **U.K. Consulate-General** in Amsterdam is at Koningslaan 44 (© 020/676-4343; tram: 2), open Monday through Friday from 9am to noon and 2 to 4pm; the U.K. Embassy in The Hague is at Lange Voorhout 10 (© 070/364-5800).

Citizens of other English-speaking countries should contact their embassies in The Hague. **Australia:** Carnegielaan 14 (© **070/310-8200**); **Canada:** Sophialaan 7, Den Haag (© **070/311-1600**); **Ireland:** Dr. Kuyperstraat 9, Den Haag (© **070/363-0993**); **New Zealand:** Mauritskade 25, Den Haag (© **070/346-9324**).

Emergencies For police assistance, an ambulance, or the fire department, call © **112.**

Holidays January 1 (New Year's Day); Good Friday; Easter Monday; April 30 (Queen's Day/*Koninginnedag*); Ascension Day; Pentecost Monday; December 25 (Christmas) and 26. The dates for Easter, Ascension, and Pentecost change each year.

Hospitals Two hospitals with an emergency service are the **Onze Lieve Vrouwe Gasthuis,** Eerste Oosterparkstraat 179 (© **020/599-9111; tram: 3, 7, 10**), in Amsterdam Oost; and the giant **Academisch Medisch Centrum (AMC),** Meibergdreef 9 (© **020/566-3333;** Metro: Holendrecht), in Amsterdam Zuidoost.

Hot Lines Rape and sexual abuse: De Eerste Lijn (© **020/612-7576**); drugs: Drug Prevention Center (© **020/626-7176**).

Information See "Visitor Information," earlier in this chapter.

Internet Access In the center, **easyEverything** (www.easyeverything.com) has two locations: Damrak 33 (© **020/320-8082;** tram: 1, 2, 4, 5, 9, 13, 16, 17, 24, 25); and Reguliersbreestraat 22 (© **020/320-6291;** tram: 4, 9, 14). Both are open 24 hours a day and access begins at 1.15€. A less-crowded choice is **Internet Café,** Martelaarsgracht 11 (© **020/627-1052;** info@internetcafe.nl; tram: 1, 2, 5, 13, 17), open Sunday through Thursday from 9am to 1am, Friday and Saturday from 9am to 3am; access is 2.75€ an hour.

Language Dutch people speak Dutch, of course, but English is the second language of the Netherlands and it is taught in the schools from the early grades, with the result that nearly everyone speaks fluently. You may speak English in Amsterdam almost as freely as you do at home, particularly to anyone in the business of providing tourist services, whether cab driver, hotel receptionist, waitperson, or store assistant.

Mail Postage for a postcard or ordinary letter to the U.S., Canada, Australia, New Zealand, and South Africa is .75€; to the U.K. and Ireland it's .45€.

Maps See "City Layout," earlier in this chapter.

Narcotics The use of narcotic drugs is officially illegal in the Netherlands, but Amsterdam allows the sale in licensed premises of up to 5 grams (.2 oz.) of hashish or marijuana for personal consumption, and possession of 30 grams (1.2 oz.) for personal use. Not every local authority in the Netherlands is as liberal-minded as Amsterdam when it comes to smoking pot—and Amsterdam is not so tolerant that you should just light up on the street, in cafes, and on trams and trains (though enough dopey people do). The possession and use of hard drugs like heroin, cocaine, and ecstasy is an offense, and the police have swept most of the downtown heroin-shooting galleries away from the tourist centers, but even in these cases the drug abusers are considered a medical and social problem rather than purely as a law-enforcement issue. On the other hand, peddling drugs *is* a serious offense. See "Smoking Coffeeshops," in chapter 9.

Newspapers & Magazines You can get the main British and Irish daily newspapers, the *International Herald Tribune, Wall Street Journal Europe,* and *USA Today,* along with *Time, Newsweek, U.S. News & World Report, Business Week, Fortune, The Economist,* and more from the **American Book Center,** Kalverstraat 185 (© 020/625-5537; tram: 4, 9, 14, 16, 24, 25), and **Waterstone's,** Kalverstraat 152 (© 020/638-3821; tram: 4, 9, 14, 16, 24, 25). Newsstands at Schiphol Airport and Centraal Station also have a big choice in international newspapers and magazines.

Pharmacies For both prescription and non-prescription medicines, you go to an *apotheek* (pharmacy). Try **Dam Apotheek** at Damstraat 2 (© 020/624-4331; tram: 4, 9, 14, 16, 24, 25). All pharmacies have the name and address of an all-night and Sunday pharmacy posted on the door.

Police Holland's emergency number to call for the police (*politie*), fire department, and ambulance is © **112.** For routine matters, police headquarters are at Elandsgracht 117 (© **0900/8844;** tram: 7, 10, 17).

Post Office Most **post offices** are open Monday through Friday from 9am to 5pm. The post office at Singel 250–256, at the corner of Raadhuisstraat (© **020/556-3311;** tram: 13, 14, 17), is open Monday through Friday from 9am to 6pm (to 8pm Thurs), and Saturday from 9am to 3pm. To mail a large package, go to the post office at Oosterdokskade 3, a large building on the right as you face Centraal Station.

Safety See "Insurance, Health & Safety," in chapter 2.

Salons In addition to beauty salons and barbershops in many major hotels, stylish hairdressers are to be found on Pieter Cornelisz Hooftstraat and on Rokin. **George en Leon,** Leidsegracht 104 (© **020/626-3831;** tram: 7, 10), and the **Hair en Beauty Center,** Rokin 140–142 (© **020/623-2381;** tram: 4, 9, 14, 16, 24, 25), are smooth performers. For something a little (or a lot) out of the ordinary, try **Hair Police,** Kerkstraat 113 (© **020/420-5841;** tram: 16, 25, 25).

Taxes There's a value-added tax (BTW) of 6% on hotel and restaurant bills (19% on beer, wine, and liquor), and 6% or 19% (the amount depends on the product) on purchases. This tax is always included in the price. People resident outside the European Union can shop tax-free in Amsterdam. Shops that offer tax-free shopping advertise with a Holland Tax-Free Shopping sign in the window, and they provide you with the form you need to recover value-added tax (VAT) when you leave the European Union. Refunds are available only when you spend more than 137€ in a store. See "The Shopping Scene" in chapter 8 for more details.

Taxis See "Getting Around," earlier in this chapter.

Telephones **To call Amsterdam:** If you're calling Amsterdam from the United States:

1. Dial the international access code: 011
2. Dial the country code for the Netherlands: 31
3. Dial the area code 20 and then the number. So the whole number you'd dial would be 011-31-20-000-0000.

To make international calls: To make international calls from Amsterdam, first dial 00 and then the country code (U.S. or Canada 1, U.K. 44,

Ireland 353, Australia 61, New Zealand 64). Next you dial the area code and number. For example, if you wanted to call the British Embassy in Washington, D.C., you would dial 00-1-202-588-7800.

For operator assistance: To make an international collect call, dial ℂ **0800/0410.** To call collect inside Holland, dial ℂ **0800/0101** (or press the "Collect" button if the phone you're using has one).

Toll-free numbers: Numbers beginning with 0800 within Holland are toll-free, but calling a 1-800 number in the States from Holland is not toll-free. In fact, it costs the same as an overseas call.

Special numbers: Watch out for the special Dutch numbers that begin with 0900. Calls to these are charged at a far higher rate than ordinary local calls. Depending who you call, they are from .25€ to .90€ a minute.

To call the United States or Canada, dial **00** (the international access code) + **1** (the country code) + the area code + the number. Other country codes are: Australia, **61;** United Kingdom, **44;** Ireland, **353;** New Zealand, **64.**

International calls, per minute, are: **U.S.** and **Canada:** .30€; **U.K.** and **Ireland:** .25€; **Australia** and **New Zealand:** .40€. You can use pay phones in booths all around town with a KPN *telekaart* (phone card), selling for 5€, 13€, and 25€ from post offices, train ticket counters, and newsstands. Some pay phones take coins, of .05€, .10€, .20€, .50€, and 1€. Use smaller coins whenever possible, at least until you are connected with the right person, as no change is given from an individual coin and once the call has begun, excess coins will not be returned when you hang up. Should there be no answer, hang up and the coin comes back to you. On both card and coin phones, a digital reading tracks your decreasing deposit so you know when to add another card or more coins. To make additional calls when you still have a coin or card inserted, briefly break the connection, and you will get a new dial tone for another call.

The area code for Amsterdam is 020. When making local calls in Amsterdam you won't need to use the area codes shown in this book. You do need to use an area code between towns and cities. The two main formats for Dutch phone numbers are for cities and large towns a three-digit area code followed by a seven-digit number, and for small towns and villages a four-digit area code followed by a six-digit number.

In the Dutch telephone system, there's a sustained dial tone, and a beep-beep sound for a busy signal. Both local and long-distance calls from a pay phone are .25€ a minute. Calls placed through your hotel switchboard or dialed direct from your room phone are usually more than twice the standard rate.

To speak with an operator, call ℂ **0800.** For information inside Holland, call ℂ **0900/8008;** for international information, call ℂ **0900/8418;** for international collect calls, call ℂ **0900/0410.**

To charge a call to your calling card, call AT&T (ℂ **0800/022-9111**); MCI (ℂ **0800/022-9122**); Sprint (ℂ **0800/022-9119**); Canada Direct (ℂ **0800/022-9116**); British Telecom (ℂ **0800/022-9944**).

Time Zone   Holland is on Central European time (CET), which is Greenwich mean time (GMT) plus 1 hour. Amsterdam is normally 6 hours ahead of New York City time and 9 hours ahead of Los Angeles time.

Tipping The Dutch government requires that all taxes and service charges be included in the published prices of hotels, restaurants, cafes, discos, nightclubs, beauty salons/barbershops and hairdressers, and sightseeing companies. Even taxi fare includes taxes and a standard 15% tip. To be absolutely sure in a restaurant, for example, that tax and service are included, look for the words *inclusief BTW en service* (BTW is the abbreviation for the Dutch words that mean value-added tax), or ask the waiter. The Dutch are so accustomed to having these charges included that many restaurants have stopped spelling it out.

Dutch waitpersons appreciate tips and rely on them to supplement their salary. To tip as the Dutch do, in a cafe or snack bar leave some small change; in a restaurant, leave 1€ to 2€, and up to a generous 5€ if you think the service was particularly good; for expensive tabs, you may want to leave more—or maybe less! An informal survey (I asked a taxi driver) reveals that Americans and British are the best tippers; the worst are the Dutch themselves.

Toilets Maybe you better sit down for this one. The most important thing to remember about public toilets in Amsterdam—apart from calling them *toiletten* (twa-*lett*-en) or "the WC" (*vay say*) and not restrooms or comfort stations—is not the usual male/female distinction (important though that is) but to *pay the person* who sits at the entrance. He or she has a saucer where you put your money. If you don't, you might have a visitor in the inner sanctum while you're transacting your business. Even if you have paid, in busy places the attendant may have forgotten your face by the time you emerge and will then pursue you out of the toilet and along the street. It's tiresome, but toilets usually costs only about .1€.

If you have a toilet emergency in the Center, the very best address to find relief is the Grand Hotel Krasnapolsky (see "In the Old Center," in chapter 4). Just breeze in as if you own the "Kras," swing left past the front desk and along the corridor, past the Winter Garden restaurant, then up a short flight of stairs. Marble washbasins and what look to be gold-plated faucets are among the wonders therein.

Transit Info For information regarding tram, bus, Metro, and train services, call ✆ **0900/9292.**

Useful Phone Numbers **Lost Property:** Call ✆ **020/560-5858** for tram, bus, and Metro; ✆ **020/557-8544** for trains and stations; and ✆ **020/649-1433** for Schiphol Airport. Don't be optimistic about your chances. There are plenty of honest Amsterdammers, but they're generally out of town when you lose something.

U.S. Dept. of State Travel Advisory ✆ **202/647-5225** (manned 24 hr.). U.S. Passport Agency ✆ **202/647-0518.** U.S. Centers for Disease Control International Traveler's Hot Line: ✆ **404/332-4559.**

See also the phone numbers for embassies and consulates, above.

Water The water from the faucet in Amsterdam is safe to drink. Many people drink bottled mineral water, called generically *spa* even though it's not all from the Belgian Spa brand.

4

Where to Stay

Is your preference old-world charm combined with luxurious quarters? Glitzy modernity with every conceivable amenity? Small, intimate, family-run hotels? A historic canal house that reflects the lifestyle of centuries past? A modern, medium-sized hotel on the fringe of inner-city hustle and bustle? A bare-bones room in a dormitory, which frees up scarce dollars for other purposes? Amsterdam has them all, and more. Some hotels share more than one of these characteristics: A common fusion is that of historic canal house on the outside and glitzy modernity with every conceivable amenity on the inside.

You probably have your own idea of what makes a great hotel. My advice is to let your choice reflect the kind of city Amsterdam is—democratic, adventurous, quirky, and always in search of that enigmatic Dutch quality, *gezelligheid,* which is the ambience that makes a place warm, cozy, friendly, and welcoming. You can find this quality at all prices levels, and especially among the moderately priced hotels owned by local people.

There are around 30,000 hotel and hostel beds available, 40% of which are in four- and five-star hotels. The city has moved in recent years to redress the balance in favor of hotels in the mid- and low-priced categories, but it is inevitably a slow process. If a particular hotel strikes your fancy but is out of your price range, it may pay to inquire if special off-season, weekend, specific weekday, or other packages will bring prices down to what you can afford.

Should your heart be set on, or your financial circumstances dictate, a low-end budget hotel, and you're arriving during almost any period between spring and fall, don't simply brush past the hotel and hostel touts at Centraal Station. Spending a minute to discuss pros and cons with them may save you long hours tramping the cobblestones or waiting in line at a VVV hotel reservations desk. They usually have photographs of the rooms they are offering, but don't commit to taking a place without first eyeballing the bricks-and-mortar reality.

HOTEL ORIENTATION

For most people, the first consideration in choosing a hotel is money: How much does a particular hotel cost, and is it worth it? Don't despair if you wish to spend less than 100€ a night for a double room with bathroom. Most Amsterdam hotels, whatever their cost, are clean and tidily furnished, and in many cases they've been recently renovated or redecorated. Shabby hotels with unhelpful staff are rare, but they do exist. If circumstance should place you in a hotel different from those recommended below, and you find an unacceptable degree of shabbiness, call around or visit a VVV tourist information office for a better bet in your price range.

All hotels have been designated according to their high-season rates. If breakfast is not included, expect to pay 5€ to 15€ and up for a continental, buffet, or full breakfast, depending on the category of your hotel. Single rates are available in many hotels, though not always for a significant reduction over double occupancy. Only those hotels with rooms that all, or nearly all, have private facilities are listed here, even in the inexpensive category, unless there are compelling reasons for including a hotel where this is not the case. Only rates that apply to rooms with bathrooms are used to determine a hotel's price category. Room rates increase on average 5% annually.

If you are traveling with kids, always ask about special rates for them. Many hotels allow a child to share their parents' room free or for a small extra charge.

Many Amsterdam hotels, in all price categories, offer significant rate reductions between November 1 and March 31, with the exception of the Christmas and New Year period. The city is as much a delight then as in the tourist-packed summer months. You'll enjoy a calendar full of cultural events, the full blossoming of many traditional Dutch dishes not offered in warm weather, and the fact that streets, cafes, restaurants, and museums are filled more with locals than with visitors.

The next consideration is location: How close is a hotel to sights, restaurants, shops, or the transportation to get to them, and what sort of neighborhood is it in? There are neighborhoods that you probably want to avoid; these might include the haunts of drug or sex peddlers. Amsterdammers accept such phenomena as facts of life, and there are really no "no-go" areas. You'll probably venture into Amsterdam's shady corners in daylight or as an evening lark, but there's no reason to spend your nights in a less-than-desirable area or worry about getting back to your room safely. The hotels described here are all decent hotels in decent neighborhoods (in the case of a few on the fringes of neighborhoods that aren't quite so decent, this is mentioned in the text).

STANDARD AMENITIES Hotel rooms without a private bathroom were once quite common in Amsterdam. A major element in the upgrading of low-cost hotels has been shoehorning bathrooms into them, and the city's canal houses and older buildings have posed a major obstacle to efforts to upgrade. One ingenious Dutch solution you may encounter is the "shower/toilet"—a combination shower stall and water closet, fully tiled, that gets the job done but inevitably results in a lot of soggy toilet paper! The term *bathroom,* by the way, is used whether the bathing facilities are a tub, tub/shower combination, shower stall, or one of those silly little shower/toilets.

You can get as much (or as little) out of your hotel-room TV as you might at home. Dutch channels show a number of American programs and air them in English with Dutch subtitles. Cable TV is firmly entrenched and many hotels have hookups. That may add CNN, BBC, MTV, Sky, and others to the menu. If you're traveling with the kids, be warned that some Dutch, German, and Luxembourg stations broadcast soft (and some not-so-soft) porn shows late at night.

RESERVATIONS This is a popular tourist city, especially during summer months and the tulip season, between early April and mid-May. You are advised always to make your reservation in advance. You can do this directly with any of the hotels below. They will often ask you to confirm by fax or e-mail and/or give your credit card number. Be sure you provide ample time for them to reply before you leave home. (See "Telephones" in "Fast Facts: Amsterdam," in chapter 3, before dialing; or write to the addresses given below.) In addition, you can reserve a hotel room through the **Netherlands Reservations Center (NRC),** Nieuwe Gouw 1, 1442 LE, Purmerend, Netherlands (© **029/968-9144;**

fax 029/968-9154; info@hotelres.nl), and you can reserve online at the NRC's Internet site: **www.hotelres.nl**.

Or, reserve with the **Amsterdam Reservation Center** (℗ **077/700-0888**; reservations@amsterdamtourist.nl), which is connected with the VVV Amsterdam tourist information office. Should you arrive in Amsterdam without a reservation, VVV Amsterdam is well organized to help you, for a moderate charge of 2.50€, plus a refundable room deposit of 2.50€. This is a nice reassurance if you prefer to freelance your itinerary, though at busy periods of the year you have to expect to take potluck. They will always find you something, even at the busiest times, but it may not be what, or where, you want.

TRANSPORTATION   Most public transportation connections given are by tram (streetcar) and most, though not all, are from Centraal Station. Never use the Metro system if there is a tram stop within similar distance from your hotel: You won't get such a good view, and the Metro is a less pleasant way to travel. Inevitably, not all hotels are right by a tram stop, so if your bags are heavy you would be better off taking a taxi right from the start.

PARKING   The entire center of Amsterdam has become a free-fire zone for marauding units of the **Dienst Parkeerbeheer (Parking Service Authority).** The locals have learned to keep their heads down and their parking meters loaded at all times. Parking is ruinously expensive, and the Parkeerbeheer will get you for sure if you try to beat the system, so either don't bring the car or stash it on the edge of town and come in by tram. See "Getting Around," in chapter 3, for more information on parking.

TIPPING   The standard 15% service charge that's included in hotel rates in Holland eliminates the need to tip under normal circumstances. Tip if you wish for a long stay or extra service, but don't worry about not tipping if that's your style. The Dutch welcome tips but don't expect them (an important distinction if you've ever been hassled by a bellboy who lit every lamp in your room until he heard the rattle of spare change).

VEXATIONS   **Mosquitoes,** which thrive in the damp conditions on and near the canals and on waterlogged reclaimed land around the city, can be a major nuisance. You can buy various plug-in devices to hold them at bay, but it's better not to let them into your room in the first place.

Amsterdam businesses in general don't much like credit cards—they offend against an ingrained Calvinist prejudice in favor of getting cash on the nail. The result in some Moderate and Inexpensive hotels is a **credit card charge,** usually 5%.

Also, the lower down the price scale you go, you may find yourself subjected to "amenities" such as tiny washbasins in which you can just about wash one hand at a time; no soap or shampoo in the bathrooms; a supplementary for orange juice at breakfast, even if the juice in question comes out of a carton— talk about being nickel-and-dimed (or dollar-and-pounded) to death.

GAY & LESBIAN HOTELS   Though by law no hotel is allowed to turn away same-sex couples—in Amsterdam such a thing is unimaginable anyway—your reception and the tourist advice you get will probably be better-tailored at gay-run accommodations. There are gay hotels aplenty in Amsterdam. Prices and facilities are pretty unexceptional—the knowledge that most guests will be out and about enjoying themselves is the probable reason for hotels not turning up the luxury level.

A Canal-House Warning

Elevators are difficult things to shoehorn into the cramped confines of a 17th-century Amsterdam canal house and cost more than some moderately priced and budget hotels can afford. Many simply don't have them. If lugging your old wooden sea chest up six flights of narrow stairs is liable to void your life insurance policy, better make sure the elevators are in place and working.

Be prepared to climb hard-to-navigate stairways if you want to save money by lodging in a hotel without an elevator. Narrow and steep as ladders, these stairways were designed to conserve space in the narrow houses along the canals. Today they're an anomaly that'll make your stay even more memorable. If you have difficulty climbing stairs, ask for a room on a lower floor.

COMPLAINTS   Standards of service are, shall we say, more relaxed in Amsterdam than, shall we say, in New York. That's not to say you won't get good, friendly service—you will—but there's a subtle subtext: Dutch service-providers just naturally assume they're doing you a favor, rather than doing their duty. This attitude surfaces most clearly when you make a complaint. You may be astonished to discover that if you have a problem with something, the fault might be attributed to you, for not being satisfied with what's being provided! And then there's the approach to making complaints adopted by some, shall we say, Americans. Rearing up on one's hind legs and hollering until the staff person gets his or her butt into gear goes down like the *Titanic* in Amsterdam. America might be the land of the free, but Dutch hotel personnel can't see much difference between slavery and what their American counterparts evidently have to do, and take. In a big international hotel, where the staff is used to the demanding "foibles" of the world's business travelers, the response is likely to be glacial but correct. But in a local hotel further down the financial food chain, watch out, you might have a stand-up fight on your hands. (We even have a report of a reader, making a reasonable complaint in a reasonable manner, being punched out by the receptionist—the hotel in question has been pulled from this book.)

1 In the Old Center

VERY EXPENSIVE

Crowne Plaza Amsterdam City Centre ★★ *Kids*   A red-coated footman greets you at the door when you arrive, and he sets the tone for everything else at this fine hotel. Relaxed luxury is perhaps the best way to describe the Crowne Plaza. Some rooms have the kind of wooden beams that are typical of canalside houses in Amsterdam. Each one comes equipped with a trouser press and there are comfortable armchairs and good desks for those of you who want to work. This hotel is ideal for tourists and expense-account travelers alike. An ongoing renovation program ensures that rooms and public spaces are kept up-to-date. **Dorrius** is one of Amsterdam's standout, Old Dutch restaurants (see chapter 5 for full details). The **Amsterdammer Bar & Patio** has the style of a typical local cafe.

Nieuwezijds Voorburgwal 5 (near Centraal Station), 1012 RC Amsterdam. © 020/620-0500. Fax 020/620-1173. www.amsterdam-citycentre.crowneplaza.com. 270 units. 335€ double; 695€ suite; add 5% city tax.

Central Amsterdam Accommodations

Club Room rates include continental breakfast. AE, DC, MC, V. Valet and self-parking 35€. Tram: 1, 2, 5, 13, 17 to Martelaarsgracht. **Amenities:** 2 restaurants (Dutch, international); bar; heated indoor pool; health club with sauna; concierge; business center; 24-hr. room service; massage; babysitting; laundry service; dry cleaning; nonsmoking rooms; executive rooms. *In room:* A/C, TV w/pay movies, dataport, minibar, coffeemaker, hair dryer, iron, safe.

The Grand Sofitel Demeure Amsterdam ★★   The Grand is indeed one of the grandest hotels in town. It's in a building that was a 15th-century convent, a 16th-century royal inn, the 17th-century Dutch Admiralty, and the 19th-century Town Hall. To reach the lobby, you walk through a courtyard with a fountain, then through the brass-and-wood revolving door. There are fresh flower arrangements on all the tables in the lobby and lounge area, where tea is served in the afternoon. You also find plenty of Art Deco style and stained-glass windows. The black-and-white marble floors are covered with Oriental rugs. All this, and only a vigorous stone's throw from the Red Light District. The individually styled and furnished guest rooms are designed to reflect the different phases of the building's illustrious past and are about the last word in plush (though some rooms put a refreshingly simple slant on this). Most have couches and armchairs; all have a personal safe and a voice-mail answering system for the telephone. The views are good too, onto the 17th-century canals, the hotel garden, or the courtyard. You can have lunch or dinner at the Art Deco, brasserie-style Café Roux, where you see an original Karel Appel mural, the *Inquisitive Children*.

Oudezijds Voorburgwal 197 (off Damstraat), 1012 EX Amsterdam. ℭ **800/228-3000** in the U.S. and Canada, or 020/555-3111. Fax 020/555-3222. www.thegrand.nl. 182 units. 360€–395€ double; from 450€ suite; add 5% city tax. AE, DC, MC, V. Parking 25€. Tram: 4, 9, 16, 24, 25 to Spui. **Amenities:** Heated indoor pool; health club; Jacuzzi; sauna; concierge; courtesy car; secretarial services; 24-hr. room service; in-room massage; babysitting; laundry service; dry cleaning. *In room:* A/C, TV w/pay movies, dataport, minibar, coffeemaker, hair dryer, safe.

Hôtel de l'Europe ★★★   On a stretch of prime riverside real estate in the city center, this elegant, old establishment is one of the Leading Hotels of the World. Its pastel-red and white facade, at the point where the Amstel River flows into the city's canal network, is an iconic element in the classic view of the city. Built in 1896, the de l'Europe has a grand style and a sense of ease, a smooth combination of aged dignity and modern comforts. Rooms and bathrooms are spacious and bright, furnished with classic good taste. Some rooms have minibalconies overlooking the river and all boast marble bathrooms. The **Excelsior** (see chapter 5 for full details), one of the toniest restaurants in town, serves breakfast, lunch, and dinner daily. **Le Relais** is a less formal setting for light lunches and dinners. Drinks and hors d'oeuvres are served daily in **Freddy's Bar** and in summer only on **La Terrasse,** overlooking the Amstel, from 11am to 1am (weather permitting).

Nieuwe Doelenstraat 2–8 (facing Muntplein), 1012 CP Amsterdam. ℭ **800/223-6800** in the U.S. and Canada, or 020/531-1777. Fax 020/531-1778. www.leurope.nl. 100 units. 335€–415€ double; suites from 445€; add 5% city tax. AE, DC, MC, V. Valet and self-parking 38€. Tram: 4, 9, 14, 16, 24, 25 to De Munt. **Amenities:** 2 restaurants (French, international); 2 bars; heated indoor pool; health club; sauna; concierge; 24-hr. room service; massage; babysitting; laundry service; dry cleaning; nonsmoking rooms. *In room:* A/C, TV w/pay movies, dataport, minibar, hair dryer, safe.

EXPENSIVE

Die Port van Cleve ★★   Fairly oozing history and charm, this hotel is near the Royal Palace and next to Magna Plaza, a big shopping center in what used to be the city's main Post Office. The hotel itself is one of the city's oldest, and started life in 1864 as the first Heineken brewery. Over the last 100 years it has

---

Kids **Family-Friendly Hotels**

Crowne Plaza Amsterdam City Centre (p. 69)   The Crowne Plaza has good and reliable amenities that are comfortable and convenient for traveling families. And it also has an indoor pool.

Estheréa (p. 81)   Though most of the rooms in this canal-house hotel are rather small, all are tastefully furnished, and a few, ideal for families, are equipped with bunk beds, always a favorite with children.

Sint-Nicolaas (p. 77)   A centrally located hotel run by the warm Mesker family, which welcomes guests into a comfortable and relaxed environment that is child-friendly.

City Hostel Vondelpark (p. 91)   An ideal choice for families traveling on a limited budget, offering a good blend of facilities, space, easygoing atmosphere, and security, in addition to a green location in the city's famous Vondelpark.

Amstel Botel (p. 77)   Although it is more common to find youthful spirits traveling alone or in small groups here, there is no reason why it wouldn't work for families, and there is the added interest for the kids of being on a ship, even if it isn't going anywhere.

---

accommodated many famous guests. The ornamental facade, complete with turrets and alcoves, is original and was fully restored in 1997. Likewise, the interior has been completely renovated, and the rooms, though relatively small, have been furnished comfortably in modern yet cozy style. You won't eat much more traditionally Dutch than in the **Brasserie de Poort,** and you can drink in the **Bodega de Blauwe Parade** watched over by Delft blue tiles.

Nieuwezijds Voorburgwal 176–180 (behind the Royal Palace), 1012 SJ Amsterdam. ✆ **020/624-4860.** Fax 020/622-0240. www.dieportvancleve.com. 120 units. TV. 215€–295€ double; 350€–525€ suite; add 5% city tax. AE, DC, MC, V. No parking. Tram: 1, 2, 5, 13, 17 to the Dam. **Amenities:** Restaurant (Dutch/international); bar; cafe; concierge; business center; limited room service; babysitting; laundry service; dry cleaning; nonsmoking rooms; executive rooms. *In room:* TV w/pay movies, hair dryer, safe.

Golden Tulip Hotel Inntel Amsterdam-Centre ✦   This fine hotel opened in 1996 as part of the redevelopment of Nieuwezijds Kolk, a small and relatively quiet side street off the Nieuwezijds Voorburgwal, not far from Centraal Station. The Inntel stands beside the spot where the remains of the 13th-century castle of the lords of Aemstel were uncovered by builders and subsequently excavated. The hotel is very modern in its design and facilities. When it opened, the Inntel was considerably less expensive than other upmarket hotels in the area, but instant popularity has allowed it to close the gap rapidly; the American buffet breakfast is no longer included in the room rate.

Nieuwezijds Kolk 19 (off Nieuwezijds Voorburgwal), 1012 PV Amsterdam. ✆ **020/530-1818.** Fax 020/422-1919. www.goldentulip.com. 236 units. 190€–270€ double; 281€ suite; add 5% city tax. AE, DC, MC, V. Tram: 1, 2, 5, 13, 17 to Nieuwezijds Kolk. **Amenities:** Bar; business center; limited room service; laundry service; dry cleaning; nonsmoking rooms. *In room:* A/C, TV w/pay movies, minibar, coffeemaker, hair dryer, safe.

Hotel Amsterdam ✦✦   Just 400m (436 yd.) from Centraal Station, this hotel, from 1911 and still owned by descendants of the original proprietors, has an 18th-century facade. Its rooms are supermodern, though, featuring thick carpets and ample wardrobe space. The entire hotel underwent renovation, completed in April 2001. Rooms at the front of the hotel tend to get more light, but are also subjected to more street noise; some have balconies. The in-house **De Roode Leeuw** restaurant serves typical Dutch cuisine and daily two-course menus. The glassed-in heated terrace overlooking the Dam is a pleasant and relaxing spot for a beer (open daily 11am–11:30pm).

Damrak 93–94 (beside the Dam), 1012 LP Amsterdam. © 020/555-0666. Fax 020/620-4716. www.hotel amsterdam.nl. 80 units. 225€–250€ double. AE, DC, MC, V. No parking. Tram: 4, 9, 14, 16, 24, 25 to the Dam. **Amenities:** Restaurant (Dutch); business center; 24-hr. room service; laundry service; dry cleaning; non-smoking rooms; executive rooms; in-house movies. *In room:* A/C, TV w/pay movies, dataport, minibar, coffeemaker, hair dryer, safe.

NH Barbizon Palace Hotel ★★   This sparkling establishment meets every criterion for the ideal Amsterdam hotel. It was built behind the facades of 19 traditional canal houses. Inside, it's fully modern, loaded with amenities, and efficient; it's also centrally located, within walking distance of Centraal Station and the Dam. Many of the rooms feature split-level designs and antique oak beams. A Roman forum may come to mind as you step into the hotel; the lobby is a long promenade of highly polished black-and-white marble floor tiles, with a massive skylight arching above. The excellent Restaurant **Vermeer** earns frequent praise from food critics. **Hudson's,** serving light food, and a late breakfast of juice, two eggs, a *broodje,* and coffee or tea from 10:30am to noon, is also pretty good.

Prins Hendrikkade 59–72 (facing Centraal Station), 1012 AD Amsterdam. © 800/327-1177 in the U.S. and Canada, or 020/556-4564. Fax 020/624-3353. www.goldentuliphotels.nl/gtbpalace. 275 units. 275€–380€ double; add 5% city tax. AE, DC, MC, V. Parking 25€. Tram: 1, 2, 4, 5, 9, 13, 16, 17, 24, 25 to Centraal Station. **Amenities:** 2 restaurants (Dutch/international); bar; health club with Jacuzzi and sauna; concierge; car-rental desk; business center; salon; 24-hr. room service; babysitting; laundry service; dry cleaning. *In room:* A/C, TV w/pay movies, minibar.

NH Grand Hotel Krasnapolsky ★★   Living it up at the Hotel Krasnapolsky, one of Amsterdam's landmark hotels, is no great trick. The Krasnapolsky is on the Dam, facing the Royal Palace. It began life as the Wintertuin ("Winter Garden") restaurant, where Victorian ladies and gentlemen sipped wine and nibbled pancakes beneath the hanging plants and lofty skylight ceiling—the Wintertuin still dominates the ground floor. The place was founded in 1866 by a Polish tailor turned entrepreneur. Its original 100 rooms had parquet floors, central heating, and electric lights—the first hotel in Holland to have them. Over the past century the "Kras" has spread over four buildings on several different levels. The sizes and shapes of the rooms vary, with some tastefully converted into individually decorated apartments. Renovations have added a new wing featuring a Japanese garden and a Dutch roof garden. The hotel's side streets lead into the Red Light District, which may not be the ideal direction to take for a casual evening stroll. There are several great dining possibilities here. The Winter Garden is the most elegant place in Amsterdam for lunch. **Brasserie Reflet** specializes in French cuisine, and there are two fine Japanese restaurants: **Edo** and **Kyo.** Certainly the most novel is the Bedouin banquet dinner at the **Shibli,** Friday through Sunday.

Dam 9 (facing Royal Palace), 1012 JS Amsterdam. © 020/554-9111. Fax 020/622-8607. www.nh-hotels.com. 468 units. 290€–340€ double; 450€–700€ suite; add 5% city tax. AE, DC, MC, V. Valet parking and self-parking 35€. Tram: 4, 9, 14, 16, 24, 25 to the Dam. **Amenities:** 4 restaurants (French, Bedouin buffet, 2 Japanese); lounge; bar; health club; concierge; business center; salon; 24-hr. room service; babysitting;

laundry service; dry cleaning; nonsmoking rooms; executive rooms. *In room:* A/C, TV w/pay movies, dataport, minibar, coffeemaker, hair dryer, iron, safe.

Radisson SAS ★★ You can't get much closer to Old Amsterdam than at this stylish hotel in the higgledy-piggledy heart of the old city. When you walk into the dazzling atrium you face the facade of a vicarage dating from 1650. Because of Amsterdam's strict preservation laws, SAS couldn't knock the building down, so they built around it and incorporated it into the new structure. Two 18th-century merchants' houses and a former paper factory complete the thoroughly renovated ensemble. The hotel offers four types of rooms. The first is typically Dutch, with oak furnishings and paneling and orange curtains. The other rooms are done in either a Scandinavian, an Asian, or an Art Deco theme. All offer a standard of comfort and style that has made the SAS a firm favorite in Amsterdam. You find a writing desk, and queen-size, king-size, or twin beds in each room. Dine in the grill-restaurant **De Palmboom** or the Mediterranean-style **Talavera;** the oak-beamed **De Pastoriebar,** in the old vicarage, handles drinks and snacks.

Rusland 17 (at the University of Amsterdam), 1012 CK Amsterdam. © 800/333-3333 in the U.S. and Canada, or 020/520-8300. Fax 020/520-8200. www.radissonsas.com. 243 units. 210€–330€ double; from 395€ suite; add 5% city tax. Buffet breakfast included in business class and suite rates. AE, DC, MC, V. Valet parking and self-parking 25€. Tram: 4, 9, 16, 24, 25 to Spui. **Amenities:** 2 restaurants (grill, Mediterranean); bar; health center with sauna; concierge; courtesy car; secretarial services; 24-hr. room service; babysitting; laundry service; dry cleaning. *In room:* A/C, TV w/pay movies, minibar, hair dryer, safe.

Renaissance Amsterdam ★★ Van Gogh liked the setting that would one day become the Renaissance well enough to paint part of it. Built around an open central courtyard in an area of old warehouses, the six-story hotel blends with the gabled facades nearby. The influence of antiquity stops at the front door, however: The Renaissance is supermodern, offering big beds, color TVs with in-house movies, electronic security, and message-retrieval systems. It's a matter of taste whether you like the hotel's transformation of the adjacent domed Lutheran Koepelkerk, into an "ultramodern conference center." The restored, strikingly beautiful old church, which dates from 1671 and was painted in 1885 by van Gogh, seems more suited to its alternative use as a dining chamber. The fine restaurant **Brasserie Noblesse** has a distinctively American slant. The **Koepelcafé** serves local dishes and the **Patio Room** serves coffee, drinks, and snacks. You can let your hair down at the Boston Club disco.

Kattengat 1 (at Singel), 1012 SZ Amsterdam. © 800/HOTELS-1 in the U.S. and Canada, or 020/621-2223. Fax 020/623-7742. www.renaissancehotels.com. 405 units. 245€–265€ double; 230€–345€ executive room; add 5% city tax. Club Room rates include continental breakfast. AE, DC, MC, V. Parking 36€. Tram: 1, 2, 5, 13, 17 to Martelaarsgracht. **Amenities:** Restaurant (international); 2 bars; health club with Jacuzzi and sauna; bike rental; concierge; business center; salon; 24-hr. room service; babysitting; laundry service; dry cleaning; nonsmoking rooms; executive rooms. *In room:* A/C, TV w/pay movies, dataport, minibar, hair dryer, iron.

Swissôtel Amsterdam ★ If you like to stay at elegant, not-too-big hotels wherever you travel in Europe, you'll be pleased by the Swissôtel Amsterdam. Opened in 1987, this hotel, like so many in Amsterdam, was built anew within the walls of a group of traditional canal-house buildings (Damrak was at one time a canal). The location is superb, just footsteps off the Dam and directly across from De Bijenkorf department store. The service is personal and thoughtful; guest rooms are large and quiet, thanks to double-glazed windows. The bathrooms are fully tiled in marble. All guest rooms and the lobby have been renovated in the last few years. You have to go elsewhere to find a health club or a hairdresser, but the Swissôtel offers very good value for money in this prime location. Restaurant **Olio** takes its inspiration from Mediterranean cuisine.

Damrak 96 (at the Dam), 1012 LP Amsterdam. ✆ 020/522-3000. Fax 020/522-3225. www.swissotel.com. 106 units. 270€ double; 350€–375€ suite. AE, DC, MC, V. No parking. Tram: 4, 9, 14, 16, 24, 25 to the Dam. **Amenities:** Restaurant (Mediterranean); bar; concierge; secretarial services; 24-hr. room service; in-room massage; babysitting; laundry service; dry cleaning. *In room:* A/C, TV w/pay movies, minibar, coffeemaker, hair dryer.

Victoria Hotel ★   You can survive quite nicely without taking taxis if you stay here, as close as you can be to Centraal Station, where most of the city's trams begin and end their routes, and where you can board a train to other parts of Holland and to Schiphol Airport. To emphasize the point, the hotel offers individual guests free first-class return train travel between Schiphol and Centraal Station. Since 1890, the elegant Victoria has been a turreted landmark at the head of Damrak. It overlooks the canal-boat piers and the stack of bikes parked outside the station. It can be noisy and tacky out on busy, neon-lit Damrak, but you won't notice that inside. Its original spacious rooms have been recently redecorated and refurnished, and the windows replaced with double-glazed panes. Rooms in the adjacent new block inevitably lack some of the atmosphere of the old. The idea of its proprietors is to give you a five-star hotel at four-star rates. All this and location, too. You can enjoy dinner or a quick lunch in the Scandinavian-look **Seasons Garden** restaurant, or take cocktails at the **Tasman Bar** and tea at the **Brasserie Vic**'s glassed-in terrace beside Damrak.

Damrak 1–5 (facing Centraal Station), 1012 LG Amsterdam. ✆ **800/670-PARK** in the U.S. and Canada, or 020/627-1166. Fax 020/627-4259. www.parkplazaeurope.com. 305 units. 315€–365€ double; 470€–505€ suite; add 5% city tax. AE, DC, MC, V. No parking. Tram: 1, 2, 4, 5, 9, 13, 16, 17, 24, 25 to Centraal Station. **Amenities:** Restaurant (international); Continental cafe; bar; small heated indoor pool; health club and spa; business center; limited room service; massage; babysitting; laundry service; same-day dry cleaning; non-smoking rooms. *In room:* A/C, TV w/pay movies, minibar, hair dryer.

MODERATE

Avenue Hotel ★   About 2 minutes from Centraal Station, this recently renovated and extended establishment has some of the style and amenities of its neighbor, the Crowne Plaza (above), at less than half the price. Part of the premises is a converted Golden Age warehouse that belonged to the V.O.C., the United East India Company. The rooms aren't huge, but they are bright and have clean furnishings, good-size bathrooms, some with a double sink.

> **Impressions**
>
> *From my favorite spot on the floor I look up at the blue sky and the bare chestnut tree, on whose branches little raindrops glisten like silver, and at the seagulls and other birds as they glide on the wind.*
> —Anne Frank (Feb 25, 1944)

Nieuwezijds Voorburgwal 33 (near Centraal Station), 1012 9599 Amsterdam. ✆ 020/530-9530. Fax 020/530-3946. www.emb.hotels.nl. 78 units. 105€–164€ double. Rates include buffet breakfast. AE, DC, MC, V. Limited street parking. Tram: 1, 2, 5, 13, 17 to Nieuwezijds Kolk. **Amenities:** Bar/brasserie; bike rental; dry cleaning. *In room:* TV w/pay movies, dataport, hair dryer.

Rho Hotel   Once you find it, you'll bless this hotel for its easy convenience. Tucked away in a side street just off the National Monument on the Dam, the Rho is housed in a building that once was the offices of a gold company and before that housed a theater dating from 1908 in the space that now holds the reception desk and breakfast area. There are elevators; the rooms are modern and

comfortable, having been recently renovated; the price is rig
quiet yet central, is one of the best in town. All rooms hav
and tour bookings are available at the reception desk, as are
for rent. Who could ask for more?

Nes 5–23 (at the Dam), 1012 KC Amsterdam. ℂ 020/620-7371. Fax 020/620-7
units. 95€–145€ double. Rates include buffet breakfast. AE, MC, V. Parking 20
to the Dam. **Amenities:** Bar, nonsmoking rooms. *In room:* TV, minibar, hair drye., ...

Sint-Nicolaas ★ *(Kids* Named after Amsterdam's patron saint, this hotel is
conveniently near the Centraal Station, in a prominent corner house with a dark
facade. It's a typical family hotel with an easygoing atmosphere, and children are
welcome. Originally the building was occupied by a factory that manufactured
ropes and carpets from sisal imported from the then Dutch colonies. It was converted into a hotel in 1980. The rather basic furnishings are more than compensated for by the ideal location and the Mesker family's friendliness.

Spuistraat 1A (at Nieuwendijk), 1012 SP Amsterdam. ℂ 020/626-1384. Fax 020/623-0979. www.hotel
nicolaas.nl. 24 units. 95€–115€ double. Rates include continental breakfast. AE, DC, MC, V. Limited street
parking. Tram: 1, 2, 5, 13, 17 to Martelaarsgracht. **Amenities:** Bar. *In room:* TV, hair dryer, safe.

Tulip Inn Dam Square ★ *(Value* This hotel is another example of putting an
old Amsterdam building to good use housing tourists. This time the old building, behind the Nieuwe Kerk, was a distillery—and a magnificent building it is.
Its granite details accentuate the brickwork and massive curve-topped doors
with elaborate hinges. Inside, the rooms are all you'll want: modern, bright,
comfortable, and attractively priced.

Gravenstraat 12–16 (at the Dam), 1012 NM Amsterdam. ℂ 800/344-1212 in the U.S. and Canada, or
020/623-3716. Fax 020/638-1156. www.tulipinndamsquare.com. 38 units. 150€ double. Rates include continental breakfast. AE, DC, MC, V. No parking. Tram: 1, 2, 4, 5, 9, 13, 14, 16, 17, 24, 25 to the Dam. **Amenities:**
Bar; dry cleaning. *In room:* A/C, TV, dataport, coffeemaker, hair dryer.

INEXPENSIVE

Amstel Botel ★ *(Kids* Where better to experience a city on the water than on
a boat-hotel? Its cabins are spread out over four decks connected by elevator. Be
sure to ask for a room with a view on the water, not on the uninspiring quay.
The boat is popular largely because of its location and rates, and for that extra
something added by sleeping on a boat. Turn left out of Centraal Station, pass
the bike rental, and you see it floating in front of you. This moored boat-hotel
has 352 beds in cabins on four decks, connected by an elevator. The bright,
modern rooms are no-nonsense but comfortable, the showers small. To get here,
leave the station and turn left, passing the bike rental—the Botel is painted
white and directly in front of you.

Oosterdokskade 2–4 (at Centraal Station), 1011 AE Amsterdam. ℂ 020/626-4247. Fax 020/639-1952. 175
units. 75€–86€ double. AE, DC, MC, V. Limited street parking. Tram: 1, 2, 4, 5, 9, 13, 16, 17, 24, 25 to Centraal Station. **Amenities:** Concierge; dry cleaning. *In room:* TV w/in-house movie channel.

Clemens ★ Fully renovated in late 1999, this hotel, a 2-minute walk from the
Anne Frankhuis, is spread over four floors in one of those typical steep-staired
Dutch buildings, with the reception and breakfast room up one flight of stairs.
It's owned and operated by a mother-and-daughter team, Dee and Emely, who
keep the fairly spacious rooms in good trim and regularly put in fresh flowers.
Nos. 7 and 8 each has a balcony facing the Westerkerk. There's room service
from noon to 10pm and each room has an unstocked refrigerator. Particularly
good and house-proud guests are in line to win a complimentary fruit basket.

ps Summer Stays: Reserve Ahead

July and August are tough months for finding hotel rooms in Amsterdam, and you are advised to reserve as far ahead as possible for this period. If you have problems getting a room, contact the VVV Amsterdam tourist information office, which can generally arrange a room somewhere though it might not be in the kind of hotel you are looking for and you might need to pay more for a room in a better-class hotel.

It can be particularly hard to find hoteliers willing to give away rooms for a single night when that might cost them a longer booking. What to do? In this circumstance a last-minute search might be called for, since a hotel that's had a last-minute cancellation would be more likely to consider single-night occupancy, but in general a last-minute search is the wrong approach.

Raadhuisstraat 39 (near to the Westerkerk), 1016 DC Amsterdam. ℭ 020/624-6089. Fax 020/626-9658. www.clemenshotel.nl. 9 units (5 with bathroom). 70€–75€ double. AE, MC, V. Limited street parking. Tram: 13, 14, 17 to Westerkerk. *In room:* TV, dataport, minibar, hair dryer, safe.

Winston ⭐ Formerly a backpackers' hotel, the Winston moved upscale by asking local artists to create paintings, photographs, and other works of what you might call art, for the halls, rooms, doors, and bathrooms. The project brought an element of whimsy to what was a rather bland lodging, giving it the character of an artist's hangout. Combine this with a location on edgy War-moesstraat, which borders the Red Light District, and you have a place with a reputation for being hang-loose and alternative. It's not entirely justified: The proprietors reserve the right to eject guests who take this too literally. Within these limits, they've done a good job of creating a democratic facility aimed mostly at young people. If you're not keen on being on a main route for charged-up groups heading into and out of the city's sin district, or on the street's sex shops and noisy bars, this won't be the place for you to rest your head. In addition to being ad hoc spaces for art exhibits, the guest rooms are sparely furnished in a modern style, vary in size, holding from two to six beds, and are clean and well-maintained. None of them have anything like a view that's worth looking out the window for. Bathrooms are small, but have all the requisite facilities, and most of those rooms that have no full bathroom do have a shower. The downstairs bar is a fun meeting place and has live music on weekends.

Warmoesstraat 129 (off Damrak), 1012 JA Amsterdam. ℭ **020/623-1380.** Fax 020/639-2308. www. winston.nl. 69 units, 25 with bathroom. 87€–92€ double with bathroom, 85€ double without bathroom. Rates include continental breakfast. AE, DC, MC, V. No parking. Tram: 4, 9, 14, 16, 24, 25 to the Dam. **Amenities:** Bar. *In room:* TV.

2 Along the Canal Belt

VERY EXPENSIVE

Blakes Amsterdam ⭐⭐⭐ The exceptional service at this intimate boutique hotel wins justified raves from its primarily American and British guests, and the Asian-influenced decor—courtesy of proprietor and British designer Anouska Hempel—is arguably the most stylish in town. Housed in a 17th-century landmark, Blakes began life as a theater (Antonio Vivaldi once conducted here) and its serene black-and-white lounge still sports the theater's original brick floor. All of the guest rooms and suites have the usual array of luxury amenities and are individually decorated in different colors and themes; no. 5, for example, is a blue Japanese-style room with a deep soaking tub and traditional sliding screens. The excellent location, in the heart of the Canal Belt, puts you within walking distance of the Leidsplein, Museumplein, and the Bloemenmarkt. My one complaint: style here occasionally trumps substance—the water fountain-style sinks in a few of the rooms look grand, but the design makes them somewhat hard to use.

Keizersgracht 384 (near Huidenstraat). 1016 GB Amsterdam. ℂ 020/530-2010. Fax 020/530-2030. www.slh.com/netherlands/amsterdam/hotel_amsbla.html. 41 units. 350€–660€ double; 800€–1,250€ suite; add 5% city tax. AE, DC, MC, V. Valet and self-parking 20€. Tram: 1, 2, 5 to Spui. **Amenities:** Restaurant (Asian/international); lounge; bar; bike rental; boat rental; concierge; 24-hr. room service; laundry service; dry cleaning. *In room:* A/C, TV/VCR w/pay movies, minibar, hair dryer, safe, CD player, bathrobe.

Hotel Pulitzer Amsterdam ★★★   The recently renovated Pulitzer has spread through 25 old canal houses, giving it frontage on the historic Prinsengracht and Keizersgracht canals. The houses date from the 17th and 18th centuries and adjoin one another, side by side and garden to garden. You walk between two houses to enter the lobby, or climb the steps of a former merchant's house to enter the ever-crowded and cheerful bar. With the exception of bare beams or brick walls here and there, history stops at the Pulitzer's many thresholds. Rooms are modern, with wickerwork furnishings, and impart an airy, expansive feeling to spaces that seem to have been shoehorned into the building. The rooms with the best views look out over either the canals or the hotel garden. The Pulitzer is big on culture, with its own art gallery, and every August the hotel sponsors a popular classical music concert performed by musicians on barges in the canal. As icing on the cake, the Pulitzer owns a restored saloon cruiser dating from 1909, which awaits your pleasure at the hotel's own jetty. The **Rendezvous Lounge** has a canalside entrance and serves lunch and snacks. Pulitzer's Bar is for a quiet drink.

Prinsengracht 315–331 (near Westermarkt), 1016 GZ Amsterdam. ℂ **800/325-3589** in the U.S. and Canada, or 020/523-5235. Fax 020/627-6753. www.luxurycollection.com/pulitzer. 230 units. 490€–590€ double; 1,025€ suite; add 5% city tax. AE, DC, MC, V. Valet parking 37€, self-parking 18€. Tram: 13, 14, 17 to Westermarkt. **Amenities:** Restaurant (Dutch/international); bar; cafe; concierge; business center; 24-hr. room service; babysitting; laundry service; dry cleaning; nonsmoking rooms. *In room:* A/C, TV w/pay movies, dataport, minibar, coffeemaker, hair dryer, safe.

EXPENSIVE

Ambassade ★★   Perhaps more than any other hotel in Amsterdam, this one, in ten 17th- and 18th-century canal houses on the Herengracht and Singel canals, re-creates the feeling of living in an elegant canal house. The pastel-toned rooms are individually styled and their size and shape vary according to the character of the individual houses. Each year one of the houses is completely renovated. Everyone who stays at the Ambassade enjoys the view each morning with breakfast in the bi-level, chandeliered breakfast room or each evening in the adjoining parlor, with Persian rugs and a stately grandfather clock ticking away. To get to some guest rooms, you cope with a typically Dutch steep and skinny staircase, though other rooms are accessible by elevator. For the nimble-footed who can handle the stairs, the rewards are a spacious room with large multipane windows overlooking the canal.

Herengracht 335–353 (near Spui), 1016 AZ Amsterdam. ℂ **020/555-0222.** Fax 020/555-0277. www. ambassade-hotel.nl. 59 units. 180€ double; 250€–315€ suite; 285€ apartment. AE, DC, MC, V. Limited street parking. Tram: 1, 2, 5 to Spui. **Amenities:** Bike rental; 24-hr. room service; massage at nearby float center; babysitting; laundry service; dry cleaning. *In room:* TV, hair dryer, safe.

Dikker & Thijs Fenice ★ On the Prinsengracht, at the intersection of the lively Leidsestraat, is this small and homey hotel whose smart but cozy character is indicated by the marble-rich lobby. The stylish facade has hosted Dikker & Thijs here since 1921. Upstairs, the spacious and tastefully styled rooms are clustered in groups of two or four around small lobbies, which makes the Dikker & Thijs feel more like an apartment building than a hotel. Welcoming touches are flowers in the rooms, a subtle but elegantly modern Art Deco decor, and double-glazed windows to eliminate the noise rising up from Leidsestraat at all hours of the day and night. But some rooms are clearly in need of renovation. Those at the front have a super view of the classy Prinsengracht. The **Prinsenkelder** restaurant and bar serves good French and Italian dinners, and the adjacent cellar bar is worth a visit.

Prinsengracht 444 (at Leidsestraat), 1017 KE Amsterdam. ℂ 020/620-1212. Fax 020/625-8986. www.dtfh.nl. 42 units. 195€–345€ double. Rates include buffet breakfast. AE, DC, MC, V. Limited street parking. Tram: 1, 2, 5 to Prinsengracht. **Amenities:** Restaurant (international); bar; bike rental; concierge; room service; in-room massage; babysitting; laundry service; dry cleaning; nonsmoking rooms. *In room:* TV, dataport, minibar, hair dryer.

MODERATE

Agora ★ Old-fashioned friendliness is the keynote at this efficiently run and well-maintained lodging, a block from the Flower Market. Proprietors Yvo Muthert and Els Bruijnse like to keep things friendly and personal. Although the hotel occupies a canal house built in 1735, it has been fully restored in an eclectic style. Furniture from the 1930s and 1940s mixes with fine mahogany antiques. Bouquets greet you as you enter, and a distinctive color scheme creates an effect of peacefulness and drama at the same time. They have installed an abundance of overstuffed furniture; nearly every room has a puffy armchair you can sink into after a wearying day of sightseeing. Upgrading of the bathrooms is proceeding apace and all beds have been recently renewed. Rooms with a canal view cost the most, but the extra few euros are worth it, though the hustle and bustle out on the street can make them somewhat noisy by day; the large family room has three windows overlooking the Singel. Those rooms that don't have a canal view look out on a pretty garden at the back.

Singel 462 (at Koningsplein), 1017 AW Amsterdam. ℂ 020/627-2200. Fax 020/627-2202. www.hotelagora.nl. 16 units, 13 with bathroom. 90€–127€ double with bathroom, 72€ double without bathroom. Rates include buffet breakfast. AE, DC, MC, V. Limited street parking. Tram: 1, 2, 5 to Koningsplein. *In room:* TV, hair dryer.

Amsterdam Wiechmann ★ It takes only a moment to feel at home in the antiques-adorned Amsterdam Wiechmann. Owned by American T. Boddy and his Dutch wife, Nicky, for a number of years, the Wiechmann is a classic, comfortable, casual sort of place, in spite of the suit of armor you encounter just inside the front door. Besides, the location is one of the best you find in this or any price range: 5 minutes in one direction is the Kalverstraat shopping street; 5 minutes in the other, Leidseplein. Most of the rooms are standard, with good-sized twin beds or double beds, and some have big bay windows. Furnishings are elegant, and Oriental rugs grace many of the floors in the public spaces. The higher-priced doubles have antique furnishings, and many have a view of the Prinsengracht. The breakfast room has hardwood floors, lots of greenery, and white linen cloths on the tables. There is a lounge and bar.

Prinsengracht 328–332 (at Looiersgracht), 1016 HX Amsterdam. ✆ **020/626-3321.** Fax 020/626-8962. www.hotelwiechmann.nl. 40 units. 120€–140€ double. Rates include continental breakfast. MC, V. Limited street parking. Tram: 1, 2, 5 to Prinsengracht. **Amenities:** Bar. *In room:* TV, safe.

Canal House ⭐   A contemporary approach to reestablishing the elegant canal-house atmosphere has been taken by the American proprietor of the Canal House Hotel. This small hotel below Raadhuisstraat is in three adjoining houses that date from 1630; they were gutted and rebuilt to provide private bathrooms and filled with antiques, quilts, and Chinese rugs. Fortunately, it's blessed with an elevator (though one that does not stop at every floor, so you may still have to walk a short distance up or down stairs), along with a (steep) staircase that still has its beautifully carved old balustrade, and overlooking the back garden, which is illuminated at night, a magnificent breakfast room that seems to have been untouched since the 17th century. Plus, on the parlor floor the proprietor has created a cozy Victorian-era saloon. It is, in short, a home away from home.

Keizersgracht 148 (near Leliegracht), 1015 CX Amsterdam. ✆ **020/622-5182.** Fax 020/624-1317. www. canalhouse.nl. 26 units. 150€–190€ double. Rates include continental breakfast. DC, MC, V. Limited street parking. Tram: 13, 14, 17 to Westermarkt. **Amenities:** Lounge; limited room service. *In room:* hair dryer.

Estheréa ⭐⭐ *(Kids)*   The Estheréa has been owned by the same family since its beginnings and is built within the walls of neighboring 17th-century canal houses. The family touch shows in careful attention to detail and a breezy but professional approach. It offers the blessed advantage of an elevator, a rarity in these old Amsterdam homes. In the 1930s the proprietors spent a lot of money on wood paneling and other structural additions; more recent proprietors have had the good sense to leave all of it in place. While it will look dated to some, the wood bedsteads and dresser-desks in fact lend warmth to the recently renovated and upgraded rooms. The room sizes vary considerably according to their location in the canal houses, and a few are quite small, though not seriously so. Most of the rooms will accommodate two, but some rooms have more beds, which make them ideal for families. The excellent small Greek restaurant **Traîterie Grekas,** next door (see chapter 5 for full details), provides room-service meals.

Singel 303–309 (near Spui), 1012 WJ Amsterdam. ✆ **020/624-5146.** Fax 020/623-9001. www.estherea.nl. 75 units. 154€–260€ double; add 5% city tax. AE, DC, MC, V. Limited street parking. Tram: 1, 2, 5, to Spui. **Amenities:** Bar; bike rental; concierge; limited room service; babysitting; laundry service; dry cleaning; nonsmoking rooms. *In room:* TV, minibar, hair dryer, safe.

Mercure Amsterdam Arthur Frommer ⭐⭐   The Mercure (once owned by Arthur Frommer) is tucked away in the canal area off Vijzelgracht. Its entrance opens onto a small courtyard off a side street that runs like an alleyway behind Prinsengracht, with a beautiful canalside mural painted along the facing wall. It's not easy to find but is well worth finding. A top-to-bottom renovation has transformed the Mercure's rooms, giving them a very stylish decor in soft pastel colors. All rooms have big double or single beds. There's a small, cozy bar.

Noorderstraat 46 (off Vijzelgracht), 1017 TV Amsterdam. ✆ **020/622-0328.** Fax 020/620-3208. www.accorhotels.com. 90 units. 120€–150€ double. AE, DC, MC, V. Limited free parking. Tram: 16, 24, 25 to Prinsengracht. **Amenities:** Babysitting; laundry service; dry cleaning. *In room:* A/C, TV, minibar, hair dryer.

Rembrandt Residence   Following the example of the Hotel Pulitzer, the Rembrandt Residence was built anew within old walls. In this case the structures are a wide 18th-century building on a canal above Raadhuistraat and four small 16th-century houses directly behind it on the Singel canal. The look of the place is best described as basic, but rooms tend to be large (in all sizes and shapes). Some still have their old fireplaces (not working) with elegant wood or marble mantels. And as you walk around, occasionally you see an old beam or pass through a former foyer on the way to your room. Hair dryers are available at the reception desk.

Herengracht 255 (at Hartenstraat), 1016 BJ Amsterdam. ✆ **020/623-6638.** Fax 020/625-0630. www. bookings.nl/hotels/rembrandt. 111 units. 100€–160€ double; 220€ executive room. AE, DC, MC, V. Limited street parking. Tram: 1, 2, 5, 13, 14, 17 to the Dam. *In room:* TV.

Seven Bridges ★★ Proprietors Pierre Keulers and Gunter Glaner have made the Seven Bridges, which gets its name from its view of seven arched bridges, one of Amsterdam's gems. Each room is individual. There are antique furnishings (Art Deco, Biedemeyer, Louis XVI, rococo), handmade Italian drapes, hand-painted tiles and wood-tiled floors, and Impressionist art posters on the walls. The biggest room, on the first landing, can accommodate up to four and has a huge bathroom with marble floor, double sinks, a fair-sized shower, and a separate area for the lavatory (the sink and shower even have gold-plated taps). The room is enormous, with high ceilings, a big mirror over the fireplace, an Empire onyx table and antique leather armchairs, and an array of potted plants. Attic rooms have sloped ceilings and exposed wood beams, and there are big, bright basement rooms done almost entirely in white.

Reguliersgracht 31 (at Keizersgracht), 1017 LK Amsterdam. ✆ **020/623-1329.** 8 units. 110€–200€ double. Rates include full breakfast. AE, MC, V. Limited street parking. Tram: 16, 24, 25 to Keizersgracht. *In room:* TV, hair dryer.

Singel Hotel ★ Style marries tradition in the elegant little Singel, near the head of the Brouwersgracht in one of the most pleasant and central locations in Amsterdam. Three renovated canal houses have been united in harmony to create this hotel. The decor is bright and welcoming. The modernly furnished rooms are spacious for a small hotel. Some of the rooms have an attractive view of the Singel canal. An elevator services the building's four floors.

Singel 13 (near Centraal Station), 1012 VC Amsterdam. ✆ **020/626-3108.** Fax 020/620-3777. www. lempereur-hotels.nl. 32 units. 120€–150€ double. Rates include buffet breakfast. AE, DC, MC, V. Limited street parking. Tram: 1, 2, 4, 5, 9, 13, 16, 17, 24, 25 to Centraal Station. *In room:* TV, hair dryer.

Toren ★ The Toren is a sprawling enterprise that encompasses two buildings, separated by neighboring houses. With so many rooms, it's a better bet than most canal-house hotels during the tourist seasons in Amsterdam. Clean, attractive, and well maintained, the Toren promises private facilities with every room, though in a few cases that means a private bathroom located off the public hall (with your own private key, however). There's a bridal suite here, complete with a blue canopy and a Jacuzzi. There's also a little private guesthouse off the garden that's done up in Laura Ashley prints. All this and a canalside location, too.

Keizersgracht 164 (near Leliegracht), 1015 CZ Amsterdam. ✆ **020/622-6352.** Fax 020/626-9705. www.toren.nl. 43 units. 120€–205€ double; 230€ suite; add 5% city tax. AE, DC, MC, V. Limited street parking. Tram: 13, 14, 17 to Westermarkt. **Amenities:** Bar; room service; babysitting; laundry service; dry cleaning. *In room:* TV w/pay movies, fax, dataport, minibar, coffeemaker, hair dryer, safe.

INEXPENSIVE

De Admiraal De Admiraal is in a building dating from 1666, part of which was originally a warehouse for spices from the East Indies unloaded on the canal quay outside, and that appeared more than 3 centuries later in the movie *Puppet on a Chain.* It still retains a nautical and exotic feel, with a bar/breakfast room that looks like an old-time sailing-ship's officer's quarters. The rooms are at all angles and places and are reached by a narrow staircase. They are simple but clean and comfortably furnished and have a fine view of the canal or adjacent Thorbeckeplein (there are some strip clubs on this otherwise pleasant little square, but it cannot be called sleazy).

Herengracht 563 (at Thorbeckeplein), 1071 CD Amsterdam. ℂ 020/626-2150. Fax 020/623-4625. 9 units. 65€–95€ double. MC, V. Limited street parking. Tram: 4, 9, 14 to Rembrandtplein. In room: TV.

De Leydsche Hof   Run by an ex-KLM purser, its greatest advantages are its location and rates, of a level that has almost vanished from Amsterdam. The accommodations are basic but well cared for and clean. The rooms all have a shower; toilets are in the hallway. You cannot get breakfast in the hotel, but there are plenty of cafes in the immediate area.

Leidsegracht 14 (off Herengracht), 1016 CK Amsterdam. ℂ 020/623-2148. No fax. 7 units, 4 with bathroom. 60€ double. No credit cards. Limited street parking. Tram: 1, 2, 5, to Koningsplein. In room: No phone.

Hegra   Housed in a 17th-century building a 5-minute walk from the Dam, this cozy little hotel has been under the same management for two generations. Robert de Vries, the proprietor, is extremely helpful and friendly. The rooms are small but tastefully furnished and have beamed ceilings. Note that there is no elevator, so you have to climb four stories if you get a room on the top floor.

Herengracht 269 (near Hartenstraat), 1016 BJ Amsterdam. ℂ 020/623-7877. Fax 020/623-8159. 11 units, 6 with bathroom. 75€–85€ double with bathroom, 60€ double without bathroom. Rates include continental breakfast. AE, DC, MC, V. Limited street parking. Tram: 1, 2, 5, 13, 14, 17 to the Dam.

Hoksbergen ★   At a tranquil point on the historic Singel canal, this inexpensive hotel in a 300-year-old canal house is not flashy or elegant, but it's bright and fresh and recently renovated, which makes it appealing to budget-conscious travelers who don't want to swap creature comforts for euros. Its central location makes it easy to get to all the surrounding sights and attractions. Rooms at the front have a canal view.

Singel 301 (near Spui), 1012 WH Amsterdam. ℂ 020/626-6043. Fax 020/638-3479. www.hotelhoksbergen. com. 14 units. 76€–90€ double. Rates include continental breakfast. AE, DC, MC, V. Limited street parking. Tram: 1, 2, 5 to Spui. In room: TV.

Keizershof ★   Owned by the genial De Vries family, this hotel in a four-story canal-house from 1672 has six rooms named after movie stars—though a greater claim to fame is that members of the Dutch royal family were regular visitors in its prehotel days. Several other touches make a stay here memorable. From the street-level entrance a wooden spiral staircase built from a ship's mast leads to the beamed rooms. Note that there's no elevator. There is, however, a television and a grand piano in the cozy lounge. In good weather, breakfast, which includes excellent omelets and pancakes, is served in the flower-bedecked courtyard. Because the hotel, which is nonsmoking, has so few rooms, you need to book well ahead.

Keizersgracht 618 (at Nieuwe Spiegelstraat), 1017 ER Amsterdam. ℂ 020/622-2855. Fax 020/624-8412. www.vdwp.nl/keizershof. 6 units, 3 with bathroom. 90€ double with bathroom, 70€–75€ double without bathroom. Rates include full breakfast. MC, V. Limited street parking. Tram: 16, 24, 25 to Keizersgracht. In room: Coffeemaker, hair dryer, safe, no phone.

Prinsenhof ★   A modernized canal house near the Amstel River, this hotel offers rooms with beamed ceilings and basic yet reasonably comfortable beds. The place has been recently refurbished, and new showers and carpets installed.

Front rooms look out onto the Prinsengracht, where colorful houseboats are moored. Breakfast is served in an attractive blue-and-white decorated dining room. The proprietors, Rik and André van Houten, take pride in their hotel and will make you feel welcome. There's no elevator, but a pulley hauls your luggage up and down the stairs.

Prinsengracht 810 (at Utrechtsestraat), 1017 JL Amsterdam. ✆ 020/623-1772. Fax 020/638-3368. www. hotelprinsenhof.com. 10 units, 3 with bathroom. 80€ double with bathroom, 60€ double without bathroom. Rates include continental breakfast. AE, MC, V. Limited street parking. Tram: 4 to Prinsengracht.

Van Haalen   If you're looking for a canal hotel decorated with the dark woods and bric-a-brac you associate with Old Holland, you'll like the Hotel van Haalen. You'll also like the friendly proprietors, who've done a lot of work around the place, including building the platform beds. Location is another advantage: The Van Haalen is near a bustling shopping street and the premier main antiques district.

Prinsengracht 520 (between Nieuwe Spiegelstraat and Leidsestraat), 1017 KJ Amsterdam. ✆ 020/626-4334. 20 units, 10 with bathroom. 95€ double with bathroom, 65€ double without bathroom. Rates include continental breakfast. No credit cards. Free parking. Tram: 1, 2, 5 to Prinsengracht. *In room:* TV.

3 Around Leidseplein

VERY EXPENSIVE

Crowne Plaza Amsterdam-American ★★★   One of the most fascinating buildings on Amsterdam's long list of monuments is this fanciful, castlelike mix of Venetian Gothic and Art Nouveau, which has been both a prominent land-mark and a popular meeting place for Amsterdammers since 1900. While the exterior of the American must always remain an architectural treasure (and curiosity) of turrets, arches, and balconies, in accordance with the regulations of the National Monument Care Office, the interior of the hotel (except that of the cafe, which is also protected) is modern and chic, though at times a bit gaudy. Rooms are subdued and refined, superbly furnished, and while some have a view of the Singelgracht, others overlook kaleidoscopic Leidseplein. They are always pink and bright, which perhaps appeals to the international rock stars who often stay here. The location, in the thick of the action and near many major attrac-tions, is one of the best in town. The famous **Café Americain** is one of the most elegant eateries in Europe (see chapter 5). There is also the **Bar Americain,** which has a closed-in terrace looking out on Leidseplein.

Leidsekade 97 (at Leidseplein), 1017 PN Amsterdam. ✆ 020/556-3000. Fax 020/556-3001. www. amsterdam-american.crowneplaza.com. 174 units. 290€–405€ double; 470€–505€ suite; add 5% city tax. AE, DC, MC, V. No parking. Tram: 1, 2, 5, 6, 7, 10 to Leidseplein. **Amenities:** Restaurant (Continental); bar; exercise room; sauna; concierge; 24-hr. room service; in-room massage; laundry service; same-day dry clean-ing. *In room:* A/C, TV w/pay movies, dataport, minibar, coffeemaker, hair dryer, iron, safe.

EXPENSIVE

NH Amsterdam Centre ★   The hotel building began life in 1927 as a YMCA to house athletes for the 1928 Amsterdam Olympic Games, and only later became a hotel. Don't worry, the smell of honest sweat has long since vanished. The Amsterdam Centre is gracious, attractive, and imaginatively arranged, with color schemes that reflect those found in the works of the late-19th-century Barbizon school of French landscape painting—restful yet distinctive tones. All rooms have been recently renovated and offer both comfort and efficiency of the kind with which frequent business travelers will be familiar. **Café Ristorante**

Bice serves Italian food, and the **Barbizon Bar Brasserie** is open for cocktails in the evening.

Stadhouderskade 7 (facing Leidseplein), 1054 ES Amsterdam. ℂ **800/344-1212** in the U.S. and Canada, or 020/685-1351. Fax 020/685-1611. www.nh-hotels.nl. 229 units. 245€–320€ double; 570€ suite; add 5% city tax. AE, DC, MC, V. Limited street parking. Tram: 1, 2, 5, 6, 7, 10 to Leidseplein. **Amenities:** Restaurant (Italian); bar; health club; concierge; salon; 24-hr. room service; laundry service; dry cleaning. *In room:* A/C, TV w/pay movies, minibar, hair dryer.

MODERATE

Orfeo   One of the city's longest-standing gay lodgings has for more than 30 years been providing basic, practical facilities and friendly, helpful service at low rates. The front desk is in a cozy and sociable lounge and there is a marble-floored breakfast room. Only three guest rooms have a full bathroom, some with charming beamed ceilings; others share shower and/or toilet. One of the perks is a small in-house Finnish sauna; and the largest concentration of city-center restaurants is right on the doorstep.

Leidsekruisstraat 14 (off Leidseplein), 1017 RH Amsterdam. ℂ **020/623-1347.** Fax 020/620-2348. www.hotelorfeo.com. 17 units, 3 with bathroom. 105€–122€ double with bathroom, 79€–83€ double without bathroom. Rates include continental breakfast. AE, MC, V. Limited street parking. Tram: 1, 2, 5 to Prinsengracht. *In room:* TV, minibar, hair dryer, safe.

INEXPENSIVE

De Lantaerne ✦   Small and inexpensive, this is perfect for long stays because for a couple of reasons it feels like home. For one, not only are the standard rooms perfectly comfortable, but there are also four studios that have kitchenettes, color TVs, and mini-refrigerators; they're perfect if you're doing Amsterdam on a budget and would like to cook some of your own meals. The other thing that makes this place homey is the breakfast room. It's bright and airy, with an exposed-beam ceiling, large windows, and red-and-white-checked tablecloths. If you happen to be sensitive to decibels (and who isn't?), watch out for noisy back rooms: In the back alley is a police station, disco bar, and movie theater. The noise is relentless, especially after 11pm.

Leidsegracht 111 (at Singelgracht), 1017 ND Amsterdam. ℂ **020/623-2221.** Fax 020/623-2683. www. channels.nl/amsterdam.html. 24 units, 19 with bathroom. 80€ double with bathroom, 65€ double without bathroom. Rates include continental breakfast. AE, MC, V. Limited street parking. Tram: 1, 2, 5, 6, 7, 10 to Leidseplein. *In room:* TV, hair dryer.

4 Around Rembrandtplein

EXPENSIVE

NH Schiller Hotel ✦✦   A historic Amsterdam gem, now fully restored, this hotel boasts a blend of Art Nouveau and Art Deco in its public spaces that is reflected in tasteful decor and furnishings in the rooms. Its sculpted facade, wrought-iron balconies, and stained-glass windows stand out on the often brash Rembrandtplein. **Café Schiller,** next door to the hotel, is one of the trendiest watering holes in town. The hotel takes its name from the painter Frits Schiller, who built it in 1912. His outpourings of artistic expression, in the form of 600 portraits, landscapes, and still lifes, are displayed in the halls, rooms, stairwells, and public areas; and their presence fills this hotel with a unique sense of vitality, creativity, and personality. Perhaps the happiest outcome of the revitalization of the Schiller is the new life it brings to the hotel's gracious oak-paneled dining room and to the Café Schiller, one of Amsterdam's few permanent, and perfectly situated, sidewalk cafes. Experience classic French and Dutch cuisine and the hotel's own beer, Frisse Frits, in the Art Nouveau **Brasserie Schiller** (see chapter 5 for more details), or join the in crowd next door for a drink amid the Art Deco splendor of the Café Schiller.

Rembrandtplein 26–36, 1017 CV Amsterdam. ℭ **020/554-0700.** Fax 020/624-0098. www.nh-hotels.nl/nhschiller. 92 units. 220€–270€ double; from 300€ suite. AE, DC, MC, V. Limited street parking. Tram: 4, 9, 14 to Rembrandtplein. **Amenities:** Restaurant (Dutch); 2 bars; health club; 24-hr. room service; babysitting; laundry service; dry cleaning. *In room:* TV, minibar, coffeemaker, hair dryer.

MODERATE

Best Western Eden ✶ The biggest hotel in its class in the center city has a great setting, in several converted 17th-century merchants' houses (and a chocolate factory) beside the Amstel River, just behind Rembrandtplein. Rooms vary quite a lot in size, with some of them on the small side. Still, they're all well cared for and have bright, modern furnishings. Many have a fine view of the river, and these are the most desirable—and most expensive—ones. The **Garden of Eden** brasserie, overlooking the river, is a good place for Dutch specialties and international menu dishes.

Amstel 144 (across the river from the Muziektheater), 1017 AE Amsterdam. ℭ **020/530-7888.** Fax 020/623-3267. www.edenhotelgroup.com. 410 units. 150€–196€ double. AE, DC, MC, V. Limited street parking. Tram: 4, 9 to Rembrandtplein. *In room:* TV w/pay movies, hair dryer, safe.

5 In the Jordaan

INEXPENSIVE

Acacia ✶ Not on one of the major canals, but in the Jordaan, facing a small canal, just a block from the Prinsengracht, the Acacia, shaped like a slice of cake, is run by Hans and Marlene van Vliet, a friendly couple who have worked hard to make their hotel welcoming, clean, and well kept, and are justifiably proud of the result. Simple, clean, and comfortable, the rooms have recently been equipped with new beds, writing tables, and chairs. They all have canal views. Breakfast is served in a triangular breakfast room. With windows on two sides, a nice view of the canal, and a breakfast of cold cuts, cheese, a boiled egg, and a choice of coffee or tea, it's a lovely way to start the morning. Two houseboats for guests on nearby Lijnbaansgracht add an authentic local touch—but what might seem like the earth moving for you may be only the wake from a passing boat roiling the water and setting your houseboat bobbing.

Lindengracht 251 (at Lijnbaansgracht), 1015 KH Amsterdam. ℭ **020/622-1460.** Fax 020/638-0748. 18 units. 85€ double; 120€ houseboat double. Rates include continental breakfast. MC, V (5% charge). Limited street parking. Tram: 3 to Nieuwe Willemstraat. *In room:* TV.

Van Onna Consisting of three canal houses, this hotel has grown over the years, but genial owner Loek van Onna continues to keep his prices reasonable. Mr. van Onna has lived here since he was a boy and will gladly tell you about the building's history. Accommodations vary considerably, with the best rooms in the newest building. However, the oldest and simplest rooms also have a great deal of charm. Whichever building you wind up in, ask for a room in front overlooking the canal.

Bloemgracht 102–104 and 108 (off Prinsengracht), 1015 TN Amsterdam. ℭ **020/626-5801.** 39 units, 30 with bathroom. 45€ double with bathroom, 35€ double without bathroom. Rates include continental breakfast. No credit cards. Limited street parking. Tram: 13, 14, 17 to Westermarkt. **Amenities:** Lounge.

6 Around Museumplein & Vondelpark

EXPENSIVE

Bilderberg Hotel Jan Luyken ★★   One block from the Van Gogh Museum and from the elegant Pieter Cornelisz Hooftstraat shopping street, the Jan Luyken is best described as a small hotel with many of the amenities and facilities of a big hotel. Everything here is done with perfect attention to detail. The Jan Luyken maintains a balance between its sophisticated lineup of facilities (double sinks and bidets, elevator, lobby bar with fireplace, and meeting rooms for business) and an intimate and personalized approach that's appropriate to this 19th-century residential neighborhood. That residential feel extends to the rooms, which look much more like a well-designed home than a standard hotel room. The proprietors are proud of the atmosphere they've created, and are constantly improving the look of the hotel.

Jan Luykenstraat 58 (near the Rijksmuseum), 1071 CS Amsterdam. ℂ 800/641-0300 in the U.S. and Canada, or 020/573-0730. Fax 020/676-3841. www.janluyken.nl. 62 units. 180€–295€ double; add 5% city tax. AE, DC, MC, V. Limited street parking. Tram: 2, 5 to Hobbemastraat. **Amenities:** Winebar; spa; concierge; 24-hr. room service; in-room massage; babysitting; laundry service; dry cleaning; nonsmoking rooms. *In room:* A/C, TV, dataport, minibar, hair dryer, iron, safe.

MODERATE

Acro ★   The Acro, in a town house on a fairly quiet street near Vondelpark and close to the main museums, tends to appeal especially to young travelers. The hotel is modern on the inside, with crisp-and-clean bedspreads and furniture and walls all colored light blue-gray. Most rooms have twin beds—some have three and some four. You find more ambience in the hotel bar than in many street cafes. The Acro is definitely value for your money.

Jan Luykenstraat 44 (near the Rijksmuseum), 1071 CR Amsterdam. ℂ 020/662-5538. Fax 020/675-0811. 65 units. 125€ double. Rates include continental breakfast. AE, DC, MC, V. Parking 25€. Tram: 2, 3, 5, 12 to Van Baerlestraat. **Amenities:** Bar. *In room:* TV, hair dryer.

AMS Hofpark Hotel ★   State-of-the-art rooms and the design and a kind of artistic flair make this place a good bet for travelers who want that extra something in their hotel. Some of the spacious rooms with large windows and modern furnishings have balconies. Club-class rooms have a minibar. For an added touch of luxury, book one of the five suites that have a Jacuzzi. There's no elevator. Koninginneweg is within easy walking distance of Vondelpark.

Koninginneweg 34–36 (at Valeriusplein), 1075 CZ Amsterdam. ℂ 800/44-UTELL in the U.S. and Canada, or 020/664-6111. Fax 020/664-5304. www.ams.nl. 107 units. 155€–172€. AE, DC, MC, V. Limited street parking. Tram: 2 to Koninginneweg. *In room:* TV, coffeemaker, hair dryer.

AMS Toro   On the fringes of Vondelpark in a quiet residential district, this beautiful hotel in a completely renovated mansion dating from 1900 is one of Amsterdam's top moderately priced choices. Both on the inside and the outside, it is as near as you can get in Amsterdam to staying in a country villa. The house is furnished and decorated with taste, combining Louis XIV and Liberty styles and featuring stained-glass windows and Murano chandeliers. The guest rooms are worthy of being featured in *Better Homes & Gardens*. The house also affords guests a private garden and terrace. It's about a 10-minute walk through Vondelpark to Leidseplein.

Koningslaan 64 (off Oranje Nassaulaan), 1075 AG Amsterdam. ℂ 020/673-7223. Fax 020/675-0031. 22 units. www.ams.nl. 185€ double. AE, MC, V. Limited street parking. Tram: 2 to Valeriusplein. **Amenities:** Laundry service; dry cleaning; nonsmoking rooms. *In room:* TV, minibar, hair dryer, safe.

Museumplein Area & Amsterdam South Accommodations

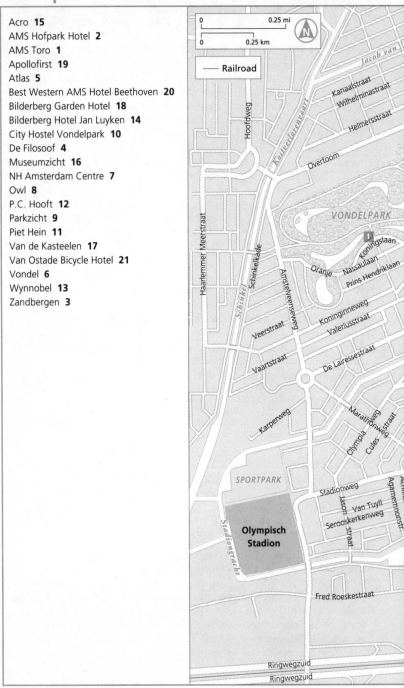

Atlas   Off Van Baerlestraat, the Atlas is a converted house with a convenient location for shoppers, concertgoers, and museum lovers. The staff backs up the homey feel with attentive service. The guest rooms are small but tidy, decorated attractively in gray with blue comforters on the beds and a welcoming basket of fruit on the desk. Leather chairs fill the front lounge, which has a grandfather clock ticking in the corner. There is also a small bar/restaurant providing 24-hour room service. Laundry and dry-cleaning service is available during the week. A hair dryer is available at the reception desk.

Van Eeghenstraat 64 (near Vondelpark), 1071 GK Amsterdam. © **020/676-6336**. Fax 020/671-7633. 23 units. 110€ double. Rates include continental breakfast. AE, DC, MC, V. Limited street parking. Tram: 2, 3, 5, 12 to Van Baerlestraat. *In room:* TV.

De Filosoof ★★ *(Finds)*   On a quiet street facing Vondelpark, this hotel might be the very place if you fancy yourself as something of a philosopher king or queen. One of the proprietors, a philosophy professor, has chosen posters, painted ceilings, framed quotes, and unusual objects to represent philosophical and cultural themes. Each room is dedicated to a mental maestro—Goethe, Wittgenstein, Nietzsche, Marx, and Einstein are among those who get a look-in—or are based on motifs like Eros, the Renaissance, astrology, and women. Rooms in an annex across the street are larger; some open onto a private terrace. Recent all-round improvements in service and facilities have raised the hotel's local rating.

Anna van den Vondelstraat 6 (off Overtoom, at Vondelpark), 1054 GZ Amsterdam. © **020/683-3013**. Fax 020/685-3750. www.hotelfilosoof.nl. 38 units. 92€–122€ double. Rates include buffet breakfast. AE, MC, V. Limited street parking. Tram: 1, 6 to Jan Pieter Heijestraat. **Amenities:** Lounge. *In room:* TV, hair dryer, safe.

Piet Hein ★   Facing Vondelpark, and close to the city's most important muse-ums, this appealing, well-kept hotel is in a villa named after a 17th-century Dutch admiral who captured a Spanish silver shipment. Its spacious rooms are well furnished and the staff is charming and professional. Half the rooms over-look the park, two second-floor double rooms have semicircular balconies, and the honeymoon suite has a water bed. The lower-priced rooms are in an annex behind the main hotel. Hair dryers are available on request.

Vossiusstraat 52–53 (off Van Baerlestraat), 1071 AK Amsterdam. © **020/662-7205**. Fax 020/662-1526. www.hotelpiethein.com. 65 units. 115€–155€ double. Rates include continental breakfast. AE, DC, MC, V. Limited street parking. Tram: 3, 5, 12 to Van Baerlestraat. **Amenities:** Bar; concierge; limited room service; laundry service; dry cleaning; nonsmoking rooms. *In room:* TV w/pay movies.

Van de Kasteelen ★   On a quiet side street not far from the Van Gogh Museum, this hotel is owned by a gracious family of Indonesian origin. The new generation, heading upmarket, has taken what had been a clean but spartan budget lodging and totally transformed the interior. You're looking effectively at a new hotel, a long way now from spartan—as the installation of an elevator symbolizes. Don't worry, though, it's still clean. The small-ish guest rooms are furnished and outfitted with a minor-key, classic elegance. Genuine-wood fur-nishings, bright and adjustable lighting, firm mattresses, and fine drapes, all indicate that some care has gone into creating a comfort zone, even if modern-design awards are unlikely. Bathrooms, which have a combined tub/shower, are large in relation to room size, with space enough for two at morning *toilette,* pro-vided neither has sharp elbows. Some rooms at the front have balconies; rear-facing rooms overlook gardens. To protect their investment from cigarette burns, ash, and smell, the proprietors have made the hotel entirely nonsmoking, a fea-ture that in this roll-your-own city should cause you to breathe a clean-air sigh of relief. A small patio-garden out back makes for a pleasant place to relax in fine weather. The location lies between tram stops, but is not overly far from them. As to rates, the upper, high-season rates might make you ponder; those for the lower, low-season look like a bargain.

Frans van Mierisstraat 34 (off Van Baerlestraat), 1071 RT Amsterdam. ✆ 020/679-8995. Fax 020/670-6604. www.hotelvandekasteelen.com. 15 units. 110€–212€ double. Rates include buffet breakfast. AE, MC, V. Limited street parking. Tram: 16 to Johannes Vermeerplein. **Amenities:** Lounge; nonsmoking rooms. *In room:* TV, dataport, minibar, hair dryer, safe.

Vondel   Named after the famous 17th-century Dutch poet Joost Van den Vondel, this five-floor hotel opened in late 1993 and has since become one of the leading three-star hotels in Amsterdam. Each room is named after one of Vondel's poems, like Lucifer or Solomon. Three of the rooms (all with sound-proof windows) are on the first floor and are ideal for travelers with disabilities. The furniture is solid, the rooms are spacious, and the service is good. This is a comfortable place, conveniently located in a quiet and popular area close to the museum area and Leidseplein.

Vondelstraat 28–30 (off Stadhouderskade), 1054 GE Amsterdam. ✆ 020/612-0120. Fax 020/685-4321. 74 units. 170€–205€ double; 275€ suite. Rates include continental breakfast. AE, DC, MC, V. Limited street parking. Tram: 1, 6 to Eerste Constantijn Huygensstraat; 3, 12 to Overtoom. *In room:* TV, minibar, hair dryer.

Zandbergen ⭐   Beside Vondelpark, this place nearly outdoes the Amstel in its use of shiny brass handrails and door handles. Rebuilt in 1979, and modernized since then, the Zandbergen has been efficiently divided into a variety of room types and sizes by the use of simple but attractive brick wall dividers between rooms. Wall-to-wall carpets and a color scheme based on bright tones of sand and blue-gray make the rooms seem more spacious and inviting, and all are outfitted with some flair and have good comfortable beds. There's also a great family-size room with a garden patio for between two and four guests. Recent improvements include new bathrooms and air-conditioning in the reception and breakfast area.

Willemsparkweg 205 (at Vondelpark), 1071 HB Amsterdam. ✆ 020/676-9321. Fax 020/676-1860. www. hotel-zandbergen.com. 21 units. 130€ double. Rates include buffet breakfast. AE, DC, MC, V. Limited street parking. Tram: 2 to Emmastraat. **Amenities:** Laundry service; dry cleaning; nonsmoking rooms. *In room:* TV, dataport, minibar, coffeemaker, hair dryer.

INEXPENSIVE

City Hostel Vondelpark ⭐ *Kids*   "The new generation of city hostel" is how the Dutch youth hostel organization describes this hostel, which opened its doors in 1998, and that's a fair description of a marvelous, great-value lodging just inside Vondelpark. The location, facing Leidseplein, could hardly be better for youthful spirits who want to be near the action. At the hostel's core is a protected monument, a former Girl's Housekeeping School. All rooms are simply but modernly and brightly furnished and all have an en suite bathroom. The four- and six-bed rooms are ideal for families traveling on a limited budget and for groups of friends. Some rooms are adapted for people with disabilities. Although the hostel is open 24 hours a day, security is taken seriously, and all guests have key cards. There are coin-operated Internet stations for those who have to surf, and the Backpacker's Lounge is a pleasant place to meet fellow travelers.

Zandpad 5 (in Vondelpark), 1054 GA Amsterdam. ✆ 020/589-8996. Fax 020/589-8955. www.njhc.org/ vondelpark. 101 units, none with bathroom. 20€–22€ dorm bed; 22€–28€ a head in room with 4–8 beds; 60€–83€ double; 2.50€ reduction for members of IYHF. Rates include continental breakfast. MC, V. No parking. Tram: 1, 2, 5, 6, 7, 10 to Leidseplein. **Amenities:** Restaurant (Continental); bike rental; coin-op washers and dryers; nonsmoking rooms. *In room:* No phone.

Museumzicht   This hotel in a Victorian house across from the back of the Rijksmuseum is ideal for museum-goers on a budget. The breakfast room commands an excellent view of the museum with its numerous stained-glass windows. Robin de Jong, the proprietor, has filled the rooms with an eclectic furniture collection, from 1930s English wicker to 1950s pieces. There's no elevator and the staircase up to reception is pretty steep.

Jan Luykenstraat 22 (near the Rijksmuseum), 1071 CN Amsterdam. ☎ 020/671-2954. Fax 020/671-3597. 14 units, 3 with bathroom. 58€ double without bathroom, 80€ double with bathroom. Rates include continental breakfast. AE, DC, MC, V. Limited street parking. Tram: 2, 5 to Hobbemastraat. *In room:* No phone.

Owl ★   If small but chic and reasonably priced seems to describe the sort of hotel you prefer, you'll be pleased to learn about the Owl, located in the pleasant residential area around Vondelpark, behind the Marriott. One of Amsterdam's best buys, the Owl Hotel has been owned by the same family since 1972 and is bright, tidy, and well kept. Rooms are not very big but are not cramped, and have all been renovated recently. The bathrooms are tiled floor to ceiling. There's also a pleasant lounge/bar overlooking a small garden.

Roemer Visscherstraat 1 (off Stadhouderskade), 1054 EV Amsterdam. ☎ 020/618-9484. Fax 020/618-9441. www.owl-hotel.demon.nl. 34 units. 92€–112€ double. Rates include buffet breakfast. AE, DC, MC, V. Limited street parking. Tram: 1, 6 to Stadhouderskade. **Amenities:** Bar; concierge; limited room service; babysitting; laundry service; dry cleaning. *In room:* TV, hair dryer.

Parkzicht   A characterful place owned and managed by the same man, Mr. Cornelissen, since 1970, this hotel features large rooms with brass beds, old Dutch wooden furniture, fireplaces in some units, and bathrooms as large as the bedrooms. Many of the guests who stay here are English-speaking—Americans, British, Australians, New Zealanders. Try to book one of the large apartment-like doubles on the second floor (no. 5 or 6), overlooking Vondelpark.

Roemer Visscherstraat 33 (off Eerste Constantijn Huygensstraat), 1054 EW Amsterdam. ☎ 020/618-1954. Fax 020/618-0897. hotel@parkzicht.nl. 14 units, 10 with bathroom. 72€–80€ double with bathroom. Rates include continental breakfast. AE, MC, V. Limited street parking. Tram: 1, 6 to Eerste Constantijn Huygensstraat; 3, 12 to Overtoom. *In room:* TV.

P. C. Hooft ★   Imagine staying on Amsterdam's most upscale shopping street, amid chic boutiques and classy restaurants, for no more than you'd pay in any other budget hotel in town. One of the spiffiest little budget lodgings in town, the P. C. Hooft seems to have picked up a sense of style from the smart shops on the street without picking up their tendency toward upscale pricing. The guest rooms are bright and tidy, and the building houses a coffeeshop, which is a handy spot to stop for a quick bite before you hit the sights or the shops. You have to climb quite a few stairs to enjoy your stay, though. Most rooms have been updated. The breakfast room, guaranteed to wake you up, is painted wild shades of orange and blue.

Pieter Cornelisz Hooftstraat 63 (near the Van Gogh Museum), 1071 BN Amsterdam. ☎ 020/662-7107. Fax 020/675-8961. 16 units, 3 with bathroom. 55€ double with bathroom, 45€ double without bathroom. Rates include continental breakfast. MC, V. Limited street parking. Tram: 2, 5 to Hobbemastraat. *In room:* TV.

Wynnobel ★ *(Finds)*   Just around the corner from the boutiques on Pieter Cornelisz Hooftstraat and only a few minutes' walk from the Rijksmuseum, the hotel overlooks a corner of Vondelpark and is owned by the Wynnobel family, who always make sure the hotel is clean and their guests are happy. One way they achieve this is by serving you breakfast in bed, if you want it. In addition, Pierre, the head of the family, plays some perfectly acceptable Gershwin, Cole Porter, and Chopin on the piano. The large rooms are furnished with old-fashioned or antique pieces. A steep but striking central stairway leads to the hotel's four floors.

Vossiusstraat 9 (at Vondelpark), 1071 AB Amsterdam. ℂ 020/662-2298. 12 units, none with bathroom. 60€–75€ double. Rates include continental breakfast. No credit cards. Limited street parking. Tram: 2, 5 to Hobbemastraat. **Amenities:** Lounge. *In room:* No phone.

7 In Amsterdam East

VERY EXPENSIVE

Amstel Inter-Continental Amsterdam ★★★   The stately Amstel, grande dame of Dutch hotels since its opening in 1867, offers the ultimate in luxury. This is the Rolls Royce of Amsterdam hotels, a place for visiting royalty and superstars hiding from eager fans. Its only possible fault is that it may seem to run a bit *too* smoothly. The hotel sports a mansard roof and wrought-iron window guards, a graceful Grand Hall, and rooms that boast all the elegance of a country manor, complete with antiques and genuine Delft blue porcelain. The Italian marble bathrooms have separate toilets and showers. The staff notes each guest's personal preferences for their next visit. The French La Rive restaurant is one of the hallowed temples of Amsterdam cuisine (see chapter 5 for details). The **Amstel Lounge, Amstel Bar & Brasserie,** and terraces overlooking the river are more informal.

Prof. Tulpplein 1 (at the Torontobrug over the Amstel River), 1018 GX Amsterdam. ℂ 800/327-1177 in the U.S. and Canada, or 020/622-6060. Fax 020/622-5808. http://amsterdam.interconti.com. 79 units. 470€–550€ double; from 750€ suite; add 5% city tax. AE, DC, MC, V. Tram: 6, 7, 10 to Weesperplein. **Amenities:** Restaurant (French); lounge; bar-brasserie; heated indoor pool; health club; Jacuzzi; sauna; concierge; limo; 24-hr. room service; massage; laundry service; dry cleaning. *In room:* A/C, TV w/pay movies, minibar.

MODERATE

Bridge Hotel ★★   The bridge in question is the famous Magere Brug (Skinny Bridge) over the Amstel River. The small and tastefully decorated hotel likely provides its guests with more space per euro than any other hotel in town. Its pine-furnished rooms seem like studio apartments, with couches, coffee tables, and easy chairs arranged in lounge areas in such a way that there's plenty of room left between them and the beds for you to do your morning exercises.

> **Impressions**
>
> *I had in my mind's eye a perfect bed in a perfect hostelry hard by the Amstel River.*
>
> —Erskine Childers, *The Riddle of the Sands* (1903)

Amstel 107–111 (near Theater Carré), 1018 EM Amsterdam. ℂ 020/623-7068. Fax 020/624-1565. www.thebridgehotel.nl. 36 units. 85€–130€; double. Rates include continental breakfast. AE, DC, MC, V. Limited street parking. Tram: 6, 7, 10 to Weesperplein. **Amenities:** Bar. *In room:* TV.

Hotel Arena ★   A converted Roman Catholic orphanage from 1890 houses a friendly, stylish, youth-oriented hotel. For all that the exterior bears a passing resemblance to Dracula's castle, the interior proves they really knew how to do an orphanage in those days. Monumental marble staircases, cast-iron banisters, stained-glass windows, marble columns, original murals—all have been faithfully restored. Spare modern rooms, some sporting timber roof beams and wooden floors, line long high-ceilinged corridors on two floors. Each room is individually decorated and styled by up-and-coming young Dutch designers. Some are split-level. Meeting and reception facilities, and spaces for art exhibits and other cultural events, signal a shift away from the Arena's history as a back-packers' rendezvous to a lodging with broader appeal. You still see kids toting backpacks, but they're a better class of backpack than those that clog corridors in the city's hostels and cheap hotels. The continental cafe-restaurant **To Dine** looks a little like an upgraded cafeteria on the inside, but has a great alfresco ter-race in the garden and an attached bar, **To Drink.** Hotel guests get a discount on concerts and dance nights in the nightclub **Tonight,** which puts up music from the 1960s onward in the old orphanage chapel. The Arena is a bit removed from the center, but isn't too far away, and the traffic is two-way, with youthful revelers heading out here to the nightspot and the outdoor cafe.

's-Gravesandestraat 51 (at Mauritskade), 1092 AA Amsterdam. ℂ 020/850-2410. Fax 020/850-2415. www.hotelarena.nl. 121 units. 102€–149€ double, 149€–173€ split-level double. Rates include buffet breakfast. AE, DC, MC, V. Free parking. Tram: 7, 10 to Korte 's-Gravesandestraat. **Amenities:** Restaurant (Con-tinental); bar; executive rooms. *In room:* TV.

8 In Amsterdam South

EXPENSIVE

Bilderberg Garden Hotel ★★★   This is the smallest and most personal five-star hotel in town. Because of its excellent **Mangerie de Kersentuin** restaurant (see below), the Garden considers itself a "culinary hotel," an idea that extends to the rooms, whose color schemes are salad-green, salmon-pink, cherry-red, and grape-blue—and you can choose whichever suits you best. The rooms themselves are furnished and equipped to the highest standards and with refined taste; only executive rooms have coffeemakers. Bathrooms are in marble, and each is equipped with a Jacuzzi tub. The Garden's spectacular lobby has a wall-to-wall fireplace with a copper-sheathed chimney. The French Mangerie de Kersentuin (Cherry Orchard) restaurant, a member of Les Etappes du Bon Goût, has an international reputation (see chapter 5 for full details) and moder-ate prices. The **Kersepit** (Cherry Pit) is a cozy bar with an open fireplace and a vast range of Scotch whiskeys.

Dijsselhofplantsoen 7 (at Apollolaan), 1077 BJ Amsterdam. ℂ 0800/641-0300 in the U.S. and Canada, or 020/570-5600. Fax 020/570-5654. www.gardenhotel.nl. 124 units. 325€ double, 370€ executive double; add 5% city tax. AE, DC, MC, V. Limited street parking. Tram: 5, 24 to Apollolaan. **Amenities:** Restaurant (French/Mediterranean); bar; concierge; business center; access to nearby health club; 24-hr. room service; in-room massage; babysitting; laundry service; same-day dry cleaning; nonsmoking rooms; executive rooms. *In room:* A/C, TV w/pay movies, fax, dataport, minibar, hair dryer, safe.

MODERATE

Apollofirst ★   The small and very elegant Apollofirst, a family owned hotel set amid the Amsterdam school architecture of Apollolaan, advertises itself as the "best quarters in town in the town's best quarter." Their claim may be debatable, but the Venman family's justifiable pride in their establishment is not. All the accommodations of this intimate hotel are quiet, spacious, and grandly fur-nished. Bathrooms are fully tiled, and rooms at the back of the hotel overlook the well-kept gardens of the hotel and its neighbors, and the summer terrace where guests can have a snack or a cocktail. The hotel's elegant **Restaurant Chambertin** is a French *fin de siècle* affair.

Apollolaan 123 (off Minervalaan), 1077 AP Amsterdam. ℂ 020/577-3800. Fax 020/675-0348. www.apollofirst.nl. 40 units. 125€–170€ double; 275€ suite. Rates include continental breakfast. AE, DC,

MC, V. Limited street parking. Tram: 5, 24 to Apollolaan. **Amenities:** Bar; 24-hr. room service; laundry service; dry cleaning. *In room:* TV.

Best Western AMS Hotel Beethoven ⭐ If you like to stay in a neighborhood atmosphere wherever you travel, make note of the AMS Hotel Beethoven. It's located in the heart of one of Amsterdam's most desirable areas, on one of its most beautiful shopping streets. The Beethoven was treated to a top-to-bottom redecoration in 1997. Plus, to the delight of local people and hotel guests, the Beethoven also gained an attractive restaurant, **Brasserie Beethoven,** that has a year-round sidewalk cafe (which closes at 7:30pm).

Beethovenstraat 43 (near Apollolaan), 1077 HN Amsterdam. ℂ 020/683-1811. Fax 020/616-0320. www.ams.nl. 52 units. 190€ double. AE, DC, MC, V. Limited street parking. Tram: 5, 24 to Apollolaan. **Amenities:** Cafe; courtesy bus; babysitting; laundry service. *In room:* TV w/pay movies, dataport, minibar, hair dryer, safe.

INEXPENSIVE

Van Ostade Bicycle Hotel ⭐⭐ The young proprietors of this establishment have hit on an interesting idea: They cater to visitors who wish to explore Amsterdam on bikes and they are helpful in planning biking routes through and around the city. You can rent bikes for 5€ daily, no deposit, and stable your trusty steed indoors. The recently renovated rooms have new carpets and plain but comfortable modern furnishings; some have kitchenettes and small balconies, and there are large rooms for families. The hotel is a few blocks from the popular Albert Cuyp street market, in the somewhat raggedy De Pijp neighborhood. An old bike hangs on the hotel's facade, and there are always bikes parked in front.

Van Ostadestraat 123 (off Ferdinand Bolstraat), Amsterdam 1072 SV. ℂ **020/679-3452.** Fax 020/671-5213. www.bicyclehotel.com. 16 units, 8 with bathroom. 99€ double with bathroom, 61€–70€ double without bathroom. Rates include continental breakfast. No credit cards. Parking 20€. Tram: 24, 25 to Ceintuurbaan. **Amenities:** Bike rental. *In room:* TV.

9 Near the Airport
VERY EXPENSIVE

Dorint Airport-Hotel Amsterdam Schiphol ⭐ Though comparisons are said to be invidious, you get many of the same amenities here for less than you'd pay at the Sheraton, and even if you do have to travel a few kilometers to get there, you do so by hotel shuttle. That said, the Dorint is no fount of Dutch tradition. Blocky and modern is the kindest thing I can say about the exterior, which is what you'd expect of a hotel in this business-park zone. The inside story is better, with rooms that bring a touch of style to their mission of lodging itinerant businesspeople. The **Wintertuin** restaurant has an international, a la carte menu. The English-style pub lounge/bar is a relaxed place for a drink.

Sloterweg 299, 1171 VB Badhoevedorp. ℂ 020/658-8111. Fax 020/658-8100. www.dorint.com/amsterdam. 220 units. 195€–240€ double; add 5% city tax. AE, DC, MC, V. Free parking. **Amenities:** Restaurant (Dutch/international); heated indoor pool; indoor and outdoor tennis courts; health club; sauna; concierge; business center; salon; 24-hr. room service; laundry service; dry cleaning. *In room:* A/C, TV w/pay movies, minibar, hair dryer, coffeemaker.

Sheraton Amsterdam Airport ⭐⭐ You could only be more convenient to the airport by lodging on the runway. There's all the comfort you would expect of a top-flight Sheraton, including soundproof rooms with big, comfortable beds, marble bathrooms with separate shower, and a well-equipped fitness center with pool. Room style ranges from modern and functional to unashamed luxury in the suites. The **Voyager** restaurant has an international, a la carte menu. The **Dutch Runway Café** serve drinks and delicatessen snacks.

Schiphol Boulevard 101 (outside Schiphol Plaza), 1118 BG Schiphol Airport. ⓒ **800/325-3535** in the U.S. and Canada, or 020/316-4300. Fax 020/316-4399. www.sheraton.com/amsterdamair. 408 units. 410€–555€ double; 890€–1,050€ suite; add 5% city tax. AE, DC, MC, V. Parking 30€. **Amenities:** 2 restaurants (international/Dutch); 2 bars; heated indoor pool; health club; sauna; concierge; business center; 24-hr. room service; babysitting; laundry service; dry cleaning; nonsmoking rooms; executive rooms. *In room:* A/C, TV w/pay movies, dataport, minibar, coffeemaker, hair dryer, safe.

Where to Dine

If cities get the cuisine they deserve, this one's ought to be liberal, multi-ethnic, and adventurous. Guess what? It is. As a port and trading city with a true melting-pot character, Amsterdam has absorbed culinary influences from far, wide, and yonder, and rustled them all up to its own satisfaction. More than 50 different national cuisines are served at its restaurants. Better yet, many of these eateries satisfy the sturdy Dutch insistence on getting maximum value out of each guilder spent.

From elegant 17th-century dining rooms to cozy canalside bistros, to exuberant taverns with equally exuberant Greek attendants to exotic Indonesian rooms attended by turbaned waiters, to the *bruine kroegjes* (brown cafes) with their smoke-stained walls and friendly table conversations, the eateries of Amsterdam confront the tourist with the exquisite agony of being able to choose only one or two from their vast numbers each day. Dutch cooking, of course, is part of all this, but you won't be stuck with *biefstuk* (beefsteak) and *kip* (chicken) every night, unless you want to be. Dutch practicality has also produced a wide selection of restaurants in all price ranges.

A relatively recent and popular trend is the emerging **grand cafe** scene. These are cafes in the, well, grand tradition of Paris, Vienna, and Rome, with lots of style, ambience, and balconies or terraces—see-and-be-seen kind of places. Grand cafes are distinguished by their emphasis on food and drink, architecture, production values, and style. The grand cafes listed below are truly grand, but there are others that use the name even though they may not be particularly impressive. The definition is an elusive one, merging into restaurants with terraces at one end and more-or-less ordinary cafes at the other.

There are a few distinctively **Dutch foods** whose availability is seasonal. Among them: asparagus, beautifully white and tender, in May; "new" herring, fresh from the North Sea and eaten raw, in May or early June (great excitement surrounds the first catch of the season, part of which goes to the queen and the rest to restaurateurs amid spirited competition); and Zeeland oysters and mussels (*Zeeuws-oesters* and *Zeeuwsmosselen*), from September to March.

Good eating out info is available on the Internet at **www.dinner-in-amsterdam.nl**.

RESTAURANT ORIENTATION

Dutch menus list appetizers, not main courses, under the title "entree." Restaurants are required to include in their prices a 15% service charge plus value-added tax (BTW) and local taxes.

HOURS   Most restaurants are open from noon to 2:30pm for lunch, and from 6 or 7 to 10 or 11pm for dinner. In general, with the exception of late-night restaurants, kitchens in Amsterdam take their last dinner orders between 10 and 11pm. Even if a restaurant is open until 11pm or midnight, you won't get served

> **Tips Good-Eats Cafes**
>
> For good, low-cost food, look out for examples of that Dutch dining insti-
> tution, the *eetcafé* (pronounced *ayt*-caff-ay). Many of these places—some
> of which are reviewed below—are essentially brown cafes (bars) with a
> hardworking kitchen attached. The food is generally unpretentious,
> mainstream Dutch (though some are more adventurous), and the price
> for their *dagschotel* (plate of the day), which might come with meat, veg-
> etable, and salad all on one large plate, is usually in the 6€ to 10€ range.

unless you arrive well before then—how much before varies with the restaurant,
and maybe with the mood of the staff, but it should be at least half an hour in
moderate and budget places, and at least an hour further upmarket. The trend
in recent years has been for restaurants to stay open later.

TIPPING   Since a 15% service charge is automatically included in the prices
shown on the menus, you needn't leave a tip beyond the amount shown on the
tab—but if you want to do as the Dutch do, round up to the next euro or two,
or in the case of a large check, up to the next 5 or 10 euros.

RESERVATIONS   On the weekends, unless you eat especially early or late,
reservations are generally recommended at top restaurants and at those on the
high end of the moderate price range. A call ahead to check is a good idea at any
time in Amsterdam, where restaurants are often small and may be crowded with
neighborhood devotees. Note that restaurants with outside terraces are always in
big demand on pleasant summer evenings; make a reservation, if the restaurant
will let you—if not, get there early or forget it.

WINE WITH DINNER   Estate-bottled imported wines are expensive in Holland, and even a bottle of modest French wine can add at least 12€ to 15€ to
a dinner tab. House wine, on the other hand—which may be a carefully selected
French estate-bottled wine—will be a more economical choice in restaurants at
any price level. Wine by the glass costs anywhere from 2€ to 5€.

LUNCH & SNACK COSTS   Unless you want it to be, lunch doesn't have to
be an elaborate affair (save that for the evening). Typical Dutch lunches are light,
quick, and cheap (see "Dutch Cuisine," below). A quick midday meal can cost
5€ to 10€. An afternoon pit stop for cake and cappuccino or pastry and tea will
set you back around 3€ to 6€.

BUDGET DINING   Eating cheaply in Amsterdam is not an impossible
dream. And, I'm happy to report, in some cases you can even eat cheaply in
style, with candles on the table, flowers in the window, and music in the air. And
though there's no such thing as a free lunch, there is the next best thing—a
dagschotel (plate of the day). The practical Dutch don't like to spend unnecessary
guilders, so almost every neighborhood has its modestly priced restaurant and
new budget places are popping up all over town like spring tulips. Another way
to combat escalating dinner tabs is to take advantage of the tourist menu that
many restaurants offer.

1 Dutch Cuisine

Dutch national dishes tend to be of the ungarnished, hearty, wholesome
variety—solid, stick-to-your-ribs stuff. A perfect example is *erwtensoep*, a thick

pea soup cooked with ham or sausage that provides inner warmth against cold Dutch winters and is filling enough to be a meal by itself. Similarly, *hutspot*, a potato-based "hotchpotch," or stew, is no-nonsense nourishment that becomes even more so with the addition of *klapstuk* (lean beef). Hutspot also has an interesting intangible ingredient—a story behind its name that's based on historical fact (see "Amsterdam's Origins," in Appendix A).

Seafood, as you might imagine in this traditionally seafaring country, is always fresh and simply—but well—prepared. Fried sole, oysters from Zeeland, mussels, and herring (fresh in May, pickled other months) are most common. In fact, if you happen to be in Holland for the beginning of the herring season, it's an absolute obligation—at least once—to interrupt your sidewalk strolls for a "green" (raw) herring with onions from a fish stall. Look for signs saying HOLLANDSE NIEUWE. These fish stalls are a great resource for snacks of baked fish, smoked eel, and seafood salads, taken on the run.

Far-ranging Dutch explorers and traders brought back recipes and exotic spices, and the popular Indonesian rijsttafel (rice table), a feast of 15 to 30 small portions of different dishes eaten with plain rice, has been a national favorite ever since it arrived in the 17th century. If you've never experienced this minifeast, it should definitely be on your "must eat" list for Holland. Should you part company with the Dutch and their love of Indonesian food, you'll find the cuisines of China, France, Greece, India, Italy, Japan, Spain, Turkey, Yugoslavia, and several other nationalities well represented.

At the top of the restaurant scale are those posh dining rooms affiliated with the prestigious **Alliance Gastronomique Néerlandaise** or the **Relais du Centre.** They're likely to be elegant and sophisticated or atmospherically old world and quaint. They will certainly be expensive. Then there are the numerous moderately priced restaurants and little brown cafes. Dutch families gravitate to the restaurants, while the brown cafes are cozy social centers with simple but tasty food, often served outside on sidewalk tables. Sidewalk vendors, with fresh herring and the ubiquitous *broodjes* (sandwiches) or other light specialties, are as popular as the brown cafes.

MEALS

The first step in getting to know Dutch gastronomy is to forget that in American restaurants the word *entree* means a main course; in Holland, an entree is an appetizer, and main courses, also known as *hoofdgerechten,* are listed separately as *vis* (fish) or *vlees* (meat), and in some restaurants, as *dagschotel* (dish of the day). The other courses you will see on Dutch menus are *soepen* (soups), *warme* or *koude voorgerechten* (warm or cold appetizers), *groenten* (vegetables), *sla* (salad), *vruchten* (fruits), *nagerechten* (desserts), *dranken* (beverages), and *wijn* (wine).

The next step is to understand that Dutch is a language of compound words, and just as Leiden Street becomes Leidsestraat—one word for two ideas—you'll notice on menus that beef steak becomes *biefstuk,* pork chop becomes *varkenscotelette,* and so on.

Similarly, you'll find listings for *gehakte biefstuk* (chopped beef) or *gebakken worst* (fried sausage). The clue is to look for the following key words and word endings as you scan a menu for basic information on the cuts of meat available and the modes of preparation of the dishes from which you are choosing:

- For cuts of meat: *-stuk* (steak or, literally, piece), *-scotelet* or *-scotelette* (chop), *-kotelet* or *-kotelette* (cutlet).

Moments (Secrets of the Rijsttafel)

The Indonesian feast **rijsttafel** is Holland's favorite meal and has been ever since the Dutch United East India Company captains introduced it to the wealthy burghers of Amsterdam in the 17th century. The rijsttafel (literally "rice table") originated with Dutch plantation over-seers in Indonesia, who liked to sample selectively from Indonesian cuisine. It became a kind of tradition, one upheld by Indonesian immi-grants to Holland who opened restaurants and, knowing the Dutch fondness for rijsttafel, made it a standard menu item. Rijsttafels are only a small part of the menu in an Indonesian restaurant, and there is a trend among the Dutch to look down on them as being just for tourists; the Dutch generally have a good understanding of Indone-sian cuisine and prefer to order an individual dish rather than the mixed hash of flavors of a rijsttafel. However, rijsttafels remain popu-lar, and many Chinese, Japanese, Vietnamese, and Thai restaurants in Holland have copied the idea.

Rijsttafel is an acquired taste, and unless you already have a stom-ach for both Chinese and Indian cooking, you may not like much of what you eat. But to be in Holland and not at least try a rijsttafel is as much a pity as it would be to miss seeing Rembrandt's *The Night Watch* while you had the chance. Besides, with more than 20 different dishes on the table, you're bound to find a few you enjoy.

The basic concept of a rijsttafel is to eat a bit of this and a bit of that, blending the flavors and textures. A simple, unadorned bed of rice is the base and the mediator between spicy meats and bland veg-etables or fruits, between sweet-and-sour tastes, soft-and-crunchy

- For modes of preparation: *gekookt* or *gekookte* (boiled), *gebakken* (fried), *gebraden* (roasted), *geroosteerd* (broiled), *gerookte* (smoked).
- For meat cooked to your taste: *niet doorgebakken* (rare), *half doorgebakken* (medium), *goed doorgebakken* (well done).

MENU CHOICES

BREAKFAST   The Dutch don't eat bacon and eggs or drink orange juice, but they eat nearly as much as Americans do in the morning. Dutch hotel restau-rants serve the same kind of breakfast the Dutch make for themselves at home, with the cost sometimes incorporated in your room rate. Bring a good appetite to the table, however, because a typical Dutch morning begins with a selection of breads—whole meal, nutty, or rye—fresh from the *warme bakker,* rusks (crunchy toasted rounds, like Zwieback), and *ontbijtkoek* (spicy gingerbread cake); a platter of cheese and sliced meats (ham, roast beef, salami); butter, jam, *hagelslag* (chocolate sprinkles), and *muisjes* (sugar-and-anise-seed sprinkles), which are a favorite with Dutch children, and *apelstroop* (apple or pear syrup); coffee (thicker and stronger than American coffee, and often served with *koffiemelk,* gunk similar to condensed milk, which does to coffee what water does to fine malt whiskey) or tea. Some hotels include a boiled egg, yogurt, a glass of fruit juice, or all three.

textures. Although a rijsttafel for one is possible, this feast is better shared by two or by a table full of people. In the case of a solitary diner or a couple, a 17-dish rijsttafel will be enough food; with four or more, order a 24- or 30-dish rijsttafel and you can experience the total taste treat.

Before you begin to imagine 30 dinner-size plates of food, it's important to mention that the dishes used to serve an Indonesian meal are small and the portions served are gauged by the number of people expected to share them. Remember, the idea is to have tastes of many things rather than a full meal of any single item. Also, there are no separate courses in an Indonesian rijsttafel. Once your table has been set with a row of low, Sterno-powered plate warmers, all 17 or 24 or 30 dishes arrive all at one time, like a culinary avalanche, the sweets along with the sours and the spicy, so you're left to plot your own course through the extravaganza. (Beware, however, of one very appealing dish of sauce with small chunks of what looks to be bright-red onion—that is *sambal badjak,* or simply *sambal,* and it's hotter than hot.)

Among the customary dishes and ingredients of a rijsttafel are *loempia* (classic Chinese-style egg rolls); *satay,* or *sateh* (small kebabs of pork, grilled and served with a spicy peanut sauce); *perkedel* (meatballs); *gado-gado* (vegetables in peanut sauce); *daging smoor* (beef in soy sauce); *babi ketjap* (pork in soy sauce); *kroepoek* (crunchy, puffy shrimp toast); *serundeng* (fried coconut); *roedjak manis* (fruit in sweet sauce); and *pisang goreng* (fried banana).

This, at any rate, is the ideal spread, but in cheaper hotels you may find a few sorry-looking, curled-up-at-the-edges slices of cheese, assorted cold meats of indeterminate provenance, and eggs boiled hard enough to sink an enemy submarine.

LUNCH & SNACK SPECIALTIES   Below are a number of dishes you may notice on lunch menus or may want to look for as typically Dutch choices for your midday meal:

Bami/Nasi Goreng & Nasi Rames   Miniature versions of an Indonesian rijsttafel (see below) that are served in a bowl on a bed of either noodles or rice, with spiced meat and possibly a fried egg or stick of satay (a grilled kebab) on top.

Bitterballen   Fried potato balls, or croquettes, that are generally quite spicy.

Broodjes   Small sandwiches on round buttered rolls, made with ham, cheese, roast beef, salami, or other fillings. They're often ordered in pairs and eaten standing up or perched at a narrow counter in a *broodjeswinkel,* or sandwich shop.

Croquetten   Fried croquettes of meat, prawns, or cheese that may be quite gooey inside but are at their best when served piping hot with a blob of mustard for dunking.

Erwtensoep Pea soup, thick and creamy and chock-full of chunks of ham, carrots, and potatoes—a meal by itself. (This is what the Dutch call a winter dish, so you may have trouble finding it on menus in summer.)

Nieuwe Haring New herring, the fresh-caught fish that is eaten whole (or chopped if you're squeamish) with minced onion at stands all over town during summer; during the rest of the year it's eaten pickled as *maatjes.*

Pannekoeken & Poffertjes Dutch pancakes that are the equivalent of French crepes, served flat on a dinner plate and topped with plain sugar, confectioners' sugar, jam, syrup, hot apples, or—typically Dutch—hot ginger sauce. Less common are pannekoeken with meat. Poffertjes are small "puffs" of a fried pancake mixture coated with confectioners' sugar and filled with syrup or liqueur.

Saucijzenbrood A Dutch hot dog, except in this case the bun is flaky pastry and the hot dog is a spicy Dutch wurst, or sausage.

Tostis Grilled ham-and-cheese sandwiches.

Uitsmijter An open-faced sandwich consisting of a slice of bread (or two), buttered and topped with cold slices of ham or roast beef and one or two fried eggs. (The name, incidentally, is the same as for "bouncer," the burly doorman at discos and clubs.)

Vlammetjes (little flames) These belong to the same general family of *borrelhapjes* (drinking snacks) as bitterballen, but are more like diminutive spring rolls which, like Napoléon, make up in fiery aggression for what they lack in size.

DINNER SPECIALTIES With the exception of one excellent taste treat—an Indonesian rijsttafel (see below)—the Dutch may seem to many tourists to be less inventive in the area of dinner specialties than they are for lunch and snacks. This is partly due to the fact that many traditional, typically Dutch dishes closely resemble dishes popular in the United States and elsewhere in Europe, but mostly it's due to modern Holland's ongoing and ever-growing (and finally, pretty tiresome) love affair with French cuisine. Here, however, are a few typically Dutch menu choices you may encounter, particularly in winter, when the stick-to-the-ribs nature of real Dutch cooking can be best appreciated:

Asperges Asparagus, the thick, white cultivated variety that grows during a 7-week season beginning with Queen's Day on April 30 and continuing until late June. Most of it comes from Limburg, so it is marketed as "the white gold of Limburg"—but most folks just call it asparagus.

Capucijners Met Spek Marrow beans with bacon.

Gember Met Slagroom The typically Dutch sweet-and-sour dessert of tangy slices of fresh ginger, topped with whipped cream.

Gerookte Paling Smoked eel, a typically Dutch appetizer, most of which come from the IJsselmeer, though many eels are now imported.

Hazepeper Jugged hare.

Hutspot A stew made of ribs of beef, carrots, onions, and potatoes, often mashed together. This is a dish with historic significance, particularly for the people of Leiden: It's the Dutch version of the stew found in the boiling pots left behind after the Spaniards were routed from their city at the end of the long siege during the Eighty Years' War.

Krabbetjes Dutch spareribs, usually beef ribs rather than pork.

Moments **In Search of Gezelligheid**

When in Amsterdam, do as the Dutch do: Look for someplace *gezellig*, and treasure it if you find it.

So what is *gezellig*, or *gezelligheid* (the state of being *gezellig*)?

Ah . . . it's a simple idea, yet one that underlines everyday life; one of those imprecise, enigmatic, and finally untranslatable-in-a-single-word concepts for a mood and an attitude that you'll recognize right away when you find it, and then you'll say with quiet satisfaction, "Ah, this place looks *gezellig*."

So what *is* it then?

The special *something* that makes a place comfortable, congenial, cozy, familiar, friendly, intimate, memorable, tolerant, warm, and welcoming. Dutch, in fact. You find it in abundance in brown cafes; in a candle-lit restaurant where the atmosphere is unforced and there's a view of a softly illuminated canal; in a Dutch home where you are made to feel one of the family; even on a packed-to-the-gills tram where everyone is in good humor and sees the funny side of the situation.

The great thing about gezelligheid is that it's free. Box some up and take it home with you.

Mosselen   Mussels, raised in the clean waters of the Oosterschelde (Eastern Scheldt) estuary in Zeeland. The mussel season begins with great fanfare in mid-August, and the first of the crop are eagerly awaited; it runs until April. The mussels are often eaten steamed in a little white wine-and-vegetable stock.

Rolpens   A combination of minced beef, fried apples, and red cabbage.

Stampot   Cabbage with smoked sausage.

Zuurkool Met Spek en Wurst   Sauerkraut with bacon and sausage.

DESSERT   Desserts at any meal lean toward fruit with lots of fresh cream, ice cream, or *appelgebak,* a lovely and light apple pastry.

2 In the Old Center
VERY EXPENSIVE

Excelsior ★★★ CONTINENTAL   One of Amsterdam's most famous restaurants derives its reputation from critically acclaimed cuisine and superb service. It's more than a little formal—more than a lot formal, by Amsterdam standards—but people who like this kind of thing will like this kind of thing. Crystal chandeliers, elaborate moldings, crisp linens, fresh bouquets of flowers, and picture windows with great views on the Amstel River, help to give this refined place a baronial atmosphere. Respectable attire (jackets for men) is required. If your budget cannot compete with that of the royalty or showbiz stars who often dine here, try the Excelsior's three-course *menu du théâtre,* which makes fine dining a little more affordable. It includes such choices as smoked eel with dill (a Dutch specialty) or marinated sweetbreads of lamb with salad for starters, filet of halibut with caper sauce or filet of veal with leek sauce as main courses, and desserts such as orange pie with frozen yogurt or raspberry bavaroise with mango

Central Amsterdam Dining

sauce. A meal here is a lovely way to start an evening at the ballet or the opera, especially as live—and soft—music is played on the grand piano every evening to get you into the mood.

In the Hôtel de l'Europe, Nieuwe Doelenstraat 2–8 (facing Muntplein). ⓒ **020/531-1777.** Reservations recommended on weekends. Main courses 28€–39€; fixed-price menus 42€–75€. AE, DC, MC, V. Mon–Fri 7–11am, 12:30–2:30pm, 7–10:30pm; Sat–Sun 7–11am, 7–10:30pm. Tram: 4, 9, 14, 16, 24, 25 to Muntplein.

Osaka ⭐ JAPANESE   The name of Japan's main port city is an appropriate one for this somewhat stiff but authentic Japanese restaurant on the 12th floor of the 13-story Havengebouw, overlooking Amsterdam harbor. Amsterdam doesn't have many tall buildings, so this place offers a grand view for dinner. Only the section where traditional Japanese food is served has the water view, however; those who go for teppanyaki get to look out over the Centraal Station and its rail-line network. But no matter where you sit, the food is worth it. This is one of the Japanese restaurants that have borrowed the Indonesian *rijsttafel* concept—a little bit of this and a little bit of that—and applied it to Japanese cuisine. Otherwise, the menu is standard Japanese, with sushi in an extensive seafood menu, and with chefs who are fast on the draw with knives and salt and pepper shakers in the teppanyaki grill section. Note that a la carte prices on the traditional menu can take you way above the top menu price listed here, depending on what choices you make.

12th floor, Het Havengebouw, De Ruijterkade 7 (beside the harbor, west of Centraal Station). ⓒ **020/638-9833.** Fixed-price menus 18€–43€. AE, DC, MC, V. Mon–Fri noon–midnight; Sat–Sun 6pm–midnight. Tram: 1, 2, 4, 5, 9, 13, 16, 17, 24, 25 to Centraal Station.

EXPENSIVE

De Silveren Spiegel ⭐⭐ DUTCH/FRENCH   The owner of this traditional old restaurant, one of the best known in Amsterdam, has introduced a fresh approach. The two houses that form the premises were built in 1614 for a wealthy soap-maker, Laurens Jansz Spieghel. It's typically Old Dutch inside, with the bar downstairs and more dining rooms where the bedrooms used to be. The whole place emanates a traditionally Dutch tidiness that's very welcoming. There's a garden in back. The menu has been updated and now offers new, finely prepared seafood and meat dishes, such as baked sole filets with wild spinach, and trilogy of lamb with ratatouille—but just as in the old days, the lamb is still Holland's finest, from Texel, and traditional Zaanse mustard is never far away.

Kattengat 4–6 (off Singel). ⓒ **020/624-6589.** Main courses 25€–30€; fixed-price menus 38€–45€. AE, MC, V. Daily 6–11pm (open for lunch by reservation). Tram: 1, 2, 5, 13, 17 to Martelaarsgracht.

Dorrius ⭐⭐ DUTCH/INTERNATIONAL   Housed in adjoining canal houses from 1890, this is one of Amsterdam's most elegant dining rooms. Its traditional atmosphere, which particularly suits quiet business discussions, is enhanced by beamed ceilings and a black-and-white marble floor. Among the specialties are fried pikeperch with raspberry sauce, and filet steak with duck liver and truffle sauce. Or you can choose from the Dorrius Classics—a list of old-fashioned Dutch dishes, including such delicacies as Zeeland oysters, home-style marrowfat peas, and braised beef with red cabbage. Although the wine list changes seasonally, you may be lucky enough to find on it some of the small production of white wines from the Slavante and Apostelhoeve wineries in the south of Holland, near Maastricht.

In the Crowne Plaza Hotel, Nieuwezijds Voorburgwal 5 (near Centraal Station). ⓒ **020/620-0500.** Main courses 16€; fixed-price menus 30€–40€. AE, DC, MC, V. Daily 6–11pm. Tram: 1, 2, 5, 13, 17 to Martelaarsgracht.

D'Vijff Vlieghen ★★ MODERN DUTCH   Among the most famous restaurants in town, the "Five Flies" occupies five canal houses (hence the name). In fact, it's an Amsterdam institution. "Who wants to eat in an institution?" I can hear you say, but I don't think you'll find any reason to knock this one. The decor is Old Dutch, though each of the nine separate dining rooms has a different character. There's the Rembrandt Room, which has five original etchings by the artist, the Glass Room, with a collection of Golden Age handmade glassware, and the Knight's Room, adorned with 16th-century armor and accouterments, to name just three. The chef is out to convey the culinary excellence inherent in many traditional Dutch recipes and products, but in an updated, French-influenced "New Dutch" form, and employing organic ingredients so far as is possible. You can enjoy quite a mouthful by choosing the *geroosteerde tamme eend op een bedje van appeltjes en tuinboontjes overgroten met een vinaigrette van rode en groene pepers* (roasted tame duck on a layer of apples and broad beans drizzled with a vinaigrette of red and green peppers). Or select from an extensive range of fish, game, and vegetarian options. And what better way to end your meal than with one of 40 brands of *jenever* (Dutch gin), including the restaurant's own.

Spuistraat 294–302 (at Spui). ✆ **020/530-4060.** Main courses 21€–30€; seasonal menu 31€–52€. AE, DC, MC, V. Daily 5:30pm–midnight. Tram: 1, 2, 5 to Spui.

Dynasty ★ CHINESE/SOUTHEAST ASIAN   Whether it's summer dining in a formal Louis XV–style canal-house courtyard garden or winter dining in a cozy cavern of exotic colors and upturned Chinese paper umbrellas, this restaurant won't disappoint. It offers an array of menu dishes, an extravaganza of flavors—Cantonese, Thai, Malay, Filipino, and Vietnamese—that take you on a virtual Cook's tour of southeast Asia. Among the intriguing possibilities is Promise of Spring, an appetizer of crisp pancakes filled with bamboo shoots and minced meat, and the delightfully named "drunken prawn," which is jumbo shrimp marinated in shoashing wine and Chinese herbs. Recommended main courses include the lobster lightly seasoned with ginger and scallions, and the Sichuan beef.

Reguliersdwarsstraat 30 (off Leidsestraat). ✆ **020/626-8400.** Main courses 18€–35€; fixed-price menus 36€–49€. AE, DC, MC, V. Wed–Mon 5:30–11pm. Tram: 1, 2, 5 to Koningsplein.

Lucius ★ SEAFOOD   Lucius, which means "pike" in Latin, has earned a reputation for fine seafood at fairly reasonable prices. Oysters and lobsters imported from Norway and Canada are the specialties. The three-course menu is also very popular. Among the half dozen or so choices featured on the chalkboard menu, you might find fish soup to start, followed by grilled plaice, Dover sole, bass, or John Dory. The spectacular seafood plate includes 6 oysters, 10 mussels, clams, shrimp, and half a lobster. The long, narrow dining room is cooled by ceiling fans and features an aquarium. In summer, chairs are placed out on the sidewalk.

Spuistraat 247 (near Spui). ✆ **020/624-1831.** Main courses 20€–40€; fixed-price menus 30€–35€. AE, DC, MC, V. Daily 5pm–midnight. Tram: 1, 2, 5 to Spui.

MODERATE

De Jaren ★ CONTINENTAL   One of the city's largest cafes, the recently refurbished, brightly lit De Jaren is fashionable without being pretentious. It occupies a solid-looking, spacious building on two stories with unusually high ceilings that served originally as bank. Many students from the nearby university who are tired of cafeteria food lunch here, and it's popular with the media crowd. De Jaren's unique selling point is not so much the fashionable set that hangs out here, but its marvelous open-air terrace beside the Amstel River, a place in the sun that is much in demand in fine weather. Occupants of those prime-time seats settle into them with a firmness of purpose that looks as if they meant to settle there permanently, but it's still worth checking out the outdoor deck, in case one of them might have fallen—or been pushed—into the river. You can enjoy everything from a cup of coffee, a beer, or a glass of *jenever* (gin) to a good salad, spaghetti bolognese, and rib-eye steak. And you can peruse the English-language newspapers while you do it.

Nieuwe Doelenstraat 20–22 (near Muntplein). ℭ **020/625-5771.** Main courses 7.50€–15€; fixed-price menus 9.50€–15€. V. Sun–Thurs 10am–1am; Fri–Sat 10am–2am. Tram: 4, 9, 14, 16, 24, 25 to Muntplein.

De Nissen DUTCH This Old Dutch-style spot has nooks and crannies that give it the atmosphere of an old wine cellar. The menu is typically Dutch and reasonably priced, and the mood is casual. Fresh fish here is a must. Try lobster *bisque* to start, fried filets of flounder as a main dish, and hot apple pie with cinnamon ice cream for dessert. At lunch, De Nissen is popular with people who work nearby, so you may have to wait for a table.

Rokin 95 (between the Dam and Muntplein). ℭ **020/624-2825.** Main courses 12€–18€; fixed-price menus 15€–22€. AE, DC, MC, V. Mon–Sat noon–9:30pm. Tram: 4, 9, 14, 16, 24, 25 to Spui.

De Poort ✦✦ DUTCH/INTERNATIONAL This restaurant, in a former beer hall, has been offering its steaks and typically Dutch dishes for more than 100 years. Its beamed and tiled Dutch-tavern dining room has recently been fully restored along with its parent hotel. De Poort still maintains a tradition that has become legendary among its patrons: Each of its steaks is numbered, and if the number on yours is a round thousand, you're the winner of a free bottle of wine. They've already served more than six million steaks! The restaurant is equally noted for its Dutch pea soup.

In the Hotel Die Port van Cleve, Nieuwezijds Voorburgwal 176–180 (behind the Dam). ℭ **020/624-0047.** Main courses 15€–22€; monthly Dutch Province menu 29€; fixed-price menu 32€. AE, DC, MC, V. Daily 7am–10:30pm. Tram: 1, 2, 5, 13, 14, 17 to the Dam.

Haesje Claes ✦ DUTCH If you're yearning for a cozy Old Dutch environment and hearty Dutch food at moderate prices, try this inviting place. Lots of nooks and crannies decorated with Delftware and wooden barrels, brocaded benches and traditional Dutch hanging lamps with fringed covers give an intimate, comfortable feel to the setting. The menu covers a lot of ground, from canapés to caviar, but you have the most luck with Dutch stalwarts ranging from omelets to tournedos, and taking in *hutspot* (stew), *stampot* (mashed potatoes and cabbage), and various fish stews, including those with IJsselmeer *paling* (eel), along the way.

Spuistraat 273–275 (at Spui). ℭ **020/624-9998.** Main courses 14€–20€; tourist menu 19€. AE, DC, MC, V. Daily noon–10pm. Tram: 1, 2, 5 to Spui.

In de Waag ✦ CONTINENTAL This cafe-restaurant is called In de Waag because it's in the Waag (see, you *can* speak Dutch). And what is the Waag? In medieval times it was the St. Antoniespoort Gate in the city walls; by the Golden Age, it had become a weigh house: De Waag. Dissections were once carried out on the top floor. Nowadays, dissections are of a culinary nature, as the castlelike structure holds one of Amsterdam's most stylish cafe-restaurants, in an area that's becoming hipper by the minute. It's an indelibly romantic place, the long banquet-style tables ablaze with candlelight in the evening. You can mix easily with other diners. The breast of Barbary duck with sesame-cracker and sherry dressing is pretty good, as is the vegetarian Kashmir bread with braised vegetables and coriander-yogurt sauce.

Nieuwmarkt 4. (©) 020/422-7772. Main courses 15€–20€. AE, DC, MC, V. Daily 10am–1am. Metro: Nieuwmarkt.

Kantjil en de Tijger ★★ INDONESIAN Unlike the many Indonesian restaurants in Holland that wear their ethnic origins on their sleeves, literally, with wait staff decked out in traditional costume, the Antelope and the Tiger is chic, modern, and cool. Moreover, it attracts customers who like their Indonesian food not only chic, modern, and cool, but good as well. The two bestsellers in this popular place are *nasi goreng Kantjil* (fried rice with pork kebabs, stewed beef, pickled cucumbers, and mixed vegetables), and the 20-item *rijsttafel* for two. Other choices include stewed chicken in soja sauce, tofu omelet, shrimp with coconut dressing, Indonesian pumpkin, and mixed steamed vegetables with peanut-butter sauce. Finish off your meal with the multilayered cinnamon cake or (try this at least once) the coffee with ginger liqueur and whipped cream.

Spuistraat 291 (beside Spui). (©) 020/620-0994. Reservations recommended on weekends. Main courses 12€–16€; rijsttafels 38€–48€ for 2. AE, DC, MC, V. Daily 4:30–11pm. Tram: 1, 2, 5 to Spui.

Le Pêcheur ★ SEAFOOD Both popular and appealing, in a frenetic neighborhood where establishments are more commonly either one or the other, Le Pêcheur has long combined elegant simplicity of presentation with a steely focus on freshness and taste. Flowers adorn the tables set on a marble floor, beneath a muraled ceiling, and there's a courtyard garden for summer dining. Dishes are prepared in Dutch, continental and international styles. In season, come for the *coquilles St-Jacques* scallops, the mussels and oysters from the southern Dutch province of Zeeland, and the house-smoked salmon. You could also try poached brill with onion sauce, fried wolffish with light mustard sauce, or sashimi. Tournedos of beef cooked to your liking are available for those who don't like seafood.

Reguliersdwarsstraat 32 (behind the Flower Market). (©) 020/624-3121. Main courses 18€–23€; fixed-price menu 34€. AE, MC, V. Mon–Fri noon–midnight; Sat 5pm–midnight. Tram: 1, 2, 5 to Koningsplein.

Lof ★★ CONTINENTAL *Finds* It's hard to pin down this fashionable, vaguely French/Italian eatery. For one thing, there's no menu. Its youthful chefs describe their creations as *cuisine spontane*—they go to the markets, spontaneously pick out whatever's fresh and takes their fancy, and equally spontaneously figure out what to do with it back at base. The results are invariably splendid. Oysters are a regular feature among three or four starters; then, choose from three main courses: meat, fish, and vegetarian; and finish with a *torte*. You dine on one of two levels, at plain tables in a cozy setting with bare brick walls, and a view of proceedings in the open kitchen.

Haarlemmerstraat 62 (near Centraal Station). (©) 020/620-2997. Main courses 9.50€–19€; fixed-price menus 26€–38€. No credit cards. Tues–Sun 6–11pm. Tram: 1, 2, 4, 5, 9, 13, 16, 17, 24, 25 to Centraal Station.

Ovidius INTERNATIONAL Though it's by no means the grandest of the grand cafes, the Ovidius is stylish, with a sufficiency of polished wood, brass railings, and mirrors, and a massive crystal chandelier. It makes for a good timeout from shopping at the stylish Magna Plaza mall. The tables are on three levels. A sign at the entrance reads, VENI, VIDI, VERBAZI, which roughly translates as "I came, I saw, I was astonished" (*verbazi* is from the Dutch *verbazen:* to be surprised). I can't promise astonishment, but the price is reasonable for an array of healthful snacks and light meals from around the globe: roast chicken and avocado, Caesar salad, Indonesian chicken satay in a spicy peanut sauce) and *vlammetjes* ("little flames," like small and spicy spring rolls), tapas, pasta, and more, along with croissants, muffins, and great coffee.

Spuistraat 137 (at Magna Plaza mall). ℂ 020/620-8977. Main courses 7.50€–15€. AE, DC, MC, V. Tues–Sat 9am–9pm; Sun–Mon 10am–9pm. Tram: 1, 2, 5, 13, 14, 17 to the Dam.

Rose's Cantina ★ TEX-MEX   Rose's attracts English-speaking guests with typical American favorites like hamburgers and meatballs, though the decor and most of the cuisine are Mexican inspired. A meal starting with tortilla chips and salsa, followed by a *plato mixto* or fried *gallinas* (roast hen with fries and red peppers), and accompanied by a Mexican beer will hit the spot. The tables are oak, the service is decent but slow—the basic rate of continental drift is a good comparison—and the atmosphere is Latin American and buzzing with good cheer. Just be careful of long waiting times for a table, during which, as likely as not, you'll sit at the bar downing one after another of Rose's deadly margaritas.

Reguliersdwarsstraat 38–40 (off Leidsestraat). ℂ 020/625-9797. Main courses 11€–22€. AE, DC, MC, V. Daily 5–midnight. Tram: 1, 2, 5 to Koningsplein.

Sarang Mas INDONESIAN   This intimate Indonesian restaurant is near the canal-boat piers, so you get a nice view while you dine on traditional Indonesian dishes, including a decent selection of rijsttafels. The pink, white, and green color scheme is a refreshing and contemporary alternative to the usual basic decor found in Indonesian restaurants. The big drawback is location: Damrak is central enough but is also the center of "tacky" Amsterdam; Sarang Mas is surrounded by sex boutiques, souvenir shops, fast-food joints, and video-game parlors. Still, the ruckus ends at the restaurant door, and Sarang Mas hasn't let its standards slip by being in a tourist ghetto.

Damrak 44 (near Centraal Station). ℂ 020/622-2105. Main courses 13€–20€; rijsttafels 27€–33€. AE, DC, MC, V. Daily 11:30am–11pm. Tram: 4, 9, 14, 16, 24, 25 to the Dam.

Treasure ★★ CHINESE   In a city with a passion for Indonesian food, it can be difficult to find traditional Chinese cuisine, let alone good traditional Chinese cuisine. Don't despair—make a beeline for Treasure, a legend in its own lunchtime (and dinnertime), rated among the best restaurants in Amsterdam by *Avant Garde.* It offers a wide array of classic Chinese choices in a classic Chinese setting, with lots of lanterns, watercolor paintings, and Chinese scripts. You can eat dishes from any of the four main styles of Chinese cooking—Beijing, Shanghai, Cantonese, and Sichuan. Look for specialties such as Beijing duck, Sichuan-style prawns (very spicy), and steamed dumplings.

Nieuwezijds Voorburgwal 115–117 (near the Dam). ℂ 020/623-4061. Main courses 9€–14€; fixed-price menus 15€–38€. AE, MC, V. Daily noon–11pm. Tram: 1, 2, 5, 13, 14, 17 to the Dam.

INEXPENSIVE

Atrium *(Finds)* DUTCH/INTERNATIONAL   Students, professors, and regular human beings in search of cheap, sustaining nosh congregate in this spectacular facility, the self-service student restaurant on the grounds of Amsterdam's old university. A courtyard between four restored buildings has been covered with a glass roof that lets in plenty of light, and plenty of hungry spirits, all year. To reach the food lines, walk up the stairs just inside the door and cross over the pedestrian bridge; at lunchtime the line is likely to extend across this bridge and down the stairs, but it moves along pretty smartly. The menu mixes standard Dutch fare like salads and pea-and-ham soup with exotic influences like filled Indonesian *bami* (noodle) and *nasi* (rice) croquettes that have themselves become Dutch standards. None of these, it must be stated, are produced to any unforgettable effect, but they're all perfectly edible and the knowledge that they're costing about as close to nothing as you're likely to get in Amsterdam for anything of reasonable quality, goes a long way toward compensating for any culinary shortcomings. An added value is the casual nature of the place, which makes it easy to share tables and strike up conversations.

Oudezijds Achterburgwal 237 (at Grimburgwal). ℂ **020/525-3999**. Main courses 3.75€–4.75€. No credit cards. Mon–Fri noon–2pm and 5–7pm. Tram: 4, 9, 14, 16, 24, 25 to Spui.

Blincker CONTINENTAL   To find this cafe-restaurant, turn into Nes (which runs parallel to Rokin) from the Dam, then turn left after the Frascati Theater. This intimate restaurant in the Frascati Theater building attracts actors, journalists, artists, and other assorted bohemians. At night the place is jammed with people around the bar. The simple but tasty fare includes lamb chops with garlic, pancakes with cheese and mushrooms, homemade pasta, and cheese fondue.

St. Barberenstraat 7 (off Rokin). ℂ **020/627-1938**. Main courses 5€–15€. AE, DC, MC, V. Mon–Sat 4pm–1am. Tram: 4, 9, 16, 24, 25 to Rokin.

Café Dulac SPANISH   This establishment used to be a bank, though it's a sure bet that none of its former staff or customers would recognize it now. The decor in the gloomily lit main room is bizarre: angels and devils on the ceilings, and skyscraper models sticking out at right angles above the bar. Still, the Dulac is one of the most popular grand cafes. There's a nice little garden terrace at the back, what's said to be the biggest pool table in Amsterdam, and a deejay on Friday and Saturday, when the lack of a true dance floor can't prevent many patrons from dancing. Friendly, youth-oriented service complements Mediterranean food specialties.

Haarlemmerstraat 118 (parallel to Brouwersgracht). ℂ **020/624-4265**. Tapas 2.95€–5.55€. AE, DC, MC, V. Sun–Thurs 4pm–1am; Fri–Sat 4pm–3am. Bus: 18, 22 to Haarlemmer Houttuinen.

Café Luxembourg ★★ INTERNATIONAL   "One of the world's great cafes," wrote the *New York Times* about this stylish grand cafe. Unlike other cafes in Amsterdam, which often draw a distinctive clientele, Luxembourg attracts all kinds of people because it offers amazingly large portions of food at reasonable prices. Soups, sandwiches, and such dishes as meat loaf are available. A special attraction is that some of the dishes are specials like the Chinese dim sum and the satay ajam (Indonesian grilled chicken in a peanut sauce). It's a good place to do breakfast with the day's papers. You're encouraged to linger in this relaxing place and read one of the many international newspapers. In summer, there's sidewalk dining.

Spui 22–24 (at Spui). ℂ **020/620-6264**. Salads and specials 8.50€–11€; lunch 4€–8.50€; main courses 8€–18€. AE, DC, MC, V. Sun–Thurs 9am–1am; Fri–Sat 9am–2am. Tram: 1, 2, 5 to Spui.

Nam Kee ★ CHINESE   Not many Dutch restaurants have made a name for themselves in the movies, but Nam Kee played a notable supporting role in the 2002 red-hot romance flick *De Oesters van Nam Kee* (*The Oysters of Nam Kee*),

> ### *Tips* **Think Japanese**
>
> Authentic Japanese sushi bars are burgeoning in Amsterdam, in part because the city and nearby infrastructure hubs like Schiphol Airport and Rotterdam harbor have become important locations for Japanese companies' European distribution centers and headquarters. Then again, the Dutch have always been fanatical about raw herring so it needed a very short imaginative leap for them to appreciate raw fish of all kinds. Whatever, here are four great *sushi* bars that wouldn't look out of place in Yokohama: **Zushi,** Amstel 20 (✆ **020/330-6882;** tram: 4, 9, 14, 16, 24, 25); **Zento,** Ferdinand Bolstraat 17–19 (✆ **020/471-5316;** tram: 16, 24, 25); **Stereo Sushi,** Jonge Roelensteeg (✆ **020/777-3010;** tram: 1, 2, 5, 14); and **Tokio Sushi,** Harlemmerdijk 28 (✆ **020/638-5677;** bus: 18, 22).

based on a novel of the same name. In the heart of the city's small but growing Chinatown, Nam Kee has a long interior with few obvious graces, little in the way of decor, and for sure no plastic Ming Dynasty knickknacks. People come here to pay modestly for food that is both authentic and excellent, from a menu with 140 items written on it. The steamed oysters with black bean sauce and the duck with plum sauce are to die for. Judging by the number of ethnic Chinese customers clicking chopsticks around, Nam Kee does okay when it comes to homeland credibility. The service is fast—not quite so fast that you'll still be eating off your plate while the waitperson is bringing it to the dishwasher, but not far away. On the bright side, this means you don't have long to wait for a table, popular though the restaurant is.

Zeedijk 111–113 at Nieuwmarkt. ✆ **020/624-3470.** Main courses 6€–16€. AE, DC, MC, V. Daily 11:30am–midnight. Metro: Nieuwmarkt.

1e Klas *Value* CONTINENTAL   For a little bit of Art Deco elegance with your budget meal, try this Centraal Station brasserie, in a lofty wood-paneled chamber with chandeliers. The place used to be the first-class waiting room. Each month there's a different special plate offered here at a rock-bottom price, and it's not the usual boring blue-plate fare. Trout, jugged hare, and coq au vin have all been the special in the recent past, always with salad, vegetable, and other appropriate accompaniments.

Platform 2B, Centraal Station. ✆ **020/625-0131.** Main courses 7.50€–11€; dish of the day 9.50€. No credit cards. Daily 8:30am–11pm. Tram: 1, 2, 4, 5, 9, 13, 16, 17, 24, 25 to Centraal Station.

3 Along the Canal Belt

EXPENSIVE

Christophe *★★* MODERN FRENCH   The star of this Michelin-star show is owner and chef Jean-Christophe Royer, who combines influences from his youth in Algeria and southwest France with his experience at top restaurants in New York, Baltimore, and Massachusetts, and a penchant for Mediterranean flourishes, to create an updated and unpretentious version of classic French cuisine. Royer serves sensuous, sophisticated food in an elegant setting featuring dark cherrywood paneling, thick carpets, rice-paper lamp shades, stately cacti by the windows, and floral paintings by contemporary Dutch artist Martin van Vreden. The food is similarly refined, using traditional Mediterranean ingredients—figs, truffles, olives, and saffron—in exciting new ways. Try the roasted milk-fed Pyrenean lamb, or roasted turbot in a light curry sauce, and finish with a light tart of prunes in Armagnac.

Leliegracht 46 (between Prinsengracht and Keizersgracht). ℂ 020/625-0807. Main courses 28€–33€; fixed-price menus 43€–53€. AE, DC, MC, V. Tues–Sat 6:30–10:30pm. Tram: 13, 14, 17 to Westermarkt.

MODERATE

Bolhoed ✿✿ VEGETARIAN   Forget the corn-sheaf 'n' brown-rice image affected by so many vegetarian restaurants, that worthy but dull message: "This stuff is good for you." Instead, garnish your healthful habits with a dash of zest. Latin style, world music, a changing program of ethnic exhibitions, evening candlelight, and a fine view of the canal from each of its two cheerful rooms distinguish a restaurant for which *vegetarian* is a tad too wholesome-sounding. Service is delivered with equal amounts of gusto and attention. Try such veggie delights as *ragoût croissant* (pastry filled with leeks, tofu, seaweed, and curry sauce), and *zarzuela*. If you want to go whole hog, so to speak, and eat vegan, most of Bolhoed's dishes can be so prepared on request, and in any case most are made with organically grown produce.

Prinsengracht 60–62 (near Noordermarkt). ℂ 020/626-1803. Main courses 12€–15€. No credit cards. Sun–Fri noon–11pm; Sat 11am–11pm. Tram: 13, 14, 17 to Westermarkt.

Breitner ✿ INTERNATIONAL   A fast, last-minute dash from here should get you to the Muziektheater or Theater Carré just in time for the evening curtain rise, but that would involve dining in unseemly haste (the expression "wolfing down" comes to mind), and undervalues the performance of the kitchen. The plush red carpet, chandelier, and a wine cupboard standing against one wall suggest timelessness, yet cool, modern decor and paintings tell a different story. Named after Amsterdam's Impressionist painter George Hendrik Breitner, this restaurant has found a way to fuse a classic French foundation with the cosmopolitan spirit of this world city. The smoked rib-eye starter with Sichuan pepper, and turbot stew with Indonesian vegetables are just two examples. Light floods in from big riverside and canalside windows.

Amstel 212 (at Herengracht). ℂ 020/627-7879. Reservations recommended at theater time. Main courses 12€–26€; fixed-price lunch 40€; fixed-price dinner 33€–44€. AE, DC, MC, V. Tues–Fri noon–2:30pm and 6–10:30pm; Sat 6–10:30pm. Tram: 4 to Keizersgracht; 9, 14 to Waterlooplein.

Café van Puffelen DUTCH/CONTINENTAL   A big cafe-restaurant near the Westerkerk. Among the menu dishes that show flair, creativity, and a seemingly inexhaustible supply of ingredients, you can try fried butterfish with a tarragon, coriander, and pesto cream sauce served on bacon and tomato spaghetti; and the main course Salad van Puffelen, served with tandoori chicken, smoked turkey, smoked salmon, roast veal, and Cajun shrimps. Other choices include vegetable platters and mozzarella with tomato. Save room for the delicious handmade chocolates that are house specialties.

Prinsengracht 377 (facing Lauriergracht). ℂ 020/624-6270. Main courses 15€–20€. AE, DC, MC, V. Mon–Thurs 3pm–1am; Fri 3pm–2am; Sat noon–2am; Sun noon–1am. Tram: 13, 14, 17 to Westermarkt.

Casa di David ✿ ITALIAN   A friend recommended Casa di David as the best Italian restaurant in Amsterdam, and she's probably right. The ambience is very romantic and typically Italian—dark paneling, red-and-white-checked tablecloths, and wine casks—but mingled with the flavor of an old wood-beamed Amsterdam canal house. There's a view of both the Singel and Herengracht canals from the restaurant's two floors. Casa di David is most famous for its freshly made in-house pasta and its pizzas for one.

Singel 426 (at Spui). ℂ 020/624-5093. Main courses 10€–15€. AE, DC, MC, V. Daily 5pm–midnight. Tram: 1, 2, 5 to Spui.

De Belhamel ★★ *Finds* CONTINENTAL   Soft classical music complements a graceful Art Nouveau setting at this two-level restaurant overlooking the photogenic junction of the Herengracht and Brouwersgracht canals. The tables fill up quickly most evenings, so make reservations or go early. The menu changes seasonally, but if you're like me you'll hope that something like, or as good as, this will be on the list: puffed pastries layered with salmon, shellfish, crayfish tails, and chervil beurre-blanc to start; and beef tenderloin in Madeira sauce with zucchini rösti and puffed garlic for a main course. You can also get vegetarian dishes. Try for a window table and take in the superb canal views. Although generally excellent, De Belhamel does have two minor flaws: The wait staff is occasionally a bit too laid-back, and when it is full, as it often is, the acoustic peculiarities of the place can drive the noise level up to about that of a boiler factory.

Brouwersgracht 60 (at Herengracht). ℂ 020/622-1095. Main courses 18€–20€; fixed-price menu 32€. AE, MC, V. Sun–Thurs 6–10pm; Fri–Sat 6–10:30pm. Tram: 1, 2, 5, 13, 17 to Martelaarsgracht.

De Kelderhof ★ CONTINENTAL   Rattan chairs, wooden tables, lots of plants, and a cobbled floor give this cellar restaurant a French Mediterranean–village atmosphere, and the French wine list adds to the feeling. The menu, though not extensive, has a good mix of soups, seafood, and grilled meat dishes, all prepared Mediterranean style. The fresh seasonal fish is close to the "heaven on earth" they claim for it, and the Caesar salad is pretty mean, too. Live music plays Wednesday through Sunday. This restaurant is a double bill: Round the corner, at Lange Leidsedwarsstraat 53–59, is Brasserie De Kelderhof (ℂ 020/638-0519), a fine fish restaurant in the style of a Portuguese *cantine.*

Prinsengracht 494 (off Leidsestraat). ℂ 020/622-0682. Main courses 15€–23€. AE, DC, MC, V. Daily 5:30–midnight. Tram: 1, 2, 5, to Prinsengracht.

De Luwte ★★ FUSION   *Graceful* is the term that seems best to sum up this fine restaurant, though that quality never descends into stiffness. It gets its grace from Florentine wall murals, floor-to-ceiling Art Deco lamps, drapes, hangings, ceiling mirrors painted with flowers and vines, a candle on each table, and not least from an elegant canalside location. And it avoids being starchy by a characteristic Amsterdam exuberance and buzz. In either of the twin rooms, try for one of the window tables that look out on the canal. The menu ranges across the globe for inspiration. Look out for items such as the vegetarian coconut curry crepes filled with spinach, lentils, and nuts; and stir-fried guinea fowl with nuts and *bok choy.*

Leliegracht 26–28 (between Keizersgracht and Herengracht). ℂ 020/625-8548. Main courses 16€–18€. AE, MC, V. Daily 6–11pm. Tram: 13, 14, 17 to Westermarkt.

Golden Temple ★ VEGETARIAN   In its fourth decade of tickling meat-shunning palates, this temple of taste is still one of the best vegetarian (and vegan) options in town. The first thing you notice when you enter is that you can actually *see* the place—the veil of cigarette smoke that obscures most

Amsterdam restaurants has been lifted here by a nonsmoking policy that adds a heavenly touch all on its own. If anything, the limpid atmosphere is a tad too hallowed, an effect enhanced by an absence of decorative flourishes that may be Zen-like in its purity but leaves you wishing for something, anything, to look at other than your fellow veggies while you wait to be served. The menu livens things up, with its unlikely roster of Indian, Middle Eastern, and Mexican dishes. This could make for an interesting game of mix-and-match if only the small print didn't all but instruct you to keep them apart. The food is ace, delicately spiced and flavored, and evidently prepared by loving hands. Multiple-choice platters are a good way to go. For the Indian *thali,* you select from constituents like *sag paneer* (homemade cheese), vegetable *korma,* and *raita* (cucumber and yogurt dip); the Middle Eastern platter has stalwarts like falafel, chickpea-and-vegetable stew, and vegetable *dolmas.* Side dishes range across items as varied as guacamole, couscous, and *pakora.* The homemade ice cream is a finger-licking good way to wind up.

Utrechtsestraat 126 (close to Frederiksplein). ℭ 020/626-8560. Main courses 6.50€–9.50€; mixed platter 12€. MC, V. Daily 5–10pm. Tram: 4 to Prinsengracht.

Het Land van Walem ✿ CONTINENTAL   Het Land van Walem may have lost a few of its accumulated brownie points since a few years ago when it was one of the hottest addresses in town, but that only means it's easier to get a seat on one of its two terraces: one outside beside the canal and the other at the back in a garden patio. The space between them isn't bad either; it was designed by Philippe Starck, with small tables in front of and beside the long bar, where daily newspapers are provided. This cafe-restaurant's standards have not slipped at all, so don't worry about being seen in yesterday's in-place. Menu items include pasta specialties, and also steak, chicken, and salads.

Keizersgracht 449 (beside Leidsestraat). ℭ 020/625-3544. Main courses 12€–20€. AE, DC, MC, V. Sun–Thurs 9am–1am; Fri–Sat 9am–2am. Tram: 1, 2, 5 to Leidsestraat.

Moko ✿ FUSION/POLYNESIAN   Experimental and trendy, Moko—the name refers to a Maori facial tattoo—has garnered mixed reviews since it replaced the beloved Kort on this prime canalside site in 2001. Be ready to go out on a limb, foodwise, and to write the experience down to, well, to experience, should it get hacked off behind you. After 10pm, you'll need to integrate music from a live deejay, who does his stuff in a lounge area beyond the central, boat-shaped cocktail bar, not right among the finely decorated dining tables. The food mixes influences from Australia, New Zealand, Asia, and Oceania with north European and Mediterranean dishes, in a free-style yet rarely overindulgent manner. Moko occupies a converted 17th-century, white-painted timber church, the Amstelkerk, but here endeth the churchly connection. Eating, design, and music intersect in a colorful, if somewhat impersonal high-tech space, in which natural materials combine with Maori-accents and images. Three coral-reef fish tanks add a touch of South Seas verisimilitude. The menu changes frequently, but these main courses provide a flavor of what's on offer: *Spiced zwaardvis en tonijn met tamari en wasabi-mayonnaise* (spiced swordfish and tuna with tamari-broth and wasabi mayonnaise), and *tomaten-risotto cake met veldchampignons, rucola en tomatenjam* (tomato risotto with portobello mushrooms, rucola, and sun-dried tomato paste). On warm summer evenings, try to get a table outdoors, on a wide, open square beside the Prinsengracht canal.

Amstelveld 12 (at Prinsengracht). ℭ **020/626-1199.** Reservations not accepted. Main courses 16€–20€. AE, DC, MC, V. May–Oct Mon–Fri 11:30am–1am, Sat–Sun 11:30am–2am; Nov–Apr Tues–Sat 11:30am–1am, Sat–Sun 11:30am–2am. Tram: 4 to Prinsengracht.

Rum Runners ☆ CARIBBEAN   In the former coach house of the Westerkerk (yes, the church) is Rum Runners, a two-level, laid-back, tropical kind of place where the atmosphere and cuisine are inspired by the Caribbean. Two gigantic bamboo birdcages greet you as you enter. You sit beneath gently circling ceiling fans and among towering potted palms that stretch to the lofty rafters. At night the reggae beat of the music often lasts until the wee hours. Try asopao, a Caribbean rice dish, or a Caribbean barbecue. You can also just drink cocktails to your heart's content and fill up on some of the best guacamole in town.

Prinsengracht 277 (beside Anne Frankhuis). ℭ **020/627-4079.** Main courses 12€–18€; fixed-price menus 18€–23€. AE, DC, MC, V. Mon–Thurs 2pm–1am; Fri–Sun 2pm–2am. Tram: 13, 14, 17 to Westermarkt.

Sluizer ☆ CONTINENTAL/SEAFOOD   Two notable restaurants (sadly, not for the price of one), stand side by side in convivial harmony. No. 45 is an old-fashioned brasserie with an eclectic menu that has a slightly French bias, in such items as *entrecôte Dijon* (steak with mustard sauce) and *poulet à la Provençal* (chicken with olives, sage, rosemary, and tomato). Next door, at nos. 41–43, the vaguely Art Deco *Visrestaurant* (Fish restaurant) has at least 10 specials daily, ranging from simple cod or eel to *coquille St-Jacques* (scallops), crab casserole, Dover sole, halibut, and octopus. Meat dishes, such as beef stroganoff and chicken supreme, also appear on the menu.

Utrechtsestraat 41–43 and 45 (between Herengracht and Keizersgracht). ℭ **020/622-6376** (Continental) or ℭ **020/626-3557** (seafood). Main courses 12€–30€; optional menu 15€. AE, DC, MC, V. Mon–Fri noon–2:30pm and 5pm–1am; Sat–Sun 5pm–1am. Tram: 4 to Utrechtsestraat.

Spanjer & Van Twist ☆☆ *Finds* CONTINENTAL   This place would almost be worth the visit for its name alone, so it's doubly gratifying that the food is good, too. The interior is typical *eetcafé* style, with the day's specials chalked on a blackboard, a long table with newspapers at the front, and the kitchen visible in back. High standards of cooking, however, put this place above others of the kind. The eclectic menu changes seasonally, but to give an idea of its range, I've come fork-to-face in the past with Thai fish curry and *pandan* rice; *saltimbocca* of trout in white-wine sauce; and artichoke mousseline with tarragon sauce and green asparagus. In fine weather, you can eat on an outdoors terrace beside the tranquil Leliegracht canal.

Leliegracht 60 (off Keizersgracht). ℭ **020/639-0109.** Reservations not accepted. Main courses 12€–15€. MC, V. Daily 10am–1am (only light snacks after 11pm). Tram: 13, 14, 17 to Westermarkt.

Tempo Doeloe ☆☆ INDONESIAN   For authentic Indonesian cuisine, from Java, Sumatra, and Bali—which doesn't leave out much—this place is hard to beat. Though its local reputation goes up and down with the tide, it's invariably busy. You dine in a *batik* ambience that's Indonesian, but restrained, and a long way short of being kitsch. The attractive decor and the fine china are unexpected pluses. Try the many little meat, fish, and vegetable dishes of the three different *rijsttafel* (rice table) options, from the 15-plate vegetarian *rijsttafel sayoeran,* and the 15-plate *rijsttafel stimoelan,* to the sumptuous 25-plate *rijsttafel istemewa.* In the big one, you get dishes like *gadon dari sapi* (beef in a mild coconut sauce and fresh coriander), *ajam roedjak* (chicken in a strongly seasoned sauce of chile peppers and coconut), *sambal goreng oedang* (small shrimps with Indonesian spices), and *atjar* (sweet-and-sour Indonesian salad). For great individual dishes, go for the *nasi koening,* or any of the vegetarian options. Finish with the *spekkoek,* a layered spice cake. One caution: When something on the menu is described as *pedis,* meaning hot, that's *exactly* what it is. A fire extinguisher would be a useful table accessory for these dishes; for an equally effective, and better-tasting alternative, order a *witbier* (white beer). But the chef doesn't rely only on killer spices; many of the flavors are subtle and refined.

Utrechtsestraat 75 (between Prinsengracht and Keizersgracht). ℂ 020/625-6718. Main courses 18€–23€; *rijsttafel* 24€–32€; fixed-price menu 27€–43€. AE, DC, MC, V. Mon–Sat 6–11:30pm. Tram: 4 to Keizersgracht.

INEXPENSIVE

De Prins ★★ *(Value)* DUTCH/FRENCH   This companionable restaurant, housed in a 17th-century canal house, has a smoke-stained, brown-cafe style and food that could easily grace a much more expensive place. De Prins offers an unbeatable price-to-quality ratio for typically Dutch/French menu items, and long may it continue to do so. The youthful clientele is loyal and enthusiastic, so the relatively few tables fill up quickly. This is a quiet neighborhood place—nothing fancy or trendy, but quite appealing in a human way. There's a bar on a slightly lower level than the restaurant. From March to September De Prins spreads a terrace out onto the canalside.

Prinsengracht 124 (at Leliegracht). ℂ 020/624-9382. Main courses 6€–13€; dish of the day 10€; specials 24€–28€. AE, DC, MC, V. Daily 10am–1am. Tram: 13, 14, 17 to Westermarkt.

Lunchcafé Singel 404 LIGHT FARE   If you find yourself growing weary of eating at local grand cafes, where they charge you an arm for ambience and a leg for lunch, Singel 404 makes an acceptable alternative. It has the blessing of simplicity and the advantage of low cost. You won't have to pretend that you're cool, or smart, or hip; you can just eat. Service is friendly and the salads and sandwiches are very good.

Singel 404 (near Spui). ℂ 020/428-0154. No credit cards. Sandwiches and salads 2.05€–7.00€. Daily 10am–8pm. Tram: 1, 2, 5 to Spui.

Pancake Bakery ★★ *(Kids)* PANCAKES   This two-story canal-house restaurant serves almost nothing but pancakes—an appropriate choice for any meal. The satisfyingly large pancakes come adorned with all sorts of toppings, both sweet and spicy, including Cajun chicken (on the spicy end of the taste spectrum), ice cream and liqueur (on the sweet end), and curried turkey with pineapple and raisins (for a little bit of both). The decor is simple, with winding staircases and exposed beams contributing to the pleasant ambience, and the windows provide a pretty view over the Prinsengracht. In the summertime you can dine outside at long wooden tables, but beware: All the syrup, honey, and sugar being passed around tends to attract bees and hornets. Nonetheless, the Pancake Bakery remains a firm local favorite, especially among children.

Prinsengracht 191 (at Prinsenstraat). ℂ 020/625-1333. Reservations required for large groups. Pancakes 4€–10€. AE, MC, V. Daily noon–9:30pm. Tram: 13, 14, 17 to Westermarkt.

Traîterie Grekas ★ GREEK   With just five tables and a small sidewalk terrace in summertime, Grekas would be more of a frustration than anything else, except that its main business is its takeout service. If you're staying at one of the hotels in this neighborhood (particularly next door at the Estheréa, to which Grekas provides room service), this place can even become your local diner. The

Kids Family-Friendly Restaurants

Pancake Bakery (p. 117)   I have yet to meet a kid who doesn't love pancakes, and this restaurant at Prinsengracht 191 (☎ **020/625-1333**) is *the* best pancake source in town. Pancakes come with various inventive toppings (sweet and savory). Suitably colorful ornaments such as umbrellas and clowns accompany child-oriented meals and desserts. Toys, children's chairs, and special menus complete the picture. There are also pancakes big enough to satisfy the most adult of tastes.

De Rozenboom   The tiny De Rozenboom, Rozenboomsteeg 6 (☎ **020/ 622-5024**), in an alley leading to the Begijnhof, serves hearty Dutch meals and has a special children's menu. Eating here is like having dinner in a doll's house.

L'Enfant Terrible   This cafe at De Genestetstraat 1 (☎ **020/612-2032**) is in a quiet residential area, not far from Leidseplein. In front is a large playroom. You can take a break and have a coffee on your own, or have lunch or dinner together with the children. There's even a playpen for the very young. The cafe also offers a babysitting service (maximum 3 hr.).

KinderKookKafé ★   Children are the chefs and waiters at this small restaurant at Oudezijds Achterburgwal 193 (☎ **020/625-3527**). With the help of some adults, they prepare dinner on Saturday and bake cookies and pies for high tea on Sunday. If your kids want to, they can join the kitchen brigade; or you can all just relax and enjoy the meal. Kids must be at least 8 years old to help with the Saturday dinner, and 5 for the Sunday bake.

New York Pizza   When your kids are longing for that all-American Italian food, head to New York Pizza, Amsterdam's answer to Pizza Hut, bright, clean, and decorated in Italy's national colors—red, white, and green. You can order three different kinds of pizza—traditional, deep pan, or whole meal. Branches are at Damrak 59 (☎ **020/639-0494**; tram: 4, 9, 16, 24, 25); Spui 2 (☎ **020/420-3538**; tram: 1, 2, 5); Reguliersbreestraat 15–17 (☎ **020/420-5585**; tram: 4, 9, 14, 16, 24, 25); Damstraat 24 (☎ **020/422-2123**; tram: 4, 9, 14, 16, 24, 25); and Leidsestraat 23 (☎ **020/622-8689**; tram: 1, 2, 5).

food is fresh and authentic, and you can choose your meal like you would in Mykonos, by pointing to the dishes you want. If there are no free tables, you can always take your choices back to your room, or eat alfresco on the canalside. Menu items are standard Greek but with a freshness and taste that are hard to beat. The moussaka and pasticcio are heavenly; the roast lamb with wine, herbs, olive oil, and bouillon is excellent; the calamari in the calamari salad seems to have come straight out of Homer's wine-dark sea; and there's a good Greek wine list, too. Takeout dishes cost a euro or two less.

Singel 311 (near Spui). ☎ 020/620-3590. Main courses 9€–11€. No credit cards. Wed–Sun 5–10pm. Tram: 1, 2, 5 to Spui.

America Online Keyword: Travel

Booked seat 6A, open return.

Rented red 4-wheel drive.

Reserved cabin, no running water.

Discovered space.

With over 700 airlines, 50,000 hotels, 50 rental car companies and ,000 cruise and vacation packages, you can create the perfect get-way for you. Choose the car, the room, even the ground you walk on.

Travelocity.com
A Sabre Company
Go Virtually Anywhere.

4 Around Leidseplein

EXPENSIVE

De Oesterbar SEAFOOD   De Oesterbar, which is more than 50 years old, is the best-known and most popular fish restaurant in Amsterdam. Its seafood is delivered fresh twice daily. The decor is a delight: all white tiles with fish tanks bubbling at your elbows on the street level, and Victorian brocades and etched glass in the more formal dining room upstairs. The menu is a directory of Dutch seafood dishes, but it also includes a few meat selections. Choices include *sole Danoise* with the tiny Dutch shrimps; *sole Véronique* with Muscadet grapes; stewed eel in wine sauce; and the assorted fish plate of turbot, halibut, and fresh salmon.

Leidseplein 10. ℘ 020/623-2988. Main courses 24€–33€. AE, DC, MC, V. Daily noon–1am. Tram: 1, 2, 5, 6, 7, 10 to Leidseplein.

MODERATE

Akbar ⚜ INDIAN   This is the best Indian restaurant in the Leidseplein area. Akbar has shifted sideways a few doors from its previous location, but is still on the same side street off the square. It's a consistently good performer across the range of Indian cuisine—tandoori, curry, vegetarian, and seafood—without being exactly outstanding in any category. The set meals are a good value, and service is friendly and prompt. There's also a takeout service.

Korte Leidsedwarsstraat 15 (off Leidseplein). ℘ 020/624-2211. Main courses 12€–21€; special Indian dinner for 1, 20€. AE, DC, MC, V. Daily 4:30pm–12:30am. Tram: 1, 2, 5, 6, 7, 10 to Leidseplein.

Aphrodite ⚜ GREEK   In an area awash with Greek restaurants that wear their Greekness on their sleeves (who doesn't like a touch of island-taverna charm?), Aphrodite stands out for putting more emphasis on taste and less on dazzling Aegean colors, fishing nets, and the lords and ladies of Olympus. Its single room is modern, restrained in its decor, and softly lit. The specialties— afelia (cubes of lamb meat in a coriander-and-wine sauce), moussaka, kleftiko (oven-baked lamb), and others—are not much different in principle from those of other Greek restaurants in the area, but are generally better prepared and served—which, after all, is difference enough.

Lange Leidsedwarsstraat 91 (off Leidseplein). ℘ 020/622-7382. Main courses 7.50€–15€. No credit cards. Daily 5pm–midnight. Tram: 1, 2, 5, 6, 7, 10 to Leidseplein.

Café Americain ⚜ CONTINENTAL   The lofty dining room here is a national monument of Dutch Art Nouveau. Since its opening in 1900 the place has been a hangout for Dutch and international artists, writers, dancers, and actors. Seductress/spy Mata Hari held her wedding reception here in her pre-espionage days. Leaded windows, newspaper-littered reading tables, bargello-patterned velvet upholstery, frosted-glass chandeliers from the 1920s, and tall carved columns are all part of the dusky sit-and-chat atmosphere. Seafood specialties include monkfish, perch, salmon, and king prawns; meat dishes include

---

Fun Fact **The Knives Are Out**

In the 1960s, satirist Gerrit Komrij described the Café Americain's famously brusque waiters as "unemployed knife-throwers."

Tips Quick Bites

To eat a *broodje* (sandwich) in a real *broodjeswinkel* (sandwich shop), go to the ever-crowded **Eetsalon Van Dobben,** Korte Reguliers-dwarsstraat 5–9 (℗ 020/624-4200; tram: 4, 9, 14), off Rembrandtplein. Other good choices are **Broodje van Kootje,** Leidseplein 20 (℗ 020/623-2036; tram: 1, 2, 5, 6, 7, 10), and Spui 28 (℗ 020/623-7451; tram: 1, 2, 5), both easily identifiable from their bright-yellow, broodje-shaped signs.

Should the shortage of good pastrami on rye in Amsterdam get to you, head out to Amsterdam South, to **Sal Meijer** ★ Scheldestraat 45 (℗ 020/673-1313; tram: 25), off Churchilllaan, a kosher sandwich shop where members of the city's Jewish community gather. The conversation and the sandwiches and other snacks are excellent. Sal's is open Sunday through Friday from 10am to 7:30pm, and delivers, depending on where you are and how much you want to order.

If you're a homesick Brit or just an admirer of traditional British fish and chips, head straight for **Al's Plaice** (get it?), Nieuwendijk 10 (℗ 020/427-4192; tram: 1, 2, 5, 13, 14, 17), where the business gets done with the requisite amounts of salt and vinegar, the pickled onions are big and juicy, and the paper wrappers all you could hope for; there's takeout service and seats inside.

If you thought Amsterdam was a bagel-free zone, think again. Some of the best bagels come from the **Gary's Muffins** chain. You can have plain, sesame, whole wheat, poppy, pumpernickel, cinnamon raisin, onion, and garlic bagels. The 20 different kinds of toppings include pesto cream cheese and tomato, and goat cheese, honey, and walnuts; the bagels range in price from 2.50€ to 7.50€. Gary's also does a takeout service. There are four Gary's Muffins: Prinsengracht 454 (℗ 020/420-1452; tram: 1, 2, 5); Marnixstraat 121 (℗ 020/638-0186; tram: 3, 10); Jodenbreestraat 15 (℗ 020/421-5930; Metro: Nieuwmarkt); and Reguliersdwarsstraat 53 (℗ 020/420-2406; tram: 1, 2, 5). The first three are open daily from 8:30am to 6 or 7pm; the fourth is open daily from noon to 3 or 4am.

Another quick-bite alternative, particularly for seriously cash-strapped budget travelers, are the branches of **Febo Automatiek** that you find all around town. They open directly on the sidewalk and look like giant streetside vending machines. Drop your euro coins in the appropriate slots and—voilà!—you have a lunch of Indonesian *nasi* or *bami goreng*, hamburger, fries, and a milk shake. I wouldn't say the portions are small, but they do have a compact form factor.

---

rack of Irish lamb and rosé breast of duck with creamed potatoes. Jazz lovers can stock up on good music and good food at the Sunday jazz brunch.

In the American Hotel, Leidsekade 97 (at Leidseplein). ℗ 020/556-3232. Main courses 16€–21€. AE, DC, MC, V. Daily 10:30am–midnight. Tram: 1, 2, 5, 6, 7, 10 to Leidseplein.

De Balie ★ CONTINENTAL   In what was once a jail, this chic theater cafe-restaurant pulls in an arty, theater-going crowd and serves them an inexpensive lunch and some great snacks in a stylish but smoky ground-floor cafe, under a high ceiling, along with beers and coffee, and simple but fine meals in a restaurant upstairs. De Balie is well placed for a dinner before or after a visit to its own theater, to the nearby Stadsschouwburg, or to one of the multiscreen movie theaters around Leidseplein.

Kleine Gartmanplantsoen 10 (off Leidseplein). ℭ 020/553-5131. Main courses 9.50€–16€; fixed-price menus 19€–25€. No credit cards. Cafe, daily 11:30am–10pm; restaurant, daily 6–10pm. Tram: 1, 2, 5, 6, 7, 10 to Leidseplein.

De Blauwe Hollander DUTCH   If you'd like a taste of sociable Dutch life, sitting shoulder to shoulder with the natives, the handful of big communal tables at this restaurant should fit the bill perfectly. De Blauwe Hollander, recently rebuilt, can be considered either a best buy as a moderate restaurant or a step-up alternative in the budget category. From a small sidewalk gallery you have a good view of the passing parade in this busy area of town, but the menu has very little that's more imaginative than roast beef, spareribs, and chicken. Everything is served with fries and a salad or vegetable.

Leidsekruisstraat 28 (off Leidseplein). ℭ 020/623-3014. Main courses 7.50€–16€; budget plate 9.50€. No credit cards. Daily 5–10pm. Tram: 1, 2, 5, 6, 7, 10 to Leidseplein.

Manchurian SOUTHEAST ASIAN   Apart from the lucky color red, the decor is minimal at this tri-level restaurant. The cuisine ranges from Cantonese, Sichuan, Beijing, and Shanghai to Thai dishes and Indonesian rijsttafels—and the Manchurian actually does a fair job of juggling these diverse types. The house specialty is crispy duck with pancakes, but also try scallion lobster or Siam prawns, Sichuan beef, or any of the sweet-and-sour dishes.

Leidseplein 10A. ℭ 020/623-1330. Main courses 17€–23€; *rijsttafel* 43€–79€. AE, DC, MC, V. Daily noon–2:45pm and 5–10:45pm. Tram: 1, 2, 5, 6, 7, 10 to Leidseplein.

INEXPENSIVE

Sherpa NEPALESE/TIBETAN   Sherpa may be a little short on the mystical tranquillity that characterizes its Himalayan homeland, but that's to be expected—it's hard for tranquillity to survive in this brash restaurants-and-bars district. Anyway, Sherpa adds a bit of culinary diversity to the area and its prices are reasonable. What's more, it's the only restaurant of its kind in Holland. You can eat "Yeti's food" (fried noodles with fried chicken and sautéed vegetables), or sample various other traditional Nepalese and Tibetan favorites.

Korte Leidsedwarsstraat 58 (off Leidseplein). ℭ 020/623-9495. Fixed-price menus 7.50€–14€. AE, DC, MC, V. Daily 5–11pm. Tram: 1, 2, 5, 6, 7, 10 to Leidseplein.

5 Around Rembrandtplein

MODERATE

Brasserie Schiller ★★ CLASSIC FRENCH/DUTCH   Beamed and paneled in well-aged oak and graced with etched-glass panels and stained-glass skylights, this 100-plus-year-old Art Nouveau landmark (not to be mistaken for the equally notable Café Schiller next door) is a splendid sight. Paintings by the artist who built the hotel, Frits Schiller, adorn the walls. Former chefs supplied the restaurant with the exact recipes and techniques used in the old days. On the classic menu you find everything from stewed eel and potato-and-cabbage casserole to T-bone steak, roast leg of lamb with mint sauce, and spaghetti bolognese.

In the NH Schiller Hotel, Rembrandtplein 26–36. ℭ 020/554-0723. Main courses 18€–23€; fixed-price menu 30€. AE, DC, MC, V. Daily 7am–10:30pm. Tram: 4, 9, 14 to Rembrandtplein.

Grand Café l'Opéra INTERNATIONAL   The main advantage of l'Opéra is that beyond its beautiful Art Nouveau facade it has probably the best and most restrained terrace in Rembrandtplein, though others are more centrally located on the square. On busy days in good weather, the Art Deco interior is a cool and quiet brasserie-style retreat, but of course on such days no one wants to go inside. The food in this cafe-restaurant is fine, if nothing to write home about. The menu items include such standards as salads, steak and mushrooms, croquettes, and mussels, and even Thai chicken curry for variation. Service, though friendly, is at times a little erratic.

Rembrandtplein 27–29. ⓒ **020/620-4754**. Main courses 14€–18€. AE, DC, MC, V. Sun–Thurs 10am–1am; Fri–Sat 10am–2am. Tram: 4, 9, 14 to Rembrandtplein.

Memories of India ⭐ INDIAN   The owner earned his spurs in the crowded London market for Indian cuisine and then brought his award-winning formula to Amsterdam. That formula is simple, really: Serve top-flight Indian cuisine in a setting that gives traditional Indian motifs a modern slant, charge moderate prices, and employ an attentive staff. Memories has won plenty of friends since it opened its doors a few years ago. The restaurant somehow manages to combine the hallowed silence of diners intent on their plates with a buzz of friendly conversation. Takeout service is available.

Reguliersdwarsstraat 88. ⓒ **020/623-5710**. Main courses 15€–20€; fixed-price menus 16€–23€. AE, DC, MC, V. Daily 5–11:30pm. Tram: 4, 9, 14 to Rembrandtplein.

Royal Café de Kroon ⭐ INTERNATIONAL   The "Royal Café" tag may be a tad overdone, but de Kroon comes close to justifying it. Along with the Café Schiller opposite, it has gone a long way toward raising the often tacky standards of Rembrandtplein. A fanciful mix of Louis XVI–style and tropical decor makes an eclectic but restful setting for the palm court orchestra that plays here on Sunday. De Kroon also has a superb enclosed balcony with a great view on the bustling square. The diverse, international menu choices range from snacks to three-course meals, and a good continental breakfast.

Rembrandtplein 17. ⓒ **020/625-2011**. Snacks 4€–12€; fixed-price menu 30€. AE, MC, V. Sun–Thurs 10am–1am; Fri–Sat 10am–2am. Tram: 4, 9, 14 to Rembrandtplein.

Tips **Late-Night Eateries**

Since the majority of restaurant kitchens in Amsterdam are closed by 10:30pm, it's good to keep these late-night addresses handy in case the munchies strike: **Bistro La Forge, De Knijp, Rum Runners,** and **Sluizer** (see "Along the Canal Belt," earlier in this chapter); and **Gary's Muffins,** Reguliersdwarsstraat 53 (see "Quick Bites," above).

INEXPENSIVE

Falafel Koning *Finds* MIDDLE-EASTERN   This tiny gem of a restaurant really needs a category all to itself: "Almost Cost-Free" comes to mind. The specialty of the house will set you back a mere 3€. It's falafel, but don't laugh—it's probably the best falafel this side of the River Jordan: mashed chick peas mixed with herbs, rolled in a ball along with what must be some magic ingredient, fried, and served in pita bread with salad. The snack bar is capable of seating about eight people at a push, plus more at a few tables outside when the sun shines.

Reguliersteeg 2 (off Reguliersstraat, opposite the Theater Tuschinski). ⓒ **020/421-1423**. Snacks and light meals 3€–6€. Daily 10am–1am. Tram: 4, 9, 14 to Rembrandtplein.

6 In the Jordaan

EXPENSIVE

Bordewijk ★★ FRENCH   This pleasantly located restaurant is often regarded as one of the best in the city. The decor is tasteful, with green potted plants offsetting the severity of the white walls and metallic black tables. Service is relaxed yet attentive, and on mild summer evenings you can't beat dining alfresco on the canalside terrace. But the real treat is the food. An innovative chef accents French standards with Mediterranean and Asian flourishes to create an elegant fusion of flavors. The menu changes often, but might include salted rib roast with bordelaise sauce, Serrano ham marinated in wine and vinegar and served with fresh pasta, pigeon cooked in the style of Bresse, or even Japanese-style raw fish. Dinner is followed by a fine selection of cheeses. The wine list is superb.

Noordermarkt 7 (at Prinsengracht). ℰ **020/624-3899.** Main courses 23€–26€; fixed-price menu 33€–43€. AE, MC, V. Tues–Sun 6:30–10pm. Tram: 1, 2, 5, 13, 17 to Martelaarsgracht.

MODERATE

Bananarama FILIPINO   There used to be four Filipino restaurants in Amsterdam, but now only Bananarama (formerly At Mango Bay) remains—a clear case of survival of the fittest. This slice of the Philippines occupies the front room of a canal house in the heart of the Jordaan. Diners enjoy delicately flavored dishes amid festive and colorful surroundings, with tropical flowers and a mural depicting an island paradise. The food also evokes the south Pacific: Main course dishes include prawns simmered in coconut milk with hints of ginger, coriander, and lemon grass; and beef marinated in honey and soy sauce. Cocktails are equally exotic. One favorite, a dangerous but tasty mixture of mango, passion fruit, lemon juice, and brandy, is humorously titled "Imelda's Shoes Plus or Minus 3,000 Ingredients."

Westerstraat 91 (off Prinsengracht). ℰ **020/638-1039.** Reservations recommended on weekends. Main courses 13€–16€; fixed-price menus 16€–20€. AE, DC, MC, V. Daily 6pm–midnight. Tram: 3, 10 to Marnix-straat.

Het Stuivertje DUTCH/FRENCH   This traditional restaurant is always crowded with people enjoying either the seasonal menu of the month or the regular menu. The latter features everything from vegetarian dishes such as broccoli soufflé to goat stew with fennel and thyme, plus more traditional items like salmon with hollandaise and breast of veal stuffed with vegetables.

Hazenstraat 58 (off Lauriergracht). ℰ **020/623-1349.** Reservations required. Main courses 9.50€–16€; fixed-price menu 22€. AE, MC, V. Wed–Sun 5:30–11pm. Tram: 7, 10 to Marnixstraat.

Hostaria ★ ITALIAN   This lively street lined with cafes and restaurants might remind you of Italy. On long summer evenings, even the ubiquitous Amsterdam cyclists have trouble picking their way through the many pedestrians out for a stroll. The Hostaria adds a little piece of authentic Italy to the scene, serving delicate homemade pasta and *secondi piatti* such as veal stuffed with Italian sausage, or duck cooked Roman style. Try the excellent *zuppa di gamberone con l'acquetta* (a plate of prawns and shellfish from the market).

Tweede Egelantiersdwarsstraat 9 (off Egelantiersgracht). ℰ **020/626-0028.** Main courses 15€–19€. No credit cards. Tues–Sun 7–10pm. Tram: 13, 14, 17 to Westermarkt.

Rakang Thai ★ THAI   A meal in this restaurant is a delight to all the senses. The dishes, many of them authentic regional specialties, are prepared with Thai

Finds Tea, Coffee, Cakes & Ice Cream

There are two sorts of cafes in Amsterdam: the museum or department-store lunchroom type and the Parisian people-watching type (the city's brown cafes are more like bars or pubs than cafes in the French or American sense). In the first category, one of the best is **La Ruche,** in De Bijenkorf department store, Dam 1 (② 020/621-8080; tram: 4, 9, 14, 16, 24, 25), a Rietveld-style cafeteria/restaurant on the second floor with a view of the Dam from its big windows.

Metz, in Metz & Co department store, Leidsestraat 34–36 (② 020/ 520-7020; tram: 1, 2, 5), at the corner of Keizersgracht, is a rooftop cafe designed by Gerrit Rietveld that offers a spectacular panorama across the rooftops of Amsterdam. Tea and a selection of cakes and sandwiches are served all day; various one-plate meals, such as grilled chicken and vegetable stew, are also available.

Near the Town Hall-Muziektheater complex, **Puccini,** Staalstraat 17 (② 020/427-8341; tram: 9, 14), is renowned for its coffee and home-made fruit tarts, cakes, and pastries. Lovers of fresh-baked goodies will appreciate **Paul Kaiser,** Wijde Heisteeg 3–5 (② 020/638-6595; tram: 1, 2, 5), between Singel and Herengracht, a bakery/coffee shop where your roll comes fresh from the oven. It has a tearoom annex (entrance at Singel 385) that serves delicious fruit pies and cakes.

Other fine tearooms are: **Berkhoff Tearoom,** Leidsestraat 46 (② 020/ 624-0233; tram: 1, 2, 5); outside Centraal Station, overlooking the inner harbor, **Smits Coffee House NZH,** Stationsplein 10 (② 020/623-3777; tram: 1, 2, 4, 5, 9, 13, 17, 24, 25), has a pleasant waterside terrace in the summer, from where you can watch the canal boats float by. **Greenwood's,** Singel 103 (② 020/623-7071; tram: 1, 2, 5, 13, 17), brings English ambience to its tea, homemade scones with jam and clotted cream, and lemon meringue pie.

A crowded spot on Saturday morning is **Kweekboom,** Reguliers-breestraat 36 (② 020/623-1205; tram: 4, 9, 14, 16, 24, 25), between Muntplein and Rembrandtplein. It's a coffee shop/candy store/pastry shop/ice-cream stand, where everything is freshly made and the management proudly displays awards won for everything from tarts, bon-bons, and butter cookies to fantasy cakes (whatever they may be). You may have to push your way to the back and wait for a table.

The best ice cream in town (now *here*'s a statement that could cause trouble) is sold by **Gelateria Italiana Peppino,** Eerste Sweelinckstraat 16 (② 020/676-4910; tram: 4, 20), near the Albert Cuyp market. Run by second- and third-generation Italian immigrants, this parlor serves up almost 100 different flavors of homemade ice cream, and great cappuccino. It's open only from March to October. Also notable is **Gelateria Jordino,** Haarlemmerdijk 25 (② 020/420-3225; bus: 18, 22), whose 30 flavors of Italian ice cream, plus chocolate cake and desserts, ought to appeal to someone.

spices, blending fierce chile peppers with more delicate flavors like ginger, coriander, and Thai basil. Bowls of delicately perfumed pandang rice accompany meals. Printed fabrics are draped along the walls and chairs are swathed in soft cottons.

Elandsgracht 29–31 (off Prinsengracht). ℂ 020/620-9551. Main courses 14€–20€; fixed-price menus 28€–38€. AE, DC, MC, V. Daily 6pm–midnight. Tram: 7, 10, 17 to Marnixstraat.

Toscanini ★ SOUTH ITALIAN   This small restaurant has a warm and welcoming ambience and excellent southern Italian food. It's popular with the artists and bohemians who inhabit this neighborhood. Toscanini has the type of unembellished country-style decor, and an open kitchen, that speak of authenticity, as does the fresh homemade food. Service is congenial but can be slow, though that doesn't seem to deter the loyal regulars, who clamor for such specialties as the delicious veal lasagna and *fazzoletti,* green pasta stuffed with ricotta, mozzarella, and mortadella. For dessert, the Italian ice cream is as good as it looks.

Lindengracht 75 (off Brouwersgracht). ℂ 020/623-2813. Main courses 15€–19€. AE, DC, MC, V. Daily 6–10:30pm. Tram: 3, 10 to Marnixplein.

INEXPENSIVE

Duende SPANISH   Dark, smoky, atmospheric, friendly—there's no better place than Duende to experience the varied palette of little dishes that are Spanish *tapas.* Take just one or two and you have a nice accompaniment to a few drinks; put five, six, or more together and you have a full-scale meal on your hands. You can pick from dozens of choices, including *tortilla española, champiñones al ajillo* (garlic mushrooms), and *calabacín a la marmera* (eggplant with seafood). Accompany them with sangria, jump into the arena of friendly conversation, and you'll be clapping your hands and stamping your feet before long. But bear in mind that though the tapas dishes are cheap individually, their cost soon adds up.

Lindengracht 62 (off Brouwersgracht). ℂ 020/420-9438. Tapas 3.50€–9.50€. No credit cards. Daily 5pm–1am. Bus: 18, 20 to Haarlemmerstraat.

7 Around Museumplein & Vondelpark
EXPENSIVE

Bodega Keyzer ★★ CONTINENTAL   Whether or not you attend a concert at the Concertgebouw, you may want to visit its next-door neighbor, Bodega Keyzer. An Amsterdam landmark since 1903—old-timers say it hasn't changed a whit through the years—the Keyzer has enjoyed a colorful joint heritage with the world-famous concert hall. Among the many stories still told here is the one about the night a customer mistook a concert soloist for a waiter and tried to order some whiskey from him. The musician, not missing a beat, lifted his violin case and said graciously, "Would a little Paganini do?" The traditional dark-and-dusky decor and highly starched pink linens add elegance to the place. The menu leans heavily to fish from Dutch waters and, in season, to game specialties, such as hare and venison. (**Note:** At this writing, Bodega Keyzer was closed for refurbishment and the phone number was out of service. The restaurant was due to re-open in the summer of 2003—and I keep my fingers crossed that all proceeds according to plan.)

Museumplein Area & Amsterdam South Dining

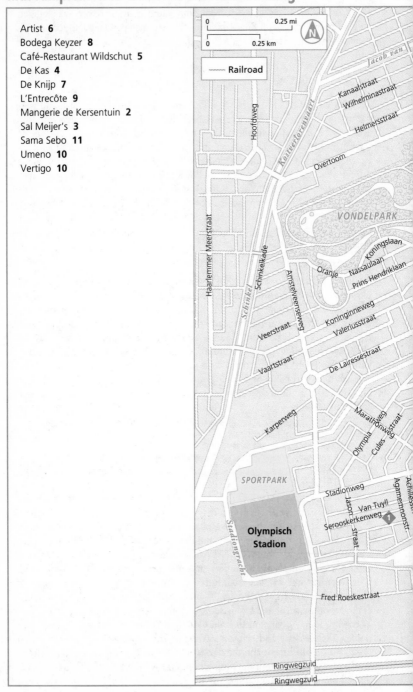

Van Baerlestraat 96 (beside the Concertgebouw). ℂ **020/671-1441.** Main courses 20€–35€; fixed-price menu 33€. AE, DC, MC, V. Mon–Sat 9am–midnight; Sun 11am–midnight. Tram: 2 to Willemsparkweg; 3, 5, 12 to Van Baerlestraat; 16 to De Lairessestraat.

MODERATE

De Knijp ☆ DUTCH/FRENCH   One of the advantages of this fine restaurant is that it's open late—its kitchen is still taking orders when chefs at many other Amsterdam restaurants are sound asleep back home. This would not count for much, of course, if the food weren't good, but De Knijp is definitely worth staying up late for, or worth stopping by for after a performance at the nearby Concertgebouw. The menu is not wildly inventive, but you might try such specialties as carpaccio with pesto, poached salmon with tarragon sauce, and goose breast with pink pepper sauce. Look also for friendly, if sometimes a little worn-out, service (this is a hardworking place), and an intimate bistro ambience, with lots of wood and tables on two levels.

Van Baerlestraat 134 (near the Concertgebouw). ℂ **020/671-4248.** Reservations required for lunch and for more than 5 people. Main courses 15€–20€; fixed-price menus 25€–35€. AE, DC, MC, V. Mon–Fri noon–3pm; daily 5:30pm–1:30am. Tram: 3, 5, 12, 24 to Museumplein; 16 to Concertgebouwplein.

Sama Sebo ☆☆ INDONESIAN   Many Amsterdammers consider Sama Sebo the best Indonesian restaurant in town, which means that the place is often filled with locals. A 23-plate *rijsttafel* that sets a standard the others try to match is served in a very Indonesian environment of rush mats and *batik*. Some of its components are hot-and-spicy but in general the effect comes from an effective blending of spices and sauces rather than from the addition of rocket-fuel to the mix. You can make your own mini-*rijsttafel* by putting together a selection from the a la carte menu, or take one big menu dish, like the *nasi goreng* or *bami goreng,* or even settle for just a snack. When the restaurant is busy, as it often is, you can either think of the quarters as convivial or cramped. A sidewalk terrace is equally as area-challenged as the interior. The takeout service is a good option if you want to eat in your hotel room, or maybe even to snack on a bench on nearby Museumplein.

Pieter Cornelisz Hooftstraat 27 (close to the Rijksmuseum). ℂ **020/662-8146.** Main courses 14€–20€; *rijsttafel* 25€. AE, DC, MC, V. Mon–Sat noon–2pm and 6–10pm. Tram: 2, 5 to Hobbemastraat.

Vertigo ☆☆ MEDITERRANEAN   If the name of this animated cafe-restaurant suggests a high location, the reality is far less giddy—in terms of altitude, at least. The reference is to Hitchcock's classic movie. In the vaulted basement of a monumental, late 19th-century villa, Vertigo shares premises with the Film Museum. Hence the portraits of screen legends on the walls and the classic scenes of movie dining on the menu. On summer days, the outside terrace on the edge of Vondelpark is a favored time-out spot for in-line skaters and joggers, and on hot days a restricted menu is served here; you can expect to share your table and make instant acquaintance of just about everyone within earshot. At other times, you can enjoy the southern European–inspired cuisine in an intimate, candle-lit setting inside. The menu, which changes every 6 to 8 weeks, has a choice of fish, meat, and vegetarian options, plus some fresh pasta varieties. If you see grilled breast of guinea fowl on the menu again, my advice is to go for it!

Vondelpark 3 (at the Film Museum). ℂ **020/612-3021.** Reservations recommended on weekends. Main courses 15€–22€. AE, MC, V. Daily 10am–1am. Tram: 1, 6 to Eerste Constantijn Huygensstraat; 2, 3, 5, 12 to Van Baerlestraat.

Tips Picnic Pick

You can pick up almost anything you might want for a picnic, from cold cuts to a bottle of wine, at the **Albert Heijn supermarket,** at the corner of Leidsestraat and Koningsplein, near Spui (tram: 1, 2, 5), open Monday through Friday from 9am to 8pm and Saturday from 9am to 6pm. Then head over to Vondelpark, only a 15-minute walk. If it's summer, you might even catch a free concert at the outdoor theater there.

Wildschut ★ CONTINENTAL   Wildschut is one of those places that keeps its chic reputation through thick and thin. The cafe-restaurant occupies a curved dining room at the junction of Van Baerlestraat and Roelof Hartstraat. Amsterdam's bold and beautiful like to see and be seen on the fine terrace in summer or amid the smoke in the brasserie-style interior in winter. It gets crowded here on Friday and Saturday evenings, so be prepared to join the standing throng while waiting for a table. The food is straightforward but good, ranging from BLTs, to vegetarian lasagna, to American rib-eye with green pepper sauce. If at all possible, try to wear something that gets you noticed—but not too much, if you get the idea.

Roelof Hartplein 1–3 (off Van Baerlestraat). ✆ **020/676-8220.** Main courses 8€–15€; fixed-price menu 25€. MC, V. Mon–Thurs 9am–1am; Fri 9am–3am; Sat 10:30am–3am; Sun 9:30am–midnight. Tram: 3, 12, 24 to Roelof Hartstraat; 5 to Joh. M. Coenenstraat.

8 In Amsterdam East

VERY EXPENSIVE

La Rive ★★★ FRENCH/MEDITERRANEAN   Cradling a pair of prestigious Michelin stars, La Rive is Amsterdam's undoubted high temple of the culinary arts, combining regional French cuisines with influences from around the Mediterranean and a taste of adventure from even further afield. Royalty, leading politicians, show-business stars, and captains of industry dine here—and you don't even need to rub shoulders with them, so discreetly far apart are the tables placed. The dining room overlooks the Amstel River, and in summer it opens onto a terrace along the embankment with a superb view of the goings-on on the water. The interior atmosphere suggests a small private library called into service for a dinner party. The walls are paneled in cherry and punctuated with tall cabinets filled with books and brass objects. Along one wall is a row of particularly romantic private booths that overlook the other tables and provide a view through the tall French windows to the water. The impeccable service and wine cellar are in the finest modern French traditions. Specialties include grilled baby abalone with citrus-pickled onion puree and garlic juice, turbot and truffles with trimmings, and grill-roasted rack of lamb with dates and Zaanse mustard.

In the Amstel Inter-Continental Amsterdam Hotel, Professor Tulpplein 1 (off Weesperstraat). ✆ **020/622-6060.** Main courses 25€–65€; fixed-price menus 68€–99€. AE, DC, MC, V. Mon–Fri noon–2pm; Mon–Sat 6:30–10:30pm. Tram: 6, 7, 10 to Sarphatistraat.

MODERATE

De Magere Brug DUTCH   This plain, down-home, cafe-restaurant, which looks out on the Magere Brug, the famous "Skinny Bridge" across the Amstel,

> *Moments* A Dinner Cruise
>
> A delightful way to combine sightseeing and leisurely dining is on a dinner cruise. During these 2½-hour canal cruises you get to enjoy a five-course dinner that includes a cocktail and wine with dinner, coffee with bonbons, and a glass of cognac or a liqueur to finish. **Holland International** (© **020/622-7788**) dinner cruises operate from April to October, daily at 8:30pm; and from November to March, on Tuesday and Thursday through Saturday at 7pm. Reservations are required. The cost is 70€ for adults, 45€ for children 4 to 12, and free for children under 4. **Rederij Lovers** (© **020/530-1090**) dinner cruises operate from April to October, daily at 7.30pm; from December to March, on Wednesday, Friday, and Saturday at 7.30pm. Reservations are required. The cost is 65€ for adults, 34€ for children 4 to 12, and free for children under 4. Boats from both companies depart from the canal tour-boat piers on Prins Hendrikkade, opposite Centraal Station.

is a good choice if you're planning to have dinner before taking in a concert, ballet, or show at the nearby Muziektheater or Theater Carré. Owner Christiaan Dijkstra, who also handles catering at the Carré, likes to keep things simple and friendly—a refreshing change from the snooty style affected by many Amstelside establishments. In addition to locals, it attracts visiting stars from the performance venues, who seem attracted by a change of pace. Rod Stewart is just one who has signed the visitors' book—"Nice ham 'n' eggs," he wrote. The food reaches higher than Rod's favorite, however. Smoked halibut, eel, and salmon steaks find a place on the menu, along with simpler fare.

Amstel 81 (near Theater Carré). © **020/622-6502.** Reservations recommended at theater time. Main courses 10€–15€. AE, DC, V. Tues–Thurs noon–1am; Fri–Sat 5pm–2am. Tram: 9, 14 to Waterlooplein.

Gare de l'Est ★★ FRENCH/MEDITERRANEAN   A distinctive detached house, with a conservatory extension and a large sidewalk terrace, originally a coffeehouse for workers at the docks, is an altogether good reason for making a trip to a part of town that is by no means fashionable. As the restaurant's name indicates, the cuisine is French, traditional, though with Mediterranean touches. Service is both relaxed and knowledgeable, and as the fixed-price menu is excellent value for money any surprises appear on your plate rather than on the check. The strict five-course formula (starter, salad, main course of meat or fish, cheese, and dessert) leaves no room for choice—except for the main course—but plenty for market-fresh ingredients and culinary creativity. How does this sound: *pulpo estofado et risotto nero* (ink-fish stew and black rice) as a starter, and roast lamb with gazpacho and farfalle as a main course?

Cruquiusweg 9 (at the East Harbor). © **020/463-0620.** Reservations recommended on weekends. Fixed-price menu 28€. No credit cards. Daily 6–11pm. Tram: 7, 10 to Zeeburgerdijk.

9 In Amsterdam South

EXPENSIVE

Mangerie de Kersentuin ★ FRENCH/MEDITERRANEAN   All cherry red and gleaming brass, the "Cherry Orchard" has floor-to-ceiling windows looking onto the residential street outside and partly screened interior windows looking into the glimmering kitchen inside. Attention to detail has made this restaurant a mecca for visiting stars. You eat with Christofle silver-plate flatware. From nouvelle cuisine and a strictly French approach to cooking, this place has progressed to its own unique culinary concept, based on French foundation with Mediterranean influences. The menu changes every 2 months, but these samples give some idea of what to expect: lamb filet prepared in goose fat with creamy salsifies, and coriander-scented vanilla sauce; sea bass sautéed with peppers, garlic, sea salt, and sesame seeds, served on stir-fried bok choy and tofu, with lemon-grass butter.

In the Bilderberg Garden Hotel, Dijsselhofplantsoen 7 (at Apollolaan). ✆ 020/570-5600. Reservations recommended on weekends. Main courses 22€–32€; fixed-price menus 34€–54€. AE, DC, MC, V. Mon–Fri noon–2pm and 6–10pm; Sat 6–10pm. Tram: 5, 24 to Apollolaan.

MODERATE

De Kas ★★ CONTINENTAL   People who dine in glass houses shouldn't throw stones. But if you have the trouble I had reserving for this oh-so-trendy eatery in a greenhouse—calling in March for June and being told that August is the earliest available date—you might want to bring along some rocks. Assuming the feeding frenzy slacks off enough to make calling worthwhile, you'll be able to see and be seen, both outside and inside. The converted 1926 greenhouse with smokestack on open ground in South Amsterdam is light, breezy, and spacious, though the atmosphere's maybe a tad too precious. You get just a couple of variations on a 3-course, daily changing fixed menu, with cheese board extra. Mediterranean-style greens and herbs come fresh from an adjacent working hot-house and the restaurant's own farm, and meat is sourced daily from nearby animal-friendly, eco-producers. Service is attentive enough that the wait staff seems to be acquainted personally with every item on your plate.

Kamerlingh Onneslaan 3 (close to Amstel Station). ✆ 020/462-4562. Reservations required. Fixed-price lunch 27€; fixed-price dinner 35€. AE, DC, MC, V. Mon–Fri noon–3pm and 6:30–10pm; Sat 6:30–10pm. Tram: 9 to Hogeweg.

Umeno JAPANESE   This intimate eatery, somewhat off the beaten track near the Olympic Stadium, is popular with local Japanese residents—you get only chopsticks to eat with. Both the food and the service make the tram ride out here worthwhile. Decor is traditional and delicate, with rice paper-covered windows, and the menu comes in a wooden box. It's generally no problem to find a seat, but as the restaurant seats only 32, it makes sense to call ahead. The sushi and sashimi are always fresh and their quality is high. Other traditional dishes include shabu-shabu, sukiyaki, yakitori, and tonkatsu.

Agamemnonstraat 27 (off Olympiaplein). ✆ 020/676-6089. Main courses 15€–26€. No credit cards. Tues–Sun noon–2pm and 6pm–midnight. Tram: 24 to Olympiaplein.

INEXPENSIVE

Artist LEBANESE   Owners Ralfo and Simon have brought a little piece of the eastern Mediterranean to Amsterdam South and presented it in a simple, authentic way at low cost with good taste guaranteed. Members of the city's Lebanese community are often seated at the tables here—always a good sign for an ethnic restaurant. Specialties include Lebanese *meze* and a selection of small dishes that adds up to a big meal, including *falafel, couscous,* and even Lebanese pizza. Many of the dishes here are vegetarian.

Tweede Jan Steenstraat 1 (off Van Woustraat). ✆ 020/671-4264. Main courses 4.50€–9.50€; fixed-price menu (*meze*) 9.50€. AE, DC, MC, V. Daily 5–11pm. Tram: 4 to Van Woustraat.

10 In Amsterdam West

MODERATE

Café-Restaurant Amsterdam ★★★ *(Finds)* CONTINENTAL   Think of it as *Amsterdam: the Restaurant,* because it's quite a performance. Based in a century-old water-pumping station, complete with diesel-powered engine, the Amsterdam has taken this monument of Victorian industrial good taste and made of it a model of contemporary good eats. You dine amidst a buzz of conviviality in the large, brightly lit, former pumping hall, which had been so carefully tended by the water workers that some of its elegant decoration didn't even need repainting. Service is friendly and the food is good and moderately priced. The fried sweetbreads are popular. If you're feeling flush, spring for a double starter of half lobster with six Zeeland oysters. The Amsterdam is a little bit out from the Center, but easily worth the tram ride.

Watertorenplein 6 (off Haarlemmerweg). ℂ 020/682-2666. Reservations recommended on weekends. Main courses 9.50€–20€. AE, DC, MC, V. Daily 11am–midnight. Tram: 10 to Van Hallstraat.

11 In Amsterdam North

MODERATE

Wilhelmina-Dok ★★ CONTINENTAL   Amsterdam is making increasing use of its vast harbor for living and working space, as the old cargo-handling installations are erased. You can dive right into the middle of this trend at this waterside eatery in Amsterdam Noord, across the IJ ship channel from Centraal Station. Getting there involves a 5-minute ferry ride followed by a 5-minute walk, but the ferry is at least free. The cafe-restaurant, which opened in 2000, is a slightly wacko-looking place on three floors (the chandeliered top-floor Kapiteinskamer [Captain's Cabin] is for groups only). Plain wood, candlelit tables, wood floors, and oak cabinets give the interior an old-fashioned maritime look, and large windows serve up views across the canal barge–speckled channel to the cruise-ship Passenger Terminal Amsterdam on the south shore. Breezy is one way to describe the impact of the prevailing westerlies, but tables on the outdoor terrace are sheltered from the wind in a glass-walled enclosure. The menu favors organic products. A couple of good choices are the *zwaardvis van de grill met saffranrisotto* (grilled swordfish with saffron rice) and the *kalfslende van de grill met gemarineerde aubergine en flageolottensalade en pesto* (grilled veal cutlets with marinated aubergines, flageolet salad, and pesto). Or, you can settle back with just a beer and a snack. On Monday evenings in August, movies are shown on an outdoor screen.

Nordwal 1 (at IJplein). ℂ 020/632-3701. Main courses 15€–17€. AE, DC, MC, V. Mon–Fri noon–midnight; Sat–Sun noon–1am. Ferry: IJveer from Pier 8 behind Centraal Station to the dock at IJplein, then go right along the dike-top path.

Exploring Amsterdam

Amsterdam offers sightseers an almost bewildering embarrassment of riches. There are miles and miles of canals to cruise and hundreds of narrow streets to wander, almost 7,000 historic buildings to see in the city center, more than 40 museums of all types to visit, diamond cutters and craftspeople to watch as they practice generations-old skills—the list is as long as every tourist's individual interests, and then some.

The city has 160 canals—more than Venice—with a combined length of 76km (47 miles), spanned by 1,281 bridges. So the first thing you should do is join the 2.5 million people every year who take a ride around the canals on one of the 70 canal tour-boats. Why? Because the water-level view of those gabled canal houses and the picturesque bridges lends meaning and color to everything else you do during your stay. Amsterdam's 17th-century Golden Age becomes a vivid reality as you glide through the waterways that were largely responsible for those years of prosperity. You view the canal houses from canal level, just as they were meant to be seen. This is also the best way to see Amsterdam's large and busy harbor. (See "Organized Tours," later in this chapter.)

SUGGESTED ITINERARIES

If You Have 1 Day

If you have only 1 day in Amsterdam, limit yourself in what you attempt. It's better to come away with a few good memories than to run around trying for a quick glimpse of everything. That doesn't mean you can't see a lot, however. The first thing you should do is invest an hour in a canal-boat trip. Don't worry for one minute about anyone who sniffs at this idea and mutters something about canal-boat tours being tourist traps. Maybe they are, but who cares? The view of Amsterdam from the water is the best you can get, and cruising is faster and a lot easier on your feet than walking.

After the boat tour, you should grab a quick lunch. How about a *broodje* at a *broodjeswinkel,* or, if you're ready to jump in with both feet, a raw herring with onions from one of the many roadside stalls?

Next you might want to do at least part of one of the walking tours listed in chapter 7. You could start with **The Golden Age Canals** tour, along Prinsengracht, Herengracht, and Keizersgracht, lined by stunning canal houses topped by step, bell, and other decorative gables, and crisscrossed by smaller canals with colorful houseboats anchored along their banks. Since you will have seen some of the main canals on your boat tour, you could instead try either the **Old Center tour** or the **Jordaan tour.** When you're finished with that, head for one of the *open* "big four" museums. Unfortunately, renovations will force the **Stedelijk Museum** and most of the **Rijksmuseum** to close in 2003 for respective periods of 2 and 5 years. (See the museum listings below for more information.) During the periods of closure, you'll fare better at the **Van Gogh Museum** and the **Anne Frankhuis.** Take a tram if you're running short on time.

After the museum, it will probably be late afternoon and you'll be pretty exhausted, so I'd suggest returning to the hotel for a drink at the bar before dinner or a nap. Since you probably had a Dutch breakfast and a Dutch lunch, you might consider going for an **Indonesian rijsttafel** at dinner.

Afterward, if you're still up for it, you really shouldn't miss having a drink in a **brown cafe**—your Amsterdam experience won't be complete without it.

If You Have 2 Days

Follow the first part of the itinerary above at a more relaxed pace. Take some notes while you're on the canal-boat tour about things you'd like to see up close later. Go for a short stroll along your favorite canal before lunch. Do the whole of one of the walking tours, visiting some of the shops and bookstores you see along the way. Save the big museums for your second day.

On the second day, you can sleep in a little because the museums don't open until later in the morning, then spend the day museum hopping. Before you leave the hotel you might want to try getting tickets to a **concert,** the **ballet,** or the **opera,** so you can attend a show in the evening. You should still be realistic about what's possible. Visiting one museum in the morning and one in the afternoon is enough. If you are keen to see the **Anne Frankhuis,** you should do that first

and go early in the morning (so much for sleeping late!), because there's always a line. After lunch, maybe in a **grand cafe,** take a tram to your second museum choice. Pick a place for dinner; this time, have a Dutch meal. Finally, go see that show.

If You Have 3 Days

Enough museums already! Today is a fresh-air day. If you want to visit the **Red Light District,** but not at night, morning is the best time to do it. Most of the weird folks have turned in for the day, and there's almost an air of innocence to the place, which actually occupies one of the prettiest parts of the old city.

Otherwise I suggest you spend the day shopping, sightseeing, and gallery hopping. Walk along **Kalverstraat** (the more modern shopping street), then perhaps stroll along **Spiegelgracht** and **Nieuwe Spiegelstraat** (antiques). Take a walk through the **Jordaan,** a lively former working-class area now filled with cafes, restaurants, and interesting little boutiques. Or take the tram to **Waterlooplein** for the flea market, or to Albert **Cuypstraat** for the great street market there. It would also be a good time to go to the **Looiersgracht Market** on an antiques hunt. If the weather is fine, have lunch on an open-air terrace and work in some people-watching.

Later, after you've had dinner take a leisurely stroll along the canals, which are particularly beautiful at night when they're lit up. A visit to a **jazz club** or **music bar** is a good way to round off your day.

If You Have 4 Days or More

You'll notice I haven't suggested a single side trip yet, even though there's an entire chapter devoted to side trips in this book (chapter 10). That's because 3 days is barely

The Canals

Amsterdam would not be the same without its canals. There might still be Golden Age architecture, trams, brown cafes and museums, and maybe its people would retain their iconoclastic outlook on life (though I doubt it), but without the mirror of water to reflect its soul the city would be a shrunken glory.

I once lived on an Amsterdam canalside. Not on one of the Golden Age canals, but still an honest-to-goodness Amsterdam canal. Barges, cabin cruisers, Frisian *skûtjes,* rowboats, all glided past my window. Often in winter I could step out my front door, jump down onto the frozen canal, strap on long-bladed *Noren,* and skate all the way to the North Sea if I wanted to.

In a way, being an outsider, I appreciate the canals more. I've happily played captain of my own water bike while Amsterdam friends I had lured aboard hid their faces for shame at being seen on such a "tourist trap." I love the glass-topped canal boats, with their view of Amsterdam from the finest vantage point of all. So don't laugh as you board one. Later, you can get down and wet on a canal-bike, or hail a water-taxi, or commandeer a passing rowboat and see how far a bunch of euros can take you. But for now, just sit back and let the 17th century flow around and through you. I never tire of the sight. To me it is quite simply the most beautiful cityscape in the world.

For information on canal tours, see "Organized Tours," later in this chapter.

---

enough to do any kind of justice to Amsterdam itself. With 4 or more days, though, the environs start to come within range.

On your first day of touring, I suggest you travel from Amsterdam to **Haarlem,** and maybe squeeze into the same day a visit to the **North Sea coast** at nearby **Zandvoort,** which has a beach, racetrack, and casino. On your second day, head to **Hoorn** on the IJsselmeer **shore.** If you're driving, take in **Volendam** and **Marken** along the way, and from Hoorn you can continue on to **Enkhuizen** and the **Afsluitdijk** (Enclosing Dike), before returning to Amsterdam.

With more time, you can alternate days spent in the city with visits to, for example, the **Bulb Fields** and **Keukenhof Gardens** if it's tulip time; **Zaanse Schans** for windmills; **Leiden** for the Pilgrim Fathers; **Delft** for Holland's royal city; **The Hague** for the seat of government; and **Rotterdam** for the world's busiest port.

1 The Big Four

Rijksmuseum ★★★   *Note:* Most of the Rijksmuseum is due to be closed for a whopping 5 years, from late 2003 to mid-2008, for renovation. During the period of partial closure, key paintings from the 17th-century Dutch Golden Age collection can be viewed in the museum's own Philips Wing, and other elements of the collection will likely be on view at other venues in the city. During

Central Amsterdam Attractions

Het IJ

De Ruijterkade

Openhaven
Front
Prins Hendrikkade

Centraal
Station

IJ-Tunnel

Canal tour
boats
Information
Post office
Railway

0   0.2 mi
0   0.2 km

27

28

29

Oosterdok

48

Nieuwendijk
Damrak
Prins Hendrikkade
Warmoesstraat
Zeedijk
Geldersekade
Kromme Waal
Waals Eilandsgracht

30

31

32

33

34

35

Oudekerks-
plein

Oude Waal

Oude Schans

36

37

Nieuwmarkt

Oudezijds Voorburgwal

Prins Hendrikkade

Kattenburgerstraat

38

Nieuwe Uilenburgerstraat

Uilenburgergracht

Nieuwe Vaar

39

40

Kloveniersburgwal
Geldersekade

Valkenburgerstraat

Hoogtekadijk

41

42

Rapenburgerstraat

Entrepotdok

Waterloo-
plein

Herengracht

47

Plantage Doklaan

43

Mr.
Visserplein

Plantage-Kerklaan

ARTIS

Nieuwe

Plantage Middenlaan

44

Rembrandt-
plein

Amstel River

Keizersgracht

Plantage Muidergracht

45

Nieuwe

Kerkstraat

Plantage Muidergracht

Nieuwe

Prinsengracht

Achtergracht

46

Nieuwe

Kerkstraat

Sarphatistraat

Utrechtsestraat

Weesperstraat

Mauritskade

Falckstraat

OOSTER-
PARK

Frederiks-
plein

Sarphatistraat

Mauritskade

Wibautstraat

Singelgracht
Stadhouderskade

Ruyschstraat

Blasiusstraat

1e Oosterparkstraat

the renovation period, you can find a complete review of the Rijksmuseum at www.frommers.com.

Stadhouderskade 42 (behind Museumplein, halfway between Leidseplein and Weteringplantsoen). ℂ **020/ 670-7047.** Admission 8.50€ adults, free for children under 18. Daily 10am–5pm. Tram: 2, 5 to Hobbemastraat; 6, 7, 10 to Weteringschans.

Van Gogh Museum ★★★   Thanks to the chauvinism of his family—in particular, his brother's wife and a namesake nephew—nearly every painting, sketch, print, etching, and piece of correspondence that Vincent van Gogh ever produced has remained in his native country, and since 1973 the collection has been housed in its own museum. To the further consternation of van Gogh admirers and scholars elsewhere in the world, all but a few of the drawings and paintings that are not in the museum's keeping hang at the Kröller-Müller Museum in the Hoge Veluwe National Park near Arnhem.

You can trace this great artist's artistic and psychological development by viewing more than 200 of his paintings displayed simply and in chronological order according to the seven distinct periods and places of residence that defined his short career. (He painted for only 10 years and was on the threshold of success when he committed suicide in 1890, at age 37.)

One particularly splendid wall, on the second floor, has a progression of 18 paintings produced during the 2-year period when Vincent lived in the south of France, generally considered to be his artistic high point. It's a symphony of colors and color contrasts that includes *Gauguin's Chair; The Yellow House; Self-Portrait with Pipe and Straw Hat; Vincent's Bedroom at Arles; Wheatfield with Reaper; Bugler of the Zouave Regiment;* and one of the most famous paintings of modern times, *Still Life Vase with Fourteen Sunflowers,* best known simply as *Sunflowers.* By the time you reach the vaguely threatening painting of a flock of black crows rising from a waving cornfield, you can almost feel the mounting inner pain the artist was finally unable to bear.

A new wing, elliptical and partly underground, designed by Japanese architect Kisho Kurokawa, opened on Museumplein in June 1999 to house temporary exhibits of work by van Gogh and other artists.

Audio tours with mobile phone-type units are available. A bunch of flat-panel iMacs on a table are used as information kiosks—some people use them for their serious purpose, while others seem content to play with the movable screens. From February 14 to June 15, 2003, the Van Gogh Museum celebrates the 150th anniversary of Vincent's birth (Mar 30, 1853) with a special exhibit of his favorite paintings.

Paulus Potterstraat 7 (at Museumplein). ℂ **020/570-5200.** Admission 7€ adults, 2.50€ children 13–17, children under 13 free. Daily 10am–6pm. Tram: 2, 3, 5, 12 to Van Baerlestraat.

⸤Tips Don't Go

Gogh is not pronounced *Go,* as many Americans incorrectly say it, but like *Khokh* (the "kh" sound is like "ch" in the Scottish pronunciation of "loch"—not "lock"). If you can pronounce van Gogh correctly, you should have no problem with Schiphol (*skhip*-ol), Scheveningen (*skheven*-ingen), and 's-Gravenhage (ss-*khraven*-hakhe; the correct full name for Den Haag: The Hague).

A New Museumplein

Three of the big four—Rijksmuseum, Van Gogh Museum, and Stedelijk Museum—are conveniently clustered around Museumplein, a big open square just south of the old city. The square has been totally transformed in recent years, and motorized through-traffic has been abolished.

Most of the rebuilt square consists of open green areas bordered by avenues of linden trees and gardens, which can be used for major outdoor events. Walkways and bike paths pass through. At the north end are sports and play areas, and a long pond that serves as an ice-skating rink in winter.

I have to say that, compared to the old Museumplein's raggedy appeal, I find the new model to be a charm-free zone, something from the Antiseptic School of urban design.

Stedelijk Museum ★★ *Note:* The Stedelijk is due to close from January 1, 2003, to March 2005 for renovation and the construction of two new wings. The following review stands in case something should happen to delay these plans. During the period of closure, elements from the museum's collection can be viewed at other venues in the city. The city's modern art museum is the place to see works by such Dutch painters as Karel Appel, Willem de Kooning, and Piet Mondrian, alongside works by the French artists Chagall, Cézanne, Picasso, Renoir, Monet, and Manet and by the Americans Calder, Oldenburg, Rosenquist, and Warhol. The Stedelijk centers its collection around the De Stijl, Cobra, post-Cobra, nouveau réalisme, pop art, color-field painting, zero, minimalist, and conceptual schools of modern art. It houses the largest collection outside Russia of the abstract paintings of Kasimir Malevich.

Architect Alvaro Siza has drawn up plans for restoring the old building as closely as possible to its original 1895 neo-Renaissance appearance, and constructing an extension on Museumplein, but no start date for the project has been announced.

In the museum cafe is a giant Appel mural. Mondrian is represented by, among other works, his *Composition in Red, Black, Blue, Yellow, and Gray* (1920), and, by way of variation, *Composition in Blue, Red, Black, and Yellow* (1922)—the gray's still there, in fact, but he chose not to mention it in the title.

Paulus Potterstraat 13 (at Museumplein). ✆ **020/573-2737.** Admission 5€ adults, 2.50€ children 7–17 and seniors, children under 7 free. Daily 11am–5pm. Closed Jan 1. Tram: 2, 5 to Van Baerlestraat; 3, 12, 16 to Museumplein.

Anne Frankhuis ★★★ In summer you may have to wait an hour or more to get in, but no one should miss seeing and experiencing this house, where eight people from three separate families lived together in near total silence for more than 2 years during World War II. The hiding place Otto Frank found for his family and friends kept them safe until, tragically close to the end of the war, it was raided by Nazi forces, and its occupants were deported to concentration camps. It was in this house that Anne kept her famous diary as a way to deal with both the boredom and her youthful jumble of thoughts, which had as

---

Fun Fact **Recreating History**

Producer David Kappes's TV mini-series on the life of Anne Frank was shot on an "amazing" recreation of Amsterdam's Prinsengracht canal during World War II—in Prague.

---

much to do with personal relationships as with the war and the Nazi terror raging outside her hiding place. Visiting the rooms where she hid is a moving and eerily real experience.

The rooms of the building, which was an office and warehouse at that time, are still as bare as they were when Anne's father returned, the only survivor of the eight *onderduikers* (divers, or hiders). Nothing has been changed, except that protective Plexiglas panels have been placed over the wall where Anne pinned up photos of her favorite actress, Deanna Durbin, and of the little English princesses Elizabeth and Margaret. As you tour the small building, it's easy to imagine Anne's experience growing up in this place, awakening as a young woman, and writing down her secret thoughts in a diary.

Get there as early as you can to avoid the lines—this advice isn't as useful as it used to be, because everybody is both giving it and heeding it, but it should still save you some waiting time. An alternative strategy if you're in town from April to August, when the museum is open to 9pm, is to go in the evening, as it is invariably quiet then—till now at any rate. A typical Amsterdam canal-house, this has very steep interior stairs. Next door at no. 265–267 is a new wing for temporary exhibits. You can see a bronze sculpture of Anne at nearby Westermarkt.

Prinsengracht 263 (beside Westermarkt). © **020/556-7100.** Admission 6.50€ adults, 3€ children 10–17, children under 10 free. Apr–Aug daily 9am–9pm; Sept–Mar daily 9am–7pm; Jan 1 and Dec 25 noon–5pm. Closed Yom Kippur. Tram: 13, 14, 17 to Westermarkt.

2 More Museums & Galleries

Allard Pierson Museum Amsterdam   The archaeological collection of the University of Amsterdam is permanently on view here, though the frequent temporary and visiting exhibits are more likely to have truly memorable pieces. In the recently installed Egyptian department you can see a model of the Pyramid of Cheops and other pyramids at Giza, and mummies and funerary and ritual objects; a computer prints out your name in hieroglyphics. Ancient Greece, Rome, Etruria, and Cyprus are among the best represented of other cultures, with pottery, sculpture, glassware, jewelry, coins, and household objects.

Oude Turfmarkt 127 (facing Muntplein). © **020/525-2556.** Admission 4.30€ adults, 3.20€ students, 1.45€ children 12–15, 1€ children 4–11, children under 4 free. Tues–Fri 10am–5pm; Sat–Sun 1–5pm. Tram: 4, 9, 14, 16, 24, 25 to Spui.

Amsterdams Historisch Museum (Amsterdam Historical Museum) ★★
Few cities in the world have gone to as much trouble and expense to display and explain their history, and few museums in the world have found as many ways to make such dry material as population growth and urban development as interesting as the latest electronic board game. Don't say you have little interest in Amsterdam's history. This fascinating museum, in the huge 17th-century Burger Weeshuis, the restored former City Orphanage, gives you a better

Catching the Museum Boat

Ever resourceful and ever aware of the transportation resource their canals represent, Amsterdammers have introduced the **Museumboot (Museum Boat),** Stationsplein 8 (© **020/530-1090**), to carry weary tourists on their pilgrimages from museum to museum. It's an easy way to travel and, for those with limited time, provides some of the advantages of a canal-boat cruise. Boats depart every 30 minutes (every 45 min. in winter) daily from 10am to 5pm from Prins Hendrikkade, in front of Centraal Station (Stop 1), and stop at key spots around the city, providing access to museums and other sights. These are:

Stop 1   Centraal Station.

Stop 2   Westermarkt: Anne Frankhuis, Theatermuseum.

Stop 3   Leidseplein: Vondelpark.

Stop 4   Museum Quarter: Rijksmuseum, Van Gogh Museum, Stedelijk Museum, Vondelpark.

Stop 5   Herengracht: Amsterdams Historisch Museum, Bijbels Museum, Flower Market.

Stop 6   Waterlooplein: Museum Het Rembrandthuis, Jewish Historical Museum, Artis, Muziektheater, Tropenmuseum.

Stop 7   Eastern Dock: Maritime Museum, NEMO.

The day ticket for the Museum Boat, which includes a discount on museum admissions of up to 50%, is 14€ for adults and 9€ for children ages 4 to 12, and free for children under 4. After 1pm, you can purchase "stop-tickets" from the boatman, the cost of which depends on the number of stops you plan at which you plan to disembark.

understanding of everything you see when you go out to explore the city on your own. Gallery by gallery, century by century, you learn how a small fishing village founded around 1200 became a major sea power and trading center.

The main focus is on the city's 17th century golden age, a period when Amsterdam was the richest city in the world, and some of the most interesting exhibits are of the trades that made it rich. You can also view many of the famous paintings by the Dutch masters in the context of their time and place in history.

There's a fascinating and beautiful scale model from around 1677 of the then new Stadhuis (Town Hall) on the Dam, now the Royal Palace, with some of its outer walls and the roof removed to give you a bird's-eye look inside.

A small room is given over to the story of local hero Jan Carel Josephus van Speyk, a Dutch naval officer during the 1830 rebellion by Belgium against Dutch rule. A boarding party of Belgian patriots who aimed to commandeer his warship in the Scheldt River off Antwerp reckoned without Van Speyk's "Don't give up the ship" disposition. He dropped his lit cigar into the ship's gunpowder magazine, setting off an explosion that blew him, the vessel, and the rebel boarders into the air and into history.

Among many other historic items are four beautiful late-15th-century altar cushions depicting the Miracle of the Host in 1345 (see "Amsterdam's Origins," in Appendix A).

Museumplein Area & Amsterdam South Attractions

Albert Cuyp Markt **8**
Amsterdamse Bos **14**
Beatrix Park **10**
Cobra Museum of Modern Art **13**
Concertgebouw **3**
Heineken Experience **7**
Martin Luther King Park **12**
Olympisch Stadion **1**
RAI Congress Center **11**
Rijksmuseum **6**
Sarphati Park **9**
Stedelijk Museum **4**
Van Gogh Museum **5**
Vondelpark **2**

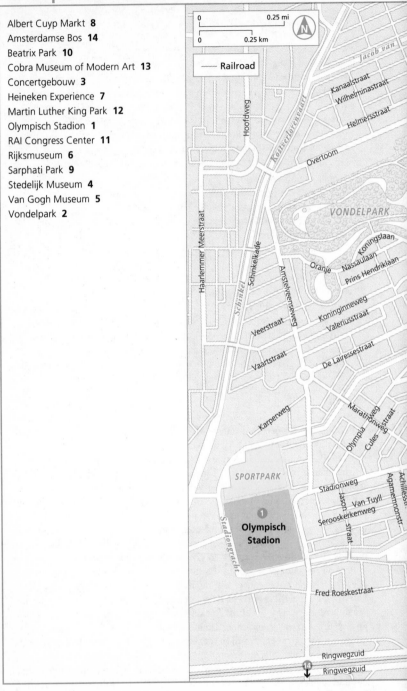

Tips **Agenda for Youth**

The monthly publication *Agenda* lists current events and information on various services available to students. If you're interested in cultural events and are under 26, go by the **Amsterdam Uit Buro (AUB) Ticketshop,** Leidseplein 26 (© **0900/0191;** www.aub.nl; tram: 1, 2, 5, 6, 7, 10), and pick up a Cultural Youth Pass for 11€. This pass gets you free admission to most museums and discounts on many cultural events. The AUB is open Monday through Wednesday and Saturday from 10am to 6pm, Thursday from 10am to 9pm, and Sunday from noon to 6pm.

You can pop into Café 't Mandje, a typical, if tiny, Amsterdam neighborhood bar. Sadly, you can't order a beer or a *jenever,* since the "cafe" is a museum exhibit. But you really can visit the museum's **David & Goliath** cafe, which has a high-beamed ceiling and lofty wooden statues of David and Goliath, salvaged from an amusement park that was a feature of Amsterdam's landscape for nearly 250 years until 1862.

When you leave the Historical Museum, cut through the **Schuttersgalerij** (Civic Guard Gallery), a narrow, two-story skylit chamber bedecked with a dozen large, impressive 17th-century group portraits of militiamen. The hours are the same as for the museum, and admission is free.

Kalverstraat 92, Nieuwezijds Voorburgwal 359, and Sint-Luciënsteeg 27 (next to the Begijnhof). © **020/ 523-1822.** Admission 6€ adults, 4.50€ seniors, 3€ children 6–16, children under 6 free. Mon–Fri 10am–5pm; Sat–Sun 11am–5pm. Closed Jan 1, Apr 30, Dec 25. Tram: 1, 2, 4, 5, 9, 14, 16, 24, 25 to Spui.

Bijbels Museum (Biblical Museum) ⭐   Taking the Good Book as a starting point, you move on to explore biblical history and geography in objects, images, and installations. The setting—twin patrician canal houses from 1662, designed by noted architect Philips Vingboons, and with a lovely courtyard garden— would be worth visiting for its historical interest alone. In 1717, Jacob de Wit painted its main ceiling with mythological scenes. The museum collection includes models of ancient Jerusalem, the Temple of Solomon, and the Tabernacle; archaeological finds from Israel, Palestine, and Egypt; and paintings of biblical scenes. Among the Bibles on display are the first Bible printed in the Low Countries, dating from 1477, and the first edition of the authorized Dutch translation, from 1637.

Herengracht 366–368 (near Spui). © **020/624-2436.** Admission 5€ adults, 2.50€ children 6–17, children under 6 free. Mon–Sat 10am–5pm; Sun 1–5pm. Tram: 1, 2, 5 to Spui.

Cobra Museum of Modern Art   You have to head out to the frankly dull dormitory suburb of Amstelveen south of Amsterdam to find one of the most exciting new museums in the country. Exciting, that is, if you like the post–World War II art of the Cobra group, who took their name from the initials of the original players' home cities: Copenhagen, Brussels, and Amsterdam. Folks like Asger Jorn, Karel Appel, and Lucebert weren't instantly popular in their day, and it's probably still stretching the term to describe them so today, but they undoubtedly changed the face of art, and here you can see how.

Sandbergplein 1–3, Amstelveen. © **020/547-5050.** Admission 4€ adults, children 16 and under free. Tues–Sun 11am–5pm. Tram: 5 to Binnenhof; light rail 51 to Beneluxbaan.

Joods Historisch Museum (Jewish Historical Museum) In 1987, this museum opened in the restored Ashkenazi Synagogue complex, a cluster of four former synagogues, in the heart of what was once Amsterdam's thriving Jewish Quarter (see below). It's home to a collection of paintings, decorations, and ceremonial objects confiscated during World War II and patiently reestablished in the postwar period. Through its objects, photographs, artworks, and interactive displays, the museum tells three intertwining stories—of Jewish identity, Jewish religion and culture, and Jewish history in the Netherlands. It presents the community in both good times and bad and provides insights into the Jewish way of life over the centuries. Leave time to appreciate the beauty and size of the buildings themselves, which include the oldest public synagogue in Europe. This is a museum for everyone—Jewish or otherwise. There are frequent temporary exhibits of international interest.

Tip: The museum cafe is a great place to have a cup of coffee and a pastry, or a light meal (kosher, too). It's quiet, inexpensive, and the food is good.

Jonas Daniël Meijerplein 2–4 (at Waterlooplein). *C* 020/626-9945. Admission 5€ adults, 3€ seniors, 2.50€ children 13–17, 1.50€ children 6–12, children under 6 free. Daily 11am–5pm. Closed Yom Kippur. Tram: 9, 14 to Waterlooplein.

Museum Amstelkring (Ons' Lieve Heer op Solder: Our Lord in the Attic) One of history's quirks is that this famously tolerant city had a law for more than 200 years, from 1578, prohibiting religious services other than those of the officially favored Dutch Reformed Church. As a result, the city's Catholics, Mennonites, Lutherans, and Jews were forced to hold services in private homes and other secret locations. This museum incorporates the best preserved of these clandestine places of worship. The Catholic church is in the attic of one of the oldest canal houses you can visit, built from 1661 to 1663 for the merchant Jan Hartman. Being able to tour a rambling old canal house makes a visit here worthwhile by itself (but note that the steep stairways can be tough to negotiate).

Worshipers entered by a door on a side street and climbed a narrow flight of stairs to the hidden third-floor church. Following Hartman's death in 1668, the

---

The Jewish Quarter

For more than 350 years, Amsterdam was a center of Jewish life, and its Jewish community was a major contributor to the city's vitality and prosperity. The Waterlooplein area was their neighborhood, where they held their market and built their synagogues. Of the five synagogues built in the 17th and 18th centuries, only the Portuguese Synagogue (see below) continued to serve as a house of worship after the devastating depletion of the Jewish population in World War II. The other buildings, sold to the city in 1955, stood unused and in great need of repair for many years. During those years, the city authorities and the curators of the Jewish Historical Collection of the Amsterdam Historical Museum were patiently reestablishing the collection of paintings, decorations, and ceremonial objects that had been confiscated during World War II.

house was bought by Jan Reynst, a Protestant merchant. Reynst planned to rent the attic as storage space, but realized he could make more money charging Catholic worshipers for continued use of their "secret" church. An 18th-century redecoration created the chapel-size church you see now, with a baroque altar, spinet-sized pipe organ, and two narrow upper balconies. It's still in use for services and concerts. Other rooms contain a trove of magnificent religious vessels, many of them in gold and silver, including monstrances made in the 17th century and another, in Art Deco style, from 1924.

Oudezijds Voorburgwal 40 (near the Oude Kerk). ℂ 020/624-6604. Admission 7.50€ adults, 3.40€ children and seniors. Mon–Sat 10am–5pm; Sun and holidays 1–5pm. Closed Jan 1, Apr 30. Tram: 1, 2, 4, 5, 9, 13, 16, 17, 24, 25 to Centraal Station.

Museum Het Rembrandthuis ⭐ To view the greatest masterpieces by Rembrandt van Rijn, you must visit the Rijksmuseum (when it re-opens), but in this house you find a more intimate sense of the artist himself. Bought by Rembrandt in 1639 when he was Amsterdam's most fashionable portrait painter, the house, which has 10 rooms, is a shrine to one of the greatest artists the world has ever known. In this house, Rembrandt's son Titus was born and his wife, Saskia, died. The artist was bankrupt when he left it in 1658. (The militia company of Captain Frans Banning Cocq portrayed in *The Night Watch* hated the artistic freedom Rembrandt had exercised on their group portrait and this helped to ruin his previously brilliant career.) Not until 1906 was the building rescued from a succession of subsequent owners and restored as a museum.

In 1998, a modern wing for temporary exhibits was added; restoration completed in 1999 has returned the old house to the way it looked when Rembrandt lived and worked there. Further work in 2000 has restored the artist's cabinet of art and curiosities, his combined living room and bedroom, and the studio he and his pupils used. The rooms are furnished with 17th-century objects and furniture that, as far as possible, match the descriptions in Rembrandt's 1656 petition for bankruptcy. His printing press is back in place, and you can view 250 of his etchings and drawings hanging on the walls. These include self-portraits and landscapes; several relate to the traditionally Jewish character of

---

Tips **Money-Savers**

One way to save money—and not just on admission to museums and attractions—is to buy the VVV Amsterdam tourist office's **Amsterdam Pass** (see "Your Passport to Amsterdam," in chapter 3).

Remember that many museums and other attractions offer reduced admission to seniors, students, and children.

If you should happen to be in the Netherlands on **National Museum Weekend,** April 12 and 13, 2003, you're in luck. Most museums in the country have free admission at this time and others charge greatly reduced admission.

If museums are high on your sightseeing agenda—and you're a resident of the Netherlands—you might find a **Museumjaarkaart (Museum Year Pass)** to be a good investment. At 30€ for adults, 25€ for those over 54, and 15€ for those under 25, the pass gives a year's free admission to 350 museums throughout the land. You can purchase it from VVV tourist offices and from many museums.

the neighborhood, such as the portrait of Rabbi Menassah ben Israel, who lived across the street and was an early teacher of another illustrious Amsterdammer, Baruch Spinoza. Opposite Rembrandthuis, appropriately, stands the Amsterdamse Hogeschool voor de Kunsten (Amsterdam High School for the Arts).

Jodenbreestraat 4 (behind Waterlooplein). ℂ 020/520-0400. Admission 7€ adults, 5€ students, 1.50€ children 6–15, children under 6 free. Mon–Sat 10am–5pm; Sun and holidays 1–5pm. Tram: 9, 14 to Waterlooplein.

> **Fun Fact A Familiar Face**
>
> Rembrandt painted about 100 self-portraits, more than any other great artist.

Museum Van Loon   The history of this magnificent patrician house, one of a matched pair dating from 1672, is a long saga of ne'er-do-well spouses and ailing orphans, of misguided inheritances and successive bankruptcies. The elegant home was owned by the Van Loon family from 1884 to 1945. On its walls hang more than 80 family portraits, including those of Willem van Loon, one of the founders of the Dutch United East India Company; Nicolaes Ruychaver, who liberated Amsterdam from the Spanish in 1578; and another, later, Willem van Loon, who became mayor in 1686. Among other treasures are a family album in which you can see tempera portraits of all living Van Loons painted at two successive dates (1650 and 1675), and a series of commemorative coins struck to honor seven different golden wedding anniversaries celebrated between the years 1621 and 1722. The house's completely restored period rooms are filled with richly decorated paneling, stucco work, mirrors, fireplaces, furnishings, porcelain, medallions, chandeliers, rugs, and more. The garden has carefully tended hedges and a coach house modeled on a Greek temple.

Keizersgracht 672 (near Vijzelstraat). ℂ 020/624-5255. Admission 4.50€ adults, 3€ students, children 12 and under free. Fri–Mon 11am–5pm. Tram: 16, 24, 25 to Keizersgracht.

Museum Willet-Holthuysen   This museum offers another rare opportunity to visit an elegant 17th-century canal house, with a beautiful garden. This particular house, built in 1687, was renovated several times before its last inhabitant gave it and its contents to the city in 1889. Among the most interesting rooms are a Victorian-era bedroom on the second floor, a large reception room with tapestry wall panels, and an 18th-century basement kitchen that's still so completely furnished and functional you could swear the cook had merely stepped out to go shopping.

Herengracht 605 (near the Amstel River). ℂ 020/523-1822. Admission 4€ adults, 2€ children 6–16, children under 6 free. Mon–Fri 10am–5pm; Sat–Sun 11am–5pm. Closed Jan 1, Apr 30, Dec 25. Tram: 4, 9, 14 to Rembrandtplein.

Scheepvaartmuseum (Maritime Museum) ★★   A bonanza for anyone who loves ships and the sea, the museum overlooks the busy harbor, and is appropriately housed in a former Amsterdam Admiralty arsenal, from 1656. Room after room is filled with boats and ship models, seascape and ship paintings, navigational instruments, prints, and old maps, including a 15th-century Ptolemaic atlas and a sumptuously bound edition of the *Great Atlas, or Description of the World,* produced over a lifetime by Jan Blaeu, the master cartographer of Holland's Golden Age. All the exhibits chronicle the country's abiding ties to the sea through commerce, fishing, yachting, exploration, and war. Among the important papers on display are several pertaining to the Dutch colonies of

Nieuw Amsterdam (New York City) and Nieuw Nederland (New York), including a receipt for the land that now surrounds the New York State capital at Albany.

A full-size replica of the Dutch United East India Company ship *Amsterdam,* which foundered off Hastings, England, in 1749 on her maiden voyage to the fabled Spice Islands (Indonesia), is moored at the wharf, as is a replica of the *Stad Amsterdam,* a three-masted iron clipper from 1854 (it may eventually be moved to Java Island in the harbor). Other ships you can see are a steam ice-breaker, a motor lifeboat, and a herring lugger; the historic Royal Barge and two towing barges are housed indoors.

You can reach the museum by taking a 20-minute walk along the historical waterfront, the Nautisch Kwartier.

Kattenburgerplein 1 (at the Eastern Dock). ℭ **020/523-2222.** Admission 7€ adults, 4€ children 6–18, children under 6 free. Tues–Sat 10am–5pm (also Mon mid-June to mid-Sept); Sun noon–5pm. Bus: 22, 32 to Kattenburgerplein.

Theatermuseum   The Netherlands Theater Institute occupies a group of adjoining 17th-century canal houses, two of which house this imaginative museum. No. 168, known as Het Witte Huis (the White House) for its whitish-gray, neoclassical sandstone facade, was built in 1638 by Philips Vingboons and sports the city's first neck gable. Dazzling interior ornamentation from around 1730 includes a spiral staircase, intricate stuccowork, and painted ceilings by Jacob de Wit. The elaborate Bartolotti House at no. 170–172, built in 1617 and 1618 by Hendrick de Keyser, famous for its ornate redbrick gable and Dutch Renaissance facade, has illuminated ceilings and other interior decoration by Jacob de Wit. In the museum, you find costumes, maquettes, masks, puppets, photographs, paintings, miniature theaters, and theatrical backdrops, covering all forms of theater, including opera and children's theater. Hands-on experience includes creating your own stage and sound effects. Book ahead for hands-on workshops for children (7–12) on Wednesday, Saturday, and Sunday afternoons.

Herengracht 168 (at Leliegracht). ℭ **020/551-3300.** Admission 3.85€ adults, 1.95€ seniors/children 7–16, children under 7 free. Tues–Fri 11am–5pm; Sat–Sun 1–5pm. Tram: 13, 14, 17 to the Dam.

Tropenmuseum (Tropical Museum) ★★   One of the city's most intriguing museums belongs to the Royal Institute for the Tropics, a foundation devoted to the study of the cultures of tropical areas around the world. Its focus reflects Holland's centuries as a landlord in such areas as Indonesia; Surinam (on the northern coast of South America); and the islands of St. Maarten, Saba, St. Eustatius, Aruba, Bonaire, and Curaçao in the West Indies. The Tropical Institute building complex alone is worth the trip to Amsterdam East; its heavily ornamented 19th-century facade is an amalgam of Dutch architectural styles: turrets, stepped gables, arched windows, delicate spires, and the monumental galleried interior court (a popular spot for concerts).

Of the exhibits, the most interesting are the walk-through model villages and city-street scenes that, except for the lack of genuine inhabitants, seem to capture a moment in the daily life of such places as India and Indonesia; the displays of tools and techniques used to produce *batik,* the distinctively dyed Indonesian fabrics; and displays of the tools, instruments, and ornaments that clutter a tropical residence. There's a permanent exhibit on people and environment in West Asia and North Africa.

Part of the premises is given over to the children-only Kindermuseum TM Junior (see "Especially for Kids," later in this chapter, for more details).

Linnaeusstraat 2 (at Mauritskade). ℂ 020/568-8215. Admission 6.80€ adults, 3.40€ children 6–17, children under 6 free. Daily 10am–5pm. Closed Jan 1, Apr 30, May 5, Dec 25. Tram: 7, 9, 10, 14 to Mauritskade.

Verzetsmuseum (Resistance Museum) ✦ Take a trip back in time to the dark days of World War II in Holland, during the Nazi occupation (1940–45). Using authentic photographs, documents, weapons, communications equipment, and other materials actually used by the Dutch Resistance, the exhibits show the ingenuity the freedom fighters brought to bear—along with courage—on the German occupation forces. A pedal-powered printing press is a good example of items that evoke the period and aim to bring it to life. The fate of Amsterdam's Jewish community, herded into a ghetto then rounded up for deportation to concentration camps, has a prominent place, as do the actions of workers who in 1941 went on strike to protest these events. Yet the museum doesn't shrink from less-palatable aspects of Holland's wartime record, like the actions of collaborators, including those who joined Dutch Nazi SS units. The museum is housed in the beautiful, neo-classical Plancius Building from 1876, which once was a social club for a Jewish choir. A program of changing exhibits takes the story beyond Holland's experience of foreign occupation, to feature resistance struggles in recent times, in Palestine for instance.

Plantage Kerklaan 61 (opposite Artis Zoo). ℂ 020/620-2535. Admission 4.50€ adults, 2.50€ children 7–15, children under 7 free. Tues–Fri 10am–5pm; Sat–Mon noon–5pm. Closed Jan 1, Apr 30, Dec 25. Tram: 6 to Plantage Kerklaan.

Woonboot Museum (Houseboat Museum) In Amsterdam, no one ever tosses away an old boat. You see many houseboats moored along the canals, on the river, and in the harbor of Amsterdam, but you won't be able to get aboard most of them unless you know the owner. The *Hendrika Maria,* a former commercial sailing ship built in 1914, is an exception. You can visit the original deckhouse where the skipper and his family lived, the cupboard bed in which they slept, and the cargo hold, now equipped as remarkably spacious and comfortable living quarters. How do you get the boat's bottom cleaned? Might you sink? What happens in winter? These and other questions are answered in models, photographs, and books.

> **Impressions**
> *This city seems to be double: one can also see it in the water; and the reflection of these distinguished houses in these canals makes this spot a fairyland.*
> —Jean-François Regnard, French writer (1681)

Opposite Prinsengracht 296 (near Elandsgracht). ℂ 020/427-0750. Admission 2.50€ adults, 2.05€ children under 152cm (59 in.). Mar–Oct Wed–Sun 11am–5pm; Nov–Dec and Feb Fri–Sun 11am–5pm. Tram: 13, 14, 17 to Westermarkt.

3 Historic Buildings & Monuments

Beurs van Berlage (Old Stock Exchange) Designed by architect Hendrik Petrus Berlage and built between 1896 and 1903, the Stock Exchange, a massive edifice of colored brick and stone enclosing three arcades roofed in glass and iron, represented a revolutionary break with 19th-century architecture. Though it's no longer the stock exchange, it's still well worth visiting as the prime example of Amsterdam School architecture, which was contemporaneous with the work of Frank Lloyd Wright in America. Today, the Beurs is used as a space for concerts, conferences, and exhibits.

Behind the Gables

Most of Amsterdam's 6,800 landmark buildings have gables. These hide the pitched roofs and demonstrate the architect's vertical show-manship in a city where hefty property taxes and expensive canalfront land encouraged pencil-thin buildings. If you can pick out Amster-dam's various gable styles without developing Sistine Chapel neck syn-drome, you can date the buildings fairly accurately.

The earliest type (ca. 1250–1550) is the wooden, triangular gable; only two of these remain, at no. 34 in the Begijnhof and at Zeedijk 1. Later developments in stone on this theme, often used on warehouses, were the early to mid-17th-century pointy spout gable and the step gable, which as the name suggests looks like a series of steps. The graceful neck gable (ca. 1640–1790) looks like a headless neck, with curlicues on the shoulders; look for the first one at Herengracht 168 (the Netherlands Theater Institute), a 1638 mansion. These were com-plemented by the less-elaborate bell gable, which looks like a cross-section of a church bell.

Walls in the Begijnhof and on Sint Luciensteeg at the Amsterdam Historical Museum have some good gable stones, including the oldest known, from 1603, showing a milkmaid balancing her buckets. Among the most lavish gables is the one with tritons blowing horns at Heren-gracht 508, and next door at no. 510 a pair of stone sea gods riding leaping dolphins.

Incidentally, the *hijsbalk*—the hook you see on many gables—might look to be ideal for a hanging (the kids maybe), but is actually used for hauling furniture. Rope and pulleys are used to get large, heavy items into and out of homes where the staircases are too narrow and steep.

Note on its facade a relief of two fishermen and a dog in a boat, depicting a legend of Amsterdam's foundation, and a modern sculpture of Count Gijsbrecht II van Amstel, who in 1204 built Amsterdam's first castle, at the Dam, set in a corner of the building facing Beursplein. This pleasant square is dotted with plane trees and 19th-century wrought-iron streetlamps. The modern Effecten-beurs (Stock Exchange) is on the eastern side of the square.

Beursplein 7 (near the Dam). ℂ 020/626-8936. Admission 3.75€ adults, 2.50€ children 5–16, children under 5 free. Mon–Fri 9am–5pm. Tram: 4, 9, 14, 16, 24, 25 to the Dam.

De Waag (Weigh House) Built in the 14th century, the city's only surviving medieval fortified gate later became a guild house. Among the guilds lodged here was the Surgeon's Guild, immortalized in Rembrandt's painting *The Anatomy Lesson* (1632), which depicts a dissection in the rarely open upper-floor The-atrum Anatomicum. Today the Waag is a multimedia center for exhibits, the-ater, and music performances. The reading table in its cafe features not only newspapers, as is common in Amsterdam, but also Internet access and a selec-tion of CD-ROMs.

Nieuwmarkt. ℂ 020/557-9898. Free admission (but some exhibits charge admission). Sun–Thurs 10am–1am; Fri–Sat 10am–2am. Metro: Nieuwmarkt.

Koninklijk Paleis (Royal Palace) ★★   One of the heavier features of the Dam is the solid, neoclassical facade of the Royal Palace (1648–55). Designed by Jacob van Campen—the Thomas Jefferson of the Dutch Republic—as a Stadhuis (Town Hall) to replace the frumpy and decayed old Gothic one that in 1652 did everyone a favor by burning down, it was designed to showcase the city's burgeoning prosperity; its interior is replete with white Italian marble. Poet Constantijn Huygens called the new Town Hall the "Eighth Wonder of the World."

Not until 1808, when Napoléon Bonaparte's younger brother Louis reigned as king of the Netherlands, did it become a palace, filled with Empire-style furniture courtesy of the French ruler. Since the return to the throne in 1813 of the Dutch House of Orange, this has been the official palace of the reigning king or queen of the Netherlands. Few of them, however, have used it for more than an occasional state reception or official ceremony (such as the inauguration of Queen Beatrix, who prefers living at Huis ten Bosch in The Hague), or as their *pied-à-terre* in the capital.

In the Vierschaar (Tribunal), magistrates pronounced death sentences watched over by images of Justice, Wisdom, and Mercy. Atlas holds up the globe in the high-ceilinged Burgerzaal (Citizens Chamber), and maps inlaid on the marble floor show Amsterdam as the center of the world. Ferdinand Bol's painting *Moses the Lawgiver* hangs in the Schepenzaal (Council Chamber), where the aldermen met. On the pediment overlooking the Dam, Flemish sculptor Artus Quellien carved a baroque hymn in stone to Amsterdam's maritime preeminence, showing figures symbolizing the oceans paying the city homage. The weathervane on the cupola takes the form of a Dutch sailing ship.

Tip: Don't miss the excellent video presentation (in English) that's shown continuously (usually in the Magistrate's Court on the second floor)

Dam. ☎ 020/620-4060. Admission 4€ adults, 3€ children 5–12, children under 5 free. Easter and June–Oct daily 11am–5pm; Nov to mid-Dec and mid-Feb to May generally Tues–Thurs 12:30–5pm (opening days and hours are highly variable; check before going). Closed mid-Dec to mid-Feb. Tram: 1, 2, 4, 5, 9, 13, 14, 16, 17, 24, 25 to the Dam.

OTHER HISTORIC SIGHTS

You may come away thinking Amsterdam is one big historic monument. Still, some buildings are more historic and monumental than others and therefore more worth going out of your way for. You won't have to go far out of your way to see **Centraal Station.** Built on an artificial island in the IJ inlet of the Zuider Zee (now the IJsselmeer), between 1884 and 1889, the station was thoroughly disliked by Amsterdammers at the time. Now it's an attraction in its own right, partly for its extravagant Dutch neo-Renaissance facade, partly for the liveliness that permanently surrounds it. The left one of the two central towers has a gilded weathervane; on the right one there's a clock. Take a little time to soak up the buzz that swirls around the station in a blur of people, backpacks, bikes,

Fun Fact **New York Loves Ya, Henry**

In 1609, Henry Hudson set sail from the Tower of Tears aboard the *Halve Maen.* He "discovered" Long Island, the Hudson River, and the future site of Nieuw Amsterdam, which would later become New York. The Greenwich Village Historical Society pinned a memorial marker to the tower in 1927.

trams, buses, vendors, pickpockets, and junkies. There should be a busker or two, maybe even a full-blown jazz or rock combo, and maybe a street organ.

Not far away, across Prins Hendrikkade at the corner of Geldersekade, is the **Schreierstoren (Tower of Tears),** from 1480, once a strong point in the city wall bristling with cannon. Its name comes from the tears allegedly shed by wives as their menfolk sailed away on voyages from which they might never return. A stone tablet on the wall shows a woman with her hand to her face. She might be weeping, but who knows what emotion that hand is really covering up?

No ambiguity surrounds the **Munttoren (Mint Tower)** on Muntplein, a busy traffic intersection at Rokin and the Singel canal. The base of the tower, from 1490, used to be part of the Reguliers Gate in the city wall. In 1620 Hendrick de Keyser topped it with an ornate, lead-covered tower, whose carillon bells sing out gaily every hour and play a one-hour concert on Friday at noon.

A monument of a different temper is the sad remains of the **Hollandsche Schouwburg,** Plantage Middenlaan 24 (© **020/626-9945;** tram 9, 14), not far from the Jewish Historical Museum and the Portuguese Synagogue. All that remains of the former Yiddish Theater, which was used by the Nazis as an assembly point for Dutch Jews who were to be deported to concentration camps, is its facade, behind which is a simple memorial plaza of grass and walkways. A granite column rising out of a Star of David emblem commemorates "those deported from here 1940–45." On a marble memorial, watched over by an eternal flame, are inscribed the 6,700 family names of the 60,000 to 80,000 deportees who passed through here, few of whom survived the war. The site is open daily from 11am to 4pm. Admission is free.

Most of Golden Age Amsterdam's wealth was generated by trade, and most of that trade was organized by the Verenigde Oostindische Compagnie (V.O.C.), based at **Oost Indisch Huis (East India House)** on Oude Hoogstraat, off Kloveniersburgwal. Dating from 1606, this former headquarters of the first multinational corporation now belongs to the University of Amsterdam, but you can stroll into the courtyard.

You might also be interested in **West Indisch Huis (West India House),** at Herenmarkt, off Brouwersgracht. On the north side of this little square is a red-brick building, built as a meat-trading hall in 1615, that in 1623 became headquarters of the Dutch West India Company, which controlled trade with the

---

Fun Fact **If I Can Make It There . . .**

In 1624, the Dutch West India Company built a fortified trading post on the tip of Manhattan Island, naming the settlement that grew up around it Nieuw Amsterdam in 1625. Two years later the company's Peter Minuit bought Manhattan Island from the Manhattoes Indians for the equivalent in cloth and trinkets of $24—surely history's smartest ever real-estate deal. Peter Stuyvesant, a stern ruler who opposed political and religious pluralism, was appointed governor in 1646. Eighteen years later he surrendered Nieuw Amsterdam to the English, who renamed it New York.

Echoes of the Dutch period remain, in Harlem, named after Haarlem, a town west of Amsterdam; Brooklyn, named after Breukelen, a village southeast of Amsterdam; Staten Island, named after the Dutch parliament, the Staten-Generaal; even the notorious Bowery, which began as the *bouwerie,* a road leading to Peter Stuyvesant's farm.

Americas. It now houses educational organizations, including the John Adams Institute, an American-oriented philosophical and literary society. In the courtyard is a statue of Peter Stuyvesant, one-legged governor of Nieuw Amsterdam (later New York City) from 1647 until the British took over in 1664. There's a sculpture depicting the first Dutch settlement on Manhattan Island, founded in 1626.

Not far from West India House is Amsterdam's first university, the **Athenaeum Illustre,** at Oudezijds Voorburgwal 231. Founded in 1631, the Athenaeum moved here in 1632, to occupy the 15th-century Gothic Agnietenkapel (Church of St. Agnes) and convent of the Order of St. Francis, whose nuns lost their place to the Dutch Admiralty after the religious upheaval of 1578. The building is now the University of Amsterdam Museum.

THE SMALLEST HOUSES

The **narrowest house** in Amsterdam (and who knows, maybe even the world) can be seen at **Singel 7.** It's just a meter (3½ ft.) wide, barely wider than the front door. It is, however, a cheat. Only the front facade is really so narrow; behind that it broadens out to more normal proportions. The genuine narrowest house is at **Oude Hoogstraat 22,** between the Dam and Nieuwmarkt. It has a typical Amsterdam bell gable and is 2m (6½ ft.) wide and 6m (20 ft.) deep. A close rival, 2.4m (7¾ ft.) wide, can be seen nearby, at **Kloveniersburgwal 26;** this is the cornice-gabled **Klein Trippenhuis,** also known as Mr. Trip's Coachman's House. It faces the elegant Trippenhuis at no. 29, which at 22m (72 ft.) is the widest Old Amsterdam house, and was built in 1660 for the wealthy merchant Trip brothers. The story goes that the coachman exclaimed one day: "Oh, if only I could be so lucky as to have a house as wide as my master's door." His master overheard this, and the coachman's wish was granted—nice work if you can get it. The house is now a fashion boutique.

OTHER MONUMENTS & SIGHTS

The **Homomonument,** on Westermarkt beside the Westerkerk church, is three granite blocks in the shape of pink triangles (the shape of the Nazi badge for homosexuals), forming a larger triangular outline. One block, a symbol of the future, points into the Keizersgracht; one, at ground level, points toward the nearby Anne Frank House; the other, a sort of plinth about 50cm (20 in.) high, points toward the offices of COC, a gay political organization). Designed by Karin Daan, the monument memorializes gays and lesbians killed during World War II and persecuted throughout the ages.

The precariously tilting **Montelbaanstoren,** the "leaning tower of Amsterdam," a fortification at the juncture of the Oude Schans and Waals-Eilandsgracht canals, dates from 1512. It is one of few surviving elements of the city's once powerful defensive works. In 1606, Hendrick de Keyser added an octagonal tower and spire.

Made of African azobe wood, the famous **Magere Brug (Skinny Bridge),** a double-drawbridge, spans the Amstel between Kerkstraat and Nieuwe Kerkstraat. This is the latest successor, dating from 1969, to the 1672 original, which legend says was built to make it easier for the two wealthy Mager sisters, who lived on opposite banks of the river, to visit each other. The footbridge, one of the city's 60 drawbridges, is itself a big draw, especially after dark, when it is illuminated by hundreds of lights. A bridge master who gets around by bike raises it to let boats through.

Though most of the **Blauwbrug (Blue Bridge)** over the Amstel at Waterlooplein looks gray to me, since a recent renovation its lanterns are once again as blue as when Impressionist artist George Hendrik Breitner painted the scene in the 1880s. The cast-iron bridge, inspired by Paris's Pont Alexandre III and opened in 1884, is named after a 16th-century timber bridge painted Nassau blue after the 1578 Protestant takeover.

The widest bridge in the old town, the **Torensluis,** Singel (at Oude Leliestraat; tram: 1, 2, 5, 13, 17), stands on the site of a 17th-century sluice gate flanked by twin towers that were demolished in 1829. Its foundations were used for what must have been a particularly damp and gloomy prison. A bronze statue on the bridge is of Multatuli, a 19th-century author, and sidewalk terraces from nearby cafes encroach onto the span.

4 Sights of Religious Significance

Religion has always played an important part in Amsterdam's history, and hundreds of churches are testimony to the great variety of religious beliefs still alive—if not always well—in the city. Most can be visited during regular services; some have open doors during weekdays so that visitors may have a look around.

Begijnhof ★★ This 14th-century cluster of small homes around a garden courtyard is one of the best places to appreciate the earliest history of the city, when Amsterdam was a destination for religious pilgrims and an important center of Catholic nunneries. The Begijnhof itself was not a convent (that was located next door, where the Amsterdams Historisch Museum now stands); it was an almshouse for pious laywomen—*begijnen*—involved in religious and charitable work for the convent. It remained in operation even after the aboutface changeover of the city from Catholicism to Protestantism in the late 16th century. The last of the *begijnen* died in 1971, but you can still pay homage to these pious women by pausing for a moment at the small flower-planted mound that lies just at the center garden's edge across from the English Reformed Church. Opposite the front of the church is a secret Catholic chapel built in 1671 and still in use. Only one of the old wooden houses from the early period remains. You're welcome to visit the Begijnhof during daylight hours. (The city's low-income seniors now reside in the old homes, and their privacy is respected after sunset.)

Gedempte Begijnensloot (at Spui). ⓒ 020/625-8853. Free admission. Daily until sunset. Tram: 1, 2, 5 to Spui.

Museum Amstelkring Although Amsterdam has been known as a tolerant city for many centuries, just after the Protestant Reformation, Roman Catholics fell into disfavor. Forced to worship in secret, they devised ingenious ways of gathering for Sunday services. In an otherwise ordinary-looking 17th-century canal house in the middle of the Red Light District is the most amazing of these clandestine churches, known to the general public as Ons' Lieve Heer op Solder (Our Lord in the Attic). The three houses making up this museum were built in the 1660s by a wealthy Catholic merchant specifically to house a church. Today they're furnished much as they would have been in the mid–18th century. Nothing prepares you for the minicathedral you come on when you climb the last flight of stairs into the attic. A large baroque altar, religious statuary, pews to seat 150, an 18th-century organ, and an upper gallery complete this miniature church.

Oudezijds Voorburgwal 40 (2 blocks north of Oude Kerk). 🕐 020/624-6604. Admission 2€ adults, 1.50€ seniors/students/children. Mon–Sat 10am–5pm; Sun and holidays 1–5pm. Closed Jan 1, Apr 30. Tram: 1, 2, 4, 5, 9, 13, 16, 17, 24, 25 to Centraal Station.

Nieuwe Kerk (New Church)   Many of this originally Catholic church's priceless treasures were removed and its colorful frescoes painted over in 1578 when it passed into the hands of Protestants, but since 1814 (when the king first took the oath of office and was inaugurated here—Dutch royalty are not crowned; Queen Beatrix, too, was inaugurated here in 1980), much of its original grandeur has been restored. The church boasts a stately arched nave, an elaborately carved altar, a great pipe organ by Jacob van Campen from 1645, and several noteworthy stained-glass windows. Look out for the carved, gilded ceiling above the choir, which survived a disastrous fire in 1645. It also holds sepulchral monuments for many of Holland's most revered poets and naval heroes. A sculpture depicts the 17th-century Dutch Admiral Michiel De Ruyter amidst the wreckage of a sea battle. Afterwards, take the weight off your feet on the sidewalk terrace of the fine cafe, the Nieuwe Café, attached to the church.

Dam (beside the Royal Palace). 🕐 020/638-6909. Admission varies with different events. Daily 10am–6pm (Thurs to 10pm during exhibits). Tram: 1, 2, 4, 5, 9, 13, 14, 16, 17, 24, 25 to the Dam.

Noorderkerk (North Church)   Recently restored, the city's first Greek cross-shaped church with central pulpit, designed by Hendrick de Keyser and dating from 1620 to 1623, was built for the poor Calvinist faithful of the Jordaan. The four triangular houses tucked into the angles of the cross weren't part of De Keyser's original plan; architect Hendrick Staets, unwilling to see so much useful space go to waste, added them after De Keyser's death in 1621. This is still a working church, with an active congregation. A plaque on the facade recalls the February 1941 strike in protest of Nazi deportation of the city's Jewish community. From May to September, a classical music recital takes place every Saturday at 2pm; admission is 5€.

Noordermarkt 44–48 (off Prinsengracht). 🕐 020/626-6436. Free admission. Mon 10:30am–12:30pm; Sat 11am–1pm (followed by an hour-long concert of chamber music); Sun (services) 10am and 7pm. Tram: 1, 2, 5, 13, 17 to Martelaarsgracht.

Oude Kerk (Old Church) ★★   This late-Gothic church—its official name is the Sint-Nikolaaskerk (St. Nicholas's Church), but nobody ever calls it that— was begun in 1250 and essentially completed with the construction of the bell tower in 1566. (There was a further "completion" in 1578, with the destruction of much of its Catholic ornamentation by Protestant reformers.) On its southern porch, to the right of the sexton's house, you will see a coat of arms belonging to Maximilian of Austria, who, with his son Philip, contributed to the porch's construction. Rembrandt's wife Saskia is buried here. The church contains a magnificent organ from 1724 and is regularly used for organ recitals.

Nowadays, the pretty little gabled almshouses around the Oude Kerk feature red-fringed windows through which can be seen the scantily dressed ladies of the Red Light District.

Oudekerksplein (at Oudezijds Voorburgwal). ✆ 020/625-8284. Church: Admission 2€ adults, 1.50€ seniors/students, children 12 and under free. Mon–Sat 11am–5pm; Sun 1–5pm. Metro: Nieuwmarkt.

Portuguese Synagogue   Sephardic Jews fleeing Spain and Portugal during the 16th and early 17th centuries established a neighborhood east of the center known as the Jewish Quarter. In 1665 they built an elegant Ionic-style synagogue within an existing courtyard facing what is now a busy traffic circle. The total cost of the magnificent building was 186,000 florins, a king's ransom in those days but a small price to pay for the city's Jewish community, whose members could worship openly for the first time in 200 years. The building was restored in the 1950s. Today it looks essentially as it did 320 years ago, with its women's gallery supported by 12 stone columns to represent the Twelve Tribes of Israel, and the large, low-hanging brass chandeliers that together hold 1,000 candles, all of which are lighted for the private weekly services.

Mr. Visserplein 3. ✆ 020/624-5351. Admission 4€ adults, 2.50€ children 10–15, free for children under 10. Apr–Oct Sun–Fri 10am–12:30pm and 1–4pm; Nov–Mar Mon–Thurs 10am–12:30pm and 1–4pm, Fri 10am–3pm, Sun 10am–noon. Closed Jewish holidays. Tram: 9, 14 to Waterlooplein.

Westerkerk (West Church)   The Renaissance-style Westerkerk holds the remains of Rembrandt and his son, Titus, and is where in 1966 Princess (now Queen) Beatrix and Prince Claus said their marriage vows. The church was begun in 1620, at the same time as the Noorderkerk, and opened in 1631. The initial designer was Hendrick de Keyser, whose his son Pieter took over after his father's death in 1621. The church's interior, light and spacious, has a fine organ. The 85m (277-ft.) tower, the Westertoren, is Amsterdam's tallest, providing a spectacular view of the city; on its top is the blue, red, and gold crown of the Holy Roman Empire, a symbol bestowed by the Austrian emperor Maximilian.

Westermarkt. ✆ 020/624-7766. Church: Free admission. May 15–Sept 15 Mon–Sat 11am–3pm; Tower: Admission 1€. June to mid-September Wed–Sat 10am–4pm. Tram: 13, 14, 17 to Westermarkt.

Zuiderkerk (South Church)   Three of Rembrandt's children were buried in the Zuiderkerk, the city's first Protestant church, designed by Hendrick de Keyser and built between 1603 and 1614. In recent years it has since succumbed to a shortage of worshipers and today houses a permanent exhibit on modern town planning in Amsterdam. From June to September you can climb the church tower on a free guided tour; these leave on the hour, Wednesday through Saturday from 2 to 4pm.

Here Today . . .

Amsterdammetjes, those much-loved, much-hated, ubiquitous anti-parking posts that in their zillions have lined streets and canalsides across the city since, well, probably since Rembrandt was a kid, are now an endangered species. They are slowly but steadily disappearing from the cityscape in favor of more space as part of a new concept in "street furniture." No doubt the scorched-earth tactics of Amsterdam's Parking Authority, which have all but eliminated parking violations, smoothed the path to their removal.

Zuiderkerkhof 72 (between Nieuwmarkt and Waterlooplein). © 020/622-2962. Free admission. Mon–Wed and Fri noon–5pm; Thurs noon–8pm. Metro: Nieuwmarkt. Tram: 9, 14 to Waterlooplein.

5 More Attractions

Heineken Experience   Five minutes into the self-guided, high-energy, multimedia tour of Heineken's old Amsterdam brewery—and still in a state of shock from having shelled out 7.50€ to get in—I was already mentally pinning Frommer's "Overrated" icon to the start of this review. Two things persuaded me not to: First, the further you go, the better it gets; second, the other visitors, most of whom (surprise, surprise) were young, male, and clearly seeking a positive user experience with the contents of a beer glass, were having a whale of a time. But the admission is steep, even if you do get two "free" glasses of Heineken beer and a "free" Heineken glass for a souvenir. It seems like a bunch of Heineken marketing whizzes came up with a brilliant wheeze, to repurpose the facility and grow the market. They get you to pay for being bombarded with Heineken's marketing message, and receiving compelling content like "Water is a vital ingredient in beer-brewing."

The experience unfolds inside the former Heineken brewing facilities, which date from 1867. Before the brewery stopped functioning in 1988, it was producing more than 100 million liters (26 million gal.) annually. The fermentation tanks, each capable of holding a million glassfuls of Heineken, are still there, along with the multistory malt silos and all manner of vintage brewing equipment and implements. You "meet" Dr. Elion, the 19th-century chemist who isolated the renowned Heineken "A" yeast, which gives the beer its taste. In one amusing attraction, you stand on a moving floor, facing a large video screen, and get to see and feel what it's like to be a Heineken beer bottle—one of a half-million every hour—careening on a conveyor belt through a modern Heineken bottling plant. Best of all, in another touchy-feely presentation, you "sit" aboard an old brewery dray-wagon, "pulled" by a pair of big Shire horses on the video screen in front of you, that shakes, rattles, and rolls on a mini-tour of Amsterdam.

It *is* fun, I have to admit. But serious types can take cold comfort from a multiscreen presentation on the evidently dire state of fresh-water resources around the world.

Stadhouderskade 78 (at Ferdinand Bolstraat). © 020/523-9666. Admission 7.50€; under 18 admitted only with parental supervision. Tues–Sun 10am–6pm. Closed Jan 1, Dec 25. Tram: 16, 24, 25 to Maria Heineken-plein.

Holland Experience   This multidimensional film and theater show takes you through the landscapes and culture of Holland at different periods of its history and today. If you've ever nervously wondered what would happen to the city if all that seawater should ever break through the defensive dikes, Holland Experience will give you a taste. In a simulated dike collapse, 80,000 liters of water pour toward you. Other exhibits include farming and fishing scenes. The show isn't as good as they could easily make it, or as the steep admission price would justify (and 80,000 liters isn't all *that* much water), but it does give you something of a nutshell picture of Holland. If you're not much into traipsing around heavy-duty cultural museums, this is a reasonably pleasant way to spend an hour or two on a rainy day. The toilets (I can vouch only for the men's) are themselves of interest; they're designed to look like the deck of a ship passing along the Dutch coast, and come complete with marine sound effects and a salt-air breeze.

Waterlooplein 17. ℂ **020/422-2233**. Admission 10€ adults, 8€ seniors, children 12 and under free. Daily 10am–10pm. Tram: 9, 14 to Waterlooplein.

Madame Tussaud's If you like your celebrities with a waxen stare, don't miss Madame Tussaud's. The Amsterdam version of the famous London attraction has its own cast of Dutch characters (Rembrandt, Queen Beatrix, Mata Hari), among a parade of international favorites (Churchill, Kennedy, Gandhi). The Amsterdam branch reopened in March 2002, after a "face-lift" that cost more than four million euros. During the refurbishment, all of the wax portraits were sent to Tussaud's Studio's in London for a makeover. Some, like David Bowie, have a complete new look. Among new figures that have been added are Kylie Minogue, Bono, and Bob Marley. Exhibits bring you "face to face" with the powerful and famous and let you step into the times, events, and moments that made them famous.

The popular Dutch 17th-century Golden Age exhibit received only minor changes. In the Grand Hall, styled to look like a reception room in Dutch manor around 1700, are images of world leaders, royalty, artists, writers, and religious leaders. Those portrayed are brought to life with memorabilia such as paintings, a smoking cigarette, or a picture of the most memorable moments of their lives. The Music Zone has a disco floor and a mix of video footage, music, and pictures illustrating the history of music from the 1950s to the present day. Then comes the Sport Gallery and its heroes of sport. Later, you get to "meet" TV personalities in the TV Studio Backstage, and in the Hall of Fame, both contemporary and legendary movie stars shine like it was premiere night. A video projected on a large wall-screen illustrates how wax portraits are created at Tussaud's Studio in London.

Dam 20. ℂ **020/622-9949**. Admission 14€ adults, 12€ seniors, 10€ children 5–15, children under 5 free. Mid-July to Aug daily 9:30am–8:30pm; Sept to mid-July daily 10am–6:30pm. Closed Apr 30. Tram: 4, 9, 14, 16, 24, 25 to the Dam.

NEMO ⭐ NEMO, a paean of praise to science and technology, is in a strikingly modern building in the Eastern Dock, designed by Italian architect Renzo Piano, which seems to reproduce the graceful lines of an ocean-going ship. The center is a hands-on experience as much as a museum, with games, experiments, demonstrations, workshops, and theater and film shows. You learn how to steer

---

𝒞 At Home in the Harbor

Amsterdam's biggest redevelopment project is under way in the Eastern Harbor Area of the IJ channel, which lies east of Centraal Station. Once a major part of Amsterdam Port, this area is now being redeveloped for housing. The city government has touted the project as "a new life on the water." The artificial islands and peninsulas of the harbor complex have been cleared of most of their warehouses and other installations; modern housing and infrastructure are taking their place. A visit here is a good way to see how Amsterdam sees its own future, away from its Golden Age heart.

At present you can reach the redevelopment zone on foot or by bus no. 28, 32, 59, or 61 to Java Eiland and KNSM Eiland.

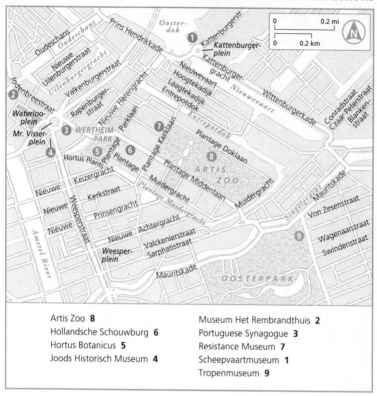

Artis Zoo **8**
Hollandsche Schouwburg **6**
Hortus Botanicus **5**
Joods Historisch Museum **4**

Museum Het Rembrandthuis **2**
Portuguese Synagogue **3**
Resistance Museum **7**
Scheepvaartmuseum **1**
Tropenmuseum **9**

a supertanker safely into port, boost your earnings on the floor of the New York Stock Exchange, and execute a complicated surgical procedure. One exhibit will even try to make you understand the basis of sexual attraction. Internet-linked computers on every floor help provide insights. IStudio Bits & Co is NEMO's digital world, in which you can play with images, sounds, text, websites, and your own imported material.

Oosterdok 2 (above the IJ Tunnel in the Eastern Dock). ✆ 0900/919-1100. Admission 10€ adults and children over 3, children under 4 free. July–Aug daily 10am–5pm; Sept–June Tues–Sun 10am–5pm. Bus: 22 to Kadijksplein.

MARKETS

There are more than 50 outdoor markets every week in Amsterdam, some of them permanent or semi-permanent, and others just passing through. For more details, see "Markets" in chapter 8, but here are three you shouldn't miss.

The **Bloemenmarkt (Flower Market)** is one of Amsterdam's stellar spots—though you might easily think it overrated, especially since it's not easy to see that it's actually floating. Still, this is probably the most atmospheric place to buy cut flowers and bulbs. Awnings stretch to cover stall after stall of brightly colored blossoms, bulbs, and potted plants. A stroll down that fragrant line is surely one of Amsterdam's most heart-lifting experiences. Looking for a bargain-basement souvenir is made easy at the **Waterlooplein Flea Market** ✦✦✦, on

Waterlooplein—naturally enough. You find all kinds of stuff here, not all of it junk, and a constant press of people with good buys on their mind. The **Albert Cuyp Markt,** on Albert Cuypstraat, is more of an everyday market for food, clothes, and other things, but is almost as colorful as the other two.

6 Green Amsterdam

Amsterdam is not a notably green city, particularly in the Old Center, where the canals are the most obvious and visible encroachment of the natural world. Still, the city as a whole has plenty of parks, including the famous **Vondelpark** ★★★, a pattern of lakes, meadows, and woodland containing 120 varieties of tree that include catalpa, chestnut, cypress, oak, and poplar. Watch out for the tasty-looking "gateau" they sell there, or you may find yourself floating above the trees: Drug-laced space-cake is an acquired taste and not everyone is ready to acquire it.

Otherwise, the Vondelpark is a fairly standard park, the site of skateboarding, Frisbee-flipping, in-line skating, model-boat sailing, soccer, softball and basketball games, open-air concerts, open-air theater performances, smooching in the undergrowth, parties, picnics, arts-and-crafts markets, and, perhaps not-so-standard, topless sunbathing. Best of all, it's free, or as the Dutch say, gratis. The Vondelpark lies generally southwest of Leidseplein, with entrances all around; the most popular is adjacent to Leidseplein, on Stadhouderskade.

You can rent in-line skates from **Rent A Skate,** Damstraat 21 (© **020/664-5091**), and tour the park in style. Including protective gear, it is 5€ an hour for adults, or 7.50€ for a half day and 13€ for a full day; for children 10 and under, 2.50€ an hour, 5€ for a half day, and 9.50€ for a full day.

After Vondelpark, the city's other parks are fairly tame, but the following still make pleasant escapes on a warm summer day: **Sarphati Park,** 2 blocks behind the Albert Cuyp Markt in South Amsterdam; **Beatrix Park,** adjacent to the RAI Convention and Exhibition Center; **Rembrandt Park** and **Erasmus Park** in the west of the city; **Martin Luther King Park,** beside the River Amstel; and the **Oosterpark,** in East Amsterdam.

To enjoy scenery and fresh air, you should head out to the giant **Amsterdamse Bos (Amsterdam Wood),** whose main entrance is on Amstelveenseweg, in the southern suburb of Amstelveen. This is nature on the city's doorstep. The park was laid out during the Depression years as a public works project. By now the trees, birds, insects, and small animals are firmly established. From the entrance, follow the path to the Roeibaan, a 2km (1¼ mile) rowing course. Beyond the western end of the Roeibaan is the Bosmuseum (© **020/676-2152**), where you can trace the park's history and learn about its wildlife. This free museum is open daily 10am to 5pm. Nearby is a big pond called the **Grote Vijver,** where you can rent boats (© **020/644-5119**), and the Openluchttheater (Open-Air Theater), which often has performances on summer evenings. In 2000, the **Kersenbloesempark (Cherry Blossom Park)** opened in the Amsterdamse Bos, its 400 cherry trees donated by the Japan Women's Club to mark 400 years of cultural ties between the Netherlands and Japan. The best way to the Amsterdamse Bos from the city center is to take tram 6, 16, or 24 to Stadionplein and then to take any bus, except the no. 23, along Amstelveenseweg to the entrance.

Hortus Botanicus (Botanical Garden) ★★   The Botanical Garden, which was established here in 1682, is a medley of color and scent, with some 250,000 flowers and 115,000 plants and trees, from 8,000 different varieties. It owes its origins to the treasure trove of tropical plants the Dutch found in their colonies of Indonesia, Surinam, and the Antilles, and its contemporary popularity to the Dutch love affair with flowers. Among its highlights are the Semicircle, which reconstructs part of the original design from 1682; the Mexico–California Desert House; the Palm House, with one of the world's oldest palm trees; and the Tri-Climate House, which displays tropical, subtropical, and desert plants.

Plantage Middenlaan 2a (near Artis Zoo). ✆ 020/625-9021. Admission 5€ adults, 3€ children 5–14, free for children under 5. Apr–Sept Mon–Fri 9am–5pm, Sat–Sun 11am–5pm; Oct–Mar Mon–Fri 9am–4pm, Sat–Sun 11am–4pm. Tram: 9, 14 to Plantage Middenlaan.

7 Offbeat & Alternative Amsterdam

RED LIGHT DISTRICT

This warren of streets and old canals (known as De Rosse Buurt or De Wallen in Dutch) around Oudezijds Achterburgwal and Oudezijds Voorburgwal by the Oude Kerk, a testament to the city's tolerance and pragmatism, is on most people's sightseeing agenda. However, a visit to this area is not for everyone, and if you're liable to be offended by the sex industry exposed in all its garish colors, don't go. If you do choose to go, you need to exercise some caution, because the area is a center of crime, vice, and drugs. As always in Amsterdam, there's no need to exaggerate the risks; and in fact the nightclubs' own security helps keep the brightly lit areas quite safe. Plenty of tourists visit the Rosse Buurt and suffer nothing more serious than a come-on from one of the prostitutes.

At night especially, however, stick to the crowded streets and be wary of pickpockets at all times. There can be a sinister air to the bunches of often weird-looking men who gather on the bridges; and there is a sadder aura around the "heroin whores" who wander the darker streets. Finally, do not take photographs of the women in the windows, many of whom don't want Mom and Dad to know how they earn a living. Men are always on the lookout, and they won't hesitate to throw your camera (and maybe your person) into the canal. (George Michael seems to have had no trouble filming the video here for his risqué 1999 cover of The Police's '70s classic *Roxanne*.)

Still, it's extraordinary to view the prostitutes in leather and lace sitting in their storefronts with their radios and TVs blaring as they do their knitting or adjust their makeup, waiting patiently for customers. The district seems to reflect Dutch pragmatism; if you can't stop the oldest trade in the world, you can at least confine it to a particular area and impose health and other regulations on it. And the fact is that underneath its tacky glitter, the Red Light District contains some of Amsterdam's prettiest canals and loveliest old architecture, plus some excellent bars and restaurants, secondhand bookshops, and other specialty shops (not all of which work the erogenous zones). For more information on the Red Light District, see also chapter 9. To get there, take tram no. 4, 9, 14, 16, 24, or 25 to the Dam, then pass behind the Grand Hotel Krasnapolsky.

OFFBEAT MUSEUMS

Erotic Museum   As its name suggests, this museum presents an allegedly artistic vision of eroticism; it focuses on prints and drawings, including some by John Lennon. There is a re-creation of a Red Light alley and an extensively equipped S&M playroom, both of which are rather antiseptic and serious. The only humorous note is an X-rated cartoon depicting some of the things Snow White apparently got up to with the Seven Dwarfs that Walt never told us about.

Oudezijds Achterburgwal 54 (Red Light District). ℂ 020/624-7303. Admission 3€. Daily noon–midnight. Tram: 4, 9, 14, 16, 24, 25 to the Dam.

Hash Marihuana Hemp Museum   Well, it wouldn't really be Amsterdam, would it, without its fascination with intoxicating weeds. This museum will teach you everything you ever wanted to know, and much you maybe didn't, about hash, marijuana, and related products. The museum does not promote drug use but aims to make you better informed before deciding whether to light up and, of course, whether to inhale. One way it does this is by having a cannabis garden in the joint (sorry) on the premises. Plants at various stages of development fill the air with an unmistakable, heady, resinous fragrance. And hemp, not plastic, could be the future if the exhibit on the multifarious uses of the fiber through the ages is anything to go by. Some exhibits shed light on the medicinal uses of cannabis and on hemp's past and present-day uses as a natural fiber. Among several notable artworks in the museum's collection is David Teniers the Younger's painting, *Hemp-Smoking Peasants in a Smoke House* (1660).

Oudezijds Achterburgwal 130 (Red Light District). ℂ 020/623-5961. Admission 5.70€. Daily 10am–5:30pm. Tram: 4, 9, 14, 16, 24, 25 to the Dam.

Sexmuseum Amsterdam   Behind its faux-marble facade, this museum is not as sleazy as you might expect, apart from one room covered with straight-up pornography. Otherwise the presentation tends toward the tongue-in-cheek. Exhibits include erotic prints and drawings, and trinkets like tobacco boxes decorated with naughty pictures. Teenage visitors seem to find the whole place vastly amusing, judging by the giggling fits at the showcases. Spare a thought for the models of early erotic photography—slow film speeds in those days made for uncomfortably long posing times!

Damrak 18 (near Centraal Station). ℂ 020/622-8376. Admission 2.50€ age 16 and over only. Daily 10am–11:30pm. Tram: 1, 2, 4, 5, 9, 13, 16, 17, 24, 25 to Centraal Station.

Torture Museum   You enter through an appropriately long and gloomy tunnel, and emerge with a new appreciation of why the framers of the U.S.

 History in the Making

Find reading about Amsterdam's history to be about as hard as digesting raw herring and onion? Relief is at hand in the new theater/restaurant **Pompoen**, Spuistraat 2 (ℂ 020/521-3000; tram: 1, 2, 5, 13, 17), which has a daily audiovisual program called *Het Mirakel van Amsterdam* (*The Miracle of Amsterdam*), in English and Dutch and projected on a cinema-size 3D screen, that recounts highlights of the city's story from 1000 to the present day. The 45-minute film takes visual material from museums and TV shows combined with animation to bring you people and events. The program plays daily on the hour from 10am to 5pm and is 7€ for adults and 5.50€ for age 18 and under.

In the evening, Pompoen offers a program of multimedia and theater productions, and jazz musicians perform most nights in the bar/restaurant.

Constitution outlawed cruel and unusual punishment. Yet o
motives of the Torture Museum—and its visitors?—are not pur
There is a horrible fascination about devices such as the Inquis
guillotine, and assorted grotesque implements of torture, pu
"redemption" favored by the civil and ecclesiastic authorities in t
past.

Singel 449 (at the Flower market). © **020/320-6642**. Admission 4€ adults, 2€ children 5–12, children under 5 free. Daily 10am–11pm. Tram: 1, 2, 5, to Koningsplein.

8 Free Amsterdam

The words *free* and *Dutch* are generally thought to mix together about as well as oil and water. Perhaps rattled by accusations that Amsterdam has grown too expensive, and by stiff competition from Prague in the young-and-alternative market, the VVV tourist office has drawn up a list of free things to see and do in the city. Here are some highlights:

- Admire 15 enormous 17th-century paintings of the Amsterdam Civic Guards, in the **Schuttersgalerij,** a covered passageway between the Begijnhof and the Amsterdams Historisch Museum.
- Visit the **Begijnhof** itself (see "Sights of Religious Significance," earlier in this chapter).
- Judge horseflesh at the **Hollandsche Manège (Dutch Stables),** at Vondelstraat 140, built in 1882 and inspired by the Spanish Riding School in Vienna.
- Cross the bridge over Reguliersgracht at Herengracht, from which you can see no fewer than **15 bridges.**
- Breathe scented air in the **Rijksmuseum Garden** and see fragments from ruined old buildings stored there.
- Find out where Amsterdam is going as a city at the permanent town-planning exhibit in the **Zuiderkerk.**
- Assess the chance of getting your feet wet, at the **Normaal Amsterdams Peil (Normal Amsterdam Level),** a fixed point against which measurements of sea level are made. Beside a bronze plaque in the passageway between the Muziektheater and the Stadhuis (Town Hall) in Waterlooplein are three glass columns filled with water. The first two show the current sea level at Vlissingen and IJmuiden; the third, 5m (15 ft.) above your head, shows the high-water mark during the disastrous floods in Zeeland in 1953. The NAP sets the standard for altitude measurements in Europe.
- Hear the **lunchtime rehearsal concerts,** from 12:30 to 1pm, at the Muziektheater (Tues) and the Concertgebouw (Wed) every week from October to June.
- Sail on the **IJ ferry** across the channel from behind Centraal Station to North Amsterdam (see "Getting Around," in chapter 3).
- Visit the **Flower Market** on the Singel (see "Markets," in chapter 8)—the flowers, however, are not free.
- Tour Europe in a single street, Roemer Visscherstraat 20–30, where the **Seven Countries Houses** were built in 1894 in the styles of Germany, France, Spain, Italy, Russia, Holland, and England.
- Stand on the **Magere Brug (Skinny Bridge)** over the River Amstel between Kerkstraat and Nieuwe Kerkstraat.

Check out the **narrowest houses** (see "Historic Buildings & Monuments," earlier in this chapter).

- Hear the music from four **17th-century carillons:** Westertoren (Tues noon–1pm); Zuidertoren (Thurs noon–1pm); Munttoren (Fri noon–1pm); and Oude Kerkstoren (Sat 4–5pm).
- Listen to the earthier performances of the **barrel organs** in the street (mixed with the rattle of money as the organ-grinder tries to persuade you to make a donation).

As well as the preceding list, the streets of Amsterdam are so filled with spectacle they constitute an ongoing, 24-hour special event all by themselves. They do, however, come into full bloom at such times as the **Spui Art Market,** from March to December, when local artists mount outdoor exhibits along the Spui. On April 30, Amsterdam, along with the rest of the country, holds a gigantic dawn-to-dawn street carnival in celebration of **Queen's Day.** In the last two weeks in May, **Floating Amsterdam** transforms the Amstel River into an outdoor theater, with performances near the Muziektheater. In August, the Prinsengracht concerts set the air ringing with music from flat-bottomed boats up and down the canal; late August, when there are folk dances on Dam Square with participants from around the world performing their own native dances; and early September, when there's a spectacular floral parade from the flower market at Aalsmeer to Amsterdam. There are free lunchtime concerts at 12:30pm on Tuesdays at the Muziektheater, and on Wednesdays in the Concertgebouw that are quite special. The program may feature chamber music, symphonic performances, or abbreviated previews of a full concert to be played to paying guests that same evening by local or visiting musical groups. In mid-April, there's no admission fee at most Amsterdam museums during National Museum Weekend, while a few charge greatly discounted fees. In the last two weeks in May, **Floating Amsterdam** transforms the Amstel River into an outdoor theater, with performances near the Muziektheater. In late August, the Prinsengracht concerts set the air ringing with music from flat-bottomed boats up and down the canal, when there are folk dances on Dam Square with participants from around the world performing their own native dances. In early September, there's a spectacular floral parade from the flower market at Aalsmeer to Amsterdam.

9 Modern Art Galleries

Visit the Stedelijk Museum for the mother of all Amsterdam modern art collections. But the Stedelijk's mission has been modified to focus more on exhibiting existing works by big names in the genre. The two galleries reviewed below aim to give new talent space to develop and to be seen.

Bureau Amsterdam   An initiative by the Stedelijk, this new gallery was described in a Dutch newspaper as a "hatchery for young artistic talent," in particular from Amsterdam. Exhibits will change constantly so I can't say what you'll be able to view on your visit, other than that the works will be by promising young artists and embrace painting, sculpture, video, installations, and performance art.

Rozenstraat 59 (off Prinsengracht). © 020/422-0471. Free admission. Tues–Sun 11am–5pm. Closed Jan 1, Apr 30, Dec 25. Tram: 13, 14, 17 to Westermarkt.

De Appel   Named after Amsterdam Cobra artist, Karel Appel, this center for contemporary art provides cutting-edge artists, both known and unknown, with space for exhibitions, projects, and research. Six presentations a year of solo or group work are backed up by interaction with the artists through lectures, discussions, and video presentations.

Nieuwe Spiegelstraat 10 (off Keizersgracht). ✆ **020/625-5651.** Admission 1.15€. Tues–Sun noon–5pm. Tram: 16, 24, 25 to Keizersgracht.

10 Especially for Kids

Kids may get a little bored at the Amsterdam art museums, but they're more likely to be interested in the **Anne Frankhuis** (see "The Big Four," earlier in this chapter). There's a section of the Tropenmuseum (see "More Museums & Galleries," earlier in this chapter) open only to children ages 6 to 12 (one adult per child is allowed); it's called **Kindermuseum TM Junior** (✆ **020/568-8300** for information). The Van Gogh Museum (see "The Big Four," earlier in this chapter) has a children's painting area on the ground floor, where budding van Goghs can get in some supervised practice. **Madame Tussaud's** (see "More Attractions," earlier in this chapter) is always fun for kids, though if they're too small they might be a little frightened by the wax statues. If all else fails, take them to **Intersphere Lasergames,** Prins Hendrikkade 194 (✆ **020/622-4809**), where in a gloomy mist-suffused futuristic world they can zap each other until the electric sheep come home. There are theater workshops at the Theatermuseum (see earlier in this chapter) for children ages 7 to 12 on Wednesday, Saturday, and Sunday afternoons.

Older kids might appreciate the sheer white-knuckle excitement of—well, of **chess,** actually. It's played with giant plastic pieces on an open-air board on Max Euweplein, named after a Dutch grandmaster, next to the Casino behind Leidseplein. They can even challenge one of the minor masters who hang around there. Finally, there are the **carillons:** Church belfries and towers throughout the city break into pretty melodies at every possible opportunity—that should hold their attention for around 30 seconds, the first time anyhow.

Artis Zoo ★★ If you're at a loss for what to do with the kids, the Artis Zoo is a safe bet. Established in 1838, the oldest zoo in the Netherlands houses more than 6,000 animals. Of course, you find the usual tigers, leopards, elephants, camels, and peacocks no self-respecting zoo can do without. Yet there's also much more, for no extra charge. There's the excellent Planetarium (closed Mon morning), and a Geological and Zoological Museum. The Aquarium, built in 1882 and renovated in the late 1990s, is superbly presented, particularly the sections on the Amazon River, coral reefs, and Amsterdam's own canals, with their fish population and burden of urban detritus. Finally, there's a children's farm, where kids help tend to the needs of resident sheep, goats, chickens, and cows. You can rest for a while and have a snack or lunch at Artis Restaurant. Artis gets 1.2 million visitors yearly.

Plantage Kerklaan 38–40. ✆ **020/523-3400.** Admission 13€ adults, 9€ children 4–11, children under 4 free. Daily 9am–5pm. Tram: 9, 14 to Plantage Middenlaan.

11 Organized Tours
CANAL TOUR-BOATS

Yes, you have to smile inanely for your boarding picture and sit through a thumbnail-sketch history in several different languages. If you are particularly unlucky (and on a boat with an open top), you'll get doused with an anarchic bucket of water while you glide under one of those romantic-looking bridges.

No matter. The canals are the best starting point to Amsterdam. Amsterdammers might scoff as they watch the fleets of glass-topped boats prowling around, but secretly they are proud of everything you will see. "I live here," you can almost hear them thinking. "All this is mine."

A typical canal tour-boat itinerary includes Centraal Station, the Harlemmersluis floodgates (used in the nightly flushing of the canals), the Cat Boat (a houseboat with a permanent population of more than 100 wayward felines), and both the narrowest building in the city and one of the largest houses still in private hands and in use as a single-family residence. Plus, you will see the official residence of the *burgomaster* (mayor), the "Golden Bend" of the Herengracht (traditionally the best address in the city), many picturesque bridges, including the famous Magere Brug (Skinny Bridge) over the Amstel, and the harbor.

Trips last approximately an hour and depart at regular intervals from *rondvaart* (excursion) piers in key locations around town. The majority of launches are docked along Damrak and Prins Hendrikkade near Centraal Station, on Rokin near Muntplein, and at Leidseplein. Tours leave every 15 to 30 minutes during the summer season (9am–9:30pm), every 45 minutes in winter (10am–4pm). A basic 1-hour tour is 8€ for adults, 6€ for children 4 to 12, and free for children under 4.

Operators of canal-boat tours are: **Amsterdam Canal Cruises** (✆ 020/626-5636); **Holland International** (✆ 020/622-7788); **Meijers Rondvaarten** (✆ 020/623-4208); **Rederij Boekel** (✆ 020/612-9905); **Rederij Hof van Holland** (✆ 020/623-7122); **Rederij Lovers** (✆ 020/530-1090)—despite its heart-shaped logo, Lovers is not necessarily for lovers only, but is named after the man who started the company; **Rederij Noord-Zuid** (✆ 020/679-1370); **Rederij P. Kooij** (✆ 020/623-3810); and **Rederij Plas** (✆ 020/624-5406). See "A Dinner Cruise," in chapter 5 and "More Evening Entertainment," in chapter 9 for information on after-dark tours.

WATER BIKES

A water bike is a boat you pedal with your feet. These craft seat two or four people and can be rented daily from 10am to 10pm in summer, and to 7pm at other times, from **Canal Bike** (✆ **020/626-5574**). Amsterdammers look down their tolerant noses at water bikers. On the other hand, tourists love the things. No prizes for guessing who has the most fun. Your water bike comes with a detailed map. It's great fun in sunny weather, and still doable when it rains and your boat is covered with a rain shield. In summer, you can even rent a water bike for evening rambles, when the canals are illuminated and your bike is kitted out with its own Chinese lantern.

The four Canal Bikes moorings are at Leidseplein (tram: 1, 2, 5, 6, 7, 10); Westerkerk, near the Anne Frankhuis (tram: 13, 14, 17); Stadhouderskade, beside the Rijksmuseum (tram: 6, 7, 10); and Toronto Bridge on Keizersgracht, near Leidsestraat (tram: 1, 2, 5). You can rent a water bike at one mooring and leave it at another. The canals can be busy with tour boats and other small craft, so go carefully, particularly when going under bridges. Rental is 7€ per person hourly for one or two people; 6€ per person hourly for three or four people. You need to leave a deposit of 50€. A booklet containing six route descriptions is 2€—see "Biking on the Water" for one that's free.

POWERBOATS

You can be the captain of your own boat and tour the canals aboard a six-seater launch with an environmentally friendly electric outboard. **Canal Motorboats**

Biking on the Water

A suggested tour by water bike: Start at the Canal Bikes mooring on Prinsengracht (at Westermarkt). Pedal south along Prinsengracht, past Lauriergracht, Looiersgracht, and Passeerdersgracht, maybe diverting into one or more of these quiet side canals if you fancy. At Leidsegracht, go straight ahead under the Leidsestraat bridge until you come to Spiegelgracht, where you turn right. Continue to the end, then left under the bridge into Lijnbaansgracht.

Turn right at the first corner into a narrow connecting canal that merges with Singelgracht in front of the Rijksmuseum. Go right along this canal, which is bordered by overhanging trees and the back gardens of waterside villas. You pass the Holland Casino Amsterdam, Leidseplein, and the American Hotel.

Keep going, past the Bellevue Theater and the De la Mar Theater, and turn right into Leidsegracht, which brings you back to Prinsengracht and the long home stretch back to Westermarkt.

(© 020/422-7007) rents open-top launches, which can go at 3½ knots on the canals, from boat docks on Oosterdokskade (tram: 1, 2, 4, 5, 9, 13, 16, 17, 24, 25), close to Centraal Station, beside the floating Chinese restaurant Sea Palace; and on Kloveniersburgwal at the Amstel River (tram: 4, 9, 14), opposite the Hôtel de l'Europe. Between April and October, the launches are available daily from 10am to dusk, or to 10pm. The rental is 18€ for the first hour, 15€ for the second hour, 10€ for the third, and 6€ for each subsequent hour. You need to show a passport or other ID and either leave a deposit of 75€ or sign an open credit card slip.

Salonboten **(saloon boats),** dating from the early 1900s, were used by doctors, lawyers, and other professionals who needed to move around town a lot and quickly. Some surviving launches have been lovingly restored and can be booked by groups of 6 to 12 people. For further information, contact **Oudhollandsche Vervoer Maatschappij** (© **020/612-9888**).

BY BIKE

You're going to look pretty conspicuous taking one of the guided tours offered by **Yellow Bike,** Nieuwezijds Kolk 29, off Nieuwezijds Voorburgwal (© **020/ 620-6940**). Why? Because you're going to be cycling on a yellow bike along with a dozen other people also on yellow bikes, that's why. In partial compensation, you have a close encounter with Amsterdam or the nearby countryside.

Two easy-ish, 6½-hour guided bike tours outside Amsterdam are offered by **Let's Go!** (© 020/600-1809). Just call the reservation number and leave your booking on the answering machine. One tour, 30km (19 miles), goes north to the IJsselmeer shore at Edam, Volendam, and Monnickendam; the other, 24km (15 miles), goes east to the castles, windmills, and fortifications of the Gooi and Vecht districts. Each tour is 25€; return ticket by train is not included.

BY BOAT

The **Historic Ferry** (© 0900/9292) plies a 2-hour furrow around the harbor and along the IJ from behind Centraal Station. It operates on Sunday from Easter to mid-October at noon, 2, and 4pm; tickets are 5€ for adults, 3€ for children.

Get closer to nature with **Wetlands Safari** (✆ **020/686-3445**), who will take you on boat tours of the watery landscapes and villages around the city. You can also board a flat-bottomed boat in the **Amsterdamse Bos (Amsterdam Woods)** on the southern edge of town.

BY TRAM

A **Tourist Tram,** an old-timer, does the sights on Sunday and public holidays from Easter to mid-September. It leaves from Prins Hendrikkade in front of Centraal Station; tickets are 5€ for adults, 3.75€ for seniors and children.

BY BUS

For many travelers, a quick bus tour is the best way to launch a sightseeing program in a strange city, and though Amsterdam offers its own unique alternative—a canal-boat ride—you might want to get your bearings on land as well. A 3-hour tour is 20€ to 30€; on most tours children 4 to 13 are charged half price. Major companies offering these and other motor-coach sightseeing trips are **The Best of Holland,** Damrak 34 (✆ **020/623-1539**); **Holland International Excursions,** Prins Hendrikkade 33A (✆ **020/625-3035**); **Keytours,** Dam 19 (✆ **020/624-7304**); and **Lindbergh Excursions,** Damrak 26 (✆ **020/622-2766**).

ON FOOT

Amsterdam Walking Tours (✆ **020/640-9072**) leads guided strolls through historic Amsterdam on Saturday and Sunday at 11am. If you'd rather guide yourself around, try **Audio Tourist,** Oude Spiegelstraat 9 (✆ **020/421-5580**), whose map-and-cassette packages allow you to "see Amsterdam by your ears." You can choose different tours lasting from 2 to 3 hours. Renting the cassette player, tape, and map is 8€ for adults, 4€ for children 13 and under, and seniors and holders of an Under-26 Pass get a 20% discount. Audio Tourist operates from April to September daily from 9am to 6pm; from October to March Tuesday through Sunday from 10am to 5pm.

BY AIRPLANE

A 30-minute bird's-eye view of Amsterdam, the tulip fields, the beaches, and nearby Volendam helps you fix the city firmly in its environs and presents quite graphically its all-important relationship with the sea. During summer months, **KLM Cityhopper,** KLM's domestic affiliate, offers Saturday- and Sunday-afternoon sightseeing flights from Schiphol Airport. For details, fares, and booking, call ✆ **020/474-7747.** If money is no object, you can also charter a chopper for an aerial tour of Amsterdam from **KLM Helikopters,** which operates big birds that usually do stuff like servicing North Sea oil rigs. For details, fares, and booking, call ✆ **020/474-7747.**

DIAMOND TOURS

Visitors to Amsterdam during the 1950s and 1960s, when the diamond business was booming, were able to go to the diamond-cutting factories of Amsterdam and take tours through their workrooms. Now you'll be lucky to see one lone polisher working at a small wheel set up in the back of a jewelry store or in the lobby of a factory building. Never mind, you still can get an idea of how a diamond is cut and polished. You need no special directions or instructions to find this sightseeing activity; you see signs all over town for diamond-cutting demonstrations. You're also on your own if you decide to buy.

A High-End Guide

"My guides are interesting people, not faceless tour operators," says René Dessing, a suave, bespectacled historian-turned-tour-operator. Dessing offers everything from architecture walks to painting classes on canal boats. His tailor-made tours aren't exactly cheap (the price depends on what you want to do), but his multilingual guides—trained art historians—can get you into private collections, the Royal Palace even when it's closed to the public, the Amsterdam School's Scheepvaarthuis (never open to the public), and plenty more places. Some clients wind up spending half their day in a cozy brown cafe. "The idea," says Dessing, "is to make new friends." Contact: **Artifex,** Herengracht 342, 1016 CG Amsterdam (© **020/620-8112**).

The major diamond factories and showrooms in Amsterdam are the **Amsterdam Diamond Center,** Rokin 1, just off the Dam (© 020/624-5787); **Coster Diamonds,** Paulus Potterstraat 2–6, near the Rijksmuseum (© 020/676-2222); **Gassan Diamonds,** Nieuwe Uilenburgerstraat 173–175 (© 020/622-5333); **Holshuijsen Stoeltie,** Wagenstraat 13–17 (© 020/623-7601); **Van Moppes Diamonds,** Albert Cuypstraat 2–6, at the daily street market (© 020/676-1242); and **Reuter Diamonds,** Kalverstraat 165 or Singel 526 (© 020/623-3500).

12 Staying Active

See also "Green Amsterdam," earlier in this chapter.

BIKING   South of the city is Amsterdamse Bos, where you can rent bikes (© **020/644-5473**) for touring the woodland's paths. Of course, you can always do as Amsterdammers do and explore all those city bridges and canals by bike (see "Bikes, Mopeds & More" under "Getting Around," in chapter 3, for rental information).

BOATING   From March 15 to October 15, you can go to Loosdrecht, outside Amsterdam, to rent sailing equipment at **Ottenhome** (© 035/582-3331). **Yacht Haven Robinson,** Dorpstraat 3, Landsmeer (© **020/482-1346**), rents rowing equipment. Canoes can be rented in the **Amsterdamse Bos,** south of the city, for use in the park only.

BUNGEE JUMPING   From **Bungy Jump** (© **020/419-6005**), from a jump point, with optional water-dip, on the IJ channel. Jump times are May and June Thursday through Sunday from noon to 9pm.

FISHING   Anglers should try the **Bosbaan** artificial pond in Amsterdamse Bos, south of the city. You can get a license there at Nikolaswetsantraat 10 (© **020/626-4988**), open Tuesday through Friday, or at any fishing supply store in the area.

GOLF   There are public golf courses in or near Amsterdam at the **Golf en Conference Center Amstelborgh,** Borchlandweg 6 (© **020/697-5000**); **Sloten,** Sloterweg 1045 (© **020/614-2402**); **Waterland Golf Course,**

Buikslotermeerdijk 141 (© **020/636-1010**); and **Spaarnwoude Golf Course,** Het Hogeland 2, Spaarnwoude (© **020/538-5599**). Call ahead for greens fees and tee times.

GYMS If don't want to neglect your exercise routine, there are several centers you can try, including **Fitness Aerobic Center Jansen,** Rokin 109–111 (© **020/626-9366**); **Garden Gym,** Jodenbreestraat 158 (© **020/626-8772**); and **A Bigger Splash,** Looiersgracht 26–30 (© **020/624-8404;** tram: 7, 10).

BOWLING If you find you just have to knock down a few pins, go to **Knijn Bowling,** Scheldeplein 3 (© **020/664-2211**).

HORSEBACK RIDING Riding, both indoor and outdoor, is offered at **Amsterdamse Manege,** Nieuwe Kalfjeslaan 25 (© **020/643-1342**); indoor riding only is available at **Nieuw Amstelland Manege,** Jan Tooropplantsoen 17 (© **020/643-2468**). Horses rented at **De Ruif Manege,** Sloterweg 675 (© **020/615-6667**), can be ridden in Amsterdamse Bos.

ICE SKATING All those Dutch paintings of people skating and sledding—not to mention the story of Hans Brinker and his silver skates—will surely get you thinking about skating on Amsterdam's ponds and canals (see "Blades on Ice," below). However, doing this won't be easy unless you're willing to shell out for a new pair of skates, since very few places rent them. One that does is **Jaap Eden Baan,** Radioweg 64 (© **020/694-9894**), where you can rent skates from November to February, and they even allow you to take them out of the rink. The Jaap Eden Baan's marvelous outdoor rink is popular in wintertime, but unless you're highly competent, watch out for the long lines of speed skaters practicing for the next Eleven Cities Race in Friesland.

IN-LINE SKATING Rent A Skate, Damstraat 21 (© **020/664-5091**), also has a rent shop for in-line skates in Vondelpark, at the Amstelveenseweg entrance (© **065/466-2262**). Why not strap your skates on for the regular **Friday Night Skate?** This attracts 3,000 skaters in the summer months. It begins at 8pm from the Filmmuseum in Vondelpark and takes a route of 15km (9 miles) through the city.

JOGGING The two main jogging areas are Vondelpark in the Center and Amsterdamse Bos on the southern edge of the city. You can also run along the Amstel River. If you choose to run along the canals, as many do, watch out for uneven cobbles, loose paving stones, and dog poop.

SAILING Sailboats and sailboards can be rented at **Duikelaars** on the Sloter-plas Lake, Sloterpark, Noordzijde 41 (© **020/613-8855**).

SALONS The **Body Tuning Clinic,** Jan Luykenstraat 40 (© **020/662-0909**), and **Vitalitae,** Nieuwezijds Voorburgwal 301 (© **020/624-4441**), will both take excellent care of the outer you.

SAUNA & MASSAGE Sauna Deco, Herengracht 115 (© **020/627-1773**), and **Oibibio Thermen,** Prins Hendrikkade 20–21 (© **020/553-9311**), are two places where, in Dutch style, you get down to the altogether in mixed facilities. At **Koan Float,** Herengracht 321 (© **020/625-4970**), you can float away the stress of a hard day's sightseeing.

TABLE TENNIS Ping-Pong to your heart's content at **Tafeltennis Centrum Amsterdam,** Keizersgracht 209 (© **020/624-5780**).

Blades on Ice

In winter, Amsterdammers watch the falling thermometer readings with the same focus as people in Aspen and Chamonix. When the temperature drops low enough for long enough, the canals become sparkling highways through the city. Skating on the canals of Amsterdam to the strains of classical music is a memorable experience. Little kiosks are set up on the ice to dispense heart-warming liqueurs. Go cautiously when skating under bridges, where the ice is usually thinner, and in general don't go anywhere the Dutch themselves don't. Few sounds can generate more adrenalin than a sudden crackling of ice when you're in the middle of a canal, but the Dutch seem to know instinctively if crepitation is cause for palpitation, just the natural rhythm of things, or time to light the afterburners and be gone.

TENNIS   You find indoor courts at **Frans Otten Stadion,** Stadionstraat 10 (✆ **020/662-8767**). For both indoor and outdoor courts, try **Gold Star,** Karel Lotsylaan 20 (✆ **020/644-5483**), and **Amstelpark Tenniscentre,** Koenenkade 8, Amsterdamse Bos (✆ **020/644-5436**), which has a total of 36 courts.

SQUASH   Squash courts can be found at **Squash City,** Ketelmakerstraat 6 (near Centraal Station; ✆ **020/626-7883**).

SWIMMING   Amsterdam's state-of-the-art swimming facility is **De Mirandabad,** De Mirandalaan 9 (✆ **020/642-8080**). This ultramodern complex features indoor and outdoor pools with wave machines, slides, and other amusements. **The Marnixbad,** Marnixplein 5 (✆ **020/625-4843**), is a glass-enclosed public pool. The **Zuiderbad,** Hobbemastraat 26 (✆ **020/679-2217**), dates from 1911. Other public pools are the **Floralparkbad,** Sneeuwbalweg 5 (✆ **020/636-8121**), and the **Sloterparkbad,** Slotermeerlaan 2 (✆ **020/611-4565**).

13 Spectator Sports

AMERICAN FOOTBALL   Yes, there's an American football league in Europe, and Amsterdam has its own franchise. The Amsterdam Admirals, complete with cheerleaders, is based at the Amsterdam ArenA (see "Soccer," below).

BASEBALL   Honk if you like baseball (the game is called *honkbal* in Holland). The Amsterdam Pirates aren't the greatest practitioners of the art, but they have their moments, as you can see at the **Sportpark,** Jan van Galenstraat 16 (✆ **020/684-8143**).

SOCCER   Soccer (called football in Europe) is absolutely the biggest game in Holland. Amsterdam's world-famous team, Ajax, is the best in Holland, and quite often the best in Europe as well. Ajax plays its home matches in a fabulous new stadium, the **Amsterdam ArenA,** ArenA Boulevard, Amsterdam Zuidoost (✆ **020/311-1333**).

7

Strolling & Biking in Amsterdam

he best way to discover Amsterdam is on foot. The first tour described here picks a way among the essential sights of the horseshoe of the city's 17th-century, Golden Age canals. Tours 2, 3, and 4 focus on the Old Center, the Jordaan, and Jewish Amsterdam, respectively.

Our fifth tour is no leisurely stroll, but a taste of that essential Amsterdam experience: biking. Bikes are a key part of the mechanism that makes Holland tick, and no trip to Amsterdam can be considered complete without some time spent in the saddle. This tour

whisks you out from the Center, along the Amstel River, to breathe fresh country air at the historic riverside village of Ouderkerk aan de Amstel.

Among Amsterdam's many enchantments is making your own discoveries by roaming wherever the fancy takes you. On each of my proposed itineraries you'll notice points of interest that aren't listed due to lack of space. It could be an unusually shaped gable, an offbeat little boutique, a gaily painted bike, a sunken canal boat, whatever. Be sure to keep your eyes wide open.

| WALKING TOUR 1 | THE GOLDEN AGE CANALS |

Start:	Herenmarkt (off Brouwersgracht).
Finish:	Amstel River.
Time:	3 hours to all day, depending on how long you linger in museums and stores along the way.
Best Times:	Begin in the morning.

The three 17th-century canals you explore on this tour—Herengracht (Gentlemen's Canal), Keizersgracht (Emperor's Canal), and Prinsengracht (Princes' Canal)—are the very heart of Golden Age Amsterdam, emblems of the city's wealth and pride in its heyday. Each one deserves at least a morning or afternoon to itself. Time being limited, we're going to combine them in one monumental effort; if you're not so rushed, by all means slice the tour up into two or three segments for a more leisurely experience.

You stroll along miles of tree-lined canals and pass innumerable old canal houses with gables in various styles (bell, step, neck, and variations), classical facades, warehouses converted to apartments, houseboats, bridges, museums, cafes, restaurants, boutiques, and offbeat stores. I'm only going to mention the most special sights and point out some insider tips along the way. This should leave you with plenty of space for making your own discoveries.

Walking Tour: The Golden Age Canals

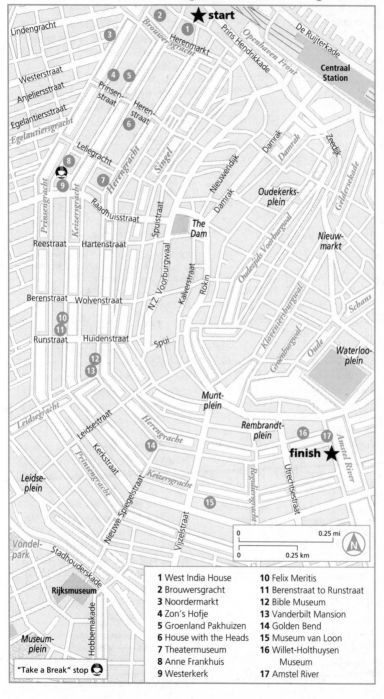

★ start

★ finish

1 West India House	10 Felix Meritis
2 Brouwersgracht	11 Berenstraat to Runstraat
3 Noordermarkt	12 Bible Museum
4 Zon's Hofje	13 Vanderbilt Mansion
5 Groenland Pakhuizen	14 Golden Bend
6 House with the Heads	15 Museum van Loon
7 Theatermuseum	16 Willet-Holthuysen
8 Anne Frankhuis	Museum
9 Westerkerk	17 Amstel River

"Take a Break" stop

The jump-off point, within easy walking distance of Centraal Station (tram: 1, 2, 4, 5, 9, 13, 16, 17, 24, 25), is at Herenmarkt, just off Brouwersgracht:

❶ West Indisch Huis (West India House)

This is the 17th-century headquarters of the Dutch West India Company that handled trade (including the slave trade) between Holland and the Americas and Africa. It later became the offices of a social-welfare organization, a Lutheran orphanage, and it now houses an educational institute (see "Historic Buildings & Monuments," in chapter 6).

Walk along tranquil, residential:

❷ Brouwersgracht (Brewers' Canal)

Humpback bridges, moored houseboats, and 17th- and 18th-century brewery *pakhuizen* (warehouses) that have been turned into apartments, combine to make this one of Amsterdam's most photogenic corners. Worth special attention on Brouwersgracht are nos. 204 and 206, "Het Kleine Groene Hert" (the Little Green Deer) and "Het Groote Groene Hert" (the Big Green Deer)—each has a gable crowned with a green-painted sculpture of a deer. Note two excellent brown cafes: Tabac, Brouwersgracht 101, and Papeneiland, Prinsengracht 2–4, for possible future reference.

On Prinsengracht, which in the 17th century was home to storekeepers and craftsmen, your first stop is:

❸ Noordermarkt

On Saturday from 10am to 3pm, this old market square hosts a Farmers' Market for "bio" (organic) products and a Bird Market. A popular flea market that overflows onto neighboring Westerstraat takes over on Monday from 7:30am to 1:30pm; clothes that were fashionable a decade and more ago are, for some reason, highly esteemed. Pause for a moment to admire the elaborate gables of the

houses at nos. 15–22, each one decorated with an agricultural image—a cow, a sheep, a chicken, and more—from the time when a livestock market was held here.

The Noorderkerk (North Church), the last masterpiece by Hendrick de Keyser, the guiding hand behind many of Amsterdam's historic churches, dominates the square. It's something of a rarity in this nominally Calvinist city, since it has a large and active congregation. A plaque on the facade recalls the February 1941 strike in protest at Nazi deportation of the city's Jewish population (see "Sights of Religious Significance," in chapter 6).

Continue along Prinsengracht to the bridge at Prinsenstraat, and cross over. A few steps back along the canal on this side is:

❹ Prinsengracht 159–171 (Zon's Hofje)

Here, you'll find a hidden almshouse surrounding a garden at the end of the passageway. You can walk discreetly (people live here) through the passageway to the garden, which has a carved plaque from a vanished clandestine church called Kleine Zon (Little Sun) that shows animals piling two-by-two into Noah's Ark.

Farther back along the canal, at nos. 89–133, is another former almshouse, Van Brienen's Hofje, from 1790 (also known as De Ster Hofje after the De Ster brewery that once occupied the site). Merchant Jan van Brienen supposedly built it in gratitude for his escape from a vault in which he had accidentally been locked. But I don't want you to have to backtrack too far, and besides, this one is usually closed, so unless you're something of a *hofje* enthusiast you can leave it alone.

Head down Prinsenstraat to Keizersgracht, named after the Austrian Emperor Maximilian, whose crown graces the summit of the Westerkerk's spire. A short detour to the left at this point brings you to the:

❺ Groenland Pakhuizen (Greenland Warehouses)

Built in 1621 to store whale oil, these are now chic apartments (nos. 40–44).

Cross the Keizersgracht bridge, noting the houseboats tied up on either side, to Herenstraat, and go right on Keizersgracht, to the:

❻ Huis met de Hoofden (House with the Heads)

At no. 123, the heads in question on the facade from 1622 by Hendrick de Keyser represent, from left to right, Apollo, Ceres, Mars, Athena, Bacchus, and Diana.

Turn left along the pretty Leliegracht side canal, then, right onto Herengracht, the ultimate Amsterdam addresses for flourishing bankers and merchants in the 17th century. Pause for a moment at the:

❼ Theatermuseum

This graceful house at Herengracht 168 was built in 1638 for Michiel Pauw, who established a short-lived trading colony in America at Hoboken, facing Nieuw Amsterdam (New York City), and named it Pavonia after his august self. Note the classical neck gable, the first example of this style in the city. The museum extends into the flamboyant Bartolotti House at nos. 170–172, built in 1617 for Guillielmo Bartolotti, who began life as homey old Willem van den Heuvel and switched to the fancy moniker after he made his bundle in brewing and banking (see "More Museums & Galleries," in chapter 6).

Backtrack to Leliegracht, noting on the corner, at Keizersgracht 176, a rare Amsterdam Art Nouveau house (1905), designed by Gerrit van Arkel, which houses Greenpeace International headquarters. Go up onto Prinsengrachtand and take a left, to the:

❽ Anne Frankhuis

This house at Prinsengracht 263 is where the young Jewish girl Anne Frank (1929–45) hid from the Nazis and wrote her imperishable diary. The earlier you get to this house the better, because the line to get in grows as the day progresses (see "The Big Four," in chapter 6).

Note the cafe/restaurant De Prins at Prinsengracht 124 on the opposite bank; for reasons of time I'm not proposing it for a break on this tour, but it is my Best Value restaurant recommendation and I strongly suggest you keep it in mind for a leisurely meal at another time (see "Along the Canal Belt," in chapter 5).

At this point, however, you may need a quick break for lunch, so pop into:

TAKE A BREAK
Rum Runners, Prinsengracht 277 (☎ 020/627-4079), a Caribbean restaurant where they serve a stiff margarita and a mean guacamole, along with other laid-back drinks and meals (see "Along the Canal Belt," in chapter 5).

Afterward, with miles and miles to go before you sleep, you may be tempted to stow away on a pedal bike from the Canal Bikes dock outside Rum Runners, but if you're staying with the program, continue a few steps to Westermarkt and its:

❾ Westerkerk

The Dutch Renaissance church by Hendrick de Keyser was begun in 1620. Hendrick's son Pieter took over after his father's death, and the church was opened in 1631 (see "Sights of Religious Significance," in chapter 6). Should you be passing between June and mid-September, from Wednesday to Saturday, you can climb to near the summit of the Westertoren, 85m (277 ft.) high, nicknamed "Lange Jan" (Long John).

Westermarkt 6 is the house where the French philosopher René Descartes lived in 1634, writing his *Treatise on the Passions of the Soul.* Descartes evidently thought he was in need of some additional passion—therefore he was—so he had an affair with his maid, which produced a child whose reality could scarcely be doubted. Also on Westermarkt are a somber bronze sculpture of Anne Frank and the pink marble triangles of the Homomonument, dedicated to persecuted gays and lesbians.

Cross over Westermarkt to Rozengracht. A short detour to the right on this busy thoroughfare would take you to the fanciful gift store Blue Gold Fish at no. 17 (see "Crafts & Curios," in chapter 8). Otherwise, continue along Prinsengracht to Reestraat, where you turn left. At Keizersgracht go right, across Berenstraat, to Keizersgracht 324:

⑩ Felix Meritis

This structure was built in 1788 by Jacob Otten Husly as the headquarters of a Calvinist philosophical society. The name (which was the group's motto) means "Happiness Through Merit," and they invited such luminaries as Czar Alexander I and Napoléon to this Palladian setting, with Corinthian columns and triangular pediment, to experience the consolations of this philosophy. The building was later the home of the Dutch Communist Party, and now hosts avant-garde theater and dance performances (see "Other Venues," in chapter 9).

On this stretch of Keizersgracht, from Berenstraat to Runstraat, instead of standing directly in front of buildings of interest, craning your neck skyward to eyeball the detail, walk along the near bank of the canal (with even-numbered houses) and look across the water to the other side, so that you can view things in panorama (in summer, leaves on elm trees along the canal screen some facades, and you might prefer to cross over for a closer look).

⑪ Berenstraat to Runstraat

The third building along from Wolvenstraat (no. 313), an office block from 1914, is almost modern in Keizersgracht-time.

Two houses along (no. 317), is the stately canalside home that belonged to Christoffel Brants, who counted Peter the Great among his acquaintances. A story goes that Peter sailed

into Amsterdam in 1716, planning to stay a night here. The Czar of All the Russias got royally drunk, kept the mayor waiting at a reception in his honor, and then removed to the Russian ambassador's residence at Herengracht 527 to sleep off his hangover.

Next door (no. 319), is a work by Philips Vingboons from 1639, as you can tell from the Latin numerals MDCXXXIX inscribed on the facade. You can compare this ornate neoclassical facade to the Theatermuseum building by the same architect, at Herengracht 168 (see above).

Note how narrow is the facade of the seventh building before Huidenstraat (no. 345A), and run your eyes over the trio of graceful neck gables on the last three houses (nos. 353–357).

At Runstraat, cross over to Huidenstraat and go along it to Herengracht. Turn right to Herengracht 366–368:

⑫ Bijbels Museum (Biblical Museum)

One of a group of four 1660s houses (nos. 364–370) with delicate neck gables, this museum was built by Philips Vingboons for timber merchant Jacob Cromhout. These houses are known as the "Father, Mother, and Twins." The museum, naturally enough, features Bibles and things biblical, but its canal house setting and painted ceilings from 1717 by Jacob de Wit are at least as interesting (see "More Museums & Galleries," in chapter 6).

Continue a few doors farther along Herengracht, to nos. 380–382:

⑬ The Vanderbilt Mansion

Well, it's not the Fifth Avenue mansion built for U.S. tycoon William H. Vanderbilt in New York, but a replica (and, as the original no longer exists, the only example) constructed in 1889 for Dutch tobacco mogul Jacob Nienhuijs. It now houses the Netherlands Institute for War Documentation. A few doors along, look for a pranksterish sequence: On the wall of Herengracht 395, a stone cat stalks its prey—a carved mouse on the facade of the next house.

Cross elegant Leidsegracht, dug in 1664 for barge traffic to and from Leiden, and cross busy Leidsestraat to the:

⓮ Gouden Bocht (Golden Bend)

You can trace the development of the rich folk's wealth and tastes as you progress up the house numbers on Herengracht, and this section, so named because of its opulent palaces, is the top of the heap. Built with old money around the 1670s, in the fading afterglow of the Golden Age, when French-influenced neoclassicism was all the rage, they are on double lots with double steps and central entrances. Compare the sober baroque facades here with the exuberant gabled houses from half a century earlier, back along the canal.

Turn right onto Nieuwe Spiegelstraat, a street lined with expensive antiques stores (at its end you can see the Rijksmuseum). Go left on the far bank of Keizersgracht to the:

⓯ Museum Van Loon

This museum (at no. 672) gives you a rare glimpse behind the gables at a patrician house of the post-Golden Age (see "More Museums & Galleries," in chapter 6).

Cross Reguliersgracht and return to Herengracht, passing through neat little Thorbeckeplein, and go right, across Utrechtsestraat,

which is a cornucopia of good restaurants and variegated stores, to Herengracht 605:

⓰ Museum Willet-Holthuysen

A patrician canal house dating from 1687, this museum is richly decorated in Louis XIV style. The table, under a big chandelier in the dining salon, is set for a meal being served more than 300 years late (see "More Museums & Galleries," in chapter 6).

Stroll to the end of Herengracht and finish your trek at the:

⓱ Amstel River

At this point, the river is thick with houseboats and canal barges. To your left is the refurbished Blauwbrug (Blue Bridge) over the river, built in 1884 on the lines of Paris's Pont Alexandre III; to your right is the famous Magere Brug (Skinny Bridge) double drawbridge.

Walking the short distance along the river to Waterlooplein, or backtracking to Utrechtsestraat, puts you on the tram net for return to your hotel. Maybe you're footsore and hungry, though, and want to eat *right now*. If the weather is fine, you can do no better than to hobble a short distance to Prinsengracht, to:

WINDING DOWN
Moko, Amstelveld 12 (☏ 020/626-1199), which has great world cuisine and a breezy sidewalk terrace (see "Along the Canal Belt," in chapter 5).

WALKING TOUR 2   **THE OLD CENTER**

Start:	The Dam.
Finish:	Prins Hendrikkade, close to Centraal Station.
Time:	2½ to 4 hours, or more, depending on how long you spend in museums, attractions, cafes, and stores (and on perusing the windows in the Red Light District).
Best Times:	If you want to visit one or more of the museums or other attractions, remember that most of them open at 10am. The morning is a good time to do the section through the Red Light District, because by then most of its bizarre night folks have crashed out for the day.

This tour takes you past some of the main city-center points of interest in the Nieuwe Zijde (New Side). It sidesteps into the Oude Zijde (Old Side), the oldest part of town, the first part of which, around the university, is a place of tranquil canals, and then weaves through the Red Light District. You might be surprised to discover that this sex-for-sale zone occupies a handsome area of 16th-century canals and gabled houses and that "ordinary" people still live here and go on the with the daily business of life—as you'll observe if you take your eyes for a moment off the barely-clad women behind the red-lit windows. I don't recommend you do the Red Light section after dark; the district is seedier and more sinister by then, and while it has its own peculiar fascination is no longer a fitting segment of a casual stroll through town.

The starting point, reached by tram 4, 9, 14, 16, 17, 24, or 25, is:

❶ The Dam
You'll look in vain for any sign of a dam on the Dam, but the city's main square is the likely site of the original dam built around 1270 on the Amstel River, that allowed Amsterdam to begin the growth trajectory that took it from backwater village to world-class watering-hole. A castle of the lords of Amstel stood here in those early days and ever since the Dam has been Amsterdam's civic heart. If that isn't enough, should you plan on feeding the city's pigeons during your visit, here's the place to do it.

You should make a leisurely circuit of the cobblestone square. Dominating the western side is the neoclassical:

❷ Koninklijk Paleis (Royal Palace)
This structure was built between 1648 and 1655 as the Stadhuis (Town Hall) and was later chosen to be an official residence of the royal family (see "Historic Buildings & Monuments," in chapter 6). A symbolic sculpture on the rooftop depicts Atlas shouldering the globe.

Cross over Mozes en Aäronstraat to the:

❸ Nieuwe Kerk (New Church)
This is the national church, where since 1814 all kings and queens of the Netherlands have been inaugurated. (Dutch monarchs are not crowned.) Built between the late 15th and the mid–17th centuries in the elaborate late-Gothic style, it often hosts temporary exhibits expensive enough to maybe make you think twice about going inside (see "Sights of Religious Significance," in chapter 6).

Outside the church, take narrow Eggertstraat at the side of the Nieuwe Cafe. On adjoining Gravenstraat, at no. 18, is:

❹ De Drie Fleschjes
A character-rich *proeflokaal* (tasting house) from 1650, this is where merchants sampled liqueurs and spirits and which now specializes in *jenever* (Dutch gin). Among a warren of tiny alleyways around here, Blaeustraat, behind a locked gate beside De Drie Fleschjes, recalls the store at nearby Damrak 46 where the 17th-century mapmaker Johannes Blaeu sold his superb world atlases.

Continue on Gravenstraat around the outer wall of the Nieuwe Kerk to Nieuwezijds Voorburgwal, from where you can look across to the Magna Plaza mall (see "Shopping A to Z," in chapter 8), in the old main Post Office building from 1908, known as De Perenberg (Pear Mountain) because of the pear-shaped decorations on its towers. You should leave shopping to another time and instead go along the front of the Nieuwe Kerk on Mozes en Aäronstraat to Damrak, casting a glance up at the painted, 15th-century wall sculpture of Sinter Claes (St. Nicholas), the city's patron, on the building just before the corner at Damrak.

Walking Tour: The Old Center

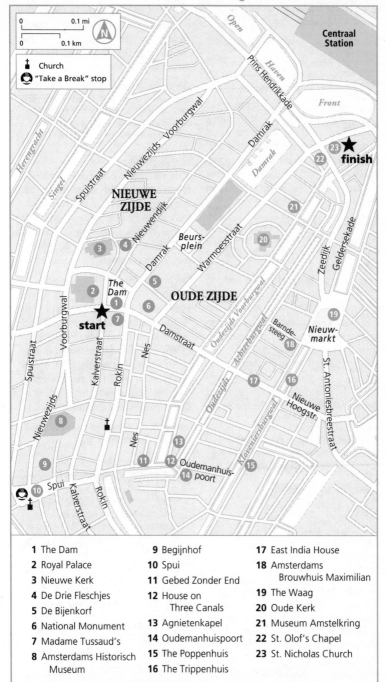

Church

"Take a Break" stop

Centraal Station

NIEUWE ZIJDE

OUDE ZIJDE

start

finish

Nieuw-markt

Beurs-plein

The Dam

Oudemanhuis-poort

1 The Dam
2 Royal Palace
3 Nieuwe Kerk
4 De Drie Fleschjes
5 De Bijenkorf
6 National Monument
7 Madame Tussaud's
8 Amsterdams Historisch Museum

9 Begijnhof
10 Spui
11 Gebed Zonder End
12 House on Three Canals
13 Agnietenkapel
14 Oudemanhuispoort
15 The Poppenhuis
16 The Trippenhuis

17 East India House
18 Amsterdams Brouwhuis Maximilian
19 The Waag
20 Oude Kerk
21 Museum Amstelkring
22 St. Olof's Chapel
23 St. Nicholas Church

Cross over busy Damrak (watch out for the trams), to Amsterdam's answer to Bloomingdale's:

❺ De Bijenkorf (The Beehive)

This is a department store from 1915 (see "Shopping A to Z," in chapter 8). In front of you is the magnificent Grand Hotel Krasnapolsky (the "Kras"). A short stroll along Damstraat at the side of the hotel would bring you right into the Red Light District—but we're not going there (not yet!). Instead, continue with this clockwise circuit of the Dam by crossing over to the:

❻ Nationaal Monument

Built in 1956 to honor the dead from World War II, this 22m (72-ft.) obelisk by J. J. P. Oud is embedded with three sculptures by J. W. Rädeler: *War*, symbolized by four male figures; *Peace*, represented by a woman and child; and *Resistance*, signified by two men with howling dogs, all flanked by two stone lions that symbolize the Netherlands. The monument is the focus of a memorial ceremony every May 4, when the Queen places a wreath on the spot. For the rest of the year it's a hangout for teens.

From here cross over to the Amsterdam Diamond Center on the corner of Rokin and go across busy Rokin (watch out for the trams) to:

❼ Madame Tussaud's

This is Amsterdam's answer to, well, to Madame Tussaud's—containing characters with a peculiarly Dutch waxen stare (see "More Attractions," in chapter 6).

Continue to Kalverstraat, and go left on this bustling, pedestrians-only shopping street lined with department stores, cheap-'n'-cheerful stores, and boutiques, and right on Sint-Luciënsteeg to the fascinating:

❽ Amsterdams Historisch Museum

A porch from 1592 that used to be the entrance to the city orphanage is now the museum entrance. The outer courtyard was for the boys and to the left are cupboards where they stored their tools. The inner courtyard was for the girls (see "More Museums & Galleries," in chapter 6).

Exit the museum through the Schuttersgalerij, a covered arcade lined with group portraits of 16th- and 17th-century militia companies, and then on Gedempte Begijnensloot to the entrance, on the right, to the:

❾ Begijnhof

This building is where devout women lived from the 14th century. No. 34, the oldest house in Amsterdam, was built in 1475 and is one of only two timber houses remaining in the city (see "Historic Buildings & Monuments," in chapter 6).

Pass between nos. 37 and 38 into:

❿ Spui

Here, you'll find a square that's both elegant and animated. At its south end is a statue of a small boy, *Het Lieverdje* (The Little Darling), supposed to represent a typical Amsterdam kid. Across the street, at no. 21, is the Maagdenhuis, the main downtown building of the University of Amsterdam.

After all that walking, you're probably ready to go up onto Spuistraat, to:

TAKE A BREAK
Café Luxembourg, Spuistraat 22–24 (℃ 020/620-6264), which the *New York Times* considers "one of the world's great cafes," for drinks and one of their renowned sandwiches or snacks (see "In the Old Center," in chapter 5).

Walk to the end of Spui, to Rokin, and cross over, past a statue of Queen Wilhelmina, a canal tour-boat dock, and the Allard Pierson Museum's sparse collection of archaeological treasures (see "More Museums & Galleries," in chapter 6). Go straight ahead on Lange Brugsteeg to Grimburgwal, in the district known as *De Wallen* (The Walls). The first street on the left, Nes, is lined with alternative theaters. You keep straight ahead, though, to:

⑪ Gebed Zonder End (Prayer Without End)

Essentially, this is an alleyway, the name of which comes from the convents that used to be here. It's said you could always hear the murmur of prayers from behind the walls.

Stay on Grimburgwal across Oudezijds Voorburgwal and Oudezijds Achterburgwal. Between these two canals is the:

⑫ Huis op de Drie Grachten (House on the Three Canals)

This is a handsome but over-restored Dutch Renaissance house from 1609.

Go a short way along the right bank of Oudezijds Voorburgwal canal to the:

⑬ Agnietenkapel

You may recognize the building at no. 231 by its elaborate ornamental gateway from 1571. This was the chapel of the St Agnes Convent until the Protestant takeover of Amsterdam. It later formed part of the Athenaeum Illustre, the city's first university, and now houses the university museum, which is not very interesting unless there's a special exhibit.

Return to the House on the Three Canals and cross the bridge to the far side of Oudezijds Achterburgwal, where you pass the Gasthuis, once a hospital and now part of the University of Amsterdam campus.

Turn right into:

⑭ Oudemanhuispoort

You'll find a dimly lit arcade that hosts a secondhand book market popular with students. Midway along, on the left, a doorway leads to a courtyard garden with a statue of Minerva. At the far end of the arcade, above the exterior doorway, is *The Liberality,* a sculpture of a seated female figure with three objects: a cornucopia (horn of plenty), symbolizing abundance; a book, symbolizing wisdom; and an oil lamp, symbolizing enlightenment. An old man and an old woman at her side represent old age and poverty. The statues were created in 1785 by city sculptor A. Ziesenis.

Turn right on Kloveniersburgwal, cross over the canal at the next bridge, and go left on the far bank of the canal, to Kloveniersburgwal 95:

⑮ The Poppenhuis

This lovely classical mansion from 1642 by Philips Vingboons was built for Joan Poppen, a dissolute grandson and heir to a rich German merchant. The youth hostel next door at no. 97 was originally a home for retired sea captains.

Continue on Kloveniersburgwal—behind the buildings to your right front as you cross Raamstraat, you'll see the tip of the Zuiderkerk spire—to Kloveniersburgwal 29:

⑯ The Trippenhuis

This house was built between 1660 and 1664 by Philips Vingboons for the Trip brothers, who were arms dealers, which accounts for the martial images and emblems dotted about the house. Originally, there were two houses behind a single classical facade, but the two have since been joined. It now houses the Royal Netherlands Academy of Science.

Backtrack to the canal bridge and cross over to Oude Hoogstraat and the:

⑰ Oost Indisch Huis (East India House)

Enter this 1606 building via a courtyard on the left side of the street. Once the headquarters of the Verenigde Oostindische Compagnie (V.O.C.), the United East India Company, the house now belongs to the University of Amsterdam (see "Historic Buildings & Monuments," in chapter 6). At Oude Hoogstraat 22, is Amsterdam's narrowest house, just 2.02m (6⅔ ft.) wide.

Back on Klovierniersburgwal, go left. At no. 26 is the Klein Trippenhuis, the narrow house of the Trip brothers' coachman (see "The Smallest Houses," in chapter 6), which now houses the Webers avant-garde fashion

store. Note a few doors along, at nos. 10–12,
the drugstore Jacob Hooy & Co., which has
been dispensing medicinal relief since 1743.
A little further along, at nos. 6–8, is the:

**⓲ Amsterdams Brouwhuis
Maximiliaan**

This is the city's smallest brewery, in a
surviving part of the 16th-century
Bethaniënklooster (Bethaniën Convent). It produces 10 different beers
and serves them from copper vats. The
nuns who once brewed their own beer
here have long since departed but
their beer-making tradition has
returned in the shape of this brewery
with a rustic-chic, wood-floored bar
and restaurant attached.

In the center of Nieuwmarkt, the large, open
square dead ahead, is:

⓳ De Waag (Weigh House)

This house was once one of the city's
medieval gates, and later the Weigh
House and guild offices (see "Historic
Buildings & Monuments," in chapter
6). It now houses a multimedia center
and a fashionable cafe-restaurant, In
de Waag (see "In the Old Center," in
chapter 5).

Take a turn around bustling Nieuwmarkt, the center of Amsterdam's
diminutive Chinatown ("Chinaham-
let" might be a better description) and
site of a Sunday antiques market in
summertime. Now, we're going to
head into the Red Light District. If
you don't want to do this, go instead
along Zeedijk at the northwest corner
of Nieuwmarkt and I'll pick you up
again further along that street. If you
have no objection to viewing the Red
Light District in all its tacky glory, take
Monnickenstraat to Oudezijds Achterburgwal and turn right, past windows
that frame prostitutes waiting for customers, or have closed curtains to sig-
nify that a deal has been done, to the
next bridge. Then, go through narrow
Oude Kennissteeg directly ahead to
Oudezijds Voorburgwal. Cross over
this canal, and to your right is the:

⓴ Oude Kerk

This was the city's first great Gothic
church. Rembrandt's wife Saskia is
buried within (see "Sights of Religious
Significance," in chapter 6). Nowadays, the pretty little gabled
almshouses around the church have
red-fringed windows through which
you can see scantily dressed hookers.

Go north on Oudezijds Voorburgwal to no. 40:

㉑ Museum Amstelkring

Here, you can visit a hidden Catholic
church in a superb example of a 17th-
century patrician canal house (see
"Sights of Religious Significance," in
chapter 6).

At the end of Oudezijds Voorburgwal, turn
right on Sint-Olofssteeg to Zeedijk. (Welcome back to anyone who passed on the
Red Light District; as compensation, you'll
surely have noticed the magnificent Bud-
dhist Fo Guang Shan He Hua Temple at Zeedijk 106–116 as you came along the street.)
Go left, to:

**㉒ Sint-Olofskapel (Saint Olof's
Chapel), at Zeedijk, 2A**

The fishermen's dog that in some legends of the city's foundation marked
the spot where Amsterdam began by
throwing up, is said to have done the
deed on the site of Saint Olof's, which
the fishermen supposedly founded in
gratitude for their escape. But the
chapel was built around 1425 and
Amsterdam dates from the end of the
12th century. You can sometimes
enter the church, which was restored
during the 1990s and re-opened as a
congress center, via a tunnel under
Zeedijk from the Golden Tulip Barbizon Palace Hotel (see below).

From here, you continue past two great
Amsterdam taverns: Het Elfde Gebod at
Zeedijk 5, which stocks 50 different kinds of
beer, and the traditional bar 't Aepje at
Zeedijk 1, in one of Amsterdam's two surviv-
ing timber houses (the other is in the Begijn-
hof, see above), from 1550. You emerge on
Prins Hendrikkade beside:

㉓ Sint-Nicolaaskerk (St. Nicholas Church), at no. 73

Opened in 1888 and restored in 2000, the city's main Catholic church has twin towers and a high, domed cupola. Inside, bronze reliefs illustrate themes from the Miracle of Amsterdam in 1345: Pilgrims on the Miracle Procession and Habsburg Emperor Maximilian, cured of a malady after a visit to the Sacrament Chapel, handing Amsterdam the imperial crown.

From here, you can get to Centraal Station just by crossing over busy Prins Hendrikkade. But before doing so, maybe a break is in order next door, at:

WINDING DOWN
Hudson's Café, in the Golden Tulip Hotel Inntel Amsterdam-Centre (see "In the Old Center," in chapter 4), Prins Hendrikkade 59–72 (✆ **020/556-4564**), a tony watering hole that serves light food and drinks.

WALKING TOUR 3   THE JORDAAN

Start:	Brouwersgracht.
Finish:	Noordermarkt.
Time:	Allow between 1½ and 2 hours.
Best Times:	Anytime, but if you want to visit one of the Jordaan's lively markets, go either on a Monday morning or on Saturday. On Monday there's a general market at Noordermarkt and along Westerstraat where you find, among other items, fabrics and secondhand clothing. On Saturday, Noordermarkt hosts a bird market and a farmer's market that has organically grown produce.

There's little in the way of "attractions" in the old working-class district called the Jordaan, but the area has a charm all its own. The neighborhood was originally built for artists, craftsmen, and tradesmen, and the old character still remains, though gentrification has left its mark.

Take the *Opstapper* bus along Prinsengracht (see "Getting Around," in chapter 3), or walk to the starting point, on:

① Brouwersgracht

A walk along this houseboat-lined canal will take you past the statue of writer Theo Thijssen (1879–1943).

Walk northwest along the canal to:

② Palmgracht

The house at nos. 28–30 hides a small courtyard behind its green door. The turnip on the gable stone is a pun on the name of a former owner, who was called "Raep," which means (you guessed it) turnip. Go left on Palmdwarsstraat, which leads to Tweede Goudsbloemdwarsstraat and Lindengracht.

Turn right and take the first street on the left, Tweede Lindendwarsstraat, to:

③ Karthuizerplantsoen

Nothing is left of the Carthusian monastery that once occupied this corner and extended toward Lijnbaansgracht. A children's playground now marks the spot where the monastery's cemetery stood. At Karthuizerstraat 11–19 is a row of neck-gabled houses from 1731, named after the four seasons: Lente, Zomer, Herfst, and Winter. Farther down this street, at nos. 69–191, is the Huiszitten Weduwenhof, a peaceful courtyard surrounded by houses that were once the homes of poor widows and are now occupied by students.

Go left on Tichelstraat, cross Westerstraat, which was once a broad canal, and continue along a string of *dwarsstraten* (side streets), Tweede Anjeliersdwarsstraat, Tweede Tuindwarsstraat, and Tweede Egelantiersdwarsstraat—it may take you longer to pronounce the names of these lively little streets, lined with cafes, restaurants, offbeat stores and boutiques, than to walk through them—to:

❹ Egelantiersgracht

Here is a quiet canal with interesting 17th- and 18th-century houses—on the way you'll see the tall spire of the Westerkerk (West Church), whose carillon breaks into cheerful song at every opportunity (see "Sights of Religious Significance," in chapter 6). There's a trio of simple bell gables at nos. 61–65, one of which has a falcon carved on the gable stone. If the door is open, you can take a peek into the Andrieshofje at nos. 107–145. A corridor decorated with blue and white tiles leads up to a small courtyard with a beautiful garden.

Retrace your steps, turn right on Tweede Leliedwarsstraat, and continue to:

❺ Bloemgracht

Along the grandest of the Jordaan canals, these three step-gabled houses at nos. 87–91 are gems. Their carved gable stones, from 1642, represent a townsman, a countryman, and a seaman. Walk back toward Prinsengracht, where again you see facing you the magnificent Westerkerk tower. This church is a symbol of the Jordaan. Just as London's Cockneys are not real Cockneys unless they were born "within the sound of Bow Bells," so Amsterdam's Jordaanees are not genuine Jordaanees unless they were born within earshot of the Westerkerk's carillon.

Turn left and walk to:

❻ Egelantiersgracht

A hardware store on this corner, at nos. 2–6, is an example of Amsterdam

School architecture from 1927. Its intricate brickwork and cast-iron ornaments were influenced by Art Deco. To the left of the store, a step-gabled house from the 1730s is decorated with sandstone ornaments.

Egelantiersgracht is a particularly good place to:

TAKE A BREAK
Though there are plenty of cafes in the Jordaan where you can rest your legs and quench your walker's thirst, the best terrace is at **Café 't Smalle,** Egelantiersgracht 12 (✆ **020/623-9617**), a *gezellig* brown cafe where the air is thick with cigar smoke, jenever vapor, and lively conversation. The place is usually packed, but you can escape the crush on the splendid waterside terrace, a perfect place to watch cyclists and cars rushing past while resting your legs on the terrace railing. The cafe serves snacks like *bitterballen* and homemade soups.

When you've finished your break, turn right off of Egelantiersgracht onto another sequence of side streets to Westerstraat:

❼ Eerste Egelantiersdwarsstraat, Eerste Tuindwarsstraat, and Eerste Anjeliersdwarsstraat

(By this time, you should be better able to deal with the length of the names, if not their pronunciation.) On the way, between Egelantiersstraat and Tuinstraat, a passage leads to the Claes Claesz Hofje (the entrance is next to a solid brick wall on the right side of Egelantiersdwarsstraat): two minuscule courtyards surrounded by even more minuscule apartments. Turn right on Westerstraat and walk toward Noordermarkt (see stop 3 in Walking Tour 1).

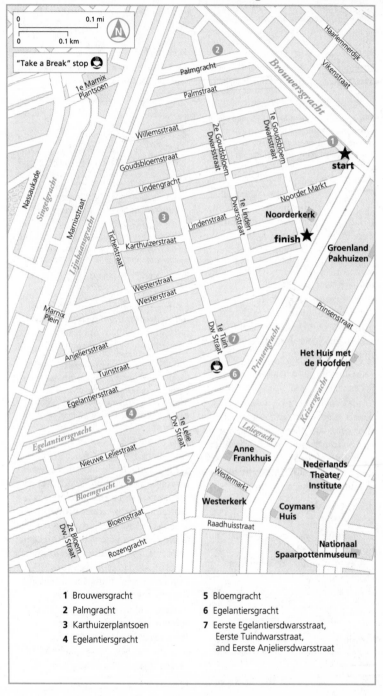

0.1 mi
0
0.1 km
0

"Take a Break" stop

start

finish

1e Marnix Plantsoen

Haarlemmerdijk

Vikenstraat

Palmgracht

Palmstraat

Brouwersgracht

Willemsstraat

2e Goudsbloem Dwarsstraat

1e Goudsbloem Dwarsstraat

Goudsbloemstraat

Lindengracht

Nassaukade

Singelgracht

Lijnbaansgracht

Marnixstraat

Karthuizerstraat

Tichelstraat

Lindenstraat

1e Linden Dwarsstraat

Noorder Markt

Noorderkerk

Groenland Pakhuizen

Westerstraat

Westerstraat

Marnix Plein

Anjeliersstraat

Tuinstraat

Egelantiersstraat

1e Tuin Dw Straat

Prinsengracht

Het Huis met de Hoofden

Prinsenstraat

Keizersgracht

Egelantiersgracht

1e Lelie Dw Straat

Nieuwe Leliestraat

Bloemgracht

Leliegracht

Anne Frankhuis

Nederlands Theater Institute

2e Bloem Dw Straat

Bloemstraat

Westermarkt

Westerkerk

Coymans Huis

Raadhuisstraat

Rozengracht

Nationaal Spaarpottenmuseum

1 Brouwersgracht
2 Palmgracht
3 Karthuizerplantsoen
4 Egelantiersgracht

5 Bloemgracht
6 Egelantiersgracht
7 Eerste Egelantiersdwarsstraat,
  Eerste Tuindwarsstraat,
  and Eerste Anjeliersdwarsstraat

WALKING TOUR 4 · THE JEWISH QUARTER

Start: Waterlooplein.

Finish: *The Dockworker,* on Jonas Daniël Meijerplein.

Time: Allow between 1½ and 3 hours, not including museum and rest stops.

Best Times: From 10am to 5pm, when the Waterlooplein flea market is open.

This area has changed almost beyond recognition since World War II, but there remain mementos and memorials of Amsterdam's once-thriving Jewish community. You can go by Metro or on tram nos. 9 or 14 to Waterlooplein, where you can enjoy the:

❶ Waterlooplein Flea Market

If you like flea-market shopping, beware: You may need to continue this tour tomorrow. In the middle of the square are the modern Muziektheater and the Amsterdam Town Hall.

Also on Waterlooplein is the:

❷ Mozes and Aäron Church

This started out as a secret church for Catholics who were forbidden to worship in public when the Calvinists rose to power in the 16th century.

Continue to the end of the street, then go left on:

❸ Jodenbreestraat

This was once the center of Jewish life in Amsterdam. Now it's mostly modern buildings, and unfortunately the right side of the street was knocked down in 1965, destroying any distinctive character that was left.

At nos. 4–6 is the:

❹ Museum Het Rembrandthuis

Rembrandt was not Jewish, but because he lived at this house (see "More Museums & Galleries," in chapter 6) in what was then a primarily Jewish neighborhood, he often painted portraits of his Jewish friends and neighbors.

Keeping the water to your right, walk down to the bridge that leads to Staalstraat, and cross over to:

TAKE A BREAK

Puccini, Staalstraat 17 (**☎ 020/427-8341**), a delightful place to stop for coffee and homemade desserts (fruit pies, cakes, and luscious pastries), which you can watch them prepare before your very eyes.

Go back over the bridge and turn right, to the:

❺ Jewish Resistance Fighters Memorial

Here, you'll find the black marble monument to those Jews who tried to resist or escape Nazi oppression and to the people who helped them.

Turn left at the monument—the Grand Café Dantzig (see below) is to your left and the Amstel River to your right—and walk toward the Blauwbrug (Blue Bridge), dead ahead. Just before the bridge, look for the outline of:

❻ Megadlei Yethomin

Starting in 1836, this was an orphanage for German and Eastern European Jewish boys. During World War II, the boys were taken to Sobibor concentration camp. After the war, the orphanage reopened, this time as a home for boys who wanted to get to Israel; it successfully placed many orphans in Israel before closing in 1955. Only the outline of the building remains today, as a memorial to the orphans and the caretaker who died in Sobibor; the rest was demolished in 1977 to make way for the Metro and later for the new Town Hall and the Muziektheater.

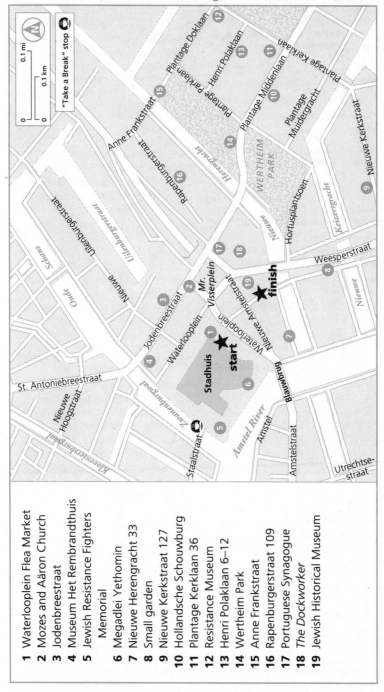

1 Waterlooplein Flea Market
2 Mozes and Aäron Church
3 Jodenbreestraat
4 Museum Het Rembrandthuis
5 Jewish Resistance Fighters
  Memorial
6 Megadlei Yethomin
7 Nieuwe Herengracht 33
8 Small garden
9 Nieuwe Kerkstraat 127
10 Hollandsche Schouwburg
11 Plantage Kerklaan 36
12 Resistance Museum
13 Henri Polaklaan 6–12
14 Wertheim Park
15 Anne Frankstraat
16 Rapenburgerstraat 109
17 Portuguese Synagogue
18 *The Dockworker*
19 Jewish Historical Museum

Continue to the Blauwbrug. Don't cross, but continue straight ahead, keeping with the river to your right. Go left on Nieuwe Herengracht just before the drawbridge and walk to:

⑦ Nieuwe Herengracht 33

This was once a Portuguese Jewish home for seniors. There was room for 10 people, and they had their own synagogue inside.

Walk to the end of Nieuwe Herengracht and turn right across Vaz Diasbrug. Take a look back down the canal as you cross the bridge—there's a picture-perfect view of canal houses and houseboats that's very typically Amsterdam. Continue along this road, which is now Weesperstraat, until you reach:

⑧ A small garden

This is a great place to sit and rest for a few minutes. The garden contains a monument to Dutch people who protected their Jewish compatriots during World War II. The memorial, from 1950, takes the shape of a white limestone altar, and has five reliefs of mourning men, women, and children.

Continue along Weesperstraat to Nieuwe Kerkstraat. Go left to:

⑨ Nieuwe Kerkstraat 127

Formerly the Metaarhuis, this is where the bodies of people who died at the Nieuwe Keizersgracht hospital were cleansed in accordance with Jewish ritual.

Walk farther along and cross the bridge at the end of Nieuwe Kerkstraat; veer to the left a bit and you'll be on Plantage Kerklaan. Walk down Plantage Kerklaan to the traffic lights and take a left on Plantage Middenlaan. To your left, at Plantage Middenlaan 24, you see the:

⑩ Hollandsche Schouwburg

Only the shell remains of this old theater (see "Other Historic Sights," in chapter 6), where many of Amsterdam's Jewish victims of the Nazi terror were processed before being transported to concentration camps. The children of some deportees who sneaked across the street to a kindergarten and saved by being taken

"underground" through the attached houses. A plaque on the school building celebrates the children's escape. Opposite the theater, you'll notice the bright primary colors of the Moederhuis (1978), a residence for single mothers, designed by Aldo van Eyck.

Go back to the traffic lights, turn left, and continue along Plantage Kerklaan. Soon, on the right side of the street, you come to:

⑪ Plantage Kerklaan 36

A plaque commemorates Jewish resistance fighters who attempted to destroy the city registers to prevent the Nazis from discovering how many Jews were in Amsterdam and where they were living. This is now part of the offices of Artis Zoo (see "Especially for Kids," in chapter 6). This brave effort could have kept thousands of Amsterdam's Jewish population from dying in concentration camps. Sadly, the attempt failed and 12 people were executed.

Stay on Plantage Kerklaan, but cross over to the other side of the street, to the:

⑫ Verzetsmuseum

The Resistance Museum at no. 61A (see "More Museums & Galleries," in chapter 6) is quite small and it eerily evokes the dark years of Amsterdam's occupation by the Nazis and the slow but sure implementation of Hitler's "Final Solution" against the city's Jewish community.

Backtrack a short way to Henri Polaklaan, where you go right, to:

⑬ Henri Polaklaan 6–12

Built in 1916, this is the former Portuguese Jewish Hospital. The pelican on the facade is a symbol of the Portuguese Jewish community.

Go left at the end of Henri Polaklaan, to Plantage Parklaan, and, on the corner of Plantage Middenlaan, go right, into:

⑭ Wertheim Park

This small park—really it's more like a large garden—is a good place for a rest, on benches around its rim. At the park's center is a memorial, by sculptor Jan Wolkers, to the victims of Auschwitz. Six large "broken" mirrors laid flat on the ground reflect a shattered sky and cover a buried urn containing ashes of the dead from the concentration camp. NOOIT MEER AUSCHWITZ (Never Again Auschwitz), reads the dedication. An information board lists, in impersonal rounded numbers, some of the gruesome statistics of the Holocaust: Of 140,000 members of Holland's Jewish community, 107,000 were deported to concentration camps, and just 5,200 returned; of the 95,000 sent to Auschwitz and Sobibor, fewer than 500 survived. One of those who perished was Anne Frank, who has a street named after her at the far end of the park.

Exit the park through the gate you came in, and go right on Plantage Middenlaan. On the other side of the street is Hortus Botanicus, the city's botanical garden (see "Green Amsterdam," in chapter 6). Keep going, across the bridge over the Nieuwe Herengracht canal. At Mr. Visserplein, turn right and walk on until you come to:

⑮ Rapenburgerstraat 109

Beth Hamidrash Ets Chaim (now the home of *NIW,* Holland's weekly Jewish newspaper) was once a center of Jewish learning where people studied Jewish law and the commentaries. The building dates from 1883; the study hall was founded in 1740.

Return to Mr. Visserplein and head to the:

⑯ Portuguese Synagogue

This will be to your left (see "Sights of Religious Significance," in chapter 6).

Make a left on Jonas Daniël Meijerplein; in the square you see:

⑰ The Dockworker

Jonas Daniël Meijerplein is where many Jews were forced to wait for their deportation to concentration camps. This bronze statue was erected in 1952 in commemoration of the 1941 February Strike by the workers of Amsterdam to protest the deportation of the city's Jewish population. The strike, one of the biggest collective actions in all of occupied Europe against the Nazi persecution, was ruthlessly suppressed.

Still on Jonas Daniël Meijerplein, visit the:

⑱ Joods Historisch Museum (Jewish Historical Museum)

This building (nos. 2–4) once housed four synagogues built by Jewish refugees from Germany and Poland in the 17th and 18th centuries (see "More Museums & Galleries," in chapter 6). Across the street from the museum is the Arsenal, which served as a storage space for munitions in the 19th century and is now part of the museum.

WINDING DOWN
Grand Café Dantzig, Zwanenburgwal 15 (✆ 020/620-9039), is a large, modern, trendy place built into a corner of the Stadhuis (City Hall) complex, with an alfresco terrace beside the Amstel River.

BIKE TOUR   **ALONG THE AMSTEL RIVER**

Start:	Waterlooplein.
Finish:	Amstel Station.
Time:	Allow between 3 and 4 hours, not including rest stops.
Best Times:	Outside of rush hour (around 8–10am and 5–7pm).

This biking route begins in the city center, and follows a scenic and relatively quiet way through the city, emerging into the countryside alongside the Amstel

River for the short but glorious hop out to the pretty village of Ouderkerk aan de Amstel.

See "Biking in Amsterdam," in chapter 3.

The nearest place to the starting point where you can rent a bike is MacBike, Mr. Visserplein 2 (② 020/620-0985; tram: 9, 14), at Waterlooplein. Prices begin at 6.50€ a day. When you've saddled up, head for:

❶ The Amstel River
The Amstel is likely to be fairly busy with waterborne traffic at this point, and houseboats are moored along both banks.

Continue to the:

❷ Magere Brug
Known as the "Skinny Bridge" over the Amstel, the Magere Brug is actually an 18th-century replacement for the original 17th-century bridge. Cross to the opposite bank and cycle south along the Amstel. On the other side of the river, you can see the Theater Carré (see "The Performing Arts," in chapter 9). Continue over Sarphatistraat, which you can easily recognize by its tram lines.

You need to detour around a break in the riverside road now, across busy Stadhouderskade, and back to the river again at:

❸ Amsteldijk
Keep pedaling south on this road, enjoying the riverside views, until you reach the **Berlage Brug (Berlage Bridge),** where you need to be more careful, as the traffic gets noticeably busier at this point.

Stay on Amsteldijk until you arrive at:

❹ Martin Luther King Park
Most of the road traffic swings away to the right on President Kennedylaan at this point, but you should stay on Amsteldijk, which gradually becomes almost rural, though with houseboats alongside the road in place of country cottages. Up ahead you'll hear a noise like a substantial storm coming your way, but you're just getting closer to the highway bridge that carries the A10 Ring Road across the river. Go

under the bridge and finally you're in the country, passing:

❺ Amstel Park
Continue to the statue of Rembrandt and a windmill at its end. Around this characteristic old Dutch scene, there'll likely be a characteristic new Dutch scene: busloads of tourists photographing Rembrandt, the windmill, themselves, and everything in sight, probably including you as you glide past. Beyond this is:

 TAKE A BREAK
't Klein Kalfje, Amsteldijk 355 (② 020/644-5338), an atmospheric little Dutch cafe-restaurant with a riverside terrace and canal barges moored alongside. The terrace is separated from the cafe by the road. There used to be a traffic sign here with an unofficial icon that indicated CAUTION: WAITER CROSSING.

The river is tranquil and scenic from now on, as you pass cottages and villas all the way to:

❻ Ouderkerk aan de Amstel
The little village has an abundance of cafes and restaurants with riverside terraces, several of them owned by Holland's first family of cuisine: the Fagels. The Fagels are a multi-generational family of chefs and restaurateurs with a high reputation in the land. If you've still got some energy left, you can put it to use exploring the village, before settling down on any one of the riverside or sidewalk terraces for something restorative.

For the return trip, change to the right bank of the river, on:

❼ Ouderkerkerdijk
This is narrower and quieter than Amsteldijk, and with almost no cars.

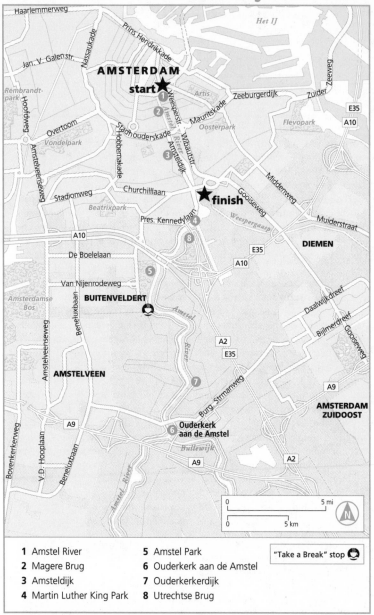

1 Amstel River	**5** Amstel Park
2 Magere Brug	**6** Ouderkerk aan de Amstel
3 Amsteldijk	**7** Ouderkerkerdijk
4 Martin Luther King Park	**8** Utrechtse Brug

"Take a Break" stop

You pass another windmill and several little hamlets along the way.

Recross the Amstel at the:

❽ Utrechtsebrug

This marks your return to Amsteldijk and busy city streets. At Berlage Brug

you can either recross the river and pedal a few hundred yards to Amstel Station, where you, your bike, and your no-doubt weary legs can board a Metro train back to Waterlooplein, or you can bike back along either bank.

8

Shopping

From its earliest days Amsterdam has been a trading city. First, trade centered on the fish that the original dammers of the Amstel caught in the rivers and the Zuider Zee; later, during the 17th century, on the spices, furs, flower bulbs, and artifacts carried back to Europe by the ships of the Dutch East and West India companies.

The fish were sold on the spot where a major department store now stands, and the early townspeople brought calves to market on the same street you will walk along to begin a shopper's walking tour through Amsterdam. The luxury items you buy today are the same sort of goods Dutch merchants sold to each other in the Golden Age of the 17th century, and the junk you buy in the flea market at Waterlooplein is much the same as it has been for hundreds of years.

Adding a modern dimension to this tradition-laden scene are the funky boutiques you find scattered around Amsterdam, and adding sparkle are the diamond cutters. Still, tradition is one thing, modern facilities are another. Amsterdam has the full range of shopping facilities, from small and highly individualistic, not to say eccentric, boutiques whose designers are often small name, through chains and department stores to malls. The Dutch themselves enjoy shopping and where possible like to take the time to seek out the more offbeat places, though they face the same time constraints as are to be found in most cities and so, more often than not, they fall back on the tried and tested.

For visitors, shopping can be an interesting extension to your experience of Amsterdam, precisely because the city center is small enough that stores and other attractions are often right beside each other. Rather than going on dedicated shopping expeditions, it may make more sense to simply drop into the nearest stores while you're involved in more weighty cultural matters. Whatever kind of shopping you prefer, you're sure to be impressed with the range of shopping possibilities Amsterdam offers.

1 The Shopping Scene

SHOPPING ORIENTATION

HOURS Regular shopping hours in Amsterdam are Monday from 10 or 11am to 6pm; Tuesday, Wednesday, and Friday from 9am to 6pm; Thursday from 9am to 9pm; and Saturday from 9am to 5pm. In recent years there has been something of a revolution in the previously restricted opening hours: Against the wishes of churches and other groups, many stores now stay open on Sunday as well, usually from noon to 5pm, and more and more supermarkets are staying open daily from 8am to 8pm, or even to 10pm.

PRICES These are fixed in Holland, with all applicable taxes included in the amounts shown on tags and counter display cards. Although end-of-season and

Tips **Tax Return**

If you live outside the European Union (EU), whatever your nationality, you're entitled to a refund of the value-added tax (VAT, or in Dutch, BTW) you pay on your purchases of 137€ or more in a store that subscribes to the refund system, in a day. On high-ticket items, the savings of 13.5% can be significant. You must export the purchases within 3 months. To obtain your VAT refund, ask for a **global refund check** from the store when you make your purchase. When you are leaving the EU, present this check, your purchases, and receipts to Customs. They will stamp the check. You can get the refund in cash or paid to your credit card at an International Cash Refund Point. At Schiphol Airport, this is the Global Refund Cash Refund Office; refunds are also available from the terminal's branch of ABN-AMRO bank. At other exit points from the EU, be sure to have Customs stamp your check and you can claim your refund later from one of 150 International Cash Refund Points worldwide. For a list of these, and for more information, contact **Europe Tax-Free Shopping,** Leidsevaartweg 99, 2106 AS, Heemstede, Netherlands (☎ **023/524-1909;** fax 023/524-6164; www.globalrefund.nl).

other special sales occur from time to time throughout the year, the practice of discounting as we know it is not a big part of the Dutch pricing system, so there's little use running from store to store trying to find a better price on ordinary consumer goods. If you want a bargain, go to the Waterlooplein flea market, though even there you find that the Dutch have much less interest in the sport of haggling—or margin in their prices—than their counterparts in countries farther south. They're simply too practical to quote a ridiculous price in the expectation that it will be cut in half or that you'll be fool enough to pay it.

DUTY-FREE ITEMS   Duty-free shopping has been abolished within the European Union. This means that if you are traveling from one member country of the EU to another, you can no longer buy duty-free goods at airports, on ferries, and at border crossings. If, however, you are traveling to or from the EU from a nonmember country, such as the United States, normal duty-free shopping rules apply. Some duty-free shopping centers, like the one at Schiphol Airport, claim to have reduced prices for intra-EU travelers to a level comparable to duty-free prices for people traveling outside the EU.

BEST BUYS

If an item in an Amsterdam store window takes your fancy or fills a specific need, buy it, of course. But often both prices and selections in Holland are too close to what you can find at home to justify the extra weight in your suitcase or the expense and trouble of shipping (prices of many consumer items in Holland are in any case often significantly higher than the same or equivalent items in the U.S.). Exceptions are the special items that the Dutch produce to perfection (delftware, pewter, crystal, and old-fashioned clocks), or commodities in which they have significantly cornered a market, like diamonds. None of these are a cheap commodity, unfortunately, and you'll want to do some homework in order to make canny shopping decisions, but if you know enough and care enough, you can find excellent values and take home beautiful, and in some cases valuable, treasures from Holland that will please you much more and much longer than the usual souvenirs. And if money is a consideration, remember that the Dutch also have inexpensive specialties, such as cheese, flower bulbs, and chocolate.

ANTIQUES Antiques lovers love Holland! And why not, when you think of all those tankards, pipes, cabinets, clocks, kettles, vases, and other bric-a-brac you see in the old Dutch paintings that still show up among the treasures of stores on Amsterdam's Nieuwe Spiegelstraat. It's the 20th century's good fortune that since the 17th century the Dutch have collected everything—from Chinese urns to silver boxes, from cookie molds to towering armoires—and should you find that while you're in Amsterdam there is a *kijkdag* (looking day) for an upcoming auction, you will realize that antiques still pour forth from the attics of the old canal houses. With 165 antiques stores in the city, there's no lack of choice.

CHEESE Holland is the Wisconsin of Europe, well known around the world for its butter and cheese (kaas). Gouda (correctly pronounced, in Dutch, *khow*-duh) and Edam (*ay*-dam) are the two Dutch cheeses most familiar to us because they have been exported from Holland for so long—since the 1700s—but once inside a Dutch cheese store, you quickly realize that there are many other interesting choices, including a nettle cheese that's a specialty of Friesland. Before you simply point to any cheese and say, "I'll take that one," you need to know that in Holland you have the choice of factory cheese, made of pasteurized milk, or *boerenkaas,* which is farm cheese that is produced in the old, careful way with fresh, unpasteurized milk straight from the cow. Boerenkaas is more expensive, of course, but it also can be expected to be more delicious. Look for the boerenkaas stamp. Another choice that you will make is between young and old cheese; it's a difference of sweetness, moistness, and a melting quality in the mouth (*jonge,* or young, cheese) and a sharper, drier taste, and a crumbly texture (*oude,* or old, cheese).

CHOCOLATE Droste, Verkade, and Van Houten are three of the best Dutch brand names to look for, or you can seek out the small specialty chocolate stores that still home-make and hand-fill the boxes of bonbons. (In fact, though no Dutch person would be unhappy to receive chocolates from these manufacturers, they themselves generally prefer handmade Belgian chocolates from such makes as Wittamer, Nihoul, Neuhaus, Godiva, and Leonidas.)

CRYSTAL & PEWTER Holland is not the only country that produces fine pewter ware and crystal, but the Dutch contribute both a refined sense of design and a respect for craftsmanship that combine to produce items of exceptional beauty and quality. Also, if you remember the classic Dutch still-life paintings and happy scenes of 17th-century family life, pewter objects are part of Holland's heritage. As with hand-painted earthenware, there are Dutch towns associated with each of these crafts and long-established firms whose names are well known as quality producers. Crystal, for example, has long been associated with Leerdam, south of Utrecht, and Maastricht, in Limburg, whose manufacturers have joined together to market under the names of **Royal Netherlands** in the United States and **Kristalunie** in Holland. To spot the genuine article, look for the four triangles of the **Royal Leerdam** label.

Traditionally, pewter was the specialty of the little town of Tiel, near Arnhem in the eastern part of Holland. Gradually, though, the old firms are disappearing, making it more difficult to find fine-spun pewter produced in the old way and in the old molds. An important shopping note on pewter is that though the Dutch government now bans the use of lead as a hardening agent, this assurance only protects you from toxicity in new pewter. Don't buy any antiques for use with food or drink. If you're not sure, look inside the pitcher or goblet; if it's light in color, it's fine; if it's dark and has a blue shine, buy it for decorative purposes only.

DELFTWARE & MAKKUMWARE   There are three types of delftware available in Amsterdam—Delftware, Makkumware, and junk—and since none of it is cheap, you need to know what the differences are among the three types and what to look for to determine quality. But first, a few words of historical background and explanation: delftware (with a lowercase *d*) has actually become an umbrella name for all Dutch hand-painted earthenware pottery resembling ancient Chinese porcelain, whether it is blue and white, red and white, or multicolored, and regardless of the city in which it was produced.

Delftware, or Delft Blue (with a capital *D*), on the other hand, refers to the predominantly blue-and-white products of one firm, **De Koninklijke Porceleyne Fles** of Delft. This is the only survivor of the original 30 potteries in Delft that during the 17th century worked overtime in that small city to meet the clamoring demand of the newly affluent Dutch for Chinese-style vases, urns, wall tiles, and knickknacks—real or reproduced, porcelain or pottery. Originally, pottery made at Delft was white, imitating tin-glazed products from Italy and Spain. During the 16th century, Chinese porcelain was imported to Holland—this was decorated in blue and was of superior quality. The Delftware factories refined their products, using a white tin glaze to cover the red clay and decorating it in blue. This Delft Blue became famous the world over. It was cheaper than Chinese porcelain and it was skillfully made. Polychrome decorations were also used, both on a white and on a black background.

Similarly, the term *makkumware* is becoming synonymous with multicolored—or polychrome—pottery, whereas Makkumware is, in fact, the hand-painted earthenware produced only in the town of Makkum in the northern province of Friesland and only by the 300-plus-year-old firm of **Tichelaars,** which was founded in 1660 and now is in its 10th generation of family management. Makkumware has a similar history to Delft Blue, though it exists only with polychrome decoration.

Delft and Makkumware are for sale in specialized stores all over the country, but it is far more interesting to go to one of the workshops in the towns themselves and see how they are made. Little has changed over the centuries, and all the decorating is still done by hand. This makes it quite pricey, but each piece is a unique product, made by craftsmen.

Copies of the products of both De Porceleyne Fles and Tichelaars are numerous, with some copies nearly equal in quality and others missing by miles the delicacy of the brush stroke, the richness of color, or the sheen of the secret glazes that make the items produced by these two firms so highly prized, and so expensive.

Your eye should tell you which pieces of pottery are worth their prices, but to be sure that yours is a *real* Delft vase, for instance, look on the bottom for the distinctive three-part hallmark of De Porceleyne Fles: an outline of a small pot, above an initial *J* crossed with a short stroke (actually, it's a combined initial, *J* and *T*), above the scripted word *Delft,* with the *D* distinctively written like a backward *C*.

To distinguish the products of Tichelaars, look for a mark that incorporates a crown above a shield showing the word *Makkum* and two scripted *T*s, over-lapped like crossed swords (or look simply for the crossed *T*s since the crown is a rather recent addition to their mark, the result of a royal honor bestowed on the company for its 300th anniversary in 1960).

DIAMONDS   Amsterdam has been a major center of the diamond-cutting industry since the 15th century and is one of the best places in the world to shop for diamond jewelry and unmounted stones in all gradations of color and quality. There are still 24 diamond-polishing workshops in the city.

Dutch jewelers generally adhere to the standards of both the Gemological Institute of America and the U.S. Federal Trade Commission, and most will issue a certificate with a diamond they sell that spells out the carat weight, cut, color, and other pertinent identifying details, including any imperfections.

Should you decide to buy a diamond, there are four factors influencing its quality that should be considered. The first is its weight, which will be stated as either points or carats (100 points equals 1 carat equals 200mg, or 3.47 grains troy). Next is the cut, which may be a classic round (brilliant) cut, a pear shape, a rectangular emerald cut, an oval, or a long and narrow double-pointed marquise. This is initially a matter of design preference rather than a factor in a stone's value; it is also, however, the test of the diamond cutter's ability to polish each of 58 facets at an angle that varies no more than half a degree from every other angle. To evaluate a diamond's cut, hold it to the light and look into the table (which is the name of the flattened top and the diamond's largest facet); if you see a dark circle, you know the stone is well cut and is reflecting light to its full capacity; if you don't, expect to pay less and to get less sparkle.

Also expect to pay more or less according to the clarity and color of a diamond. The clarity can be reliably evaluated only by a jeweler, who uses a loupe, or small eyeglass, to magnify the stone 10 times; the fewer the imperfections, the better the diamond and the higher the price (and, by the way, only a stone with *no* visible imperfections at that magnification can be described as "perfect" according to the guidelines of the Gemological Institute). Likewise, the whiter the diamond, the better the quality and the greater its value. To see for yourself whether a stone you are considering is closer to white than yellow or even brown, hold it with tweezers and look at it from the side, against a pure background (do this preferably in daylight through a north window, and never in direct sunlight). But don't expect to see blue unless you're looking at what a diamond dealer calls a "fancy" (a colored diamond), similar to the yellow Tiffany diamond or the deep-blue Hope.

FLOWER BULBS   Nothing is more Dutch than a tulip, and no gift to yourself will bring more pleasure than to take home some bulbs to remind you of Holland all over again when they pop up every spring. You may have a problem making your choices, however, since there are more than 800 different varieties of tulip bulbs available in Holland, not to mention more than 500 kinds of daffodils and narcissi, and 60 different varieties of hyacinth and crocus. Many growers and distributors put together combination packages with various amounts of bulbs that are coordinated according to the colors of the flowers they will produce, but it's great fun—since so many bulbs are named for famous people—to put together your own garden party with Sophia Loren, President Kennedy, Queen Juliana, and Cyrano de Bergerac!

Say It With Flowers

Holland has long had a close relationship with flowers. It's not merely that the tulip fields around Lisse are a springtime blaze of color that attracts admirers from around the world. If it were, the flower frenzy could be written off as "just business," good for bringing in the tourists. Flowers have deeper roots in this land of flat green polders. Amsterdam's floating flower market is only the best-known example of a sales network that makes a flower store one of the vital services in Dutch towns and villages.

Maybe because so many people live side-by-side in such a small, well-ordered country, flowers provide a breath of fresh air, a touch of the natural world when much of the environment is artificial. A Dutch house without flowers would be like Edam without the cheese. Window boxes, vases, balconies, rooftop terraces, gardens—all are pressed into service.

No visit to a dinner party or to friends or relatives would be complete without an accompanying bunch of flowers. You can forget the wine or the pralines, but not the bouquet. And Dutch men don't share the macho hang-up that some nationalities have at being seen carrying flowers in public.

You might not know what kind to buy though, as it is difficult to choose from the incredible variety of shapes and colors offered in Holland. Some bulbs flower early in January; others wait until the warmer months of May or June. Knowing this, you can choose bulbs with different flowering times, so you can enjoy their bloom over a long period in spring. In Amsterdam, you can't do better than to buy them from the floating Flower Market on the Singel Canal (see below).

If you worry about the failure rates or bug-ridden bulbs, don't! The Dutch have been perfecting their growing methods and strengthening their stock for more than 400 years, and as in everything they do, perfection is not simply a standard to strive for, it's an obligation. Do check before buying, however, since not all bulbs are certified for entry into the United States. Packages are marked; look for the numbered phyto-sanitary certificate attached to the label—it allows you to import the bulbs into the United States.

OLD-FASHIONED CLOCKS   It's true that the Swiss make the finest clocks in the world, but what they do well for the inner workings, the Dutch do well for the outside, particularly if you like a clock to be old-fashioned, handcrafted, and highly decorated with figures and mottoes or small peekaboo panels to show you the innards.

There are two types of clocks that have survived the centuries and the shift in Dutch taste to more contemporary timepieces. One is the Zaandam clock, or Zaanseklok, from the small city across the harbor from Amsterdam, which is identified by its ornately carved oak or walnut case and brass panels, its tiny windows on the dial face, and the motto *Nu Eick Syn Sin,* which basically translates from Old Dutch as "To Each His Own." The other popular clock style is the Friese Stoelklok, or Frisian clock, which is even more heavily decorated, customarily with hand-painted scenes of the Dutch countryside or ships at sea (that may even bob back and forth in time with the ticks) or possibly with both motifs and a smiling moon face.

GREAT SHOPPING AREAS

The easiest way to approach shopping in Amsterdam is to devote a day to the project, put on your most comfortable shoes, and walk. You can window-shop all the way from the Dam to the Concertgebouw if you have the stamina, and as long as you remember a few key jogs in the path, you won't even need to consult a map. A few shopping streets are pedestrians-only, some are busy thoroughfares, and others are peaceful canal-side esplanades or fashionable promenades, but each segment in this ever-growing network of commercial enterprises has developed its own identity or predominant selection of goods as a specialty. To get you on your way, here are three suggested shopping walks:

If you're looking for jewelry, trendy clothing, or athletic gear, begin at the department stores at the Dam and follow Kalverstraat to Heiligeweg; turn right there and continue shopping until you reach the Leidseplein. (Heiligeweg becomes Leidsestraat after it crosses the Koningsplein, but it's really one long street, so you can't possibly get lost.)

If you're feeling rich or simply want to feast your eyes on lovely things (fashion, antiques, and art), begin at the Concertgebouw and walk along Van Baerlestraat toward Vondelpark; turn right on the elegant Pieter Cornelisz Hooftstraat. At the end of the street, by the canal, turn right again and walk to the Rijksmuseum, then turn left across the canal. Straight ahead is the Spiegelgracht, a small and quiet bit of canal that's the gateway to the best antiques-shopping street in Amsterdam, if not in all of Europe.

Finally, if your idea of a good day of shopping includes fashion boutiques, funky little specialty stores, and a good browse through a flea market or secondhand store, cut a path from west to east through the old city by beginning at the Westermarkt and crisscrossing among the canals. Reestraat, Hartenstraat, Wolvenstraat, and Runstraat are particularly good choices with lots of fun stores, including one that boasts Europe's largest selection of ribbons and braid, and another with elaborately painted toilet bowls. At the Dam you can take Damstraat and its continuations (Oude Doelenstraat, Hoogstraat, and Nieuwe Hoogstraat) to St. Antoniesbreestraat (and its continuation, Jodenbreestraat) to Nieuwe Uilenburgerstraat to Waterlooplein and the market. Or at the Dam, follow Rokin to the Muntplein and walk from there, or take tram no. 9 or 14 to the stop for the Muziektheater/Waterlooplein.

To plan your own shopping route through Amsterdam, here are brief descriptions of the major shopping streets and what you can expect to find along each of them:

KALVERSTRAAT This is the busiest stretch of pedestrian shopping in the city. At one end is the Dam with its department stores; at the other end, the Muntplein traffic hub. In between, Kalverstraat is a hodgepodge of shopping possibilities. Punk-tinged boutiques for the young and athletic-shoe emporiums are side-by-side with stores selling dowdy raincoats and conservative business suits, bookstores, fur salons, maternity and baby stores, and record stores.

The big and busy **Vroom & Dreesman** department store has its main entrance on Kalverstraat, as does the elegant **Maison de Bonneterie en Pander;** also along the way are **Benetton** and **Fiorucci,** plus everything in the way of fast food from *frites* to *poffertjes*. The more conservative and well-established fashion stores for men and women on Kalverstraat are **Maison de Vries, Claudia Sträter,** and **Austin Reed;** for leather goods, **Zumpolle** offers elegant and high-quality handbags and leather suitcases. Something big, brash, and new on Kalverstraat is the **Kalvertoren Shopping Center,** a multistory mall with 45 stores, cafes, and restaurants, including the cheap 'n' cheerful department store **Hema.**

ROKIN   Parallel to Kalverstraat and also running from the Dam to the Muntplein is Rokin, one of the busiest tram routes in the city. Along here you will find art galleries and antiques stores, and elegant fashion boutiques such as **Le Papillon** for fitness/dance wear, **Jan Jensen** for shoes, **Emmy Landkroon** and **Sheila** for haute couture, or the straightforward chic of **Agnès B.**

HEILIGEWEG & LEIDSESTRAAT   The fashion parade that begins on Kalverstraat continues around the corner on Heiligeweg, across the Koningsplein and along Leidsestraat, all the way to the Leidseplein. But the mood changes: The stores are more elegant, and instead of a sprinkling of fast-food outlets and souvenir stores, you find congenial cafes and airline ticket offices. Along the way, look for **Esprit** and **Khymo** for men's and women's fashion; **Pauw Boutique, Cora Kemperman,** and **Agnès B** for women's fashion; **Smit-Bally** for shoes; the Amsterdam branches of **Studio Haus** for modern china and crystal and **Cartier** for gold and silver; the **Amsterdam Diamond Center** and **Rokin Diamonds** for, guess what? **Metz & Co.,** a dry-goods store at the corner of the Keizersgracht; and for men's and women's fashions, **Meddens** on Heiligeweg. **Morris** has suede and leather on Leidsestraat; **Crabtree & Evelyn** has its usual array of fragrant soaps, sachets, and cosmetics; and **Shoe-Ba-Loo** has, you guessed it, a choice selection of shoes.

PIETER CORNELISZ HOOFTSTRAAT & VAN BAERLESTRAAT   Pieter Cornelisz Hooftstraat (known locally as "P. C. Hooftstraat," or just as "the P. C. Hooft," pronounced *"pay say hoaft"*) is the (diminutive) Madison Avenue of Amsterdam, where well-dressed and well-coiffed Amsterdammers buy everything from lingerie to light bulbs. Along its 3 short blocks you find stores selling furniture, antiques, toys, shoes, chocolates, Persian rugs, designer clothes, fresh-baked bread and fresh-caught fish, china, books, furs, perfume, leather goods, office supplies, flowers, and jewelry. And around the corner on Van Baerlestraat are more boutiques, shoe stores, and enough branches of the major banks to guarantee that you can continue to buy as long as your traveler's checks hold out. Worth special mention are **Edgar Vos, Frans Molenaar, Tim Bonig, Rob Kroner, Jacques d'Ariege, DKNY, Laurèl,** and **Gimmicks, Pauw Boutique,** and at the corner of Van Baerlestraat, **Azurro,** all for women's fashions; **Pauw Junior** on Van Baerlestraat for children's clothes; branches of **Emporio Armani, Hobbit, Rodier Paris, MacGregor,** and **Society Shop** for men's fashions; and **Godiva Chocolatier** for handmade pralines. Van Baerlestraat continues southward onto Beethovenstraat, which is rich in boutiques, delicatessens, cafes, and specialty grocers.

NIEUWE SPIEGELSTRAAT & SPIEGELGRACHT   This is the antiques esplanade of Amsterdam, and though it covers only a short 4-block stretch of street-plus-canal, it's one of the finest antiques-hunting grounds in Europe. At one end of this shopping street is the Rijksmuseum; at the other, the Golden Bend of the Herengracht Canal, where Amsterdam's wealthiest burghers once kept house. It seems that, now that these beautiful gabled homes have been turned over to banks and embassies, all the treasures they contained have simply found their way around the corner to the antiques stores. Among the items you might expect to see are dolls with china heads, rare editions of early children's books, Indonesian puppets, Persian tapestries and rugs, landscape paintings, prints, reproductions and modern art, brass Bible stands and candlesticks, copper kettles, music boxes, old Dutch clocks, and, of course, the little *spiegels,* or mirrors, that give this street its name, and which the Dutch use beside upper-story windows to see who's knocking at their door.

AMSTELVEEN   Amstelveen is a new town built around an old village in the polderland south of Amsterdam. Think of modern, clean, efficient living in a garden city. The shopping center here has many of the nonspecialist types of outlets—department stores, boutiques, toy stores, and the like—that you find in Amsterdam. Here, however, they're in an enclosed mall and you can get around them all a lot quicker. So if you don't like shopping, but can just about tolerate it if you get through it quickly, this may be the place for you. Take the no. 5 tram from Centraal Station to the terminus, which is right beside the Amstelveen shopping center; the journey lasts about 25 minutes.

OTHER SHOPPING AREAS

For more antiques stores, look along the Prinsengracht between Leidsestraat and Westermarkt, or visit the **Kunst- & Antiekcentrum de Looier** (see "Shopping A to Z," below). For the up-and-coming funky boutiques of Amsterdam, look among the canals east and west of the Dam, or in the nest of streets beyond the Westermarkt known as the **Jordaan.**

2 Shopping A to Z

Here is a selection of interesting stores in Amsterdam, some of which you might not otherwise have found. It can save you time and trouble with your shopping list or simply provide interesting stores to visit.

ANTIQUES

A. van der Meer   For more than 30 years, A. van der Meer has been a landmark amid the fashionable stores of Pieter Cornelisz Hooftstraat and a quiet place to enjoy a beautiful collection of antique maps, prints, and engravings. And 17th- and 18th-century Dutch world maps by the early cartographers Blaeu, Hondius, and Mercator are a specialty. Also, there is a small collection of Jewish prints by Picart and 18th-century botanicals (pictures of flowers) by Baptista Morandi and 19th-century works by Jacob Jung, mostly of roses. There are also 19th-century lithographs of hunting scenes by Harris. Open Monday through Saturday from 10am to 6pm. Pieter Cornelisz Hooftstraat 112. ✆ 020/662-1936. Tram: 2, 3, 5, 12 to Van Baerlestraat.

Premsela & Hamburger   Opposite the Allard-Pierson Museum, this fine jewelry and antique silver establishment—purveyors to the Dutch court—opened in 1823. Inside their brocaded display cases and richly carved cabinets is a variety of exquisite and distinctive items. You can find decorative modern and antique silver objects and Old Dutch silver fashioned by 17th-century crafters. Feast your eyes on an 18th-century perpetual calendar, a silver plaque depicting the entrance to an Amsterdam hospital, and a variety of sterling silverware. Their workshop designs, makes, and repairs jewelry. Open Monday through Friday from 9:30am to 5:30pm. Rokin 98. 🕿 **020/624-9688** or 020/627-5454. Tram: 4, 9, 14, 16, 24, 25 to Spui.

ART

Galleries abound in Amsterdam, particularly in the canal area near the Rijksmuseum, and a quick look at the listings of their exhibitions proves that Dutch painters are as prolific in the 20th century as they were in the Golden Age. The VVV Tourist Information Office publication *What's On in Amsterdam* is your best guide to who is showing and where; your own eye and sense of value will be the best guide to artistic merit and investment value.

On the other hand, posters and poster reproductions of famous artworks are an excellent item to buy in Amsterdam. The Dutch are well known for their high-quality printing and color-reproduction work, and one of their favorite subjects is Holland's rich artistic treasure trove, foreign and domestic. Choose any of the three major art museums as a starting point for a search for an artistic souvenir, but if you like modern art—say, from the Impressionists onward—you will be particularly delighted by the wide selection at the **Stedelijk Museum,** Paulus Potterstraat 13 (🕿 **020/573-2911**); and if you particularly like van Gogh, the **Van Gogh Museum,** Paulus Potterstraat 13 (🕿 **020/570-5200**), is another good source of reproductions. And at **Museum Het Rembrandthuis,** Jodenbreestraat 4 (🕿 **020/624-9486**), you can buy a Rembrandt etching for 15€ or 20€ mounted; it's not an original, of course, but it is a high-quality modern printing produced individually, by hand, in the traditional manner from a plate that was directly and photographically produced from an original print in the collection of Rembrandthuis. Or for something simpler and cheaper to remind you of the great master, Het Rembrandthuis also sells mass-printed reproductions of the etchings, or small packets of postcard-sized reproductions in sepia or black and white on a thick, fine-quality paper stock (including a packet of self-portraits).

Perhaps you're more interested in an artistic, rather than photographic, view of Amsterdam or the Dutch countryside. **Mattieu Hart,** which has been in its location on the Rokin since 1878, sells color etchings of Dutch cities.

Here are just a few of Amsterdam's 140 or so galleries that hold contemporary and modern art, photography, sculpture, and African art.

Animation Art   Got a favorite cartoon character? Well, Animation Art has original drawings and cell-paintings of all different kinds of cartoons. A fun place for the kid in everyone. Open Tuesday through Friday from 11am to 6pm, Saturday from 11am to 5pm, and Sunday (not in Jan or Feb) from 1 to 5pm. Berenstraat 19 (between Keizersgracht and Prinsengracht). 🕿 020/627-7600. Tram: 1, 2, 5 to Spui.

Galerie Carla Koch   For ceramics and glassware, this gallery employs some of the raciest design talent in Amsterdam, meaning that their products are always different and always interesting, if inevitably not to everyone's taste. Open Monday to Saturday noon to 6pm. Prinsengracht 510. 🕿 020/639-0198. Tram: 1, 2, 5 to Prinsengracht.

Italiaander Galleries   There's a permanent exhibition of primitive art from around the world, particularly from Africa and Asia, and all sorts of ethnic jewelry. Open Wednesday to Saturday noon to 5:30pm. Prinsengracht 526. 🕿 020/625-0942. Tram: 1, 2, 5 to Prinsengracht.

BOOKS

American Book Center   You'll swear you never left the States when you see the array of best-sellers and paperbacks in the American Book Center on Kalverstraat near Muntplein, which claims to be the biggest U.S.-style book store on the European continent. Plus, there are magazines (risqué and otherwise) and hardcover editions, hot off the presses. Prices are higher than you'd pay at home, but the selection beats any airport or hotel gift store, with categories ranging from ancient civilizations, astrology, and baby care to science, science fiction, and war. Students and teachers can get 10% off simply by showing a school ID. Open Monday through Wednesday and Friday and Saturday from 10am to 8pm, Thursday from 10am to 10pm, and Sunday from 11am to 6pm. Kalverstraat 185. ✆ 020/625-5537. Tram: 4, 9, 14, 16, 24, 25 to Muntplein.

Athenaeum Booksellers   You can't miss this place. It's always crowded with book lovers, students, and scholars. The Athenaeum is best known for its non-fiction collection and has books in a number of different languages. There are magazine stands on the sidewalk. The store is open Monday through Wednesday and Saturday from 9:30am to 6pm; Thursday from 9:30am to 9pm; Sunday from noon to 5:30pm. Spui 14–16. ✆ 020/622-6248. Tram: 1, 2, 5 to Spui.

De Slegte   You won't find too many books in English here—most are in Dutch or other languages—but you find some, and if you collect books as a hobby, you might run across a real gem. It's probably one of the biggest, most-often-visited bookstores in Amsterdam. Open Monday from 11am to 6pm, Tuesday through Friday from 9:30am to 6pm, and Saturday from 8am to 6pm. Kalverstraat 48–52. ✆ 020/622-5933. Tram: 4, 9, 14, 16, 24, 25 to the Dam.

English Bookshop   On the edge of the Jordaan, this small bookstore has a wonderful selection of books in English, mainly fiction and biography, and a small selection of British magazines. Occasionally, you can find a great book at a discount. Open Tuesday through Friday from 1 to 6pm and Saturday from 11am to 5pm. Lauriergracht 71. ✆ 020/626-4230. Tram: 7, 10, 17 to Elandsgracht.

Evenaar   Since you are traveling, you may be in the mood for travel literature. Evenaar, which is close to Spui, sells not only travel guides but also a wide range of travel literature and large-format photo books on travel and anthropology, and secondhand and antique travel books. Open Monday through Friday from noon to 6pm, Saturday from 11am to 5pm. Singel 348. ✆ 020/624-6289. Tram: 1, 2, 5 to Spui.

Waterstone's Booksellers   Waterstone's is a British chain that has a large stock of fiction and nonfiction titles. You'll probably be able to find almost anything you're looking for on one of the three floors here. Open Monday from 11am to 6pm, Tuesday, Wednesday, and Friday from 9am to 6pm, Thursday from 9am to 9pm, Saturday from 9am to 7pm, and Sunday from 11am to 5pm. Kalverstraat 152. ✆ 020/638-3821. Tram: 1, 2, 4, 5, 14, 16, 17, 24, 25 to Spui.

CARS

Ten Cate Fiat   Ah, the Fiat 500! What the T-Bird was to the States, the diminutive Cinquecento was to Europe. No matter that when you wanted to overtake you found it easier to get out, pick the car up under your arm, and run with it. You could park one anywhere, and Italians always did. Henk ten Cate and his team are Fiat 500 enthusiasts, and they will sell or lease you an exceedingly little piece of lovingly restored automotive history. You might even be able to take it home in your hand-baggage. Their showroom is worth visiting just for the sight of dozens of Cinquecentos lined up side by side. Open Monday through Friday from 9am to 5pm, Saturday from 11am to 3pm. Weesperzijds 143. ☎ **020/668-6373**. Tram: 12 to Amstel Station.

CIGARS, PIPES & SMOKING ARTICLES

Holland is one of the cigar-producing centers of the world. Serious smokers know that Dutch cigars are different, and drier, than Cuban or American smokes. It's partly because of the Indonesian tobacco and partly because of the way the cigar is made, but whatever the reason, Dutch cigars can be a pleasant change for American tobacco enthusiasts.

P G C Hajenius   This store has been Amsterdam's leading purveyor of cigars and smoking articles since 1826, first with a store on the Dam and then since 1915 in its present elegant headquarters. Cigars are the house specialty and the stock includes a room full of Havanas. Hajenius sells the long, uniquely Dutch, handmade clay pipes you see in old paintings and that are a good gift idea, and ceramic pipes, some painted in the blue-and-white Chinese-inspired patterns of Delftware. You also find lighters, cigarette holders, clippers, and flasks. Open Monday through Wednesday and Friday and Saturday from 9:30am to 6pm, Thursday from 9:30am to 9pm, Sunday from noon to 5pm. Rokin 92–96. ☎ **020/ 623-7494**. Tram: 4, 9, 14, 16, 24, 25 to Spui.

Smokiana & Pijpenkabinet   This place stocks a vast range of pipes from the antique, to the exotic, to the downright weird. It's where to buy that unique pipe, into which the tobacco can be tamped with an air of deliberate insouciance, and the resulting fug flaunted in the faces of nonsmokers everywhere. Open Wednesday through Saturday from noon to 6pm. Prinsengracht 488. ☎ **020/ 421-1179**. Tram: 1, 2, 5 to Prinsengracht.

CLOCKS

Victoria Gifts   Dutch clockmakers turn out timepieces with soft-toned chimes in exquisite Old Dutch–style handcrafted cases covered with tiny figures and mottoes, insets of hand-painted porcelain, and hand-painted Dutch scenes. This small store is a happy hunting ground for these treasures. It also has a good stock of Delftware, embroidered flags, chocolates, and other quality gifts at reasonable prices. Open in summer Monday through Saturday from 9am to 8pm; in winter, Monday through Saturday from 9am to 8pm. Prins Hendrikkade 47 (opposite Centraal Station). ☎ **020/427-2051**. Tram: 1, 2, 4, 5, 9, 13,16, 17, 24, 25 to Centraal Station.

CRAFTS & CURIOS

Blue Gold Fish *(Finds*   "Dive into the pool of fantasy," say the owners of this colorful store and gallery. There's no real rhyme or reason to the items for sale. They cover a wide range of ceramics, jewelry, household items (including colorful lamps in the "Aladdin's Corner"), textiles, all of them running the stylistic gamut from kitsch to chic. Still, there's unity in diversity in the more-or-less fantastic design sensibility that goes into each piece. Open Monday through Saturday from 11:30am to 6:30pm. Rozengracht 17 (opposite Westerkerk). ☎ **020/623-3134**. Tram: 13, 14, 17 to Westermarkt.

Cortina Papier   If you'd like the kind of personal journal that would have looked good in *The English Patient* and *Dances with Wolves*, this is the place for you. Cortina does fancy notebooks, agendas and address books, and nice lines in writing paper, envelopes, and other such products. Open Monday from 1 to 6pm, Tuesday through Friday from 11am to 6pm, and Saturday from 11am to 5pm. Reestraat 22 (between Prinsengracht and Keizersgracht). ✆ **020/623-6676**. Tram: 13, 14, 17 to Westermarkt.

E Kramer Candle Shop   This place provides illumination for everything from a romantic candlelit dinner to a wake, while filling all kinds of temporary and mobile lighting requirements in between. Some of the candles are little melting works of art and some are outrageously kitschy, but all will shed some light on your activities. The store also sells scented oils and incense, and even repairs dolls. Open Monday through Friday from 10am to 6pm, Saturday from 10am to 5pm. Reestraat 20 (between Prinsengracht and Keizersgracht). ✆ **020/626-5274**. Tram: 13, 14, 17 to Westermarkt.

La Savonnerie   This is the kind of clean-living store that a raffish place like Amsterdam can't get enough of. You can buy artisanal soap in all kinds of shapes and sizes. How about a soap chess set, soap alphabet blocks, and soap animal shapes? You can buy personalized soap and even make your own soap. Open Tuesday through Friday from 10am to 6pm (8pm on Thurs in summer), Saturday from 10am to 5pm. Prinsengracht 294 (corner of Elandsgracht). ✆ **020/428-1139**. Tram: 7, 10, 17 to Elandsgracht.

Magic Mushroom Gallery   How to define this place that seems to tread a thin line? It sells "natural drugs" and "psychoactive mushrooms" that are much better for you, so they say, than illegal narcotics. Improve your sex life with Yohimbe Rush and Horn E; boost your energy with Space Liquid and Herbal Booster; grow your own Mexican mushrooms; then unwind with After Glow and Rapture. Open Monday through Saturday from 9:30am to 6pm. Singel 524 (near Muntplein). ✆ **020/422-7845**. Tram: 4, 9, 14, 16, 24, 25 to Muntplein.

Nieuws Innovations   This store is a source for all kinds of offbeat souvenirs, such as pens in the shape of fish, lipsticks, and (perhaps too near the bone for Amsterdam) syringes; washcloths in the form of hand-glove puppets; spherical dice; finger massage sets; and many other hard-to-define but colorful little bits and pieces. Open Monday from 1:30 to 6:30pm; Tuesday, Wednesday, and Friday from 10am to 6:30pm, Thursday from 10am to 9pm, Saturday and Sunday from 11am to 6pm. Prinsengracht 297 (at Westermarkt). ✆ **020/627-9540**. Tram: 13, 14, 17 to Westermarkt.

Pakhuis Amerika   All kinds of American souvenirs and antiques, imported from the United States, and just waiting to be paid for, wrapped, and brought straight back home again—and all for much more than you would have paid for them in the States! If nothing else, it's a kind of museum—your heritage (as Europeans see it) all together in one place. Open Monday through Saturday from 11am to 8pm. Prinsengracht 541 (at Runstraat). ✆ **020/639-2583**. Tram: 1, 2, 5 to Prinsengracht.

't Winkeltje   This place sells knickknacks such as colored bottles and glasses; modern versions of old tin cars and other children's toys from the 1950s and earlier; big plastic butterflies; lamps shaped like bananas; and many other such useful things. A little bit of this and a little bit of that. Open Monday from 1 to 5:30pm, Tuesday through Friday from 10am to 5:30pm, and Saturday from 10am to 5pm. Prinsengracht 228 (at Leliegracht). ✆ **020/625-1352**. Tram: 13, 14, 17 to Westermarkt.

DELFTWARE

Focke & Meltzer   This main branch of a popular chain is the best one-stop store you'll find for authentic Delftware and Makkumware, Hummel figurines, Leerdam crystal, and a world of other fine china, porcelain, silver, glass, and crystal products. Open Monday through Friday from 9:30am to 5:30pm and Saturday from 9:30am to 5pm. Gelderlandplein 149, Buitenveldert. © 020/644-4429. Tram: 5, 51 to A. J. Ernststraat.

Heinen   You can save considerably on hand-painted pottery and have the fun of seeing the product made at these stores, owned by a father-and-son team who sit inside their canal-house windows, quietly painting the days away. You get quality and a good selection of useful, well-priced items. Jaap (father) and Jorrit (son) both paint in five techniques: blue and white (Delft), polychrome (Makkum), Japanese Imari, Kwartjes (a modern-looking Delft with blue, red, and gold), and Sepia (brown and red). They are official dealers of De Porcelyne Fles and Tichelaars and have a third store, in Volendam, at Haven 92. Open Monday through Saturday from 9:30am to 6pm. Prinsengracht 440 (at Leidsestraat). © 020/627-8299. Tram: 1, 2, 5, to Prinsengracht. Spiegelgracht 13. © 020/421-8360. Tram: 6, 7, 10 to Spiegelgracht.

DEPARTMENT STORES

De Bijenkorf   De Bijenkorf is Amsterdam's best-known department store, and the one with the best variety of goods. A recent renovation changed this once-frumpy little dry-goods emporium into Amsterdam's answer to New York's Bloomingdale's. On the ground floor, you find the usual ranks of cosmetic counters in the center section, plus a men's department and odds and ends such as socks and stockings, handbags and belts, costume jewelry, and stationery. And umbrellas—plenty of umbrellas! On upper floors there's everything from ladies' fashions to *dekbedden* (down comforters), plus a bookstore, several eating spots, and even a luggage section where you can pick up an extra suitcase or tote bag to take home your purchases. Records, color TVs, shoes, clothing, personal effects, appliances—it's all here. Open Monday from 11am to 6pm; Tuesday, Wednesday, and Friday from 9:30am to 6pm; Thursday from 9:30am to 9pm; and Saturday from 9am to 6pm. Dam 1. © 020/621-8080. Tram: 4, 9, 14, 16, 24, 25 to the Dam.

Hema   Hema is the Woolworth's of Amsterdam, selling things like socks, toothbrushes, chocolate, cookies, and cheeses. If you can't figure out where to find something, your best bet is to look here. Open Monday from 11am to 6pm, Tuesday through Friday from 9:30am to 6pm, and Saturday from 9am to 6pm. Kalvertoren Shopping Center, Kalverstraat. © 020/626-8720. Tram: 4, 14, 16, 24, 25 to Muntplein.

Magna Plaza   Magna Plaza is not actually a department store, but a mall, located amid the extravagant Gothic architecture of the former central Post Office. The Plaza's floors are filled with stores of all kinds and yet it's small enough to function as a kind of department store. Spuistraat 168 (behind the Dam's Royal Palace). © 020/626-9199. Tram: 1, 2, 5, 13, 14, 17 to the Dam.

Marks & Spencer   This is a branch of the popular British store chain, whose specialties are clothes of good quality in their class, even if they are not always very imaginative—the underwear is particularly good! It also has a food hall with a reputation for quality, freshness, and convenience. Open Monday from 11am to 6pm, Tuesday, Wednesday and Friday from 10am to 6pm, Thursday from 10am to 9pm, Saturday 9:30am to 6pm and Sunday from noon to 6pm. Kalverstraat 66–72. ✆ 020/531-2468. Tram: 4,5, 9, 14, 16, 24, 25 to the Dam.

Metz & Co This dramatic store, founded in 1740, is now owned by Liberty of London. It sells furniture, fabrics, kitchenware, and other traditional department-store items. The cupola and cafe are worth stopping for. Open Monday from 11am to 6pm and Tuesday through Saturday from 9:30am to 6pm. Keizersgracht 455 (at Leidsestraat). ✆ 020/520-7020. Tram: 1, 2, 5 to Keizersgracht.

Peek and Cloppenburg Peek and Cloppenburg is a different sort of department store—or perhaps a better description is that P&C is an overgrown clothing store. Open Monday from noon to 6pm and Tuesday through Saturday from 9:30am to 6pm. Dam 20. ✆ 020/623-2837. Tram: 4,5, 9, 14, 16, 24, 25 to the Dam.

Vroom & Dreesman Less polished and pretentious than Metz & Co., and highly successful as a result, this is the Amsterdam branch of Vroom & Dreesman, a Dutch chain of department stores that pop up in key shopping locations all over Holland. It's a no-nonsense sort of store with a wide range of middle-of-the-road goods and prices and services to match. Open Monday through Saturday from 9am to 6pm. Kalverstraat 201–221 and 212–224 (near the Muntplein). ✆ 020/622-0171. Tram: 4, 9, 14, 16, 24, 25 to Muntplein.

DIAMONDS
The following stores offer diamond-cutting and polishing tours, and sales of the finished product: **Amsterdam Diamond Center,** Rokin 1 (✆ 020/624-5787), open Friday through Wednesday from 10am to 6pm, Thursday from 10am to 6pm and 7 to 8:30pm; **Coster Diamonds,** Paulus Potterstraat 2–4 (✆ 020/676-2222), open daily from 9am to 5pm; **Gassan Diamonds,** Nieuwe Uilenburgerstraat 173–175 (✆ 020/622-5333), open daily from 9am to 5pm; **Stoeltie Diamonds,** Wagenstraat 13–17 (✆ 020/623-7601), open daily from 9am to 5pm; and **Van Moppes Diamonds,** Albert Cuypstraat 2–6 (✆ 020/676-1242), open daily from 9am to 5pm.

FASHIONS
WOMEN'S
Paris may set the styles, but young Dutch women—and some of their mothers—often know better than the French how to make them work. Whatever the current European fashion rage is, you can expect to see it in store windows all over Amsterdam, and in all price ranges. Some boutique faithfuls claim that they buy Paris designer fashions in Amsterdam at lower-than-Paris prices, but one quick check will tell you that designer wear is still expensive, whether you pay in guilders, francs, or hard-earned dollars.

It's more fun to ferret out the new, young crop of Dutch designers who regularly open stores in unpredictable locations all over town. Boutiques and their designers change rapidly with the tides of fashion, but the current top names and locations along the Rokin are: **Carla V., Sheila de Vries, Jan Jansen** (shoes), **Agnès B** (women's fashions), and **Puck & Hans,** whose pseudo-Japanese look catches the eye as you walk along.

Also stop by **The Madhatter,** Van der Helsplein 4 (✆ 020/664-7748), for handmade hats; **Mô,** Overtoom 336 (✆ 020/689-4369), for leather apparel (menswear also); and **Eva Damave,** Tweede Laurierdwarsstraat 51c (✆ 020/627-7325), for knitwear.

Maison de Bonneterie   Here you find exclusive women's fashions, and Gucci bags and Fieldcrest towels and a star-studded cast of brand names on household goods and personal items. Open Monday from 1 to 5:30pm and Tuesday through Saturday from 10am to 5:30pm. Rokin 140–142. ℂ 020/626-2162. Tram: 4, 9, 14, 16, 24, 25 to Rokin.

MEN'S

In addition to the department stores listed above, you can find men's fashions at **Tie Rack,** Heiligeweg 7 (ℂ **020/627-2978**), and **Guus de Winter,** Linnaeusstraat 197 (ℂ **020/694-0252**). If you're into fancy, colorful sweaters, check out those of former cabaret performers Greg and Gary Christmas, at their boutique **Backstage,** Utrechtsedwarsstraat 67 (ℂ **020/622-3638**).

CHILDREN'S

Children's clothing stores are everywhere. Among them are **'t Schooltje,** Overtoom 87 (ℂ **020/683-0444**), which carries expensive but cute clothes for babies and children (well into the teen years); and the more affordable **Spetter Children's Fashion,** Van den Helstraat 53 1e (ℂ **020/671-6249**).

FOOD & DRINK

De Waterwinkel   Quality, purity, and beauty are the watchwords at the tastefully designed Water Shop. More than 100 varieties of mineral water from all over the world are on sale, ranging from ordinary, everyday water to designer water. Some of the bottles are miniature works of art in themselves. This is a store whose liquid assets are its stock-in-trade. Open Monday through Wednesday, Friday, and Saturday from 9am to 6pm, Thursday from 9am to 9pm. Roelof Hartstraat 10. ℂ 020/675-5932. Tram: 3, 5, 12, 24 to Roelof Hartplein.

H. Keijzer   H. Keijzer, which was founded in 1839, specializes in tea and coffee. It sells 90 different kinds of tea and 22 coffees. Consider taking home several 100-gram packets of teas from different parts of the tea-growing world: Ceylon Melange (or Delmar Melange), an English-style blend from Sri Lanka; Darjeeling First Flush, from India; Yunnan, from China; and Java O.P. (Orange Pekoe), from Indonesia. All of these teas are popular with the Dutch. For a nice gift, select from an assortment of tea boxes, among them a small box with a picture of the store and other buildings. Open Monday through Friday from 8:30am to 5:30pm and Saturday from 8:30am to 5pm. Prinsengracht 180.ℂ 020/624-0823. Tram: 13, 14, 17 to Westermarkt.

H P de Vreng en Zonen   This traditional distillery creates Dutch liqueurs and gins according to the old-fashioned methods, sans additives. Try the Old Amsterdam jenever or some of the more flamboyantly colored liquids, like the bright green plum liqueur *Pruimpje prik in.* Some supposedly have aphrodisiac power. A chance to see the collection of 15,000 miniature bottles alone makes a visit worthwhile. Open Monday through Saturday from 10am to 5pm. Nieuwendijk 75. ℂ 020/624-4581. Tram: 1, 2, 5, 13, 17 to Martelaarsgracht.

Jacob Hooy & Co *(Finds)*   You feel you've stepped back into history if you visit Jacob Hooy & Co. This store, opened in 1743 and operated for the past 130 years by the same family, is a wonderland of fragrant smells that offers more than 500 different herbs and spices and 30 different teas, all sold loose, by weight. Health foods, homeopathic products, and natural cosmetics are also on sale. Everything is stored in wooden drawers and wooden barrels with the names of the contents hand scripted in gold. Across the counter are fishbowl jars in racks containing 30 or more different types of *dropjes* (drops or lozenges) that range in taste from sweet to sour to salty. Open Monday from noon to 6pm, Tuesday through Friday from 8am to 6pm, and Saturday from 8am to 5pm. Kloveniersburgwal 10–12. ✆ 020/624-3041. Metro: Nieuwmarkt.

Patisserie Pompadour   The counter display here is amazing. It groans under the weight of around 50 luscious pastries and tarts, complemented by endless dollops of whipped cream. You can enjoy these genuine Dutch treats in the exquisite Louis XVI tearoom or wrapped to go. Open Tuesday through Friday from 9:30am to 5:45pm and Saturday from 9am to 5:30pm. Huidenstraat 12. ✆ 020/623-9554. Tram: 1, 2, 5 to Spui.

GAY

Boekhandel Vrolijk   The city's main bookstore for gays and lesbians stocks a wide range of books, many of them in English. It's invariably cheaper to buy here than at the gay sections of general bookstores, but still is likely to be more expensive than at home. Paleisstraat 135 (at the Dam). ✆ 020/623-5142. Tram: 1, 2, 4, 5, 9, 13, 14, 16, 17, 24, 25.

Mr B   This airy store is world famous for high-quality leather goods, from basic trousers and chaps to more revealing and fetish wear. The store window's display of accessories for the S/M, leather and rubber guys, regular exhibitions of erotic art, and a great selection of piercing jewelry, ensures many a gaping tourist. Visiting tattoo and piercing artists from around the world make guest appearances for the real connoisseurs. There are cards and postcards to greet the friends you left behind. Open Monday through Friday from 10am to 6:30pm (Thurs to 9pm), Saturday from 11am to 6pm. Warmoesstraat 89 (Red Light District). ✆ 020/422-0003. Tram: 1, 2, 4, 5, 9, 13, 14, 16, 17, 24, 25 to Centraal Station.

HABERDASHERY

H J van de Kerkhof   The walls of this store are lined with spools of ribbon and cord, and its notebooks are filled with examples of patches and appliqués. There are key tassels and tiebacks in all sizes, including very large "canal house" size. Open Monday through Friday from 9am to 6pm and Saturday from 10am to 5pm. Wolvenstraat 9–11. ✆ 020/623-4666. Tram: 1, 2, 5 to Spui.

HOUSEHOLD

Kitsch Kitchen   The name just about says it all. You'll probably want to put on your shades before entering the world of glaringly bright colors that characterize Kitsch Kitchens' utensils and fittings in plastic, enamel, and papier-mâché.

Tips **Night Owls**

A local *avondwinkel* (night store) is a resource not to be ignored for keeping you stocked with things to munch after normal hours. Suppose you feel like an evening "at home" in your hotel, watching television or whatever, and you either don't fancy the room-service menu or your hotel doesn't provide this service. There is sure to be a night store close to the hotel (ask at the front desk). Many can prepare take-out meals to about the same standard as you would find in a typical Dutch *eetcafé,* for 10% to 20% less than the restaurant price, and they often sell fresh delicatessen items. Hours are usually from 5 to 11pm or midnight.

From Ships to Shops

KNSM-Eiland (KNSM Island; named after the Dutch initials of the old Royal Dutch Steamship Line that was based there), in the redeveloping Eastern Harbor area, now has a streetload of design and interior design stores. These include **Pilat & Pilat,** KNSM-Laan 19 (✆ **020/419-3670**), for furnishings by modern designers; Pol's Potten, KNSM-Laan 39 (✆ **020/419-3541**), for work by hip young designers; **Keet in Huis,** KNSM-Laan 303 (✆ **020/419-5958**), for lifestyles for children; and **World of Wonders,** KNSM-Laan 293–295 (✆ **020/418-4067**), for fabrics and furnishings.

Kitsch Kitchens has extended its market by opening a second store, **Kitsch Kitchen Kids,** Rozengracht 183 (✆ **020/622-8261**), aimed at children. Open Monday through Friday from 10:30am to 6pm, Saturday from 10am to 6pm. Eerste Bloemdwarsstraat 21. ✆ 020/428-4969. Tram: 13, 14, 17 to Westermarkt.

JEWELRY

BLGK Edelsmeden   This store is run by a group of jewelry designers who produce and sell affordable jewelry with character. Each designer has his or her own slant on things. Some of their pieces represent a new and fresh spin on classic forms, while others are more innovative and imaginative. Open Tuesday through Friday from 11am to 6pm, Saturday from 11am to 5pm. Hartenstraat 28. ✆ 020/624-8154. Tram: 13, 14, 17 to Westermarkt.

Galerie Ra   Marvelous contemporary designs and materials turn jewelry into an art form here. Owner Paul Derrez specializes in stunning modern jewelry in gold and silver, and goes a bit further, turning feathers, rubber, foam, and other materials into pieces that he describes as "playful." Open Tuesday through Friday from 10am to 6pm, Saturday from 10am to 5pm. Vijzelstraat 90. ✆ 020/626-5100. Tram: 16, 24, 25 to Keizersgracht.

MARKETS

Amsterdammers are traders to the tips of their fingers, as you quickly see if you visit a street market. It's not that the Dutch will bargain for hours like a Moroccan in his souk or follow you around a square pulling bigger and brighter samples from beneath a poncho, like a bowler-hatted Ecuadorian. No, the Dutch street merchants exhibit their enthusiasm for trade in a more stolid way—simply by being permanent. Many of Amsterdam's open-air salesmen are at their stalls, vans, tents, and barges of the city's 26 markets 6 days a week, 52 weeks a year. In all, there are more than 50 outdoor markets every week in Amsterdam and its outlying neighborhoods, and on any given day, except Sunday, you have a choice of several.

The **Waterlooplein Flea Market,** Waterlooplein (tram: 9, 14), is the classic market of Amsterdam, perhaps of all Europe. It's often said that in the market's glory days before World War II, you could find amazing antiques among the junk and possibly even a proverbial dusty Rembrandt. Today your luck is more apt to run in the opposite direction. Most of the merchants now work out of tents, and some sell *patates frites met mayonnaise* (french fries, eaten Dutch style, with mayonnaise) from vans that are a long way from the pushcarts of yesteryear; but among the old CDs and leather jackets, you still find cooking pots, mariner's telescopes, coal scuttles, bargain watches, nuts and bolts, and decent prints of Dutch cities. The market is open Monday through Saturday from 10am to 5pm.

On a row of permanently moored barges, the **Bloemenmarkt (Flower Market),** Singel (tram: 4, 9, 14, 16, 24, 25), at Muntplein, sells a selection of fresh-cut flowers, bright- and healthy-looking plants, ready-to-travel packets of tulip bulbs, and all the necessary accessories for home gardening. Tulips here cost a few cents less than at the flower stands around town. Otherwise, the floating Flower Market doesn't quite live up to its billing as a prominent local tourist attraction. The market is open Monday through Saturday from 10am to 6pm.

You find just about anything and everything your imagination can conjure up at the 350 stalls of the colorful, kilometer-long **Albert Cuyp Markt,** Albert Cuypstraat (tram: 16, 24, 25). Different types of foods, clothing, flowers, plants, and textiles are all for sale. The market is open Monday through Saturday from 10am to 4pm.

The Friday **book market** at Spui (tram: 1, 2, 5) usually has around 25 different booths that offer secondhand books. Often you can find some great deals (even for books in English), perhaps even a rare book or two. Just about any subject is available, both fiction and nonfiction. The market is open Friday from 10am to 4pm.

> *Tips* **Floral Tributes**
>
> Should you be invited to the home of an Amsterdammer, buy flowers to take along with you. That's what the Dutch themselves do.

Kunst- & Antiekcentrum de Looier, Elandsgracht 109 (℃ 020/624-9038; tram: 7, 10, 17), is a big indoor antiques market spread through several old warehouses along the canals in the Jordaan. Individual dealers rent small stalls and corners to show their best wares. The old armoires and other pieces of heavy Dutch traditional furniture are too large to consider buying, but many dealers also offer antique jewelry, prints and engravings, and the omnipresent Dutch knickknacks. De Looier is open Saturday through Wednesday from 11am to 5pm, Thursday from 11am to 9pm.

Local artists come and show off their wares at the **Thorbecke Sunday Art Market,** Thorbeckeplein (℃ 075/670-3030; tram: 4, 9, 14). Picking your way through the artists' tables, you find sculptures, ceramics, paintings, graphics, jewelry, and mixed-media pieces. The market runs from March to December, Sunday from 11am to 6pm.

The **Boerenmarkt (Farmer's Market)** at Noordermarkt (tram: 3, 10), also known as the Bio Market, caters to Amsterdam's infatuation with health foods and natural products. It takes place Saturday from 8am to 2pm.

Other markets you might enjoy visiting include the **Textile Market** (at Noordermarkt, on Prinsengracht), on Monday morning; the **Garden Market** (at Amstelveld, on Prinsengracht near Vijzelstraat), on Monday; the **Stamp Market** (at the post office), on Wednesday and Saturday afternoons; and the **Bird Market** (at Noordermarkt, on Prinsengracht), which on Saturday morning displays a selection of caged birds.

MUSIC

Free Record Shop   The records themselves aren't free, sadly, but the large ground floor and basement of this store hold an incredible number of cassettes, compact discs, and videos at competitive prices. Open daily from 9am to 6pm

(Thurs 9am–9pm). Kalverstraat 230. ✆ **020/625-7378**. Tram: 4, 9, 14, 16, 16, 24, 25 to Muntplein.

SEX

Amsterdam's free and easy—you could even say laid-back—attitude to the mysteries of the flesh has spawned a vast range of stores devoted to satisfying customers' needs, whether real or pure fantasy. Many of these stores are down-and-dirty, sleaze-ball kinds of places, but not all. Here are a couple with a sense of style.

Absolute Danny   The name comes from its owner, Danny Linden, a graduate of the Fashion Academy and the Academy of Fine Arts, who brings her artistic sensibilities to bear on the erotic lifestyle her store supports. You find everything from sexy tableware (if you can imagine such a thing) to S/M clothing and accessories, with the main lines covering sexy lingerie and erotic clothing in leather and latex. Open Monday through Saturday from 11am to 9pm. Oudezijds Achterburgwal 78. ✆ **020/421-0915**. Tram: 4, 9, 14, 16, 24, 25 to the Dam.

Condomerie Het Gulden Vlies   The Golden Fleece condom store stocks a vast range of these items, in all shapes, sizes, and flavors, from regular brand labels to flashy designer fittings, all but guaranteeing your apparel of choice. The store claims to be the world's first specialized condom store—the start of a whole new protection racket. There is probably no significance whatsoever in the fact that the store is located on the edge of the Red Light District. Open Monday through Wednesday, Friday, and Saturday from noon to 6pm, Thursday from noon to 8pm. Warmoesstraat 141. ✆ **020/627-4174**. Tram: 4, 9,14, 16, 24, 25 to the Dam.

TOYS

Some museum gift stores are good sources for toys and other children's knickknacks. Try the stores at the **Scheepvaartmuseum (Maritime Museum),** Kattenburgerplein 1 (✆ **020/624-6601**), for model ships; the **Theatermuseum,** Herengracht 168 (✆ **020/623-5104**), for masks, costumes, and minitheaters; **NEMO,** Oosterdok 2 (✆ **020/531-3233**), for all kinds of scientific toys and gadgets; and the **Tropenmuseum,** Linnaeusstraat 2 (✆ **020/568-8215**), and **Artis Zoo,** Plantage Kerklaan 38–40 (✆ **020/523-3400**), for model animals and ecological stuff.

Ever wished that your kids would take an interest in the sweet, wholesome kinds of things that children ought to like—instead of getting their kicks from zapping aliens, surfing the Web, and watching MTV? Try taking them to the stores below.

Bell Tree   Bell Tree is the place to find treasures for kids. The toys here don't blink, bleep, or run out of battery juice—many of them are actually made from wood! And they're not just modern versions of the kind of playthings that Grandma and Grandpa knew and loved, but real up-to-the-minute gear. Open Monday from 1 to 6pm, Tuesday through Saturday from 10am to 6pm. Spiegelgrscht 10–12. ✆ **020/625-8830**. Tram: 6, 7, 10 to Spiegelgracht.

Kinderfeestwinkel   The name means "Children's Party Shop," and that's just what it is. Everything that a child could possibly want for celebrating the big moments in life, such as birthdays. Open Tuesday through Saturday from 10am to 6pm. Eerste van der Helststraat 15. ✆ **020/470-4791**. Tram: 16, 24, 25 to Albert Cuypstraat.

9

Amsterdam After Dark

Nightlife in Amsterdam, like an Indonesian *rijsttafel,* is a bit of this and a bit of that. The cultural calendar is full, but not jammed. There's a strong jazz scene, good music clubs, and enjoyable English-language shows at the little cabarets and theaters along the canals. The club and bar scene can be entertaining if not outrageous; the dance clubs may indeed seem quiet and small to anyone used to the flash of clubs in New York City, Los Angeles, or London. However, the brown cafes—the typical Amsterdam pubs—have never been better. And there's always the movies. Amsterdam is one of the few cities on the European continent where you can see first-run blockbuster hits from the United States with their English soundtracks intact.

As you go around, look up to admire the elegant gables (illuminated from 30 min. after sundown to 11:30pm) or look down to watch the flickering reflections of the street lamps on the canals. The evening hours are a magic time in Amsterdam; if nothing else has brought you around, a sparkling ripple on the water can make you fall hopelessly in love with the city.

ENTERTAINMENT ORIENTATION

INFORMATION   Your best source of information on nightlife and cultural events is *What's On in Amsterdam,* the VVV Tourist Office's monthly program guide in English, which costs 2€. It provides a complete cultural guide to Amsterdam, day by day, with listings for concerts and recitals, theater, cabaret, opera, dance performances, rock concerts, art films, film festivals, special museum and art gallery exhibitions, and lots more. Many hotels have copies available for guests, in some cases for free, or you can get one at the VVV offices (see chapter 3 for addresses and hours). There is also the free monthly listings magazine *Uitkrant,* in Dutch, which you can pick up at many performance venues.

MAIN NIGHTLIFE AREAS   **Leidseplein,** hot and cool at the same time, is the center of Amsterdam's nightlife, with some of the city's most popular restaurants, bars, and nightspots all within dancing distance of each other. Leidseplein never really closes, so you can greet the dawn and start again. **Rembrandtplein** is a brash and brassy square that really comes alive at night, when it's awash with neon. Although it has a more downmarket reputation than Leidseplein, this area often seems even more intent on having fun, and there are enough cool and sophisticated places to go around. These two areas are connected by Reguliersdwarsstraat, which has some good cafes, including a few gay cafes, and also several fine clubs and restaurants. The **Rosse Buurt (Red Light District)** serves up its own unique brand of nightlife, and adjoining this is **Nieuwmarkt,** which is rapidly becoming a popular, if somewhat alternative, hangout.

TICKETS   If you want to attend any of Amsterdam's theatrical or musical events (including rock concerts), make it your first task on arrival to get tickets.

Box office information is given below. **Amsterdam Uit Buro (AUB) Ticket-shop,** Leidseplein 26 (✆ **0900/0191;** amsterdam.aub.nl); tram 1, 2, 5, 6, 7, 10), can reserve tickets for almost every venue in town; it also handles reservations in advance from abroad. The office is open Monday through Wednesday and Saturday from 10am to 6pm, Thursday from 10am to 9pm, and Sunday from noon to 6pm. The VVV Amsterdam tourist information office (see chapter 3 for addresses and hours) can also reserve tickets, and charges 2.50€ for the service. Most upmarket and many mid-level hotels will reserve tickets as well.

HOURS & PERFORMANCE TIMES   Concert, theater, opera, and dance performances generally begin at 8:15pm; jazz concerts begin at 11 or 11:30pm. Jazz clubs and music spots are usually open from 10pm to 2am, and as late as 4am on weekends. Dance clubs open at 10 or 11pm and close at 4am on weeknights and 5am on weekends.

DRINK PRICES   With the exception of the dance clubs, nightclubs, and other high-ticket nightspots in Amsterdam, you can expect to pay 1.50€ to 3€ for a beer or a Coke and 1.50€ to 3€ for *jenever* (Dutch gin, the national drink; try it at least once, *without* ice). To order your favorite whiskey and water will probably cost you at least 4€, and a mixed cocktail can be as much as 10€. But, remember, these are average prices around town; the cost at a brown cafe (bar) could be less and a hotel bar could charge more.

DRESS CODE   If you intend to go to the opera, a classical music concert, or the theater, don't worry about what to wear, since Amsterdam has a very informal dress code—no code at all, really. Of course, you might want to dress up, and in fact many people do, but you'll never be turned away for being "improperly" dressed.

SAFETY   Wherever you wander in Amsterdam after dark, it's wise to be mindful of your surroundings. Fortunately, Amsterdam's less desirable citizens tend to congregate in the less desirable neighborhoods, and none of the nightspots described here are in a problem area, though taxis are advised in a few cases.

For personal safety in the Red Light District, stick to the main streets and the crowds. It's asking for trouble to go off on your own at night down some of those very narrow and dark side streets and connecting lanes between the canals—some are so narrow that you literally have to squeeze past people. The main streets are usually busy and quite brightly lit (what with all those red lights and neon signs) and most clubs have their own security, since they have a vested interest in not having their customers mugged. Remember, though, that the kinds of industries active here tend to attract less savory types, including muggers, pickpockets, drug dealers, junkies, street prostitutes and their pimps, and

---

Tips **That's the Ticket**

If you're interested in cultural events and are under age 26, go by the **Amsterdam Uit Buro (AUB),** Kleine-Gartmanplantsoen 21 (✆ **0900/0191;** tram: 1, 2, 5, 6, 7, 10), just off Leidseplein, and pick up a **CJP** (Cultural Youth Pass) for 11€. This pass grants you free admission to most museums and discounts on most cultural events. The AUB is open Monday through Wednesday and Saturday from 10am to 6pm, Thursday from 10am to 9pm, and Sunday from noon to 6pm.

weird folks in general. But there are also plenty of tour groups who seem to be having a great time, judging by all the laughing they do as they walk around.

1 The Performing Arts

CLASSICAL MUSIC

Amsterdam's top orchestra—indeed one of the world's top orchestras—is the famed **Royal Concertgebouw Orchestra,** which performs mainly in the Concertgebouw, but can also be found giving an occasional open-air concert in the Vondelpark. The Concertgebouw Orchestra can produce any of the great classical pieces at the tap of a baton, yet it is also willing to go out on a limb from time to time with modern and experimental works. The city's other full orchestra, the **Netherlands Philharmonic Orchestra,** fondly known as the NedPho, isn't far behind its illustrious cousin, if behind at all. It performs in the Beurs van Berlage, its main venue, and in the Concertgebouw. The NedPho has found its niche in a somewhat adventurous repertoire, which often includes opera collaborations. In addition, at either of these venues you may well catch one of Holland's other top orchestras, such as The Hague's **Residentie Orchestra** and the **Rotterdam Philharmonic,** and visiting orchestras from abroad.

When it comes to chamber music, the **Netherlands Chamber Orchestra, Amsterdam Baroque Orchestra,** and **Orchestra of the Eighteenth Century** provide plenty of possibilities, often playing with authentic period instruments and ably supported by the **Netherlands Chamber Choir.** Students of the **Sweelinck Conservatorium** fit themselves in at all possible times and places. You often hear these outfits in the Recital Hall of the Concertgebouw, the Beurs van Berlage, or in one of Amsterdam's historic churches (for information on venues, see below).

OPERA

Productions by the **Netherlands Opera** dominate the schedule at the Muziektheater. Although less well known internationally than the Royal Concertgebouw Orchestra or either of Holland's major dance companies, the Netherlands Opera has its own well-known performers and a devoted following. In recent years, under the artistic direction of Pierre Audi, it staged a successful Monteverdi trilogy before moving confidently on to Wagner's *Ring* cycle.

DANCE

The Dutch take pride in the growing international popularity and prestige of their major dance companies. The **Dutch National Ballet,** home-based at Amsterdam's Muziektheater, has a repertoire of both classical and modern works,

Arts Adventure

This is a cultural program designed to extend the regular flow of cultural events into the previously dormant months of July and August—precisely the time when most tourists visit the city. The program includes more offbeat and informal events across the full range of the arts than would be the case with the main (Sept–June) cultural program of opera, ballet, and classical music. Further information is available from VVV tourist information offices and the **Amsterdam Uit Buro** (see "Entertainment Orientation," above).

many by choreographers George Balanchine and Hans van Manen. The **Nether-lands Dance Theater,** choreographed by Czech artistic director, Jirí Kylián, is based in The Hague but frequently comes to the Muziektheater. Both compa-nies are generally accompanied by the specialized **Netherlands Ballet Orchestra.**

THEATER

Amsterdammers speak English so well that Broadway and London road shows and English-language touring companies sometimes make Amsterdam a stop on their European itineraries. It's even possible that you'll find a production of Shakespeare's *Hamlet* or Agatha Christie's *The Mouse Trap* here. However, many of the theater-going opportunities in Amsterdam are more experimental and avant-garde, and most of them are in Dutch.

MAJOR CONCERT HALLS & THEATERS

Beurs van Berlage   The former home of the Amsterdam Beurs (Stock Exchange) now has the **Netherlands Philharmonic Orchestra (the NedPho)** and the **Netherlands Chamber Orchestra** under its roof. What was once the trading floor of the Exchange, built in 1903 by H. P. Berlage, has since 1988 been a concert venue with two halls—the 665-seat Yakult Zaal and the 200-seat AGA Zaal. Holland's **Concertzender** classical radio station is based here. Damrak 243 (near the Dam). ✆ **020/627-0466.** Tickets 7.50€–20€. Box office Tues–Fri 12:30–6pm, Sat 12:30–5pm, and 1¼ hr. before performances begin. Tram: 4, 9, 14, 16, 24, 25 to the Dam.

Carré   This big, plush theater on the banks of the River Amstel used to be a full-time circus, but now the clowns and animals are infrequent visitors, though spectacles such as The Flying Karamazov Brothers fill some of the gaps. In addi-tion to opera, dance, and ballet, look out for Dutch-language productions of top Broadway and London musicals—*Les Misérables, The Phantom of the Opera, Miss Saigon, Evita, Cats,* and *42nd Street* have all been on the bill. Top names in the world of rock and pop perform here, but the biggest names now strut their stuff at Amsterdam ArenA (see below). Get your tickets as far in advance as pos-sible because the hottest shows sell out quickly. Amstel 115–125. ✆ **020/622-5225.** Tickets 10€–125€. Box office Mon–Sat 10am–7pm, Sun 1–7pm. Tram: 6, 7, 10 to Weesperplein.

Concertgebouw   The Concertgebouw (Concert Building) is one of the most acoustically perfect concert halls in the world and home base of the Royal Con-certgebouw Orchestra. Musical performances have a distinctive richness of tone that is as much a pleasure for the performer as for the audience. During the musical season (Sept–Mar) and the annual Holland Festival, the world's greatest orchestras, ensembles, conductors, and soloists regularly perform here. Concerts and recitals are scheduled every day and often there's a choice of two programs at the same time on the same evening: one in the Grote Zaal, or Great Hall, and the other in a smaller recital hall, the Kleine Zaal, or Little Hall. Don't worry about your location—every seat in the Grote Zaal has a clear view. It's even pos-sible to sit on the stage, behind the performers; tonal quality is slightly altered there, however, so seats are cheaper.

There are free lunchtime rehearsal concerts at 12:30pm (or thereabouts) on Wednesday in the Concertgebouw. The program may feature chamber music, symphonic performances, or abbreviated previews of a full concert to be played to paying guests that same evening. Concertgebouwplein 2–6. ✆ **020/671-8345.** Tickets 13€–100€; summer concerts (Aug) 25€. Box office daily 9:30am–7pm, until 8pm for same-day tickets; phone orders 10am–3pm. Tram: 3, 5, 12 to Museumplein; 16 to Concertgebouwplein.

Muziektheater   In the 1980s, the construction of this superbly equipped 1,600-seat auditorium sparked street riots that sent tear gas drifting across what is now the stage. Today, it's the performances that cause a stir. The Muziektheater is one of the city's stellar performance venues and home base of the highly regarded Netherlands Opera and Dutch National Ballet. There are "musical lunches" during the concert season—free 30-minute concerts on some Tuesdays at 12:30pm (doors open at 12:15pm). Waterlooplein 22 (beside the River Amstel). ℭ **020/625-5455.** Tickets 20€–60€. Box office Mon–Sat 10am–6pm, Sun 11:30am–6pm. Tram: 9, 14 to Waterlooplein.

Stadsschouwburg   Recently renovated, the plushly upholstered, 950-seat Municipal Theater is the city's main venue for mainstream Dutch theater. It also mounts Dutch, and occasionally English, productions of international plays, both classic and modern. You can also take in opera and ballet here. The baroque theater from 1894, stands on the site of earlier theaters that were destroyed by fire. Performances usually start at 8pm. Leidseplein 26. ℭ **020/624-2311.** Tickets 8€–40€. Tram: 1, 2, 5, 6, 7, 10 to Leidseplein.

OTHER VENUES

In addition to the big four, there are plenty of other venues in Amsterdam. No fewer than 42 of the city's churches are equipped with organs, some of them historic works of art in their own right. Four churches in particular—the **Engelse Kerk,** Begijnhof 48 (ℭ **020/624-9665**); **Nieuwe Kerk,** the Dam (ℭ **020/626-8168**); **Oude Kerk,** Oudekerksplein 23 (ℭ **020/625-8284**); and **Waalse Kerk,** Walenpleintje 157 (ℭ **020/623-2074**)—are regularly in use for baroque chamber music and organ recitals, as is the **Sweelinck Conservatorium,** Van Baerlestraat 27 (ℭ **020/666-7641**).

Theaters, some of which occasionally feature performances in English, include **De Balie,** Kleine Gartmanplantsoen 10 (ℭ **020/623-2904**); **Bellevue Theater,** Leidsekade 90 (ℭ **020/624-7248**), which also hosts modern dance; **De Brakke Grond,** at the Vlaams Cultureel Centrum, Nes 43 (ℭ **020/626-0044**), which otherwise has mostly Flemish theater; **Felix Meritis,** Keizersgracht 324 (ℭ **020/626-2321**); **Frascati,** Nes 63 (ℭ **020/626-6866**), which focuses on modern theater; the multicultural **Melkweg** (see below); **Nieuwe de la Mar,** Marnixstraat 404 (ℭ **020/623-3462**); and the new **Westergasfabriek,** Haarlemmerweg 8–10 (ℭ **020/581-0425**), a multipurpose arts complex in an old gas works. **De Stalhouderij,** Eerste Bloemdwarsstraat 4 (ℭ **020/626-2282**), is a tiny place that puts on only English-language theater. For open-air theater in summer, there's the **Vondelpark Openluchttheater,** Vondelpark (ℭ **020/673-1499**).

A MULTIDIMENSIONAL VENUE

Melkweg *Finds*   A sometime hippie haven in an old dairy factory, the Melkweg (Milky Way) constantly reinvents its multimedia persona. Inside, you find a reasonably priced international restaurant (Eat@Jo's), coffee shop, bar, art center, dance floor, cinema, theater, concert hall, photo gallery, and exhibition space. You need to take out temporary membership before they let you in, but it's worth it. International big-name groups perform here, and deejays spin a musical mix that ranges from ska to house. Friday night is club night for the Electric Circus, a multimedia music extravaganza. In June, the club hosts the World Roots Festival, a world music concert series that features Caribbean and African bands. The Melkweg's organizers have always embraced liberalism and experimentalism, and its theater tends to showcase new groups, both international and local. You can take in comedy, multicultural, and gay and lesbian theater. The entire set-up is a throwback to Amsterdam's glory days in the '60s, but is big enough, and wise enough, to accommodate the latest trends as well. Lijnbaansgracht 234A (near Leidseplein). ℰ 020/531-8181. Cover 5€–10€ plus 2.50€ monthly club membership. Box office Mon–Fri 1–5pm, Sat–Sun 4–6pm. Tram: 1, 2, 5, 6, 7, 10 to Leidseplein.

A COMEDY THEATER

Boom Chicago *(Finds)*   For several years, Boom Chicago has been bringing delightful English-language improvisational comedy to Amsterdam. *Time* magazine compared it to Chicago's famous Second City comedy troupe. Dutch audiences don't have much problem with the English sketches; they often seem to get the point ahead of the native English speakers in attendance. Spectators are seated around candlelit tables for eight people and can have an excellent dinner and a drink while they

> **Impressions**
> I often think the night is more richly colored than the day.
>   —Vincent van Gogh, letter to his sister Wilhelmina, 1888

enjoy the show. The restaurant is open at 7pm, and meals cost 13€ to 15€ per person. Leidseplein Theater, Leidseplein 12. ℰ 020/530-7300. 7.50€–9.50€. Box office daily noon–8:30pm. Tram: 1, 2, 5, 6, 7, 10 to Leidseplein.

2 The Club & Music Scene

CONTEMPORARY MUSIC

De IJsbreker   For the latest in high-tech, electronic music, and anything else that goes out on a musical limb, this is the place. A very good cafe, with a shaded terrace overlooking the Amstel, adds to the club's appeal. Weesperzijde 23 (beside the Amstel River). ℰ 020/668-1805. Cover 7.50€–13€. Tram: 3 to Wibautstraat.

JAZZ & BLUES

Jazz, Dixieland, and blues may be American musical forms, but Europeans— and certainly the Dutch—have adopted them with gusto. July is the best month of the year for a jazz lover to travel to Europe. That's when three major festivals are scheduled almost back-to-back in France, Switzerland, and Holland, including the 3-day **North Sea Jazz Festival,** P.O. Box 87840, 2508 DE, The Hague (ℰ 070/350-1604), held each year at the Congresgebouw in The Hague. It's a convention of the biggest names in the international jazz world, with more than 100 concerts—involving more than 600 artists—scheduled in 10 halls in 3 days.

Described below are a few of the jazz hangouts that dot Amsterdam's cityscape.

Alto Jazz Café   A regular quartet plays jazz nightly to a diverse crowd in this small, comfortable cafe. There are also guest combos and occasionally blues as well—the music is always top-notch. On Wednesday evening, the noted saxophonist Hans Dulfer plays, sometimes accompanied by his equally noted daughter Candy. Korte Leidsedwarsstraat 115 (off Leidseplein). ℰ 020/626-3249. No cover. Tram: 1, 2, 5, 6, 7, 10 to Leidseplein.

Bimhuis   This has been the city's premier jazz and improvisational spot for the past 20 years. "Bim," as locals affectionately call it, regularly features top European and American artists in a relaxed but serious atmosphere. You won't feel that you can't have a conversation, but you won't have to struggle to hear the music either. Tuesday night is workshop night; Sunday, Monday, and Wednesday concerts are rare. Oudeschans 73–77 (near the Rembrandthuis). ℂ 020/623-3373. No cover. 10€–18€. Tram: 9, 14 to Waterlooplein.

Bourbon Street   Bourbon Street, a wonderful little club for jazz, blues, and funk, hosts local talent and guests from the States and elsewhere. There's a cover charge for well-known jazz groups or musicians. The music, which tends toward Dixieland and mainstream jazz, plays well into the night. Leidsekruisstraat 6–8 (off Leidseplein). ℂ 020/623-3440. No cover, except for special acts. Tram: 1, 2, 5, 6, 7, 10 to Leidseplein.

Joseph Lam Jazz Club   This jazz nook beside the harbor offers Dixieland and bebop performed by local and little-known touring ensembles. The crowds tend to be mixed, consisting of couples on dates, hard-core jazz cats in berets, musicians, and younger jazz fans. The free jazz jam sessions on Sunday, which feature more experimental fare and acid jazz, are especially popular. Van Diemenstraat 8 (west of Centraal Station). ℂ 020/622-8086. Cover 5€ Sat only. Bus: 35 to Van Diemenstraat.

Maloe Melo   This small club isn't the Mississippi Delta, but Amsterdam's "home of the blues" features live blues every night and is generally packed. The music's quality varies but a pleasantly intimate setting and an eager audience make for a good time. Lijnbaansgracht 163. ℂ 020/420-4592. Cover 3€. Tram: 7, 10, 17 to Elandsgracht.

ROCK & POP CONCERTS

Nothing changes faster in Holland—or exhibits more variety—than the pop music scene, whether the latest craze is rock, reggae, new wave, or whatever. Performers en route to (or from) world-class stardom always seem to turn up in Amsterdam, and few of their shows have difficulty selling out. Big stars and large-scale productions are occasionally featured at **Carré,** Amstel 115–125 (ℂ 020/622-5225), or, in the case of rock stars, at **Amsterdam ArenA,** ArenA Boulevard, Amsterdam Zuid-Oost (ℂ 020/311-1313), the Ajax soccer club's new stadium in the southeastern suburbs, which has a sliding roof to keep out the ubiquitous Dutch rain (Metro: Strandvliet/ArenA). For ticket information, contact **Ticketline** (ℂ 0900/300-125) or **Mojo Concerts** (ℂ 015/212-1980).

DANCE CLUBS

For local residents, the club scene in Amsterdam is generally a "members only" situation. But as a tourist, you can simply show up and, as long as your attire and behavior suit the sensibilities of the management, you shouldn't have any problems getting past the bouncer. Drinks can be expensive—a beer or Coke averages 5€, and a whiskey or cocktail, 8€—but you can nurse one drink while you dance your feet off, or down a quick beer and move on if the crowd or the music mix is not your style.

The places listed below are some of the most popular at press time, and in Amsterdam these things don't change very quickly. But don't hesitate to ask around for new places once you get here. Of course, you can always consult the trusty *What's On in Amsterdam* for listings.

Akhnaton   Jazz, African bands, and salsa are featured regularly at a spot that caters to a youthful, multiethnic, hash-smoking crowd of joyful dancers. Nieuwezijds Kolk 25 (near Centraal Station). ℂ 020/624-3396. Cover 3€–5€. Tram: 1, 2, 5, 13, 17 to Martelaarsgracht.

Amnesia   Trance-house and hard-core may be part of the history of dancing by the time you read this, but if they aren't yet, this is the place to come to grips with them. This determinedly youth-oriented disco is in the Red Light District. Oudezijds Voorburgwal 3 (near Nieuwmarkt). ✆ 020/638-1461. Cover 5€–8€. Metro: Nieuwmarkt.

Back Door   Enter here for some of the best musical soul food around for an over-25 crowd with a limitless appetite for hip-shaking funk and soul. Along with soul you can hoof it to '60s and '70s music. This place is best approached late, *very* late, because the action doesn't really heat up until after 3am. Amstelstraat 32 (off Rembrandtplein). ✆ 020/620-2333. Cover 5€–8€. Tram: 4, 9, 14 to Rembrandtplein.

Club Arena   A former orphanage chapel with frescoed walls is the atmospheric if unlikely setting for one of the city's hottest clubs. Deejays rustle up music from the '60s to the '90s that draws a surprisingly youthful crowd to the Timezone club nights, where funk, soul, and New York disco reign. 's Gravesandestraat 51 (near the Tropenmuseum). ✆ 020/850-2400. Cover is 6€–7.50€. Tram 7, 10 to Korte 's-Gravesandestraat.

De Duivel   Other nightclubs in Amsterdam play some hip-hop, but De Duivel is the only one to serve up rap classics and contemporary hip-hop tunes to the baggy-jeans set nightly. Reguliersdwarsstraat 87. ✆ 020/626-6184. No cover. Tram: 16, 24, 25 to Keizersgracht.

Escape   Large and popular, and with a choice of several dance floors, all with flashing lights and a great sound system. On Saturday, the Chemistry club night, helmed by local deejays and an occasional big international name, takes over. Rembrandtplein 11 (✆ 020/622-1111) Cover 7€–17€, free for students on Thursday. Tram: 4, 9, 14.

iT   A legend in its own nighttime, this extravagantly gay disco-club also does mixed nights where everybody performs with gay abandon in a raunchy atmosphere. Anything can happen, and usually does. The crowd is young, and the music is young, with techno and house being especially popular. There are occasional drag shows, and there's a room that's quieter and more conducive to conversation, or whatever. Amstelstraat 24 (near Rembrandtplein). ✆ 020/625-0111. Cover 6€–10€. Mixed nights Thurs, Sun. Tram: 4, 9, 14 to Rembrandtplein.

Mazzo   It sometimes seems that Mazzo has been around forever. Who knows? Maybe Rembrandt discoed here. Its longevity has a lot to do with keeping up with the latest trends while providing something for everyone—though not on the same night. You find just about every kind of club music style on offer here at some time or other. Rozengracht 114 (near Westermarkt). ✆ 020/626-7500. Cover 6€–10€. Tram: 13, 14, 17 to Westermarkt.

Odeon   Your feet might not know what to do at first amid the graceful surroundings of this converted 17th-century canal house. The period ceiling paintings and stucco decor seem more suited to minuets than disco moves. You can dance to jazz, funk, house, techno, R&B, and classic disco here—all at the same time, as there are three different floors. Singel 460 (near Muntplein). ✆ 020/624-9711. Cover 2.50€–5€. Tram: 1, 2, 5 to Koningsplein.

Paradiso   An old church has been transformed to present an eclectic variety of music. A dark and somewhat forbidding exterior belies the bright inside. You might catch some great acts here before they become really famous, or some already established international stars. The majestic interior has lofty ceilings and a high balcony encircling the room, affording excellent views of the central dance floor. The club has extremely popular theme nights, which range from jazz to raves to disco. The VIP Club on Friday night is stylish. Weteringschans 6–8 (near Leidseplein). ✆ 020/626-4521. Cover 8€–22€. Tram: 1, 2, 5, 6, 7, 10 to Leidseplein.

Sinners in Heaven This is a seriously trendy club. The great and the good of the Dutch film, theater, and TV scene like to see and be seen here (especially seen). Every second Sunday of the month you can dance here to R&B, hip-hop, and swing. Wagenstraat 3–7 (off Rembrandtplein). ✆ 020/620-1375. Cover 5€–10€. Tram: 4, 9, 14 to Rembrandtplein.

West Pacific Step on the gas for hip-hop and Latin dance at this cavernous place, in the unlikely setting of the Westergasfabriek, a disused gas plant in the Westerpark district west of Centraal Station, that's now a cultural center, restaurant, and bar (open longer hours than the dance club). This place was born hip—as a club, not as a gas plant—and has stayed that way, so it's often crowded and hard to get in. Haarlemmerweg 6–10 (west of Centraal Station). ✆ 020/597-4458. Cover 5€–8€. Tram: 10 to Van Halstraat.

3 The Bar Scene

BROWN CAFES

Anyone who's sipped a frothy Heineken knows the Dutch can brew beer. But you haven't really tasted Dutch beer until you've tasted it in Holland, served Dutch style in a real *bruine kroeg*, or brown cafe. These traditional Dutch bars are unpretentious, unpolished institutions, filled with camaraderie, somewhat like pubs in London or neighborhood bars in the United States. In a brown cafe, pouring another beer is much more important than dusting off the back bottles on the bar. In fact, the Dutch beer-pouring process itself is part of the charm of these places; it's a remarkable ritual of drawing a beer to get as much foam as possible and then using a wet knife to shave the head between a series of final fill-ups.

Even if you're not a beer lover, venturing into a brown cafe in Amsterdam will give you a peek into the everyday life of the city. You find brown cafes on almost every corner in the old neighborhoods of the city, and you can't miss them. Most have lacy curtains on the bottom half of the window, and perhaps a cat sleeping in the sun on the ledge. In winter the front door will be hung with a thick drape to keep out drafts; you may still find it there long into spring. Once you're inside, you find the smoky, mustard brownness that's unique to an Amsterdam brown cafe, the result of years—no, centuries—of thick smoke and warm conversation.

There may be booths or little tables sprinkled around the place, but the only spots of color and light will be the shining metal of the beer tap and, perhaps, a touch of red still showing in the Persian rugs thrown across the tables (that practice is typically Dutch, if you recall the old paintings) to catch sandwich crumbs and soak up beer foam. You feel the centuries of conviviality the minute you walk in the door of a really old, really *brown* brown cafe. Some have been on their corners since Rembrandt's time, haunted by the ghosts of drinkers past. The best of them are on the Prinsengracht, below Westermarkt, at the Dam, at Leidseplein, on Spui, or with a bit of looking, on tiny streets between the canals.

Café Chris Café Chris opened in 1624 and has been going strong ever since. It's said to be the place where the builders of Westerkerk were paid every week

or two. There are a lot of curious old features to this bar that keep drawing people year after year, including the quirky toilet in the bathroom, which, oddly,
flushes from outside the door. On Sunday night loud opera music engulfs the
bar, attracting a cultured bohemian crowd. Bloemstraat 42 (near Westermarkt). ℂ 020/
624-5942. Tram: 13, 14, 17 to Westermarkt.

Café 't Smalle   Café 't Smalle is a wonderfully cozy spot where you're highly
unlikely to get a seat, or even see one. It was opened by Pieter Hoppe in 1786
as a liquor distillery and *proeflokaal* (tasting house). If you really want an authentic brown cafe experience, you should at least try to stop by. 't Smalle has
expanded its area of operations to the water's edge, with a fine terrace on the
Egelantiersgracht, and to the water itself, on a boat moored alongside. Egelantiersgracht 12 (at Prinsengracht). ℂ 020/623-9617. Tram: 13, 14, 17 to Westermarkt.

De Druif   This is one of those places that not too many people know about.
De Druif ("The Grape") is located on the waterfront and is mainly frequented
by a friendly local crowd. The bar's mythology has it that the Dutch naval hero,
Piet Heyn, was a frequent patron (he lived nearby); however, as happens so
often when good beer is at hand, this seems to be a tall tale come of wishful
thinking—the bar opened in 1631 and Heyn died in 1629. Rapenburg 83 (behind
the Eastern Dock). ℂ 020/624-4530. Bus: 22 to Prins Hendrikkade.

De Karpershoek   Opened in 1629, this bar was once a favorite hangout of
sailors and seamen. The floor is covered with sand, as it was in the 17th century.
Martelaarsgracht 2 (facing Centraal Station). ℂ 020/624-7886. Tram: 1, 2, 5, 13, 17 to Martelaarsgracht.

De Vergulde Gaper   This place is a double delight. In bad weather you can
retreat into the warm, cozy brown cafe atmosphere indoors, and in good weather
you can sit on a terrace beside the Prinsengracht—if you can get a seat. There's
an unseemly dash whenever a table becomes free. Prinsenstraat 30 (at Prinsengracht).
ℂ 020/624-8975. Tram: 1, 2, 5, 13, 17 to Martelaarsgracht.

Gollem   More than 200 different beers are on sale in this ever-popular brown
cafe near Spui. Many of them are international, and in particular, Belgian
favorites, but look for some weird-and-wonderful brews from around the world.
Raamsteeg 4 (off Spui). ℂ 020/626-6645. Tram: 1, 2, 5 to Spui.

Hoppe   Standing room only is often the space situation here and the crowds
sometimes even overflow onto the sidewalk. It seems that, quite by accident,
Hoppe has become a tourist attraction. Locals love this spot, which dates from
1670, and often pass through for a drink on their way home. A convivial atmosphere and authentic decor make it a great place to while away an afternoon. It's
worth stopping by just to see it. Spui 18–20. ℂ 020/420-4420. Tram: 1, 2, 5 to Spui.

In de Wildeman   Tucked away in a medieval alley, this wood-paneled *bier-
proeflokaal* (beer tasting house) dates from 1690. The tile floor and rows of

---

(Fun Fact   Lost Art?

Today's Amsterdammers are no more than a pale shadow of their
esteemed ancestors when it comes to quaffing beer. In 1613 there were
518 taverns in the city, one for every 200 or so inhabitants. Today the ratio
has slipped to one per 725. It seems that the 17th century was a golden
age in more senses than one.

bottles and jars behind the counters are remnants of its earlier days, when it functioned as a distillery. Today it serves 17 draught and 200 bottled beers from around the world. There is a separate room for nonsmokers. Kolksteeg 3 (off Nieuwezijds Voorburgwal). © 020/638-2348. Tram: 1, 2, 5, 13, 17 to Nieuwezijds Kolk.

Reijnders It would be hard for a cafe in this prime location not to be something of a tourist trap—but Reijnders has succumbed only a little to this temptation and can perhaps be forgiven. This is a brown cafe with a long and noble tradition, outstanding looks, and a glassed-in front porch that offers a great vantage point for viewing the comings and goings of Leidseplein. Leidseplein 6. © 020/623-4419. Tram: 1, 2, 5, 6, 7, 10 to Leidseplein.

't Loosje This is a friendly place in the up-and-coming Nieuwmarkt area, popular with students, artists—and guidebook writers. It was built around 1900 and was originally used as a waiting room for the horse-drawn tram. The walls are still ornamented with tiles from that period and a painting of the South Holland Beer Brewery. There are lots of beers on tap. Nieuwmarkt 32–34. © 020/627-2635. Metro: Nieuwmarkt.

BONUS PICKS

As brown cafes are such an important part of the Amsterdam experience, in addition to my 10 favorites described above, here are 10 other great choices: **Bern,** Nieuwmarkt 9 (© 020/622-0034); **Eijlders,** Korte Leidsedwarsstraat 47 (© 020/624-2704); **De Eland,** Prinsengracht 296 (© 020/623-7654); **De Engelbewaarder,** Kloveniersburgwal 59 (© 020/625-3772); **Het Molenpad,** Prinsengracht 653 (© 020/625-9680); **Kalkhoven,** Prinsengracht 283 (© 020/624-9649); **Oranjerie,** Binnen Oranjestraat 15 (© 020/623-4611); **Papeneiland,** Prinsengracht 2 (© 020/624-1989); **De Reiger,** Nieuwe Leliestraat 34 (© 020/624-7426); and **Tabac,** Brouwersgracht 101 (© 020/622-4413).

TASTING HOUSES

There are only three major differences between a brown cafe and a *proeflokaal,* or tasting house: what you customarily drink, how you drink it, and who owns the place. The decor will still be basically brown and typically Old Dutch—and the age of the establishment may be even more impressive than that of its beer-swilling neighbors—but in a tasting house you traditionally order jenever (Dutch gin, taken "neat," without ice) or another product of the distillery that owns the place. Then, to drink your choice of libation, custom and ritual decree that you lean over the bar, with your hands behind your back, to take the first sip from your well-filled *borreltje* (small drinking glass).

Brouwerij 't IJ In addition to the usual features, this proeflokaal has a fascinating location—it's situated in an unused windmill in the city's old harbor area—and a small brewery. You can take guided tours of the beer-making facilities (Fri at 4pm), and then taste the brewery's Pilzen (5% alcohol by volume), Mug Bitter (5%), Pasij (7%), or Zatte (8%) brews. One popular new Brouwerij 't IJ concoction is Columbus, a hearty wheat beer that's reddish, flavorful, strong (almost 10% alcohol by volume), and the new brew of choice among many Amsterdam barflies. Funenkade 7 (at Zeeburgerstraat). © 020/684-0552. Tram: 6, 10 to Mauritskade.

D'Admiraal This tasting house has a small and pleasant outdoor cafe patio. There are also sofas and big comfortable armchairs inside—oh yes, and 15 different *jenevers* and 55 liqueurs, plus a fair Dutch dinner and snacks menu.

Message in the Bottle

The process of conversing with the locals in a bar is smoothed if you can bandy about some Dutch drinking terminology. The most common word for a glass of *jenever* (Dutch gin) is a *borrel* (*bo*-rel) or the diminutive *borreltje* (*bo*-rel-che), though other terms such as *hassebassie* (*hass*-uh-bassie), *keiltje* (*kyle*-che), *piketanussie* (*pik*-et-an-oossee), *recht op neer* (*rekht op near*), and *slokkie* (*slok*-ee) are also used. Avant-garde imbibers may ask for an "uppercut" to prove their international credentials. A glass of *jenever* filled to the brim, as tradition mandates that it must be, is called a *kamelenrug* (cam-ay-len-rookh), meaning "camel's back," or an *over het IJ-kijkertje* (*over het eye kyk*-erche), meaning "view over the IJ (a water channel at Amsterdam)."

Jenever is often ordered with a beer chaser. The barkeep will then place the *kopstoot* (*cop*-stoat), meaning "knock on the head," of a *stelletje* (*stel*-etche), meaning "couple," on the bar. Beer or *pils* (*pilss*) in a small glass is called a *colaatje pils* (co-la-che *pilss*); *kabouter pils* (ka-*bou*-ter *pilss*), meaning "dwarf beer"; or a *lampie licht* (*lam*-pee likht), meaning "little lamp." Ale in a large glass is known as a *bakkie* (*bak*-ee) or a *vaas,* which means jar or vase.

So if you breeze into a brown cafe, park yourself at the bar, and call for a "Recht op neer borrel, make sure it's a proper over het IJ-kijkertje, put a kopstoot with it, a colaatje if you please, and set up a bakkie for later while you're at it," you should get on swimmingly (of course, they might also send for the men in white coats).

Herengracht 319 (along the canal near Oude Spiegelstraat). ✆ 020/625-4334. Tram: 1, 2, 5 to Spui.

De Drie Fleschjes   Not much has changed in this tidy and charming tasting house ("The Three Little Bottles") since it opened in 1650, except that in 1816 Heindrik Bootz liqueurs took over and have been tasted here ever since. There are 52 wooden casks along the wall facing the bar. Open Monday through Saturday from noon to 8:30pm, Sunday from 3 to 8pm. Gravenstraat 18 (off the Dam, behind the Nieuwe Kerk). ✆ 020/624-8443. Tram: 1, 2, 4, 5, 9, 14, 16, 24, 25 to the Dam.

De Ooievaar   This tiny place, the smallest proeflokaal in Holland, sells jenevers and Oudhollandse liqueurs. It's a pleasant place, with a bright bar area to offset the brown walls and wooden casks. Sint Olofspoort 1 (at the Zeedijk). ✆ 020/625-7360. Tram: 1, 2, 4, 5, 9, 13, 16, 17, 24, 25 to Centraal Station.

't Doktertje   This antiques-filled tasting house is near Spui, the main square of the Student Quarter. Ask to sample the homemade *boeren jongen* and *boeren meisjes,* the brandied fruits—raisins and apricots—that are traditional introductions to "spirits" for Dutch *jongen* and *meisjes,* boys and girls. Rozenboomsteeg 4 (off Spui). ✆ 020/626-4427. Tram: 1, 2, 4, 5, 9, 14, 16, 24, 25 to Spui.

Wynand Fockink *(Finds)*   Don't waste your breath—regulars here know all about the little English pronunciation bomb hidden in the Dutch name. This popular *proeflokaal* dates from 1679. Aficionados of the 50 varieties of Dutch

Great Dutch Drinks

The Dutch are famous for their gin, or *jenever,* and their beer. The former is a fiery, colorless liquid served ice cold to be drunk "neat"—it's not a mixer. You can get flavored jenever—from berry to lemon—and just as with cheese, you can get *oude* or *jonge* (old or young) jenever, and every bar has a wide selection of most or all of the above on its shelves. Jonge is less sweet and creamy than the oude variety, but both are known for their delayed-action effectiveness.

As for **beer,** you can get the regular Heineken, Grolsch, or Amstel—called *pils* in Amsterdam, or you can try something different as you make the rounds of the brown cafes (the world-renowned Dutch beer halls). I happen to like the *witte* (white) beer, which is sweeter than pils. Or, on the opposite end of the spectrum, you can have a Belgian dark beer, like De Koninck or Duvel, or a white beer like Hoegaarden. (Belgian beers are very popular in Holland and are, in general, better made, more "artisanal," than the native brews.)

There are also very good Dutch liqueurs, such as Curaçao and Triple Sec.

jenever and 70 traditional liqueurs on display often have to maneuver for elbow-room to raise their glasses. One of the attractions here that wows visitors is the collection of liqueur bottles on which are painted portraits of every mayor of Amsterdam since 1591. That ought to set your pulse racing. Open daily from 3 to 9pm. The attached *lunchlokaal* is, as its name implies, open for lunch. Pijlsteeg 31 (off the Dam). ✆ 020/639-2695. Tram: 4, 9, 14, 16, 24, 25 to the Dam.

MODERN CAFES

Amsterdam has many contemporary cafes that are neither brown cafes nor your friendly neighborhood watering holes (many examples of both categories are acceptably trendy in themselves). You may hear some contemporary cafes described as "white cafes," as distinct from brown cafes. You may also hear talk of the "coke-trail circuit," though that's a bit passé nowadays.

Besides the cafes listed below, you might want to check out Amsterdam's "Grand Cafes," reviewed in chapter 5: Café Dulac, De Jaren, Café Luxembourg, De Balie, Grand Café l'Opera, Het Land van Walem, Ovidius, and Royal Café de Kroon.

Bayside Beach Club "Life's a beach," they say, at the Beach Parties in this Florida-style bar-restaurant-dance place. The waitresses here in minimalist Stars-and-Stripes bikinis seem to have been specially chosen for, shall we say, aesthetic purposes; but lest the establishment be accused of sexism, let me hasten to add that the male staff also seems to have been selected from an International Male catalog. There's live music and deejays on two different levels. Sunday is ladies night (free cocktails and an all-male revue). Halve Maansteeg 4–6 (near Rembrandt-plein). ✆ 020/620-3769. Tram: 4, 9, 14 to Rembrandtplein.

Café Dante This is art gallery chic. The owners cover the walls with a different exhibition of modern art every month. Feel free to wander in and around. Spuistrat 320 (at Spui). ✆ 020/638-8839. Tram: 1, 2, 5 to Spui.

Café Schiller   It may be a little unfair to include Schiller in this designation, with its implication of trendiness. Schiller's style seems timeless. A bright glassed-in terrace on the square and a finely carved Art Deco interior make a good setting for the friendly, laid-back atmosphere, good food, and lively crowd of artistic and literary types. Rembrandtplein 36. ℂ 020/624-9864. Tram: 4, 9, 14 to Rembrandtplein.

Frascati   Frascati belongs to a category similar to Schiller's, except that in this case its own good looks are complemented by a theatrical bent. The surrounding neighborhood is rife with alternative theater, and Frascati is a major player in this minor league. Nes 59 (behind Rokin). ℂ 020/624-1324. Tram: 4, 9, 14, 16, 24, 25 to Spui.

Kanis en Mailand   On a redeveloped island named KNSM Eiland in the old Eastern Docks Area, the cafe takes its moniker from a clever Dutch play on words—or more accurately on sounds. Equally inventive is a time-warp design that lets you step from 1990s functional urban architecture on the outside into a "traditional" brown cafe interior. The illusion is genuine enough that K&M has become a near classic on the city's cafe roster and a legend in its own lunchtime for freshly made snacks. Levantkade 127. ℂ 020/418-2439. Bus: 32 to Levantkade.

Seymour Likely   Woe unto you if you enter here wearing out-of-date duds. And it's no use wailing that they were the latest and hippest thing only yesterday—that's the whole point. The lips of all those beautiful young things inside that aren't curled around a glass, or each other, will be curled into a sneer. Cruel it may be, but you can always withdraw and try your luck across the road at Seymour Likely's offspring, Seymour Likely 2, which attracts a slightly older crowd. Nieuwezijds Voorburgwal 250 (near Amsterdam Historical Museum). ℂ 020/627-1427. Tram: 1, 2, 5, 13, 17 to Nieuwezijds Voorburgwal.

ENGLISH, IRISH & SCOTTISH PUBS

Balmoral   This pub specializes in hunting lodge atmosphere, tartanry, and malt whiskey—of which it has 50 varieties. You almost expect to see a kilted piper sinking a wee dram at the bar while drawing a bead on a pheasant with a silver-chased fowling piece. In the Balmoral Hotel, Nieuwe Doelenstraat 26. ℂ 020/622-0722. Tram: 4, 9, 14, 16, 24, 25 to Muntplein.

Mulligans Irish Music Bar   Both the Irish music and the *craic* (pronounced like "crack"—Irish crack is fast wit and good conversation, not that other stuff) here have been pretty good since it opened in 1988. Bring an instrument and you may be allowed to play. Amstel 100 (off Rembrandtplein). ℂ 020/622-1330. Tram: 4, 9, 14 to Rembrandtplein.

Three Sisters Grand Pub   There's an English-style pub on the first floor, with lots of snug corners for conversation about Shakespeare or Manchester United over pints of warm ale (they have cold beers too), and a New York Steakhouse upstairs. Leidseplein 2. ℂ 020/428-0428. Tram: 1, 2, 5, 6, 7, 10 to Leidseplein.

JORDAAN CAFES

The Jordaan is Amsterdam's iconoclastic working-class district. It has suffered from the depredations of gentrifiers, demolition experts, and cleaner-up-ers, but still retains its distinctive style and preoccupation with its own collective navel. Cafes here are old style, colorful, and working class (a bit like London's

Smoking Coffeeshops

Tourists often get confused about the city's smoking "coffeeshops." Well, it's simple, if controversial: You go to a coffeeshop to buy and smoke cannabis. Though technically illegal, the practice is tolerated. For coffee and a snack you go to a *cafe* or an *eetcafé*—usually, though, the coffee sold in a "coffeeshop" is surprisingly good, considering it's only an excuse for selling something else.

Licensed and controlled, coffeeshops not only sell hashish and marijuana, but also provide a place where patrons can sit and smoke it all day if they so choose—they're one reason why most of Amsterdam's drug aficionados are laid-back and gooey-eyed, as opposed to scary-dangerous and wild-eyed.

Each coffeeshop has a menu listing the different types of hashish and marijuana it sells, and the tetrahydrocannabinol (THC) content of each. Hashish comes in two varieties: white and black. The black hash is usually more powerful, but both are pretty strong. Local producers, who are tolerated so long as they don't go in for in large-scale production (some of their wares are used in pain relief), have developed a Super Skunk hash that is said to be better than imported stuff from Lebanon and Morocco. Connoisseurs say the best has a strong smell and is soft and sticky. A 5-gram bag costs from 3€ to 8€, depending on the quality. Coffeeshops also have hashish joints (*stickie*) for sale, rolled with tobacco.

Coffeeshops are not allowed to sell alcohol, so they sell coffee, tea, and fruit juices. You won't be able to get any food, so don't expect to grab a quick breakfast, lunch, or dessert. You're usually allowed to smoke your own stuff, so long as you buy a drink.

Some of the most popular smoking coffeeshops are **The Rookies,** Korte Leidsedwarsstraat 145–147 (✆ **020/694-2353**); **Borderline,** Amstelstraat 37 (✆ **020/622-0540**); and the shops of **Bulldog** chain, which has branches around the city (the **Bulldog Palace** is at Leidseplein 15; ✆ **020/627-1908**). Like the John Travolta character Vincent Vega in *Pulp Fiction,* you'll find it's mostly fellow high-seeking tourists you'll be gazing at through the fug of bitter-smelling smoke that passes for an atmosphere in these places.

Toker's tip: Don't buy on the street. You stand a fair chance of being ripped off, the quality will be questionable, and there may be unpleasant additives. For more details, including coffeeshop reviews, pick up a copy of the English-language *Mellow Pages* for 3€ from "good" bookstores.

Cockney pubs). You might even get a singsong of incredibly schmaltzy old Dutch songs about stolen kisses behind the windmill.

Café Nol   A bit younger and cooler than your average Jordaan cafe, but the young folks like to sing along as well, you know. Westerstraat 109 (near Noordermarkt). ✆ **020/624-5380.** Tram: 3, 10 to Marnixplein.

Café Rooie Nellis The decor here has to be seen to be believed—and even then you might not. This place has been owned by the same family for generations; it's real down-home Jordaan. Laurierstraat 101 (off Prinsengracht). ✆ 020/624-4167. Tram: 13, 14, 17 to Westermarkt.

De Twee Zwaantjes The two swans of the cafe's name would find it hard going to spread their wings here, but in this intimate little place you're brought face-to-face with the Jordaanese in all their glory. Prinsengracht 114 (at Egelantiersgracht). ✆ 020/625-2729. Tram: 13, 14, 17 to Westermarkt.

COCKTAILS WITH A VIEW

Ciel Blue Bar Even a low-rise city like Amsterdam has a high-rise hotel with a rooftop cocktail lounge. This one is located on the 23rd floor. The drink prices are a little higher than what you'd find at ground level, but the view is worth the cost. From a comfortable vantage point in Amsterdam South, the big picture windows provide a sweeping panorama that takes in the city's residential neighborhoods, the river, and the harbor. Ciel Blue is a particularly enchanting place to be in the evening, when the sun is setting and the lights are beginning to twinkle on in the houses near the hotel. In the Hotel Okura Amsterdam, Ferdinand Bolstraat 175. ✆ 020/678-7111. Tram: 25 to Ferdinand Bolstraat.

GAY & LESBIAN BARS

The gay scene in Amsterdam is strong, and there is no lack of gay bars and nightspots in town. Below are listings of some of the most popular spots for gay men. For lesbians, the scene is a little more difficult to uncover. Places that are hot now might not be later, so you might want to call or visit **COC,** Rozenstraat 14 (✆ **020/623-4079**), the office/cafe headquarters of the Organization of Homosexuals in the Netherlands. The office and telephone lines are open daily from 10am to 5pm. More information should be available from the **Gay and Lesbian Switchboard** (✆ 020/623-6565).

Most of the city's gay bars are in well-defined areas. For frivolous, old-style camp, look along the Amstel near Muntplein and on Halvemaansteeg. You find trendier places along Reguliersdwarsstraat. Casual locals head for Kerkstraat, on both sides of Leidsestraat.

Lesbian bars are more thinly spread, from the longstanding Vive-la-Vie near Rembrandtplein, to the brown-cafe atmosphere of Saarein in the Jordaan, to the hipper Getto, a mixed bar and restaurant on Warmoesstraat (see listings below for details).

Amstel Taveerne One of the city's oldest and most traditional gay bars, this is the kind of place where about an hour after happy hour everyone starts singing popular songs. Although the songs are in Dutch, the crowd welcomes visitors from other countries, so don't be afraid to sing along. Amstel 54 (off Rembrandtplein). ✆ 020/623-4254. Tram: 4, 9, 14 to Rembrandtplein.

Café April It's said that every gay visitor to Amsterdam goes here at least once, so you're likely to make friends that hail from around the world. A light menu is served. **April's Exit,** an affiliated dance club at Reguliersdwarsstraat 42 (✆ **020/625-8788**), is close by, and

> **Impressions**
> I just wanna get, like, stoned out of my head all day.
> —Young American, overheard entering a coffeeshop

For Women Only

Amsterdam is very much a center of women's activism, and there are many women's centers around the city. **Vrouwenhuis (Women's House), at Nieuwe Herengracht 95 (✆ 020/625-2066)**, has a cafe that opens on Wednesday from noon to 5pm and Thursday from noon to 9pm.

---

many people from the Café April head over after happy hour. Reguliersdwarsstraat 37 (near the Flower Market). ✆ 020/625-9572. Tram: 1, 2, 5 to Koningsplein.

Cockring   The most popular gay disco in town generally lays down no-nonsense, hard-core, high-decibel dance and techno music on the dance floor. More relaxed beats in the sociable upstairs bar make a welcome break. Warmoesstraat 96 (Red Light District). ✆ 020/623-9604. Tram: 4, 9, 14, 16, 24, 25 to the Dam.

Getto   This 3-year-old bar and restaurant attracts an equal mix of boys and girls with its hip interior and such events as "Club Fu" karaoke (first Mon of every month) and bingo (every Thurs). There is an eclectic dinner menu inspired by food from around the world, whether vegetarian or a Cajun crocodile steak, and the kitchen stays open until 11pm. Open Wednesday, Thursday, and Sunday from 5pm to 1am, Friday and Saturday from 5pm to 2am. Warmoesstraat 51 (Red Light District). ✆ 020/421-5151. Tram: 1, 2, 4, 5, 9, 13, 14, 16, 17, 24, 25 to Centraal Station.

Saarein   Once a female-only enclave with a feisty atmosphere, the bar is now open to both genders and has livened up a bit. Attractions include pool, darts, and pinball. The recent change in atmosphere has included the addition of food, with a well-priced dinner menu of continental fare from 6pm to 9:30pm. Open Sunday through Thursday from 5pm to 1am, Friday and Saturday from 5pm to 2am. Elandstraat 119 (Jordaan). ✆ 020/623-4901. Tram 7, 10, 17 to Marnixstraat.

Spijker   This longstanding neighborhood bar attracts a casual crowd that extends a friendly welcome to visitors. The pinball machine and pool table are sociable focal points, and side-by-side video screens show an amusing juxtaposition of cartoons and erotica. Lively bar staffers keep the atmosphere relaxed with a varied selection of music and stiff drinks, and happy "hour" draws the crowds in daily from 5 to 7pm. Open Sunday through Thursday from 1pm to 1am, Friday and Saturday from 1pm to 3am. Kerkstraat 4 (corner with Leidsegracht). ✆ 020/620-5919. Tram: 1, 2, 5 to Prinsengracht.

Vive-la-Vie   This lesbian bar celebrated its 20th anniversary in 2000. The place attracts a young, lively crowd before club-hopping time, and lipstick isn't forbidden. The sidewalk terrace offers excellent summertime relaxation and a fine view of the flocks of tourists in neighboring Rembrandtplein. Open Sunday through Thursday from 2:30pm to 1am, Friday and Saturday from 3pm to 3am. Amstelstraat 7 (off Rembrandtplein). ✆ 020/624-0114. Tram: 4, 9, 14 to Rembrandtplein.

Web   Behind its corrugated metal facade, this popular after-work drinks venue has a raunchy atmosphere and plenty of walk space. Tuesday is "beer bust" and Wednesday evening is prize-draw night. On Sunday evening at 7pm you can line up for a food buffet. Open Sunday through Thursday from 2pm to 1am, Friday and Saturday from 2pm to 2am. St. Jakobsstraat 6 (at Nieuwendijk). ✆ 020/623-6758. Tram: 1, 2, 5, 13, 17 to Nieuwezijds Kolk.

4 The Red Light District

Prostitution is legal in Holland, and in Amsterdam most of it is concentrated in the Red Light District. Even if you don't want to play, this is a place you may want to see at night, when the red lights reflect from the inky surface of the canals. Lots of visitors come here out of curiosity or just for fun. There's no problem with wandering around, and you don't need to worry much about crime as long as you stick to the busier streets—and keep an eye out for pickpockets. While you can josh with the hookers behind the windows, taking pictures of them is a no-no; large and observant men are always on the lookout and will have no qualms about throwing your camera (and maybe you) into the canal. Visiting women going around in groups of two or more won't be noticed any more than anyone else, but a single female might be subject to misrepresentation.

The Red Light District, known in Dutch as the *Rosse Buurt,* isn't very big. The easiest way in is on Damstraat, beside the Krasnapolsky Hotel on the Dam. Then stick to the main drag on Oudezijds Voorburgwal, as far north as the Oude Kerk, the venerable Old Church, which stands watch over this passable representation of Sodom and Gomorrah. If you don't mind the weird-looking, sad-sack males and the "heroin whores" hanging around on the bridges, you can go further in, to the parallel canal, Oudezijds Achterburgwal, and the cluster of good bars and restaurants, many of the latter Chinese, at Nieuwmarkt.

You pass lots of red-fringed window parlors populated by women, few of them Dutch, who favor a minimalist dress style, and who tap (or pound) on the windows as likely looking customers go by. Then, there are peep-show joints with private cabins; dark and noisy bars; theaters offering a popular form of performance art; bookshops filled with the illustrated works of specialists in a wide

 Rooms With a View

The most celebrated Amsterdam bordello is **Yab Yum,** Singel 295 (© 020/624-9503; open daily 8am–4am), in a 17th-century canalside mansion. Taxi drivers, who get a hefty tip if they deposit you there, love Yab Yum (named for a goddess of love from the *Kama Sutra*).

The women, all Dutch, well educated, well spoken, gorgeous, and between ages 18 and 24, are strictly moonlighting. Most are reportedly flight attendants, nurses, students, and housewives. The clientele is businessmen, jet-setters, and kinky couples into threesomes or orgies.

A bouncer leads you up the stairs and rings a buzzer. An elegant man initiates you into the establishment's mysteries. The interior is replete with stalagmite chandeliers, pin-cushion red-velvet walls, gold encrustations, etched-glass nudes, a lounge with a splashing Venus fountain, and a U-shaped bar where the ladies perch on stools. The price: about 100€ to get in, and 200€ to 600€ for champagne while you chat.

Innocent entertainment—and expense—can stop there. If it doesn't, you follow a faux leopard-skin carpet leading to luxury rooms fitted out like the extravagant whorehouses of Hollywood Westerns but with whirlpool tubs.

range of interpersonal relationships; video libraries; and dedicated apparel and appliance stores.

Without going into detail about the services on offer in the Red Light District, here are a couple of places that have shown an enduring popularity with visitors.

Bananenbar   Bananas are an essential prop in the nightly drama here, and audience participation is encouraged. Needless to say, the show is mainly of interest to males on temporary vegetarian diets. Let your sense of taste be your guide. Oudezijds Achterburgwal 37. Ⓒ 020/622-4670. Tram: 1, 2, 4, 5, 9, 13, 16, 17, 24, 25 to Centraal Station.

Casa Rosso   In its own words, Casa Rosso puts on "one of the most superior erotic shows in the world, with a tremendous choreography and a high-level cast." Not everyone would describe it in those exact words, perhaps, but this is the local market leader in live shows. Oudezijds Achterburgwal 106–108. Ⓒ 020/627-8943. Tram: 4, 9, 13, 14, 16, 24, 25 to the Dam.

5 More Evening Entertainment

EVENING CANAL-BOAT TOURS

Even if you took the daytime canal-boat tour, come back for cocktails. Special candlelit wine-and-cheese cruises operate nightly year-round, except for December 31. Wine and cheese are served as you glide through the canal district, which is quiet and calm at night. It's a leisurely, convivial, and romantic way to spend an evening in Amsterdam. Operators include **Holland International** (Ⓒ 020/622-7788) and **Rederij Lovers** (Ⓒ 020/530-1090). Boats depart from the canal tour-boat piers on Prins Hendrikkade, opposite Centraal Station. The 2-hour cruises are 25€ for adults, 15€ for children 4 to 12, and free for children under 4. Reservations are required.

CINEMA

In most European cities it's either difficult or impossible to find a theater showing undubbed American and British films, but in Amsterdam you'll find a dozen or more first-run features, most of them Hollywood's finest, in English with Dutch subtitles. Program information is available in English in the free weekly *Film Agenda* brochure, which you can pick up at movie theaters, hotels, and cafes, and in Dutch in the bimonthly magazine *Preview* and the monthly newspaper-style *Filmkrant*, both of which are available at the cinemas. Admission prices are around 8€, depending on the day, the time, and the movie, and you

---

Through a Glass, Clearly

A simple and free evening pleasure is walking along the canals and looking into the houses as you pass. You may think I'm making the shocking suggestion that you window-peep, but in Amsterdam it's not peeping. The Dutch take great pride in their homes and they keep their curtains open in the evening because they want you to see how tidy and *gezellig* (cozy, homey, warm, and inviting) their living quarters are. This doesn't mean you're meant to linger on the sidewalk, gawping through the windows, but a leisurely stroll past a canal house and a peek inside at the decor is okay.

can reserve tickets in advance for a small charge. Don't worry if you're a few minutes late getting to your seat: A string of commercials and trailers always precedes the main feature (except at the art-house cinemas).

Note: If all of a sudden there's a break in the film, which happens at some movie theaters, don't fret; it lasts about 15 minutes, and is called a *pauze.* If you aren't used to intermissions in the middle of movies, it can be incredibly annoying, especially as it seems always to come at an arresting moment on screen, but at least it gives you time to visit the toilet, buy an ice cream, or—if you must—grab a smoke.

The following are the major movie theaters of Amsterdam, many of them multiplexes, and most of which screen first-run Hollywood films: **Bellevue Cinerama Calypso,** Marnixstraat 400 (✆ 0900/1458; tram: 1, 2, 5, 6, 7, 10); **Cinecenter,** Lijnbaansgracht 236 (✆ 020/623-6615; tram: 1, 2, 5, 6, 7, 10); **Cinema De Balie,** Kleine-Gartmanplantsoen 10 (✆ 020/553-5100; tram: 1, 2, 5, 6, 7, 10); **Cinema Amstelveen,** Schouwburg, Stadsplein 100, Amstelveen (✆ 020/547-5175; tram: 5); August Allebéplein 4 (✆ 020/615-1243); **City,** Kleine-Gartmanplantsoen 13–25 (✆ 0900/1458; tram: 1, 2, 5, 6, 7, 10); **De Uitkijk,** Prinsengracht 452 (✆ 020/623-7460; tram: 1, 2, 5); **Kriterion,** Roetersstraat 170 (✆ 020/623-1708; tram: 6, 7, 10); **Pathé ArenA,** ArenA Boulevard 600 (✆ 0900/1458; Metro: Bijlmer); **Pathé De Munt,** Vijzelstraat 15 (✆ 0900/1458; tram: 4, 9, 14, 16, 24, 25); and **Tuschinski,** Reguliersbreestraat 34 (✆ 0900/1458; tram: 4, 9, 14)—the Tuschinski is well worth a visit to view its extravagant Art Deco style alone; on the upper balconies you sit on plush chairs and can sip champagne during the movie.

Art-house, international, and lesser-known films are screened at **Desmet,** Plantage Middenlaan 4A (✆ 020/627-3434; tram: 6, 9, 14); **Film Museum,** Vondelpark 3 (✆ 020/589-1400; tram: 1, 3, 6, 12); **Het Ketelhuis,** Westergasfabriek, Harlemmerweg 8–10 (✆ 020/684-0090; bus: 18, 22); **Rialto,** Ceintuurbaan 338 (✆ 020/676-8700; tram: 3); **Smart Cinema,** Eerste Constantijn Huygensstraat 20 (✆ 020/427-5951; tram: 3, 12); and **The Movies,** Haarlemmerdijk 161 (✆ 020/638-6016; tram: 3).

CASINOS

The Holland Casinos group operates the only legal casinos in Holland. Amsterdam's is the **Holland Casino Amsterdam,** in the Lido, Max Euweplein 62 (✆ **020/521-1111**), near Leidseplein. There are casinos in other towns as well, including the beach resort of Zandvoort, 30 minutes by train from Centraal Station (see chapter 10). This is European gambling, with emphasis on the quiet games of roulette, baccarat, and blackjack, though there are abundant one-armed bandits, which the Dutch call "fruit machines," and blackjack, poker, and bingo machines (start saving your euro coins!). You need correct attire to get into a casino in Holland (jacket and tie or turtleneck for men), and you also have to bring your passport to register at the door. The minimum age to gamble is 18. Admission is 3.50€. Casinos are open from 1:30pm to 2am.

10

Side Trips from Amsterdam

Amsterdam is the brightest star of a small galaxy of cities and towns that together form what the Dutch call the Randstad (Rim City), a budding megalopolis. Stretching from Amsterdam to Rotterdam, the Randstad contains these two cities plus The Hague, Utrecht, Haarlem, Leiden, and Delft, and two-thirds of the country's 15 million people.

The area offers a number of interesting possibilities for a day outside the city. It won't be a day in the country,

exactly, but you don't have to go far from Amsterdam to see tulips, windmills, and cheese markets. You can climb tall towers, visit interesting museums, ride a steam train, tour the world's largest harbor, and see giant locks and tiny canals. If you're historically minded, you'll want to explore sites associated with the Pilgrims (who lived in Holland for years before sailing to the New World on the *Mayflower*).

EXCURSIONS ORIENTATION

BUS TOURS Among the major Amsterdam-based sightseeing companies are: **Best of Holland Excursions,** Damrak 34 (℃ **020/623-1539**); **Holland International Excursions,** Prins Hendrikkade 33A (℃ **020/625-3035**); **Keytours,** Dam 19 (℃ **020/624-7304**); and **Lindbergh Excursions,** Damrak 26 (℃ **020/ 622-2766**). They provide a variety of half- and full-day tours into the surrounding area, particularly between April and October; in addition, there are special excursions at tulip time and at the height of the summer season. Rates vary a bit from company to company and with the particular tour on offer. Typical half-day tours are 16€ to 25€ and full-day tours 33€ to 40€; children 4 to 13 are charged half fare, and children under 4 travel free.

Two tours offered year-round are the Grand Holland Tour, an 8-hour drive that includes the Aalsmeer flower auction, The Hague and its sea coast resort Scheveningen, Delft, and Rotterdam; and a 6½-hour trip to see the decorated houses and the (occasionally) costumed villagers of Volendam and Marken on the shore of the IJsselmeer (IJssel Lake, formerly the Zuider Zee, an inland sea), with stops at the windmills of Zaanse Schans and a cheese farm along the way. An additional tour, available during tulip time (late Mar to late May), is a 4½-hour or 9-hour drive through the flower fields of the Bollenstreek (Bulb District) and to Keukenhof Gardens. (See the following pages for information on most destinations named here.)

Other tours, generally available only between April and October (though some are year-round), include one to Delft, The Hague, and Scheveningen; an 8-hour trip along the IJsselmeer shore and across the Afsluitdijk (Enclosing Dike) to Friesland; a 4½-hour tour via Zaanse Schans to Edam (a cheese town, with no market); and a 5-hour trip to visit the Alkmaar cheese market and the 17th-century port of Hoorn.

CAR RENTAL   To rent a car for an excursion outside Amsterdam, rates begin at around 45€ a day for a no-frills, subcompact car with a stick shift and unlimited mileage. You pay as much as 180€ a day for a fully equipped luxury car such as a BMW. Gas is around 1.20€ per U.S. gallon for Super (leaded) and 1.10€ for Euro (unleaded).

Rates vary among companies, as do the makes of their cars, the rental plans available, and extra services (some companies, for example, have free car delivery to your hotel). Call around until you find the car, and the deal, that best suits your plans.

The major car-rental firms with offices in Amsterdam are: **Avis,** Nassaukade 380 (✆ **020/683-6061;** tram: 1, 6); **Budget,** Overtoom 121 (✆ **020/612-6066;** tram: 1, 6); **Europcar,** Overtoom 197 (✆ **020/683-2123;** tram: 1, 6); and **Hertz,** Overtoom 333 (✆ **020/612-2441;** tram: 1, 6). All of these firms also have desks at the airport.

TRAIN SERVICES   With a few exceptions, you can easily travel by train to the cities and towns described in this chapter and, once there, walk or take public transportation to the major sights. Dutch cities are not large and train stations are located within a few blocks of the center of town, with buses or trams parked out front. The trains of **Nederlandse Spoorwegen (Netherland Railways)** run frequently throughout the day from Amsterdam Centraal Station to many of the cities mentioned in the following pages (and there's limited night service to some destinations). For example, trains depart at least every half hour to Alkmaar, to Rotterdam, and to Haarlem. Trip times are short: Rotterdam, the most distant destination in this chapter, is just an hour away from Amsterdam Centraal Station; Zaandam, the nearest, is just 8 minutes.

Fares are reasonable. A *dagretour* (1-day round-trip ticket at about 10%–20% savings) to Haarlem is just 6€; to Leiden, 14€; and to Rotterdam, 25€.

You can get information from train stations. For telephone information, the information office of **Netherland Railways** (✆ **0900/9292**) is open Monday through Friday from 7am to 11pm and Saturday, Sunday, and holidays from 8am to 11pm. *Note:* Be sure to check the time of the late trains back to Amsterdam; service is limited after midnight.

BIKES   Holland has 16 million people and 11 million bikes, so you better believe the Dutch are born in the saddle. To fully engage in the Dutch experience, you positively have to climb aboard a bike and head out into the wide green yonder. You can rent bikes at many train stations around the country to tour the local highlights (and at many places in Amsterdam—see "Getting Around," in chapter 3). The tourism authorities have marked out many biking tour routes and have published descriptive booklets and maps, available from VVV offices.

A great suggestion for a longer tour is to bike around the IJsselmeer, the big lake north of Amsterdam (see "Cycling Along the IJsselmeer Shore," later in this chapter). This tour, following a narrow track between the polders and the lake, is a perfect Dutch experience.

Biking in Holland is safe, easy, and pleasant. Almost all roads have designated bike paths, often separated from the road by a screen of trees or bushes, and there are separate traffic lights and signs for bikers. (Mopeds, called *brommers* in Holland, and motor scooters also use the bike tracks.) One thing that can prove an unpleasant surprise for those who think an absence of hills makes for easy

Side Trips: The Randstad

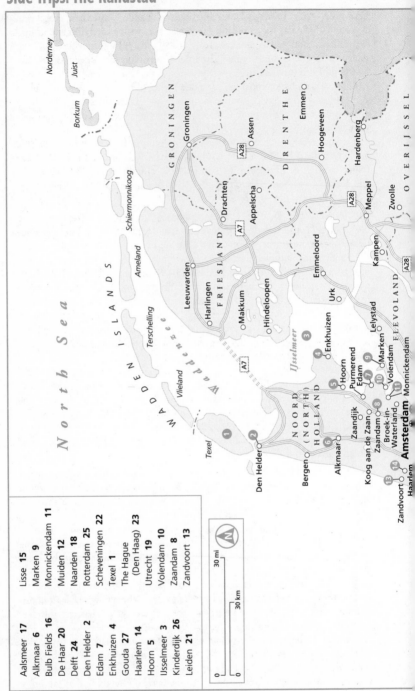

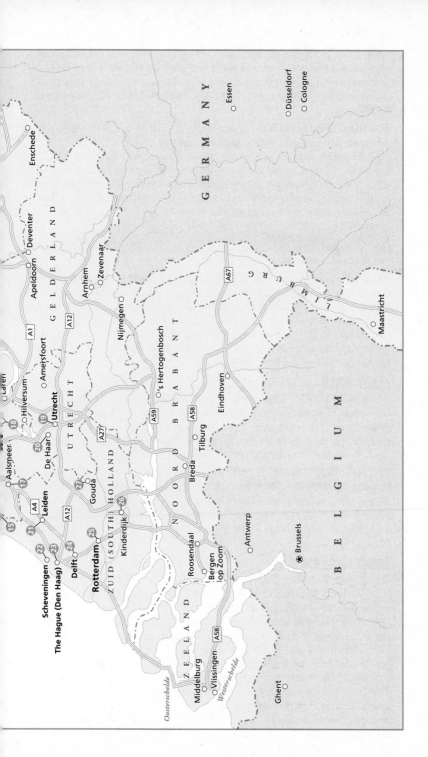

riding is that in a totally flat landscape nothing blocks the wind—which is fine when the wind is behind you and not so fine when it's blowing in your face.

A company that offers great out-of-town (and in-town) biking excursions is **Yellow Bike,** Nieuwezijds Kolk 29 (© **020/620-6940**), off Nieuwezijds Voorburgwal.

TOURIST INFORMATION Anywhere you travel in the Netherlands you can expect to find a local **VVV Tourist Information Office,** usually either near the train station or at the town's main square. If you're driving, you'll see blue-and-white VVV signs posted along major routes into town to direct you to the office. VVV offices are open during regular business hours, including Saturday in many places; hours are sometimes extended in cities and large towns, and during the busy spring and summer seasons.

1 Haarlem ⟨★⟨★

18km (11 miles) W of Amsterdam

If you have only 1 day to travel beyond Amsterdam, spend it in Haarlem. This city of music and art is just a 20-minute train journey from Centraal Station. It's the gateway to the reclaimed Haarlemmermeer polder land, near the beaches and the bulb fields, in the heart of an area dotted with elegant manor houses and picturesque villages. Haarlem is home to two of Holland's finest museums. A trip to Haarlem can easily be combined with one to nearby Zandvoort, which is on the same railway line (see below).

ESSENTIALS

GETTING THERE There are trains departing at least every half hour from Amsterdam Centraal Station to Haarlem; journey time is 20 minutes. Buses depart every 15 minutes or so from outside Amsterdam Centraal Station to Haarlem, but they take longer than the train and there seems no benefit in using them. By car from Amsterdam, take N5/A5.

VISITOR INFORMATION VVV Haarlem, Stationsplein 1, 2011 LR, Haarlem (© **0900/616-1600**; fax 023/534-0537; www.vvvzk.nl), just outside the train station. The office is open October through March, Monday through Friday from 9:30am to 5:30pm and Saturday from 10am to 2pm; April through September, Monday through Friday from 9:30am to 5:30pm and Saturday from 10am to 4pm.

WHAT TO SEE & DO

Traditionally, Haarlem is the little sister city of Amsterdam. It was where Frans Hals, Jacob van Ruysdael, and Pieter Saenredam were living and painting their famous portraits, landscapes, and church interiors during the same years that Rembrandt was living and working in Amsterdam. The finest attraction in the city is the **Frans Hals Museum** ★★★, Groot Heiligland 62 (© **023/511-5775**), which may well be a high point of your trip to Holland. The galleries here are the halls and furnished chambers of a former home, and the famous paintings by the masters of the Haarlem school hang in settings that look like the 17th-century houses they were intended to adorn. Among other pieces is a superb dollhouse from around 1750, though "doll-house" seems an inadequate description for an exquisitely detailed miniature replica of an Amsterdam merchant's canal house. This is a beautiful place to spend an hour or two at any time. The museum is open Tuesday through Saturday from 11am to 5pm, and

(i) Information

— Railway

Haarlem Station

ATTRACTIONS ●
Frans Halsmuseum **7**
Grote Kerk (Church of St. Bavo) **2**
Teylers Museum **5**
Woltheus Cruises **6**

DINING ◆
Café Mephisto **1**
De Pêcherie Haarlem aan Zee **4**
Jacobus Piek **3**

0   0.1 mi
0   0.1 km

Sunday and holidays from noon to 5pm; closed January 1 and December 25. Admission is 5.40€ for adults, 4€ for seniors, and free for children under 19.

Handel and Mozart both made special visits to Haarlem just to play the magnificent, soaring Christian Müller organ of the former St. Bavo's Cathedral, the **Grote Kerk,** Oude Groenmarkt 23 (© **023/532-4399**). Walking to the town center from Haarlem station, you catch only glimpses of the church, but the moment you reach the market square it's revealed in all its splendor. Finished in 1520 after a relatively short building period (130 years), it has a rare unity of structure and proportion. The elegant wooden tower is covered with lead sheets and adorned with gilt spheres. The interior is light and airy, with whitewashed walls and sandstone pillars. Look for the tombstone of painter Frans Hals, and for a cannonball that has been embedded in the wall ever since it came flying through a window during the siege of Haarlem in 1572 and 1573.

And, of course, don't miss the church's famous **Christian Müller Organ,** built in 1738. You can hear it at one of the free concerts given on Tuesday and Thursday from April to October. It has 5,068 pipes and is nearly 98 feet tall, and when it's going flat out it will blow your socks off. The woodwork was done by Jan van Logteren. Mozart played the organ in 1766 when he was just 10 years old. When you see it, you may be dumbstruck at the thought of little Wolfie reaching for one of its 68 stops. St. Bavo's is open Monday through Saturday from 10am to 4pm. Admission is 1.50€ for adults and 1€ for children under 14.

From St. Bavo's, it's an easy walk to the oldest and perhaps the most unusual museum in Holland, the **Teylers Museum,** Spaarne 16 (© **023/531-9010**). Here you find a curiously diverse collection of displays: drawings by Michelangelo, Raphael, and Rembrandt (which are shown on a rotating basis); fossils, minerals, and skeletons; and instruments of physics and an odd assortment of inventions, including the largest electrostatic generator in the world (built in 1784) and a 19th-century radarscope. The museum is open Tuesday through Saturday from 10am to 5pm, and Sunday and holidays from noon to 5pm; closed January 1 and December 25. Admission is 4.50€ for adults, 1€ for children 5 to 18, and free for children under 5.

As in Amsterdam, an ideal way to see the city is by canal boat. These are operated by **Woltheus Cruises,** whose jetty is on the River Spaarne at the Gravensteenbrug (© **023/535-7723**). Boats leave every hour for a cruise around the canals. Cruises, from April to October at 10:30am, noon, 1:30, 3, and 4:30pm, are 6.50€ adults, 4€ children 3 to 11, and free for children under 3.

NEARBY SIGHTS

The little village of **Spaarndam,** north of Haarlem, and reached by bus from outside Haarlem train station, is picturesque enough to warrant a visit just for the scenery, but its main claim to fame is a monument to a fictional character who has become an everlasting symbol of Holland and the Dutch people. You remember, of course, Young Pieter (of *Hans Brinker or the Silver Skates* by Mary Mapes Dodge, 1865), who saved Haarlem from disaster when he plugged a hole in the dike with his finger and steadfastly refused to leave until help came at the end of a long night. Because this fictional boy's heroic act so caught the imagination of people around the world, the Dutch government erected a **memorial** in 1950, dedicating it to the courage of Dutch youth.

Other attractions near Haarlem include the graciously restored 18th-century manor house and country estate, **Beeckestijn,** in the town of Velsen-Zuid near IJmuiden (open Wed–Sun noon–5pm); and the **Museum de Cruquius,** Cruquiusdijk 27 (© **023/528-5704**), a steam-driven water mill and land-reclamation museum at Heemstede. It's open from March to October, Monday through Friday from 10am to 5pm, Saturday, Sunday, and holidays from 11am to 5pm. For early birds, the **fish auctions** at IJmuiden, Halkade 4, are held Monday through Friday from 7 to 11am.

WHERE TO DINE

Café Mephisto DUTCH/INTERNATIONAL   You get reasonably priced meals at this brown cafe, where the decor is Art Nouveau and the music leans toward classic jazz. The kitchen turns out a respectable chicken satay and other soul food staples.

Grote Markt 29. © 023/532-9742. Main courses 6.50€–11€. No credit cards. Sun–Thurs 9am–2am; Fri–Sat 9am–3am.

De Pêcherie Haarlem aan Zee ✦✦ SEAFOOD   You can just about smell the fresh breeze from the North Sea at this fine seafood restaurant facing Haarlem's Grote Kerk. You sit in wooden booths on chairs that have brightly colored canvas backings, like deck chairs. The menu features oysters, crab, prawns, and various fish dishes, all of which go well with the crisp house white wine.

Oude Groenmarkt 10. ✆ **023/531-4848.** Main courses 15€–22€. MC, V. Mon–Sat noon–midnight; Sun 5pm–midnight.

Jacobus Pieck DUTCH/INTERNATIONAL ✦   This popular cafe-restaurant has a lovely shaded terrace in the garden for fine-weather days, while inside it's bustling and stylish. Outside or in, you find excellent food for reasonable prices and friendly, efficient service. At lunchtime they serve generous sandwiches and burgers, and their salads are particularly good. Main dinner courses range from pastas and Middle Eastern dishes to wholesome Dutch standards.

Warmoesstraat 18. ✆ **023/532-6144.** Main courses 7.50€–15€. AE, MC, V. Mon–Sat 10am–11pm; Sun noon–11pm.

2 Zandvoort

26km (16 miles) W of Amsterdam

If you feel like drawing a breath of fresh sea air and you don't have much time for it, do what most Amsterdammers do: Head for Zandvoort. On the North Sea coast just west of Haarlem, Zandvoort is brash and brassy in summer, though it often looks forlorn in the off-season. Yet even in winter it's a long-standing Amsterdam tradition to take the train here, walk up and down along the shore for an hour or so, then, head for one of the town's cafes. If you're in quick-look mode, Zandvoort can easily be combined with Haarlem as a day trip, as both are on the same railway line from Amsterdam.

ESSENTIALS
GETTING THERE   You get to Zandvoort easiest by train from Amsterdam Centraal Station. Trains leave every hour; transfer at Haarlem (where the Zandvoort train is usually waiting on the adjacent platform); during summer extra trains go direct from Centraal Station. In either case, journey time is 30 minutes. Buses leave every 30 minutes from outside Centraal Station to Zandvoort, but they take longer than the train. By car go via Haarlem, on N5/A5/N200, but beware of frequent long traffic lines in summer.

VISITOR INFORMATION   VVV Zandvoort, Schoolplein 1, 2042 VD, Zandvoort (✆ **023/571-7947;** fax 023/571-7003; www.vvvzk.nl), opposite the bus station in the center of town. The office is open October through March, Monday through Friday from 9:30am to 12:30pm and 1:30 to 5pm, Saturday from 10am to 12:30pm and 1:30 to 3:30pm; from April to mid-July and from mid-August to September, Monday through Saturday from 9am to 5pm; from mid-July to mid-August, Monday through Saturday from 9am to 7pm.

WHAT TO SEE & DO
There is not much more to Zandvoort than its **beach,** but what a beach! In summer, this seemingly endless stretch of smooth sand is lined with dozens of temporary beach cafe-restaurants and discos. Holland's prurient picture magazines publish seasonal articles about the antics of the *Jongens van Zandvoort* (Kids of Zandvoort), which are not much more than an excuse to show as many topless

girls as possible. Besides the mainstream beaches, there are gay and naturist beaches, where the shocking sight of a clothed or even partially clothed individual can generate considerable moral outrage.

Windsurfing is pretty good at Zandvoort, which hosts international competitions in this sport, and in catamaran sailing.

At its northern end, beyond the suburb of Bloemendaal aan Zee, the beach runs into industrial IJmuiden, easily identified by the smokestacks of the Hoogovens steel plant. Water quality in this stretch of the North Sea probably leaves something to be desired, and sand in suspension gives it a muddy look.

Circuit Park Zandvoort, Burg van Alphenstraat 63 (© **023/574-0740**), in the north of the town a short distance from the beach, used to be the venue for the Dutch Formula One Grand Prix motor race. Holland's Formula One fans live in hope that a Dutch Grand Prix will once again cleave the sea air with supercharged noise and one day their prayers might be answered. But up to the time of writing, local people's reluctance to revisit the problems the event allegedly caused when it was held here have kept a long-term ban in force. For now the circuit hosts only smaller events. If you come on a summer weekend, you might find a Formula Three training session or a Porsche meeting under way.

Equally racy, though less noisy, is **Holland Casino Zandvoort,** Badhuisplein 7 (© **023/574-0574**), in the center behind the seafront promenade. This is one of only 10 legal casinos in Holland, with roulette, blackjack, and more. The dress code here is "correct" (collar and tie for men), and the minimum age is 18. You need your passport to get in. Casino Zandvoort is open daily from 1:30pm to 2am. Entry is 3€.

More tranquil pursuits can be found by walking through the extensive sand dunes of the **Kennemer Duinen** and **Amsterdamse Waterleiding Duinen** around the town. Reinforced by native vegetation, the dunes play an important part in the sea defense system and have been designated nature reserves. You can have an active fresh-air experience here, strolling along pathways through the woods on the landward side and westward across the dunes toward the sea. A variety of flora occupies this relatively small area, and the beach is never far away if the call of the sea proves too strong.

In town, there are casual shopping, eating, and drinking possibilities.

⌐Tips Hot Jets

For a fast-moving kind of excursion, try a ride to the seacoast on a Russian-built jetfoil operated by the dramatically named **Fast Flying Ferries** (© 020/639-2247). Just as Russian helicopters look a bit ponderous and clunky compared to sleek Western choppers, so do Russian jetfoils look oddly different, but they get the job done. FFF runs a scheduled service through the North Sea Canal between Amsterdam and IJmuiden on the North Sea coast. The jetfoils leave from Pier 7 behind Centraal Station every half hour from 7am to 10am and 4 to 7:30pm, and every hour from 10am to 4pm; the trip to IJmuiden takes 30 minutes. Fares are 4.15€ one-way and 7.10€ round-trip for adults, and 2.50€ one-way and 4.15€ round-trip for children age 4 to 11; children under 4 go free.

---

3 The IJsselmeer ✦

Only in Holland could you say, "This used to be a sea." The IJsselmeer, a large lake on Amsterdam's doorstep, actually was once a sea, the Zuider Zee (as in the words of the song, "by the side of the Zuider Zee . . ."), until the Dutch decided they didn't want it to be one any longer because it was always threatening to flood Amsterdam (remember that Amsterdammers don't like water in their *jenever*). So in the 1930s, workers blocked off the mouth of the Zuider Zee with a massive dike, the Afsluitdijk, running from North Holland to Friesland, and that was that. Nowadays, in the sea's place, there is a freshwater lake, the IJsselmeer (pronounced *eye*-sselmeer). The long shoreline of this great lake is a scenic and popular escape from Amsterdam.

The IJsselmeer is an important stopover point for migrating birds and a feeding resource for indigenous species. It provides much-needed space for satisfying the growing demand for marine leisure time—amateur admirals who command fleets of old sailing ships, sailboats, powerboats, and canoes consider the lake their home waters.

Some of Holland's most emblematic places—Hoorn, Edam, Marken, Urk, Stavoren—lie along its shores. Cyclists test both speed and endurance against its 400km (248-mile) circumference, whirring round in bright lycra blurs or plodding along the dike-top, immersed in wind, rain and shine. The painter's light washes through the clouds, gleaming on the hull-studded lake and bouncing off windmill blades. Almost lost in luminous mists, a Frisian *skûtsje* under full sail looks like a swan spreading its wings.

VOLENDAM, MARKEN & MONNICKENDAM
18km (11 miles), 16km (10 miles), and 12km (7½ miles) NE of Amsterdam

There are differences between Volendam and **Marken** ✦—one is Catholic, the other Protestant; one is on the mainland, the other on a former island; one has women wearing white caps with wings, the other has women wearing caps with ribbons—but Volendam and Marken have been combined on bus-tour itineraries for so long that they seem to have contributed a new compound word to the Dutch language. Unfortunately, *volendammarken* will probably come to mean "tourist trap," or perhaps, "packaged Holland and costumes to go." Nonetheless, it's possible to have a delightful day in the bracing air of these waterside communities, where residents go about their daily business in traditional dress.

ESSENTIALS
GETTING THERE   You get to Volendam and Monnickendam by separate buses, respectively every half hour and every hour, from outside Amsterdam Centraal Station; the Monnickendam bus continues to Marken. Journey time to Volendam is 35 minutes; to Monnickendam 30 minutes; to Marken 45 minutes. When driving to Marken, which was once an island, you cross a 3km (2-mile) long causeway from Monnickendam. You need to leave your car in a parking lot outside the main hamlet before walking through the narrow streets.

VISITOR INFORMATION   **VVV Volendam,** Zeestraat 37, 1131 AA, Volendam (✆ **029/936-3747;** fax 029/936-8484; www.volendam.com), beside the harbor; and **VVV Monnickendam/Marken** at Nieuwpoort 15, Monnickendam (✆ **029/965-1998**). Open times for both offices are Monday through Friday from 9am to 5pm, Saturday from 9am to 4pm.

WHAT TO SEE & DO

Volendam, a small town that lost most of its fishing industry when the enclosure of the Zuider Zee cut it off from the North Sea, is geared for tourism in a big way. It has souvenir shops, boutiques, gift shops, and restaurants in full swing during summer months. Still, its boat-filled harbor, tiny streets, and traditional houses have an undeniable charm. If you must have a snapshot of yourself in the traditional local costume, this is the place to visit. Tourism isn't a bad alternative to fishing—it brings lots of people to town to see such attractions as the **fish auction,** the **diamond cutter,** the **clog maker,** and the **house** with a room entirely wallpapered in cigar bands.

Marken used to be an island until a narrow causeway was built connecting it with the mainland, and it remains as insular as ever. This is a tiny green village of houses on stilts grouped around an equally tiny harbor. It's smaller and quieter than Volendam, and more rural, with clusters of farmhouses dotted around the polders and a candy-striped **lighthouse** on the IJsselmeer shore. This town does not go all over gushy for the tourists; it merely feeds and waters them, and allows them to wander around its pretty streets. Occupants of Marken's green-and-white houses occasionally wear traditional dress, as much to preserve the custom as for the tourists who pour in daily. There's a typical **house** open as a sort of museum and a **clog maker,** who usually works in the parking lot in summer.

In case you feel a bit uncomfortable gawking at the picturesque locals as they go about their daily routine of hanging out laundry, washing windows, and shopping for groceries, take comfort. This is a village that lost its livelihood when access to the open sea was cut off (some of the fishing boats that now sail the IJsselmeer hoist dark-brown sails as a sign of mourning for their lost sea fishing), and tourism has become an alternative industry, with a tax levied on every tour, which goes directly into the village coffers.

Monnickendam, in contrast to its two neighbors, doesn't pay much attention to tourists at all, but gets on with its own life as a boating center and with what's left of its fishing industry, as you can see in its busy **harbor.** Visit the **Town Hall,** at Noordeinde 5, which began life as a private residence in 1746, and step inside to admire the elaborately decorated ceiling. Then take a walk through streets lined with gabled houses and make a stop to admire the 15th-century late Gothic **Sint-Nicolaaskerk,** at Zarken 2.

WHERE TO STAY

If you want to overnight in Volendam or Monnickendam in traditional style, ask at their VVV offices about staying on one of the old wooden IJsselmeer *boters* and *skûtsjes* (sailing ships) moored in the harbor (this option is generally not available in Marken). It makes for a romantic, if somewhat cramped, way to spend the night. Another good bet is the:

Hotel Spaander ✿ This old-fashioned hotel has a real harbor flavor to go with its waterfront location. The public spaces have an Old Dutch interior look; the rooms, however, are modern, brightly furnished, comfortable, and attractive. There's a heated indoor pool and a fitness center. The hotel's two dining rooms and outside terrace cafe are excellent restaurant choices. Meals average 45€, without wine.

Haven 15–19 (north end of the harbor), 1131 EP Volendam. © 029/936-3595. Fax 029/936-9615. 84 units. 82€–118€ double. Rates include breakfast. AE, DC, MC, V. **Amenities:** Restaurant (Dutch); bar. *In room:* TV.

WHERE TO DINE

De Taanderij ★ DUTCH/FRENCH   This little *eethuis* at the end of the harbor is great for lunch or a traditional Dutch treat of *koffie en appelgebak met slagroom* (coffee with apple pie and cream) or *poffertjes* (small fried pancake "puffs" coated with confectioners' sugar and filled with syrup or liqueur). Seafood dishes are also served. The inside is an elegant and cozy interpretation of old Marken style. When the weather is good, a terrace will be spread onto the harborside, where you can absorb the sunshine, the tranquil view over the Gouwzee, and of course the luscious goodies on the menu.

Havenbuurt 1, Marken. ℂ 0299/602-206. Main courses 15€–20€; snacks 3€–13€. AE, MC, V. Apr–Sept Tues–Sun 11am–10pm; Oct–Mar Tues–Sun 11am–7pm.

HOORN ★★

32km (20 miles) NE of Amsterdam

GETTING THERE   Hoorn is the home of Willem Cornelis Schouten, who in 1616 rounded South America's southernmost tip, which he promptly dubbed Kap Hoorn (Cape Horn). Trains depart at least every hour from Amsterdam Centraal Station to Hoorn; journey time is 1 hour. There are buses every hour or so leaving from outside Amsterdam Centraal Station, but they take much longer than the train. By car from Amsterdam, take E22 north.

VISITOR INFORMATION   VVV Hoorn, at Veemarkt 4, 1621 JC, Hoorn (ℂ 0900/403-1055; fax 022/921-5023; www.vvvhoorn.nl), between Hoorn train station and the town center. The office is open May through August Monday from 1 to 6pm, Tuesday through Wednesday and Friday from 9:30am to 6pm, Thursday from 9:30am to 9pm, Saturday from 9:30am to 5pm; September through April, Monday from 1 to 5pm, Tuesday through Saturday from 9:30am to 5pm. It can furnish information on Hoorn's many historic buildings and interesting houses, and a delightful *Walking in Hoorn* booklet.

WHAT TO SEE & DO

While in Hoorn (pronounced *hoarn*) visit the Westfries Museum, Rode Steen 1 (ℂ 022/928-0028). This beautiful 1632 building holds 17th-century artifacts brought from Indonesia by ships of the United East India Company (V.O.C.), armor, weapons, paper cuttings, costumes, toys, naive paintings (which embody a style that is deliberately "childlike"), coins, medals, jewels, civic guards' paintings, porcelain, and a second-floor exhibit that details the town's maritime history. There are also tapestries and 17th- and 18th-century period rooms. A collection of Bronze Age relics is exhibited in the basement. The museum is open April through September, Monday through Friday from 11am to 5pm, Saturday from 2 to 5pm, Sunday from noon to 5pm; October through March, Monday through Friday from 11am to 5pm, Saturday and Sunday from 2 to 5pm. Admission is 4€ for adults, 2€ for seniors and children 16 and under.

During July there's an interesting craft market in the marketplace every Wednesday, with demonstrations and items for sale; and during the summer an antique steam train (ℂ 022/921-4862) takes tourists from Hoorn to Medemblik, a small IJsselmeer town nearby. Tickets are 8.35€ round-trip for adults, 6.35€ for children 4 to 11, and free for children under 4. The 8th-century Radboud Castle (ℂ 022/754-1960) in Medemblik, which was fortified in 1288 against possible rebellion from those troublesome Frisians, has been restored to its original state and is well worth a visit. The castle is open from May 15 to

May 31 and from September 1 to September 14, Monday through Saturday from 10 am to 5pm, and Sunday from 2 to 5pm; from June to August, daily from 10 am to 5pm; from September 14 to April, Sunday from 2 to 5pm. Admission is 2.50€ for adults, 1.25€ for children 5 to 13, and free for children under 5.

WHERE TO DINE

De Hoofdtoren ✩ DUTCH   Boat-lovers will want to sit on the terrace of this cafe-restaurant in an old defense tower, in the midst of the busy harbor, surrounded by traditional IJsselmeer sailing ships and by pleasure boats large and

---

 Cycling Along the IJsselmeer Shore

It's possible to cycle from Amsterdam to Hoorn and return to Amsterdam by train in a day, so long as you're fit, healthy, and ready for some vigorous pedaling. Watch out for the wind—if it's blowing strongly in your face, you may prefer to go another day. You can turn back at various logical places on this route, but once you're beyond the halfway point you're really committed to going all the way to Hoorn.

Still with me? Okay, board the IJ ferry at the pier behind Centraal Station and cross to Amsterdam North. Take Durgerdammerdijk, the road that runs east alongside the lakeshore, to **Durgerdam,** a lakeside village huddling below water level behind its protective dike, its roofs sticking up over the top. You can either pedal beside the houses or venture up onto the dike-top path, past **Uitdam,** with a fine view over the polders to your left and the lake studded with the sails of old-style IJsselmeer *boter* and *skûtsje* sailing ships to your right.

Beyond Uitdam, turn right onto the causeway that leads to **Marken.** You could instead turn left toward Monnickendam, which bypasses Marken and means less cycling. In summer you can take a boat, the *Marken Express,* from Marken harbor across to Volendam, a half-hour trip, with boats leaving every hour. This, in turn, means bypassing **Monnickendam.** Or, retrace your route back across the causeway from Marken and stay on the lakeside road to Monnickendam. Pass through Monnickendam, keeping to the shore, then on through **Katwoude** to **Volendam.** If you've had enough, this is a good place to take a break before cycling back to Amsterdam.

If you're still with the program, go inland a short way from the lakeside dike to **Edam,** famed for its Edammer cheese (see "The Cheese Towns," later in this chapter, for more details). Turn right at the canal bridge at Damplein in Edam, and back along the canal to regain the IJsselmeer shore.

Ahead of you is a straight run north on the lakeside road through the polders. The villages of **Warder, Eteresheim,** and **Scharwoude** are your "checkpoints" on the way to **Hoorn.** You may be ready to flop aboard a train going anywhere by now, but should you have some puff left, visit Hoorn's beautiful inner harbor, the Binnenhaven. Then follow the green-painted signs, pointing first to the VVV office, then to the station, for the train ride back to Amsterdam.

small. The tower, which dates from about 1500, protected the harbor entrance and its interior retains many antique features. Traditional Dutch fare and grilled specialties, both meat and fish, are served at dinner. During the day, there is a lunch and snacks menu.

Hoofd 2. ✆ 022/921-5487. Main courses 9.50€–28€. AE, DC, MC, V. Daily 10am–10pm.

De Waag ✪ FRENCH This grand cafe in the monumental Weigh House from 1609 is open all day, for breakfast, lunch, and dinner. It stands on a square that is among the most beautiful in the country, surrounded by 17th-century buildings from the town's heyday. You can still see the antique weighing scales in the wood-beamed interior.

Rode Steen 8. ✆ 022/921-5195. Main courses 8.50€–17€. MC, V. Daily 10am–1am.

ENKHUIZEN ✪
44km (28 miles) NE of Amsterdam

A great herring fleet of some 400 boats once sailed out of Enkhuizen harbor, and then came the Enclosing Dike, closing off the North Sea. Now Enkhuizen looks to tourism and pleasure boating for its livelihood, and its population has declined from 30,000 in its 17th-century heyday to a mere 13,000 today. Enkhuizen has no train station, but there are buses every hour or so from Hoorn train station. By car from Amsterdam, drive via Hoorn. **VVV Enkhuizen,** Tussen Twee Havens 1, 1601 EM, Enkhuizen (✆ 022/831-3164; fax 022/831-5531; www.enkhuizen.nl), at the harbor, is open November through March, Tuesday through Friday from 9am to 12:30pm and 1 to 3pm; April through October, daily from 9am to 5pm.

WHAT TO SEE & DO
From the Enkhuizen–Lelystad dike parking area you can take a ferry over to one of Holland's finest museums, the open-air **Zuiderzeemuseum** ✪✪, Wierdijk 12–22 (✆ 022/835-1111), dedicated to recreating the historic way of life on the shores of the old Zuider Zee. Its two sections, indoor and outdoor, feature many exhibits, of which the most dramatic are 130 complete old buildings: Old farmhouses, public buildings, stores, and a church from around the sea have been moved here from lakeside villages. They've been brought together to form a cobblestone-street village, as well as examples of the fishing boats, which provided the incomes on which villagers depended. The museum is open April through June and September through October, daily from 10am to 5pm; July through August, daily from 10am to 6pm; closed January 1 and December 25. Admission is 10€ for adults, 8€ for seniors, 6.50€ for children 3 to 18, and free for children under 3.

4 The Zaanstreek
16km (10 miles) NW of Amsterdam

Much of this district is now taken up with shipping and industry, but nestled in its midst is the charm of the Zaanse Schans, near Zaandam, a planned replica village made up of houses moved to the site when industrialization leveled their original locations. Although most of these houses are inhabited by the sort of Amsterdam expatriates who can afford and appreciate their historic timbers (and have the patience for the pedestrian traffic from the tour buses), a few can be visited as museums. It may all look familiar because you have seen pictures of the windmills and green wooden houses in many a Holland brochure; but it's hard to believe that until a century or two ago, not even the ground on which everything stands existed.

Wood was the foundation of wealth along the Zaan River in the 16th and 17th centuries. The burgeoning Dutch merchant-shipping fleet and navy needed the timber, and the invention of a wind-powered sawmill provided the power. The wood was also used to build the Zaan's distinctive green-painted houses, and it is these as well as windmills, including one that makes mustard, which are recalled in the Zaanse Schans open-air museum.

ESSENTIALS

GETTING THERE Trains and buses depart every 20 minutes or so to Zaandam from Amsterdam Centraal Station; the train is the Alkmaar train to Koog-Zaandijk Station, from where Zaanse Schans is around a 10-minute walk. By car from Amsterdam, take A8 north.

VISITOR INFORMATION VVV **Zaanstreek/Waterland,** Gedempte Gracht 76, 1506 CJ, Zaandam (© **075/616-2221;** fax 075/670-5381; www. zaanstreekwaterland.nl), on the main shopping street, between the train station and the town center. The office is open Monday through Friday from 9am to 5:30pm and Saturday from 9am to 4pm.

WHAT TO SEE & DO

To the pleasure of just walking through the **Zaanse Schans,** add a visit to four different kinds of **windmills:** One for lumber, one for paint, one for vegetable oil, and one for the renowned Zaanse mustard. At one time the industrious people of the Zaanstreek had almost 500 windmills working for them. Only 12 have survived, including these 4. A short tour of one shows you just how these wind machines worked; they're open for visitors at varying hours from late March to October. Stop at the **18th-century grocery** that was the beginning of Holland's largest supermarket chain (Albert Heijn) and the old-style **bakery,** visit the **clog shop** to see how the wooden shoes called *klompen* are made, and take a **mini-cruise** on the River Zaan. Most individual museums are open daily from 10am to 5pm (tour buses full of visitors turn up all the time on organized day trips). Admission varies from 4€ to 5€.

Several other points in the Zaanstreek are worth a visit. At **Koog-aan-de-Zaan** there's a 1751 windmill museum, **Het Pink.** At **Zaandijk** you can explore an 18th-century **merchant's home** furnished in the old Zaanse style.

Nearby **Zaandam,** the main town of the district, was an important shipbuilding center in the 17th century. In 1697 Peter the Great of Russia worked incognito for a few days at a Zaandam shipyard, studying shipbuilding methods with craftsmen whom he, an avid nautical student, considered the world's best. He stayed at the humble timber home of a local blacksmith, Gerrit Kist. The

---

Tips Get Your Clogs On

Clogs are still a fixture in many farming areas, where they're much more effective against wet and cold than leather shoes or boots. They're also a tourist staple, and if you plan to buy a pair, Zaanse Schans is a good place to do it. Traditionally, those with pointed toes are for women and rounded toes are for men. All must be worn with heavy socks, so when buying, add the width of one finger when measuring for size.

Czar Peter House (Czaar Peterhuisje), Krimp 23, enclosed in a brick shelter contributed by Czar Nicholas II in 1895, contains souvenirs of Peter's stay, including an exhibit on his life and the small bed into which the 2.1m (7-ft.) tall Czar of All the Russias squeezed himself. Peter visited Zaandam again in 1698 and twice in 1717, each time paying Kist a visit. A **statue** of the czar at work on a boat stands in Damplein, the town's main square.

WHERE TO DINE

De Hoop op d' Swarte Walvis ✭ DUTCH/INTERNATIONAL   This gourmet restaurant with a mouthful of a name sits amid-the green-painted Zaanse Schans houses, with a glass pavilion and terrace overlooking the River Zaan and the waterside villas on the opposite bank. You can expect an unforgettable treat, with subtle mixtures of superior produce (it is owned by the same company as the Netherlands' biggest supermarket chain) cooked and prepared to perfection.

Kalverringdijk 15. ✆ **075/616-5629.** Lunch 35€; 5-course dinner 48€. AE, DC, MC, V. Mon–Sat noon–2:30pm, 6–10pm.

5 The Flower Centers

The first tulip bulbs were brought to Holland in 1592 by the botanist Carolus Clusius, who planted them at the Hortus Botanicus in Leiden, but never got to see the first plants flower—they were stolen by rivals. Tulips soon became highly popular, especially among the aristocracy. Trading in bulbs was a lucrative business and prices soared to ridiculous heights. During the 17th-century's "Tulip Mania," a single bulb could be worth as much as a canal house complete with garden and coach house. Today, the bulbs are more affordable, but competition to produce new strains is still fierce. The place to see them in their full glory is the Keukenhof Gardens at Lisse, where vast numbers of tulips and other flowers create dazzling patches of color. Combine your visit with a trip through the bulb fields between Leiden and Haarlem, for which VVV offices provide a detailed "Bulb Route."

KEUKENHOF GARDENS ✭✭

Flowers at their peak and the **Keukenhof Gardens,** Stationsweg 166A, Lisse (✆ **025/246-5555**) both have short seasons, but if you're here in the spring, you'll never forget a visit to this park. It's a meandering 70-acre wooded green in the heart of the bulb-producing region, planted each fall by the major Dutch growers (each plants his own plot or establishes his own greenhouse display). Then, come spring, the bulbs burst forth and produce not hundreds of flowers, or even thousands, but millions (almost eight million at last count) of tulips and narcissi, daffodils and hyacinths, bluebells, crocuses, lilies, amaryllis, and many others. The blaze of color is everywhere in the park and in the greenhouses, beside the brooks and shady ponds, along the paths and in the neighboring fields, in neat little plots and helter-skelter on the lawns. Keukenhof Gardens claims to be the greatest flower show on earth—and it's Holland's annual spring gift to the world.

The park is open from late March to mid-May only, daily from 8am to 7:30pm. There are special train/bus connections via Haarlem and the nearby town of Leiden. Admission is 12€ for adults, 5.50€ for children 4 to 11, and free for children under 4. There are four cafes where you can grab a quick lunch so that you don't have to go running around looking for a place to eat when you'd rather be enjoying the flowers.

BULB FIELDS

The largest bulb growers are in the northern corner of the South Holland province and the southern part of North Holland, with the heaviest concentration along the 40km (25-mile) Haarlem–Leiden drive. The organized Dutch make finding the different growers easy, with a signposted **Bolenstreek (Bulb District)** route that covers about 60km (38 miles). They suggest that you plan to drive it during weekdays, when stalls along the roads sell flower garlands (do as the natives do and buy one for yourself, another for the car).

Each year from mid-March until the end of April, the bulb fields between Leiden and Haarlem cover 12,370 hectares (30,600 acres) with tulips, narcissi, hyacinths, and more. To get there from Amsterdam, you can either drive first to Haarlem, then south on N208, through Hillegom, Lisse, and Sassenheim; or drive south on A4 (E19) past Schiphol Airport to the Nieuw-Vennep junction, and northeast on N207.

Just one of many bulb growers, the **Frans Roozen Bollentuinen,** Vogelenzangseweg 49, Vogelenzang (✆ **023/584-7245**), a few kilometers south of Haarlem on the N206, provides excellent guided tours that illuminate the ins and outs of growing tulips and getting them to market. Their **Tulip Show** is open daily from late March to late May from 8am to 7:30pm, and their **Summer Show** from July until early October, Monday through Friday from 9am to 5pm. Admission is 3€, and your hosts have no objection whatever to you buying some of their products.

If you are interested in the original plants, a specialized tulip garden in Limmen, 30km (18 miles) northwest of Amsterdam, has re-created some of the older varieties. Here you can see the flowers that are so prominent in the floral displays painted by 17th-century artists—fancifully shaded in flaming patterns and with names like Semper Augustus or Bruin Anvers. You find the garden, the **Hortus Bulborum,** at Zuidkerkerlaan 23 in Limmen. It's open in April and May.

AALSMEER FLOWER AUCTION

16km (10 miles) SW of Amsterdam

Growing flowers and plants is a year-round business that nets 2 billion euros a year at the **Aalsmeer Bloemenveiling (Aalsmeer Flower Auction)** ✻, Legmeerdijk 313 (✆ **029/739-2185**), in the lakeside community of Aalsmeer, near Schiphol Airport. It's one of seven Dutch auction houses that between them handle 60% of the world's cut-flower exports. Every year, in ten million transactions, the auction, sells 5 billion flowers and 500 million plants, from 8,000 nurseries. So vast is the auction house that 120 soccer fields would fit inside.

Get there early to see the biggest array of flowers in the distribution rooms and to have as much time as possible to watch the computerized auctioning process, which works basically like the old "Beat the Clock" game on television—the first one to press the button gets the posies. In keeping with a Dutch auctioneering philosophy that demands quick handling for perishable goods, the bidding on flowers goes from high to low instead of proceeding in the usual direction of bidding—up. Mammoth bidding clocks are numbered from 100 to 1. The buyers sit in rows in the five auditorium-style auction halls; they have microphones to ask questions and buttons to push to register their bids in the central computer (which takes care of all the paperwork). As the bunches of tulips or daffodils go by the stand on carts, they are auctioned in a matter of seconds. The first bid, which is the first one to stop the clock as it works down from 100 to 1, is the only bid. Around 600 lots change hands every hour. Whether or not its tactics are really for the sake of the freshness of the flowers, the Aalsmeer Flower Auction is smart Dutch business.

The auction is Monday through Friday from 7:30 to 11am. Admission is 4€ for adults, 2€ for children 6 to 11, and free for children under 6. Bus no. 172 takes you there from Amsterdam Centraal Station. To drive there, take A4 (E19) south to the Hoofddorp junction, then go southeast on N201.

> **Impressions**
>
> *Aalsmeer is an auction house in the sense that Shanghai is a city or Everest a mountain.*
>   —National Geographic
>   (Apr 2001)

6 The Cheese Towns

ALKMAAR
30km (19 miles) NW of Amsterdam

GETTING THERE   Trains depart at least every hour from Amsterdam Centraal Station to Alkmaar, and buses every half hour or so. By car from Amsterdam, take A8 and A9 north, via Zaanstad.

VISITOR INFORMATION   VVV Alkmaar, Waagplein 2, 1811 JP, Alkmaar (© 072/511-4284; fax 072/511-7513; www.vvvalkmaar.nl), in the town center. The office is open Monday from 10am to 5:30pm, Tuesday and Wednesday from 9am to 5:30pm, Thursday from 9am to 9pm, Friday from 9am to 6pm, and Saturday from 9:30am to 5pm.

WHAT TO SEE & DO
Every Friday morning during the long Dutch summer season there's a steady parade of tourists leaving Amsterdam to visit the **Alkmaar Cheese Market** ★, in the small city of Alkmaar, northwest of Amsterdam, and it's quite a show they're on their way to see.

Cheeses are piled high on the cobblestone square and the carillon in the **Weigh House** tower drowns the countryside in Dutch folk music. Around the square dart the white-clad cheese carriers whose lacquered straw hats tell you which of four sections of their medieval guild they belong to: red, blue, yellow, or green. Carriers are so proud of their standards that every week they post on a "shame board" the name of any carrier who has indulged in profanity or has been late arriving at the auction. The square is filled with sightseers, barrel organs, souvenir stalls, and a tangible excitement.

The bidding process is carried on in the traditional Dutch manner of hand clapping to bid the price up or down, and a good solid hand clap to seal the deal. Then, once a buyer has accumulated his lot of cheeses, teams of guild members move in with their shiny, shallow barrows and, using slings that hang from their shoulders, carry the golden wheels and balls of cheese to the Weigh House for the final tally of the bill. The market takes place from mid-April to mid-September, Friday from 10am to noon.

While you're in Alkmaar, there are a few other attractions you may want to see, including the **Old Craft Market** (also held on Fri 10am–noon); the **House**

with the Cannonball, a souvenir of the Spanish siege; and the **Remonstraat Church,** a clandestine church in a former granary.

EDAM
18km (11 miles) NE of Amsterdam

A short way inland from the IJsselmeer and about 5km (3 miles) north of Volendam, Edam has given its name to one of Holland's most famous cheeses. Don't expect to find it in the familiar red skin, though—that's for export. In Holland the skin is yellow. This pretty little town (pronounced *ay*-dam) is centered around canals you cross by way of drawbridges, with views on either side of lovely canal houses, beautiful gardens, and canalside teahouses.

ESSENTIALS
GETTING THERE   Edam has no train station, but buses depart every hour or so from Amsterdam Centraal Station.

By car from Amsterdam, drive via Volendam (see "The IJsselmeer," earlier in this chapter).

VISITOR INFORMATION   VVV Edam, Stadhuis (Town Hall), Damplein 1, 1135 BK, Edam (© **029/931-5125;** fax 029/937-4236; www.vvv-edam.nl), in the town center. The office is open May through October, Monday through Saturday from 10am to 5pm; November through April, Monday through Saturday from 10am to 3pm.

WHAT TO SEE & DO
This was once a port of some prominence, and a visit to the **Captain's House,** just opposite the Town Hall, gives you a peek not only at its history but also at some of its most illustrious citizens of past centuries (look for the portrait of Pieter Dirksz, one-time mayor and proud possessor of what is probably the longest beard on record anywhere). Take a look at the lovely "wedding room" in the Town Hall, and if you visit during summer months, don't miss the cheese-making display at the **Kaaswaag (Weigh House).** The **Speeltoren (carillon tower)** tilts a bit and was very nearly lost when the church to which it belonged was destroyed. The carillon dates from 1561.

GOUDA
40km (25 miles) S of Amsterdam

Try to come here on a Thursday morning between 9am and noon during July and August, when the lively Gouda (pronounced *khow*-dah) cheese market brings farmers driving farm wagons painted with bright designs and piled high with round cheeses in orange skins. It's an altogether different scene from the market in Alkmaar.

ESSENTIALS
GETTING THERE   Trains depart every hour from Amsterdam Centraal Station, via Leiden or Rotterdam, to Gouda. By car from Amsterdam, take A4 and N207 south.

VISITOR INFORMATION   VVV Gouda, Markt 27, 2801 JJ, Gouda (© **0900/468-3288;** fax 018/258-3210; www.vvvgouda.nl), is open April through May and September through October, Monday through Saturday from 9am to 5pm; June through August, Monday through Saturday from 9am to 5pm, Sunday from noon to 5pm; November through March, Monday through Friday from 9am to 5pm, Saturday from 10am to 4pm.

WHAT TO SEE & DO

If you arrive on **cheese market day** ★★, walk to the back of the **Stadhuis (Town Hall),** where you can sample the famous Gouda cheese. This gray stone building, with stepped gables and red shutters, is reputed to be Holland's oldest Town Hall, and parts of its Gothic facade date from 1449.

Gouda has been the center of a thriving **clay pipe industry** since the 17th century. One local style of pipe has a pattern on the bowl that's invisible when the pipe is new and only appears as the pipe is smoked and darkens; it's called a "mystery pipe," because the designs vary and the buyer never knows what the design will be. Gouda is also noted for its **candles.** Every year, from the middle of December, the market and the Town Hall are lit by candles.

Holland's longest church, and one of its most majestic, **Sint-Janskerk (Church of St. John)** ★, Achter de Kerk 16 (© 018/251-2684), south of the Markt, holds 64 beautiful stained-glass windows, with 2,412 panels. Some date back as far as the mid-1500s. To see the contrast between that stained-glass art of long ago and the work being carried out today, take a look at the most recent window, no. 28A, commemorating the World War II years in Holland. The church is open March through October, Monday through Saturday from 9am to 5pm; November through February, Monday through Saturday from 10am to 4pm. Admission is 1.60€ for adults, .70€ for children under 12.

The monumental **Waag (Weighing House)** ★, Markt 35–36 (© 018/252-9996), from 1668, is Gouda's pride. An exhibit inside uses interactive audiovisual media to tell the story of cheese. You get to know all about the manufacturing process, from grass through cow through milk to cheese, and have a chance to taste the finished product. It also explains Gouda's importance as a center of Dutch dairy production. The museum is open April through October, Tuesday through Wednesday and Friday through Sunday from 1 to 5pm, and Thursday from 10am to 5pm. Admission is 2€ for adults, 1.50€ for seniors, 1€ for children under 12 (free for small children).

For fascinating demonstrations of the centuries-old craft of making beautiful pottery and clay pipes, visit the **Adrie Moerings Pottenbakkerij & Pijpenmakerij (Pottery and Pipemaker),** Peperstraat 76 (© 018/251-2842). At this interesting factory, just a 5-minute walk from Markt, you can watch the work going on and visit the pottery exposition and viewing room. This is a good place to pick up a uniquely Dutch memento of your visit. The factory is open Monday through Friday from 9am to 5pm, and Saturday and holidays from 11am to 5pm. Admission is free.

The **Catharina Gasthuis Museum,** Oosthaven 10 (© 018/258-8440), Gouda's municipal museum, is in a 1665 mansion and former hospital. The jewel of its collections is a gold chalice that Countess Jacqueline of Bavaria presented to the Guild of Archers in 1465. Its whereabouts were unknown for more than a century before it was recovered in the Town Hall's attic and brought here. There are also colorful guild relics, antique furniture, and a terra-cotta plaque with a Latin inscription proclaiming that the humanist Erasmus may have been born in Rotterdam but was conceived in Gouda. The museum is open Monday through Saturday from 10am to 5pm, and Sunday and holidays from noon to 5pm. Admission is 2.50€ for adults, 1.80€ for seniors, and free for children under 18.

During the 18th century, the **De Moriaan Museum,** Westhaven 29 (© 018/258-8440), was the home of a Gouda merchant who sold spices, tobacco, coffee, and tea. The interior of his shop remained unchanged over the centuries.

Going through to the back rooms, you find a large pipe collection. Upstairs is a beautiful display of *plateel,* a colorful local pottery that is Gouda's answer to Delftware. The museum is open Monday through Friday from 10am to 5pm, Saturday from 10am to 12:30pm and 1:30 to 5pm, and Sunday and holidays from noon to 5pm. Admission is 2.50€ for adults, 1.80€ for seniors, and free for children under 18.

You can go out on the platform of the **Molen De Roode Leeuw (Red Lion Windmill),** Vest 65 (✆ **018/252-2041**), west of the Markt, and watch the vanes swish past, while inside, the huge wooden cogwheels and beams work the millstones. Built in 1727 and completely renovated, this grain mill is again grinding away happily. You can buy flour ground in the mill. The mill is open Thursday from 9am to 2pm, and Saturday from 9am to 4pm. Admission is 1.20€ for adults, and .60€ for children.

WHERE TO DINE
Mallemolen ⭐ CLASSIC FRENCH   This excellent traditional restaurant is on what's known as "Rembrandt's corner." There's an ancient windmill on the same street. The restaurant has an Old Dutch look, though the cuisine is chiefly French. Dishes include tournedos with goose liver in a red-wine sauce.

Oosthaven 72. ✆ **018/251-5430.** Reservations recommended. Main courses from 28€; 3-course fixed-price dinner 30€. AE, DC, MC, V. Tues–Fri noon–2pm; Tues–Sun 5pm–midnight.

7 Den Helder & Texel Island

64km (40 miles) N of Amsterdam

Den Helder, at the tip of North Holland Province, is Holland's most important naval base and the site of its Royal Naval College.

DEN HELDER
ESSENTIALS
GETTING THERE   Trains depart at least every hour from Amsterdam Centraal Station to Haarlem, via Alkmaar. Buses depart every half hour or so from outside Alkmaar train station. By car from Amsterdam, take A9 and N9 North, via Alkmaar.

VISITOR INFORMATION   VVV **Den Helder,** Bernhardplein 18 (✆ **022/362-5544;** fax 022/361-4888; vvv.denhelder@trif.nl), next to the train station. The office is open Monday from 1 to 6pm, Tuesday through Friday from 9:30am to 6pm, and Saturday from 9:30am to 5pm.

WHAT TO SEE & DO
You can visit the **Den Helder Navy Museum (Helders Marinemuseum),** Hoofdgracht 3 (✆ 022/365-7535), which holds exhibits illustrating the Dutch Royal Navy's history, and take a look at the state shipyards. Among the ships on display is the warship *De Schorpioen,* an impressive sight to behold. It was built in France for the Dutch Navy in 1868. Although it's now safely chained to the quayside, this steam-driven vessel was once a warship to be reckoned with. Its secret weapon was a ram below the water line that could deal fatal blows to enemy ships. The steam engine still works, and you can visit the restored captain's cabin and crew's quarters. While you're in naval mode, visit the **Dorus Rijkers Lifeboat Museum** (Reddingmuseum Dorus Rijkers), Bernhardplein 3 (✆ 022/361-8320), which chronicles the history of the service. The National Fleet Festival is held at Den Helder for 3 days during July.

Walking on Water

At low tide, the Wadden Sea, between the northern coast of Holland and the **Wadden Islands,** virtually disappears. The muddy seabed becomes visible, and seabirds feast on mollusks in the sand. At times like these, the Wadden Islands seem even closer to the mainland, and if you feel like walking the mudflats, you can join a *Wadlopen* (Wadden Walking) trip and plow your way across to one of the islands. **Don't attempt this without an official guide (there is a very real danger of being caught by the fast incoming tide); with a guide, it is perfectly safe.**

Several companies, both in Groningen and Friesland, organize guided trips from May to early October. These range from a relatively easy round-trip on the flats to more difficult walks to the islands. Wear shorts and close-fitting ankle-high shoes or boots. The trips are very popular; groups are often as large as 75 to 100 people, with about seven guides to look after you. Weather permitting, you start walking at ebb tide, which can be at the crack of dawn. Soon the safe mainland looks far away, and you may feel lost in the middle of a salty mire trying to suck your feet in deeper with every step. But you get used to it, and your attention will be drawn to the unusual landscape as you realize that this is actually the bottom of a sea that you're walking on, and that in a few hours all this will have disappeared under water again. If you're lucky, you might encounter some seals gallivanting in pools left by the retreating tide or sunbathing on the flats. When you finally reach the island, you have to wait for high tide to be able to go back by boat.

Advance booking is necessary, and prices range from around 10€ to 25€ per person. Longer trips can take about 8 hours (including the wait for the boat). For information and reservations, contact the **Wadloopcentrum Pieterburen** (✆ 059/552-8300) in Pieterburen (Groningen) or **Wadloopcentrum Friesland** (✆ 051/845-1491) in Holwerd (Friesland).

AFSLUITDIJK (ENCLOSING DIKE)

It's impossible to grasp just what a monumental work this great barrier that begins 18km (11 miles) east of Den Helder and separates the Waddenzee from the IJsselmeer is until you've driven its 30km (19-mile) length. Dr. Cornelis Lely came up with the plans in 1891, but work was delayed for 25 years as he tried to convince the government to allocate funds for its construction.

Massive effort and backbreaking labor went into this 300-foot-wide dike that stands a full 21 feet above mean water level, keeps back the sea, and converted the salty Zuider Zee into the freshwater IJsselmeer. Midway along its length, at the point where the dike was completed in 1932, there's a **monument** to the men who put their backs to the task and a memorial to Dr. Lely. Stop for a light snack at the cafe in the monument's base and pick up an illustrated booklet that explains the dike's construction. Nondrivers will find both a biking path and a pedestrian path along the dike.

TEXEL

66km (41 miles) N of Amsterdam

During the summer months, it's a great idea to take the 20-minute ferry trip from Den Helder to Texel (pronounced *tess*-uhl), a quiet, family-oriented resort island in the Waddenzee. Texel is the biggest and most populated of the Wadden Islands—with a permanent population of less than 14,000, that's not saying much—and the only one that can be reached directly from North Holland Province (though a tourist ferry operates between the north of Texel and neighboring Vlieland island May–Sept). It has the serenity intrinsic to islands, even allowing for the many visitors who pour in during summer. Beaches, boating, cycling, and bird-watching are the big attractions here, yet eating, drinking, and partying have their place too.

ESSENTIALS

GETTING THERE   The TESO company's car ferries *Molengat* and *Schulpengat* sail every hour at peak times from Den Helder to 't Horntje on Texel—a half-hour trip—from 6:35am (8:35am on Sun and public holidays) to 9:35pm. Reservations are not accepted. There is a connecting bus service every hour from Den Helder railroad station to the ferry terminal.

VISITOR INFORMATION   VVV Texel, Emmalaan 66, 1790 AA, Den Burg (© 022/231-2847; fax 022/231-4129; www.texel.net), just off N501, the main road into town from the ferry harbor. The office is open April through November, Monday through Thursday from 9am to 6pm, Friday from 9am to 9pm, Saturday from 9am to 5:30pm (July–Aug, also Sun 10am–1:30pm); December through March, Monday through Friday from 9am to 6pm, Saturday from 9am to 5pm.

WHAT TO SEE & DO

Unlike some of the Wadden Islands, cars are allowed on Texel, but there's no doubt that the best way to get around and to respect the island's environment is to go by bicycle. Bikes can be brought over free on the ferry, or rented from dozens of outlets in the island's "capital," **Den Burg,** and from the other villages dotted around the coast.

Some 300 bird species have been observed on Texel, of which around 100 breed here. A short list of the star performers includes oystercatchers, Bewicks swans, spoonbills, Brent geese, avocets, marsh harriers, snow buntings, ringed plovers, kestrels, short-eared owls, and bar-tailed godwits. They can be seen in one of the three protected **nature reserves** that are open to the public: the **Schorren, Bol,** and **Dijkmanshuizen** reserves. Visitors must enter on guided tours organized by the **Natuurmonumenten,** Polderweg 2, De Waal (© 022/ 231-8757); call evenings only.

Nature trails through areas belonging to the **Staatsbosbeheer (State Forest Authority)** abound in the dunes and wooded areas, and can be freely visited as long as you stick to the marked paths. Guided tours of some of these areas are organized by **Ecomare,** Ruyslaan 92, De Koog (© 022/231-7741). Ecomare's visitor center is also a seal rehabilitation facility—the waters around Texel used to be rich in seals until their numbers were greatly reduced by a virus in 1988. Ecomare assists with their recovery by caring for weak and injured seals until they are strong enough to be returned to the sea. A bird rehabilitation scheme does the same for avian life threatened by pollution and other hazards. Ecomare also offers temporary exhibits.

8 Castle Country

MUIDEN

13km (8 miles) E of Amsterdam

The perfect starting point for a lovely day in the Middle Ages is the **Rijksmuseum Muiderslot,** near the small town of Muiden at Herengracht 1 (*©* **029/ 426-1325**). This is a turreted, fairy-tale-princess sort of castle—complete with moat—that perches on the far bank of the river Vecht, just 13km (8 miles) east of Amsterdam. Go there to see where Count Floris V was living when he granted toll privileges and thereby officially recognized the small, new community of "Aemstelledamme" in 1275, and where he was murdered just 20 years later. By car from Amsterdam, take the Muiden junction of A1 (E231) east of Amsterdam. There is no VVV office in Muiden.

Muiderslot is where poet P. C. Hooft found both a home and employment—and, I suppose, inspiration for romantic images and lofty phraseology—when he served as castle steward and local bailiff for 40 years in the early 17th century. The castle is furnished essentially as Hooft and his artistic circle of friends (known in Dutch literary history as the Muiden Circle) knew it, with plenty of examples of the distinctly Dutch carved cupboard beds, heavy chests, fireside benches, and mantelpieces. The castle is open from April to September, Monday through Friday from 10am to 5pm and Sunday from 1 to 5pm (last tour at 4pm); from October to March, Saturday and Sunday from 1 to 4pm (last tour at 3pm). Admission is 5€ for adults, 3.75€ for seniors and children 4 to 12, and free for children under 4.

NAARDEN

19km (12 miles) E of Amsterdam

Just beyond Muiderslot is the still-fortified small town of Naarden, where, much in the spirit of locking the barn door after the horse was gone, the local inhabitants erected their beautiful star-shaped double fortifications after the town was brutally sacked by Don Frederick of Toledo and his boys in the late 16th century.

Trains depart to Naarden every hour or so from Amsterdam Centraal Station. By car from Amsterdam, take A1 (E231) east. **VVV Naarden,** Adriaan Dortsmanplein 1B, 1411 RC, Naarden (*©* **035/694-2836;** fax 035/694-3424), inside the walls of the old town. The office is open May through October, Monday through Friday from 10am to 5pm, Saturday from 10am to 3pm, and Sunday from noon to 3pm; November through April, Monday through Saturday from 10am to 2pm.

Beneath the Turfpoort Bastion, you can visit the casemates (the artillery vaults) at the **Nederlands Vestingmuseum (Dutch Fortification Museum),** Westwalstraat 6 (*©* **035/694-5459**), open from Easter to October, Tuesday through Friday (Mon also in summer) from 10:30am to 5pm and Saturday, Sunday, and holidays from noon to 5pm; from November to Easter Sunday from noon to 5pm. Admission is 5€ for adults, 4€ for seniors, 3€ for children 5 to 15, and free for children under 5.

Also see the 15th-century **Grote Kerk,** on Marktstraat (*©* **035/694-9873**), renowned for its fine acoustics and annual performances of Bach's *St. Matthew Passion.* The Grote Kerk is open from June to September daily from 1 to 4pm.

DE HAAR

29km (18 miles) SE of Amsterdam

One of the more richly furnished castles you can visit in Holland—and one that's still owner-occupied part of the year—is **Kasteel de Haar,** Kasteellaan 1 (© **030/677-1275**), at Haarzuilens near Utrecht. Like most castles, De Haar has had its ups and downs—fires and ransackings and the like—over the centuries, but thanks to an infusion of Rothschild money in the early 1900s, it now sits in all its 15th-century moated splendor in the middle of a gracious Versailles-like formal garden. Its walls are hung with fine paintings and precious Gobelin tapestries of the 14th and 15th centuries; its floors are softened with Persian rugs; and its chambers are furnished in the styles of Louis XIV, XV, and XVI of France. The castle is open from March 1 to August 19 and from October 12 to November 15, Monday through Friday from 11am to 4pm and Sunday and public holidays from 1 to 4pm (these dates and times are subject to constant change, so phone before going). Admission is 8€ for adults, 5€ for children 5 to 12, and free for children under 5. The castle is a few kilometers south, then west, from the Maarssen Junction of the A2 (E35) Amsterdam-Utrecht expressway.

9 The Hague ★★

63km (43 miles) SW of Amsterdam

Amsterdam may be the capital of the Netherlands, but The Hague ('s-Graven-hage, or more commonly Den Haag, in Dutch) has always been the seat of government and the official residence of the Dutch monarchs, whether or not they chose to live there. (Juliana, when she was queen, preferred to live near Utrecht, whereas Queen Beatrix has chosen Huis ten Bosch in The Hague Woods as her home.) In 1998 the city celebrated its 750th anniversary—it was in 1248 that Count William II of Holland was crowned king of the Romans in the German city of Aachen, but he chose to live at the Binnenhof Palace in what is now The Hague.

The Hague, only 63km (43 miles) from Amsterdam, is a beautiful and sophisticated city full of parks and elegant homes, with an 18th-century French look that suits its role as the diplomatic center of the Dutch nation and the site of the International Court of Justice (housed in the famous Peace Palace). Among the city's attractions are a number of fine antiques shops and a weekly antiques and curios market from May to September, on Thursday and Sunday from 10am to 5pm; from October to May, on Thursday from noon to 6pm. (An ironic counterpoint to The Hague's genteel image is that it has the worst reputation in Holland for soccer-related hooliganism—some supporters of FC Den Haag behave like Visigoths on match days.)

ESSENTIALS

GETTING THERE   The Hague makes an easy day trip from Amsterdam, with frequent train and bus service. Be advised that The Hague has two major train stations, Centraal and Hollands Spoor; most of the sights are closer to Centraal Station, but some trains only stop at Hollands Spoor. A "Schiphol Line" offers fast rail service (30 min.) to Amsterdam's airport. When driving from Amsterdam, take A4.

Scheveningen is about 4.8km (3 miles) from The Hague. Take tram lines 1 and 9 from Den Haag Centraal Station to Gevers Deynootplein, or drive via A44 and follow the signs.

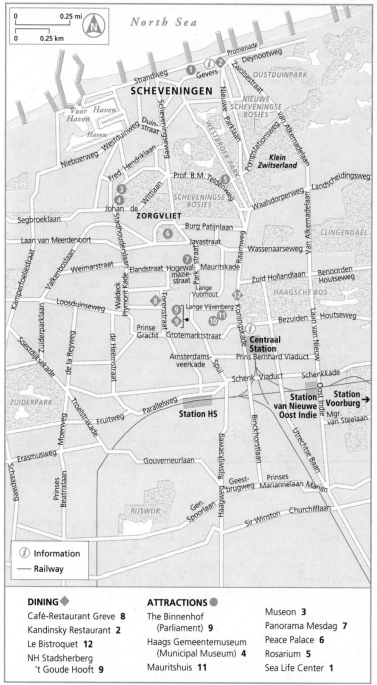

North Sea

0   0.25 mi
0   0.25 km

N

Strandweg
Gevers
Promenade
Deynootweg
Zwolsestraat
OUSTDUINPARK

SCHEVENINGEN

Nieuwe Parklaan
NIEUWE SCHEVENINGSE BOSJES

Voor Haven
Haven
Haven

Nieboerweg
Westduinweg
Duin-straat
Scheveningseweg

WESTBROEK PARK

Pompstationsweg
van Alkemadelaan

Fred. Hendriklaan

Prof. B.M. Teldenweg

Klein Zwitserland

③
④
Johan de
Wittlaan
SCHEVENINGSE BOSJES

⑤

Stadhouderslaan

Waalsdorperweg
Landscheidingsweg

Segbroeklaan

ZORGVLIET
Burg Patijnlaan
⑥
Javastraat

CLINGENDAEL

Laan van Meerdervoort
Weimarstraat
Elandstraat
Hogewal-mazie-straat
Mauritskade
⑦
Park-straat
Wassenaarseweg

van Alkemadelaan

Kamperfoeliestraat
Valkenboslaan
Waldeck
Pymont Kade
de Heemstraat

Lange Voorhout
⑧
Torenstraat
Lange Vijvenberg
⑨
⑨
⑩⑪
⑫
Koningskade

Zuid Hollandlaan
Benoorden Houtseweg
HAAGSCHE BOS
Bezuiden Houtseweg
Laan van Nieuw Houtseweg

Loosduinseweg

Soestdijksekade
Zuiderparklaan
de la Reyweg

Prinse Gracht
Grotemarktstraat
Amsterdams-veerkade
Spui
Prins Bernhard Viaduct

Centraal Station
ⓘ

ZUIDERPARK
Troelstrakade
Fruitweg
Parallelweg
Schenk   Viaduct
Schenkkade

Station van Nieuwe Oost Indie
Oost Indie
Station Voorburg →
Mgr. van Steelaan

Moerweg

Binckhorstlaan
Utrechtse Baan

Station HS

Erasmusweg
Schaapweg
Prinses Beatrixlaan

Gouverneurlaan
RIJSWIJK
Gen. Spoorlaan
Haagweg
Rijswijkseweg
Geest-brugweg
Prinses Mariannelaan Marian
Sir Winston Churchilllaan

ⓘ Information
—— Railway

VISITOR INFORMATION Tourist information is available from **The Hague Visitors & Convention Bureau,** Nassaulaan 25 (© **070/361-8820;** fax 070/361-5459), and from **VVV Den Haag,** Koningin Julianaplein (© **0900/ 340-3505;** fax 070/347-2102; www.denhaag.nl), in front of Centraal Station; open from September to June Monday through Saturday from 9am to 5:30pm; July and August Monday through Saturday from 9am to 5:30pm, Sunday from 11am to 5pm.

WHAT TO SEE & DO

Perhaps the most notable attraction of The Hague is the impressive **Binnenhof,** or Inner Court, a complex of Parliament buildings located at Binnenhof 8A (open Mon–Sat 10am–4pm). You can join a tour to visit the lofty, medieval **Ridderzaal (Hall of the Knights),** in which the queen delivers a speech from the throne each year. If you're in Holland on the third Tuesday in September, be sure to be there to see her arrive and depart in her real golden coach—like Cinderella—drawn by high-stepping royal horses; it's quite a spectacle. Depending on the volume and urgency of governmental business, you can tour one or the other of the two chambers of the **States General,** the Dutch Parliament. The last guided tour starts at 3:45pm and is 2.50€ or 3€ for adults, 2€ or 2.50€ for seniors and children 13 and under, depending on the exact tour being offered at the time. It's requested that you book in advance by telephone (© **070/364-6144**) if you intend to take the guided tour—call ahead in any case to make sure tours are being given on the day you intend to visit. Admission to the Parliament exhibit in the reception room of the Hall of Knights is free.

Adjacent to the Binnenhof Parliament complex is the elegant Italian Renaissance-style **Mauritshuis** ✦✦✦, Korte Vijverberg 8 (© **070/302-3435**), which was built in 1644 as the architecturally innovative home of a young court dandy and cousin of the Orange-Nassaus. Today this small palace is officially known as the **Koninklijke Prentenkabinet (Royal Picture Gallery)** and is the permanent home of an impressive art collection given to the Dutch nation by King Willem I in 1816. Highlights include 13 Rembrandts, three Frans Hals, and three Vermeers (including the famous *View of Delft*), plus hundreds of other famous works by such painters as Breughel, Rubens, Steen, and Holbein (including his famous portrait of Jane Seymour, third wife of Henry VIII of England). The gallery is open Tuesday through Saturday from 10am to 5pm and Sunday from 11am to 5pm. Admission is 7€ for adults, 3.50€ for seniors, and free for children under 19.

If you have an interest in royalty and palaces, take a ride on bus no. 4; its route passes four Dutch palaces built during the 16th and 17th centuries, including Palace Huis ten Bosch, the home of Queen Beatrix (no visits are permitted).

Venture beyond the city center to visit the famous **Peace Palace,** Carnegieplein 2 (© **070/302-4137**), donated by Andrew Carnegie as a home for the International Court of Justice and the Permanent Court of Arbitration. The palace is open for hourly guided tours from June to September, Monday through Friday from 10am to 4pm; from October to May, from 10am to 3pm. Tours are 3.50€ for adults and 1.80€ for children under 13.

Also stop at the impressive center of popular sciences, **Museon,** Stadhouderslaan 41 (© **070/338-1338**), which is open Tuesday through Friday from 10am to 5pm, and Saturday, Sunday, and holidays from noon to 5pm; closed January 1 and December 25. Admission is 6€ for adults, 3€ for children 4 to 12, and free for children under 4.

The **Haags Gemeentemuseum (Municipal Art Museum)** ★★, Stadhouder-slaan 41 (© **070/338-1111**), was designed by Hendrik Petrus Berlage (1927–34) and possesses a world-famous collection of works by Piet Mondrian (1872–1944), including his last work, *Victory Boogie Woogie* (1943), inspired by New York. The museum is open Tuesday through Sunday from 11am to 5pm; closed January 1 and December 25. Admission is 7€ for adults, 5.50€ for seniors, and free for children under 13.

Not far away in the Scheveningen Woods is the enchanting **Maduro-dam** ★★, George Maduroplein 1 (© **070/416-2400**), a miniature village in 1-to-25 scale that represents the Dutch nation in actual proportions of farmland to urban areas. It presents many of the country's most historic buildings in miniature, with lights that actually work, bells that ring, and trains that run efficiently—as all do in Holland. It's open from January to mid-March and from September to late December from 9am to 6pm; from mid-March to June from 9am to 8pm; July and August from 9am to 10pm. Admission is 10€ for adults, 9€ for seniors, 7€ for children 4 to 11, and free for children under 4.

In the **Rosarium** in Westbroekpark, more than 20,000 roses bloom each year between July and September. The grounds are open daily from 9am to 1 hour before sunset.

If you don't have time to visit Scheveningen (see below) from The Hague, you can still see the resort town, sort of, at The Hague's **Panorama Mesdag,** a superb 120-yard-long panoramic painting of the resort as it was in 1880, done in the style of The Hague school. It can be seen at Zeestraat 65, The Hague (© **070/364-4544**), Monday through Saturday from 10am to 5pm, Sunday and holidays from noon to 5pm; closed December 25. Admission is 4€ for adults, 3€ for seniors, 2€ for children 4 to 13, and free for children under 4.

SCHEVENINGEN

So close to The Hague is the beach resort and fishing port of **Scheveningen** that it seems to be part of the same city. Scheveningen exhibits a curious combination of costumed fishermen's wives (they only dress up in their traditional Dutch garb for special events, such as *Vlaggetjesdag*—Flag Day—in mid-May when the first of the new season's herring are landed) near the harbor and tuxedoed croupiers from the casino across from the beautifully restored 19th-century **Kurhaus Hotel.** This is probably the most chic seacoast resort in Holland (though that is not necessarily saying much), with a full cast of international-name boutiques and upscale restaurants.

Tourist information is available from **VVV Scheveningen,** Gevers Deynootweg 1134 (© **0900/340-3505;** fax 070/361-5495; www.denhaag.com), at the Palace Promenade shopping mall.

The attractions of Scheveningen are no longer limited to bicycling on the dunes, deep-sea fishing in the North Sea, and splashing in the waves at the beach or in a wave pool (an indoor/outdoor heated swimming pool that has mechanically produced surf). The city's indoor amusements, which have long included blackjack and roulette at the **Holland Casino Scheveningen,** Kurhausweg 1 (© **070/306-7777**), opposite the Kurhaus Hotel, have been supplemented by video games and pinball machines at the beautiful old Scheveningen Pier jutting out into the North Sea, shopping and noshing at the Palace Promenade shopping mall, and, of course, fish dinners at the restaurants around the harbor (where you just might catch a glimpse of a fisherman's wife wearing the traditional costume of Scheveningen). The beach and bathing zone is called Scheveningen Bad—but it looks pretty good to the Dutch.

Sea Life Scheveningen, Strandweg (aka the Boulevard) 13 (© **070/354-2100**), takes you under the sea in an aquarium with a walk-through underwater tunnel, from where you can see the denizens of the deep, including sharks, swimming around above your head. The aquarium is open daily from 10am to 6pm (10am–8pm in July and Aug). Admission is 7.75€ for adults, 5.25€ for children 4 to 11, and free for children under 4.

WHERE TO DINE

Café-Restaurant Greve ✸ MEDITERRANEAN   What was once a car showroom is now a popular cafe-restaurant. The large windows of the cafe look out on lively Torenstraat; the restaurant is more intimate with low ceiling, candlelight, and wooden tables. There's a small a la carte menu, but together with the list of daily specials it's very difficult to make a choice. You can choose a dish either as a starter or as a main course, which is an ideal solution for small appetites (or when you just want a taste from every dish on the menu!). Fish and lamb dishes, like bouillabaisse or lamb cutlets with feta cheese and ouzo sauce, are popular.

Torenstraat 138. © **070/360-3919.** Main courses 13€–16€; 3-course dinner 23€. AE, DC, MC, V. Cafe daily 10am–1am; restaurant Mon–Sat 6–11pm, Sun 6–10pm.

Kandinsky Restaurant ✸✸ FRENCH/MEDITERRANEAN   Save your most special Scheveningen meal for this small, exquisite restaurant, officially opened by Mme Claude Pompidou, widow of the late French president. Beside the beach, the dining room overlooks the sea and its decor features signed lithographs by abstract artist Wassily Kandinsky. The cuisine here is classic French plus some Italian and other Mediterranean variations, and you can order vintage wines by the glass. The Kurhaus serves a lavish buffet daily for 45€ for lunch and 53€ to 63€ for dinner, both spread in the gorgeous Kurzaal area, where dancing is added to dinner on Friday and Saturday nights at only slightly elevated prices.

In the Steigenberger Kurhaus Hotel, Gevers Deynootplein 30, Scheveningen. © **070/416-2636.** Main courses 23€–38€; 5-course *menu du chef* 55€. AE, DC, MC, V. Mon–Fri noon–2pm; daily 6–10:30pm. No lunches served July–Aug.

Le Bistroquet ✸ CONTINENTAL   This small, popular restaurant in the city center is one of The Hague's finest, its quietly elegant dining room featuring lovely table settings. The menu, though short, is to the point, and covers lamb, fish, and poultry dishes. A fine Dutch menu choice is the three variations of Texel lamb with roasted garlic and a basil sauce. Seafood checks in with an excellent halibut prepared in a lemon crust and served with asparagus, cannelloni stuffed with scallops, and a parsley sauce.

Lange Voorhout 98. © **070/360-1170.** Reservations required. Main courses 19€–33€; fixed-price menus 29€–45€. AE, DC, MC, V. Mon–Fri noon–2pm and 6–10:30pm; Sat 6–10:30pm.

NH Stadsherberg 't Goude Hooft ✸✸ DUTCH/CONTINENTAL   There's a definite old Dutch flavor to this wonderful, large, happy cafe-restaurant overlooking the city's old market square, yet its 1600s exterior cloaks a 1939 interior installed after a disastrous fire. In fact, the establishment's history dates back to 1423, and it was originally a tavern before being transformed in 1660 into a coffeehouse, and finally a cafe-restaurant from 1939. The wooden beams, brass chandeliers, and rustic chairs and tables blend harmoniously with the stained-glass windows, medieval banners, and wall murals. Some of the rooms that divide the interior are nonsmoking. There's a large sidewalk cafe on the "Green Market" square, pleasant on sunny days, and an extensive menu covers everything from snacks to light lunches to full dinners. Look out for fine menu dishes like the Guinea fowl with thyme sauce and the red perch with saffron sauce. This also is a good place to drop by for a cocktail and snack, or just for a beer or a coffee.

Dagelijkse Groenmarkt 13. © **070/346-9713**. Main courses 14€–20€; fixed-price menus 16€–24€; coffee table 15€–16€. AE, DC, MC, V. Mon noon–6pm; Tues–Wed and Fri–Sat 10am–7pm; Thurs 10am–9:30pm; Sun 11am–6pm.

10 Rotterdam

75km (51 miles) S of Amsterdam

For a change from the thick blanket of history in and around Amsterdam, consider a visit to this modern Dutch city. Here, instead of the usual Dutch web of little streets and alleyways, there's a spacious and elegant shopping mall; and instead of Amsterdam's miles of winding canals, there's the biggest and busiest ocean harbor in the world.

Rotterdam is a fascinating place to see and experience, particularly when you consider that this city was a living monument to Holland's Golden Age until it was bombed to rubble during World War II. At the war's end, rather than try to re-create the old, Rotterdammers looked on their misfortune as an opportunity and approached their city as a clean slate. They relished the chance—unique in Holland—to create an efficient, elegant, and workable modern city and the results are a testimony to their ability to find impressive solutions to their problems. (Rotterdammers are said to be born with their sleeves already rolled up.)

By the time the workers had finished, they had dredged a long deep-water channel and filled in the shallow banks of the estuary that connected the city with the North Sea to create a 32km (20-mile) long harbor called the **Europoort** (pronounced the same as "port" in English) that now handles more cargo and more ships every year than any other port in the world (250 million tons of cargo annually). You may think that visiting a harbor is boring business on a vacation, but Rotterdam's makes any other harbor you've ever seen look like a Fisher-Price toy! One of the most memorable sights in Holland is the ship-jammed channel of Rotterdam harbor. Container ships, bulk carriers, tankers, sleek greyhounds of the sea, and careworn tramps, all are waited on by a vast retinue of machines and humans. Trucks, trains, and barges, each carrying its little piece of the action, hurry outward from the hub only to be drawn back again as if by gravity. Rotterdam is the pump that replenishes Europe's commercial arteries.

ESSENTIALS

GETTING THERE Two trains run each hour around the clock from Amsterdam to Rotterdam's Centraal Station; the trip takes 50 minutes. Buses from Amsterdam arrive at Centraal Station. When driving from Amsterdam, take A4 to The Hague, then A13 to Rotterdam.

VISITOR INFORMATION VVV Rotterdam, Coolsingel 67 (© **0900/403-4065**; fax 010/413-0124; www.vvv.rotterdam.nl), on the corner of Stadhuisplein, is reached by tram no. 1, or the Stadhuis stop of the Metro. The office is

Rotterdam

DINING ◆

Brasserie Henkes' **3**

Grand Café-Restaurant
Engels **4**

ATTRACTIONS ●

Boymans-van Beuningen
Museum **5**

De Dubbelde
Palm-boom
(Double Palm Tree
Historical Museum) **2**

Zakkendragershuisje
(Sack Carriers'
Guild House) **1**

Spido Harbor Trips **6**

open Monday through Thursday from 9:30am to 6pm, Friday from 9:30am to 9pm, Saturday from 9:30am to 5pm, and Sunday (Apr–Sept) from noon to 5pm.

WHAT TO SEE & DO

The first thing to do in Rotterdam is to take a **Spido Harbor Trip** (via Metro to Leuvehaven station; ② **010/275-9988**). Departures are every 30 to 45 minutes from 9:30am to 5pm, April through September; two to four times per day, October through March. The season of the year will determine how much of the vast Europoort you'll be able to see, but it's an unforgettable experience to board a boat that seems large in comparison to the canal launches of Amsterdam—two tiers of indoor seating and open decks—and then feel dwarfed by the hulking oil tankers and container ships that glide like giant whales into their berths along the miles of docks. The basic harbor trip, offered year-round, is a 75-minute tour of the city's waterfront; between April and September, it's possible to take an extended (2¼-hr.) trip daily at 10am and 12:30pm; and on a limited schedule in July and August, you can make all-day excursions to the sluices of the Delta Works and along the full length of the Europoort. Prices vary according to the trip, but run from 7.70€ to 25€ for adults, 4.75€ to 13€ for children 3 to 11, and free for children under 3. There's a music/dinner cruise offered from April to November that is 50€, which includes the cruise, a welcome cocktail, a four-course meal, two glasses of wine, and coffee. Reservations are needed.

On dry land, the **Boymans-van Beuningen Museum,** Museumpark 18–20 (② **010/441-9400**), is another of Holland's treasure troves of fine art. In this case, however, Dutch painters share wall space with an international contingent that includes Salvador Dalí and Man Ray, Titian and Tintoretto, Degas and Daumier. Plus, there are fine collections of porcelain, silver, glass, and Delftware. The museum houses a gift shop and a restaurant where you can have a quick lunch. The museum is open Tuesday through Saturday from 10am to 5pm and Sunday and holidays from 11am to 5pm; closed January 1, April 30, and December 25. Admission is 6€ for adults, 3€ for seniors, and free for children under 18.

Not all of Rotterdam is spanking new. A neighborhood the German bombers missed is the tiny harbor area known as **Delfshaven (Harbor of Delft),** where the Puritan Separatists known as the Pilgrims embarked on the first leg of their trip to Massachusetts. This is a pleasant place to spend an afternoon. You can wander into the church in which the Pilgrims prayed before departure, peek into antiques shops and galleries, and check on the progress of housing renovations in this historic area.

Two interesting places to visit in Delfshaven are the **Sack Carriers' Guild House,** Voorstraat 13–15 (② **010/477-2664**), where artisans demonstrate the art of pewter casting, and the adjoining warehouses that make up **De Dubbelde Palm-Boom (Double Palm Tree Historical Museum),** Voorhaven 12 (② **010/ 476-1533**), which displays objects unearthed during the excavations of Rotterdam. Both are open Tuesday through Friday from 10am to 5pm, Saturday, Sunday, and public holidays from 11am to 5pm (closed New Year's Day and Apr 30).

WHERE TO DINE

Brasserie Henkes ★ CONTINENTAL   Henkes' Brasserie is an ideal place to appreciate the special atmosphere of old Delfshaven. The waterside terrace invites you to while away a sunny afternoon, interrupted only by a leisurely stroll down the harbor, then to return for dinner. Inside, the old Henkes' *jenever* (Dutch gin) distillery has been completely transformed; the interior now features the furnishings of a 19th-century Belgian insurance bank. The warm woodwork and brass chandeliers create a dining room on a grand scale. You can enjoy seafood and meat dishes, or seasonal specialties like venison with a chocolate-port sauce.

Voorhaven 17 (in Delfshaven). © 010/425-5596. Main courses 17€–19€; fixed-price 25€. AE, DC, MC, V. Daily 11:30am–midnight; kitchen closes at 10pm.

Grand Café-Restaurant Engels INTERNATIONAL This marvelous eatery is actually a complex of four restaurants, each dedicated to a different international cuisine: Don Quijote (Spanish), Tokaj (Hungarian), The Beefeater (British), and Brasserie Engels (Dutch/Continental). Tokaj and Don Quijote offer live music. There's an a la carte menu (full dinners, light meals, sandwiches, omelets, snacks) and a vegetarian menu.

Stationsplein 45 (next to Centraal Station, in the Groothandelsgebouw). © 010/411-9550. Main courses 13€–20€; fixed-price dinner in Don Quijote and Tokaj and Sun brunch in Brasserie Engels 20€; Carvery buffet in the Beefeater 20€–23€. AE, DC, MC, V. Daily 8am–1am.

THE WINDMILLS OF KINDERDIJK

There are three things that stir the soul of a true Hollander: the Dutch flag, the Dutch anthem, and the sight of windmill sails spinning in the breeze. There are 19 water-pumping windmills at Kinderdijk, a tiny community between Rotterdam and Dordrecht; that means 76 mill sails, each with a 14-yard span, all revolving on a summer day. It's a spectacular sight and one of the must-sees of Holland. The mills are in operation on Saturday afternoon in July and August from 2:30 to 5:30pm; the visitor's mill is open from April to September, Monday through Saturday from 9:30am to 5:30pm.

To get there, board a train from Rotterdam's Centraal Station to Rotterdam's Lombardijen Station; from there, take bus no. 154 to Kinderdijk. If you're driving, take the N207 toward Bergambacht and then board the ferry across the river Lek. On the other side, turn right and follow the road along the river toward Kinderdijk.

11 Utrecht

42km (26 miles) SE of Amsterdam

When the Dutch Republic was established in the late 16th century, Utrecht was one of its more powerful political centers, having been an important bishopric since the earliest centuries of Christianity in Holland. As a result, this is a city of churches; there are more restored medieval religious structures here than in any other city in Europe. Most are in the old heart of town, including the beautiful Domkerk and its adjacent Domtoren, or Dom Tower, the tallest in Holland (and worth a climb). Two other church buildings, the St. Agnes and Catherine Convents, now house two of Utrecht's many fine museums; for centuries these structures filled a variety of roles (orphanages, hospitals, and so on) during the period of Protestant influence in the Netherlands.

Also unique to Utrecht is its bi-level wharf along the Oude Gracht Canal through the Center, where restaurants, shops, and summer cafes have replaced the hustle and bustle of the commercial activity of former times, when Utrecht was a major port along the Rhine.

Commerce continues to be the city's major focus, as you quickly realize if you arrive by train. Centraal Station is in the Hoog Catherijne (High Catherine)—a vast, multitiered, indoor shopping mall that spreads over a 6-block area and traverses both a multilane highway and the web of railway tracks. Another part of the complex is Jaarbeursplein, which holds a 40-room exhibit hall built especially to house the annual Utrecht Trade Fair, at which Dutch industry has presented its best products every year since 1916.

ESSENTIALS

GETTING THERE Trains depart at least every half hour from Amsterdam Centraal Station to Utrecht. By car from Amsterdam, take A2 south.

VISITOR INFORMATION **VVV Utrecht,** Vinkenburgstraat 19, 3512 AA Utrecht (© **0900/128-8732;** fax 030/236-0037; www.12utrecht.nl). The office is open Monday through Wednesday and Friday from 9:30am to 6:30pm, Thursday from 9:30am to 9pm, Saturday from 9:30am to 5pm, Sunday (in summer and occasionally in winter) from 10am to 2pm.

WHAT TO SEE & DO

Don't let Utrecht's modern face dampen your interest in visiting this well-preserved 2,000-year-old city. To tour the city, take a **canal-boat ride,** with Rederij Lovers (© **030/231-6468**) or Rederij Schuttevaer (© **030/272-0111**), who leave from Nieuwekade; tours are Monday through Sunday every hour on the hour from 11am to 5pm. At the end of the trip, visit **'t Hoogt,** Hoogt 4, at the corner of Slachstraat. This 17th-century burgher's house is now an art cinema. It's open Monday through Sunday from noon to 1am, and admission is 5€ per screening.

The major attraction in Utrecht is **Domplein,** where, if you have the stamina and the inclination, you can climb the 465 steps to the top of the **Domtoren,** or Dom Tower (© **030/286-4540**). Guided tours take place every hour from May to September daily from 10am to 5pm; from October to April Saturday and Sunday from noon to 5pm. Admission is 6€ for adults, 4€ for children 11 and under.

Also, visit the **Domkerk** cathedral (© **030/231-0403**), which took almost 3 centuries to build, from 1254 to 1517. The original Romanesque structure was replaced bit by bit; first the choir, then the tower, and finally the nave and transepts. The nave collapsed during a violent storm in 1674 and was never rebuilt; the choir and transepts survived and remain disconnected from the tower. Standing in the cloisters and looking up at the church, you get some impression of how imposing this cathedral must have been. The interior bears traces of the fierce wave of iconoclasm that spread over Holland in the second half of the 16th century. There's a battered altarpiece in one of the side chapels, and a sandstone Holy Sepulcher, dated 1501, shows a defaced Christ in a tomb under a badly damaged Gothic arch. The Domkerk is open from May to September, Sunday from 2 to 4pm, and Monday through Saturday from 10am to 5pm; from October to April, Monday through Saturday from 11am to 4pm. Admission is free.

Other worthwhile sights nearby are the **Bisschopes Hof,** or Bishop's Garden (open daily 11am–5pm), and the **Dom Kloostergang,** a cloister arcade built in the 15th century, with magnificent stained-glass windows depicting scenes from the legend of St. Martin. Information on any of the sights on or near the Domplein can be obtained by calling © **030/231-0403.**

Utrecht

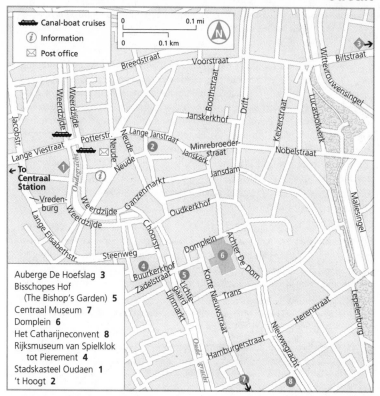

Canal-boat cruises
Information
Post office

Auberge De Hoefslag **3**
Bisschopes Hof
(The Bishop's Garden) **5**
Centraal Museum **7**
Domplein **6**
Het Catharijneconvent **8**
Rijksmuseum van Spielklok
tot Pierement **4**
Stadskasteel Oudaen **1**
't Hoogt **2**

In another medieval church, visit the merry **Rijksmuseum van Spielklok tot Pierement (National Museum from Music Box to Street Organ),** Buurkerkhof 10 (✆ **030/231-2789**), where you can hear and see 600 different music makers. The museum is open Tuesday through Saturday from 10am to 5pm, and Sunday and holidays from noon to 5pm. Admission is 6€ for adults, 3€ for children 4 to 12, and free for children under 4.

Also, be sure to see the exceptional collection of medieval religious art at **Het Catharijneconvent,** Lange Nieuwstraat 38 (✆ **030/231-3835**). It's open Tuesday through Friday from 10am to 5pm, and Saturday and Sunday from 11am to 5pm. Admission is 6€ for adults, 3€ for children 4 to 12, and free for children under 4.

The **Centraal Museum,** Nicolaaskerkhof 10 (✆ **030/236-2362**), has a ship from Utrecht that dates from 1200, a number of paintings of the Utrecht artistic school of the 16th century, and a dollhouse that dates from 1680. There's an impressive collection of Dutch modern art and Dutch 20th-century applied art—the De Stijl group—displayed in the former artillery mews on the grounds of the museum. The museum is open Tuesday through Sunday from 11 to 5pm. Admission is 6.75€ for adults and 3€ for children 13 and under.

An important item in the Centraal Museum collection is the **Rietveld-Schroder House,** Prins Hendriklaan 50, built in 1924 and designed by Gerrit Rietveld according to the ideas of the De Stijl group. The Rietveld-Schroder

House is open Wednesday through Saturday from 11am to 5pm and Sunday from noon to 5pm, or by appointment.

WHERE TO DINE

de Hoefslag ★★ INTERNATIONAL/FRENCH   This beautiful dining spot, located on wooded grounds just a little northeast of Utrecht, is considered by many to be Holland's top restaurant. Amsterdammers think nothing of driving the 48km (30 miles) down here for dinner. There's a Victorian garden feel to the lounge, while the dining room is reminiscent of an upscale hunting lodge, with lots of dark wood, an open hearth, and ceiling-to-floor doors opening to the terrace. The de Hoefslag changes its menu daily, setting specials after the chef has returned from the market. The seafood is superb, as are pork, lamb, and game dishes.

Vossenlaan 28, Bosch en Duin. ✆ **030/225-1051.** Fixed-price menus 43€–60€. AE, DC, MC, V. Mon–Sat noon–2:30pm and 5:30–9:30pm.

Stadskasteel Oudaen CONTINENTAL   This medieval town castle has been transformed into a culinary palace. Downstairs, in what once was the main hall, you can sit in the cafe and savor beer brewed on the premises, according to medieval recipes. Upstairs is the restaurant "Tussen hemel en aarde" ("Between heaven and earth"), with its original fireplace still intact and a rustic tile floor. The menu changes weekly, according to what is freshest and in season.

Oudegracht 99. ✆ **030/231-1864.** Main courses 18€–23€; fixed-price menus 27€–38€. AE, DC, MC, V. Cafe daily 10am–2am; restaurant Mon–Sat 5:30–9pm.

12 Three Historic Art Towns: Delft, Leiden & Laren

DELFT ★★
54km (34 miles) SW of Amsterdam

Yes, this is the home of the famous blue-and-white porcelain, and you can visit the factory of De Porceleyne Fles where it is produced, but don't let Delftware be your only reason to visit. The small, handsome city is quiet and intimate, with flowers in its flower boxes and linden trees bending over gracious canals. The cradle of the Dutch Republic, Delft is still the burial place of the royal family, and the birthplace and inspiration of artist Jan Vermeer, the 17th-century master of light and subtle emotion.

ESSENTIALS

GETTING THERE   There are frequent rail and bus connections to Delft from Amsterdam and Rotterdam. Delft is connected to The Hague by tram. By car, Delft is just off A13, the main Rotterdam–The Hague motorway.

VISITOR INFORMATION   VVV Delft, Markt 83–85, 2611 GS, Delft (✆ **015/212-6100;** fax 015/215-8695; www.vvvdelft.nl), in the center of town. The office is open from April to September, Monday through Saturday from 9am to 5:30pm, and Sunday from 11am to 3pm.

WHAT TO SEE & DO

The house where Vermeer was born, lived, and painted is long gone from Delft, as are his paintings. The artist's burial place, the **Oude Kerk (Old Church)** ★, Roland Holstlaan 753 (✆ **015/212-3015**), is noted for its 27 stained-glass windows by Joep Nicolas. You should also visit the **Nieuwe Kerk (New Church)** ★★, Markt (✆ **015/212-3025**), where Prince William of Orange and

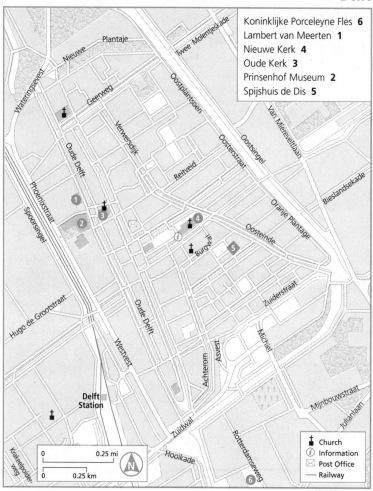

all other members of the House of Orange-Nassau are buried. It's open April through October, Monday through Saturday from 9am to 6pm; November through March, Monday through Saturday from 11am to 4pm. Admission is 4€ for adults, 2€ for children 3 to 12, and free for children under 3.

The **Prinsenhof Museum** ✦ St. Agathaplein 1 (© **015/260-2358**), on the nearby Oude Delft Canal, is where William I of Orange (William the Silent) lived and had his headquarters in the years when he helped found the Dutch Republic. This is where he was assassinated in 1584 (you can still see the bullet holes in the stairwell). Today, the Prinsenhof is a museum of paintings, tapestries, silverware, and pottery, and is the site of the annual Delft Art and Antiques Fair, held in late October or early November. The museum is open Tuesday through Saturday from 10am to 5pm, and Sunday and holidays from 1 to 5pm; closed January 1 and December 25. Admission is 3.50€ for adults, 3€ for children 12 to 15, and free for children under 12.

In the same neighborhood you can see a fine collection of old Delft tiles displayed in the wood-paneled setting of a 19th-century mansion museum called **Lambert van Meerten,** Oude Delft 199 (© **015/260-2358**). The museum is open Tuesday through Saturday from 10am to 5pm, and Sunday and holidays from 1 to 5pm; closed January 1 and December 25. Admission is 2.50€ for adults, 2€ for children 12 to 15, and free for children under 12.

To see a demonstration of the traditional art of making and hand-painting Delftware, visit the factory and showroom of **Koninklijke Porceleyne Fles,** Rotterdamseweg 196 (© **015/251-2030**), founded in 1653. It's open April through October, daily from 9am to 4:30pm; November through March, Monday through Friday from 9am to 4:30pm, and Saturday through Sunday from 11am to 1pm. Admission is 2.50€ for adults and free for children under 13.

WHERE TO DINE

Spijshuis de Dis ★★ DUTCH   Some of the best Dutch cooking in the country is dished up at this atmospheric restaurant east of the market. Look out for traditional plates presented in modern variations. These include *Bakke pot*—a stew made from three kinds of meat (beef, chicken, and rabbit) in a beer sauce, served in the pan; VOC mussels (named after the Dutch initials for the United East India Company), prepared with garlic and spices such as ginger and curry; and asparagus in season (May–June). Steaks and lamb filet are other specialties. If you're feeling especially decadent, opt for a luscious dessert of vanilla ice cream with hot cherries, whipped cream, and cherry brandy.

Beestenmarkt 36 (2 blocks from the Markt). © **015/213-1782**. Main courses 13€–23€; fixed-price menu 27€. AE, MC, V. Thurs–Tues 5–9:30pm.

LEIDEN
36km (23 miles) SW of Amsterdam

Historians may know that the Pilgrim Fathers lived here for 11 years before sailing for North America on the *Mayflower*. Leiden's proudest homegrown moment came in 1574, when it was the only Dutch town to withstand a Spanish siege. This was the birthplace of the Dutch tulip trade in 1594, and of the painters Rembrandt and Jan Steen, and it is the home of the oldest university in the Netherlands. Finally, with 14 museums, covering subjects ranging from antiquities, natural history, and anatomy to clay pipes and coins, Leiden seems perfectly justified in calling itself "Museum City."

ESSENTIALS
GETTING THERE   There are frequent trains from Amsterdam; the station is northwest of the town center (about a 10-min. walk). By car, take A4.

VISITOR INFORMATION   VVV Leiden, Stationsweg 2D, 2312 AV, Leiden (© **0900/222-2333;** fax 071/516-1227; www.leidenpromotie.nl), just opposite the train station. It is open Monday through Friday from 9am to 5:30pm, Saturday from 10am to 2pm.

WHAT TO SEE & DO
Probably the best way to tour the town is to cruise its canals or follow one of four special city **walking tours.** One tour, called "The Pilgrim Fathers" (see below), makes a large circle around the old center of the city; the others—"Town Full of Monuments," "In the Footsteps of Young Rembrandt," and "Along Leiden's Almshouses"—make shorter circuits that can easily be combined to give

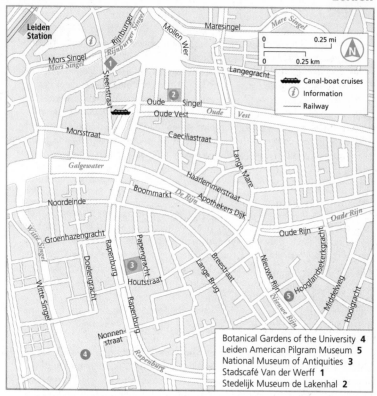

Botanical Gardens of the University **4**
Leiden American Pilgram Museum **5**
National Museum of Antiquities **3**
Stadscafé Van der Werff **1**
Stedelijk Museum de Lakenhal **2**

you a comprehensive look at the sights near the university. The tours are organized by the VVV and are from 2€ to 5€.

The **Rijksmuseum van Oudheden (National Museum of Antiquities)** ★★, Rapenburg 28 (℃ **071/516-3163**), which houses the 1st century A.D. Temple of Taffeh, presented by the Egyptian government as a gift to the Dutch nation for its assistance in saving monuments before the construction of the Aswan High Dam. The museum is open Tuesday through Friday from 10am to 5pm, Saturday and Sunday from noon to 5pm; closed January 1, October 3, and December 25. Admission is 4€ for adults, 3€ for seniors and children 6 to 18, and free for children under 6.

Also noteworthy, the **Hortus Botanicus (Botanical Gardens)** (Hortus Botanicus) of the university, Rapenburg 73 (℃ **071/527-7249**), from 1587—that's more than 400 years of blooming flowers! The gardens are open April through September, daily from 10am to 6pm; October through March (closed last week in Dec and Jan 1), Monday through Friday and Sunday from 9am to 4pm. Admission is 4€ for adults, 2€ for children 4 to 12, and free for children under 4.

To touch base with those courageous but humble Pilgrim Fathers, pick up the VVV brochure **A Pilgrimage Through Leiden: A Walk in the Footsteps of the Pilgrim Fathers.** The walk starts at the **Lodewijkskerk,** which was used as a

---

Fun Fact Roots of a Love Affair

In the spring of 1594, a highly respected yet perennially disgruntled botanist, Carolus Clusius, strode purposefully into the Hortus Botanicus, his research garden at the University of Leiden. He stopped beside a flower bed where an experiment begun the year before was coming to fruition, and cast a critical eye over some little splashes of color nodding their heads in the spring breeze. Clusius was no great admirer of humanity, but flowers were something else, so we may suppose that his dyspeptic disposition softened for a moment as he paused to admire the first tulips ever grown in Holland. A nation's love affair with a flower had begun.

---

meeting place by the cloth guild. William Bradford, who later became governor of New Plymouth, was a member of this guild. The walk takes you past the house on William Brewstersteeg (formerly Herensteeg) where William Brewster's Pilgrim Press published the religious views that angered the Church of England. Plaques at **Sint-Pieterskerk** (in a small square off Kloksteeg) memorialize the Pilgrims, in particular Rev. Jon Robinson, who was forced to stay behind because of illness and is buried in this church (an almshouse, the Jean Pesijnhofje, in Kloksteeg, now occupies the house in which he died). Special Thanksgiving Day services are held each year in honor of the little band of refugees who worshipped here.

At the **Leiden American Pilgrim Museum,** Beschuitsteeg 9 (© **071/512-2413**), you can hear a recorded commentary on the Pilgrims and see photocopies of documents relating to their 11-year residence in Leiden. The museum is open Wednesday through Saturday from 1 to 5pm. Admission is 4€ for adults and free for children under 5.

On the other side of town, visit the **Stedelijk Museum de Lakenhal,** Oude Singel 32 (© **071/516-5360**), to view works by local heroes Rembrandt and Jan Steen, and others, plus period rooms from the 17th to 19th centuries, and temporary modern art exhibits. Also on parade is Leiden's pride and joy: a copper stew pot said to have been retrieved by a small boy who crawled through a chink in the city wall just minutes after the lifting of the Spanish siege. He found this very pot full of boiling stew in the enemy's camp and brought it back to feed the starving inhabitants. Ever since, stew has been a national dish and is still traditionally prepared for the Leiden city holiday, October 3, which is the anniversary of its liberation; every year on this day *haring en witte brood* (herring and white bread) are distributed, just as they were in 1574. The museum is open Tuesday through Friday from 10am to 5pm, and Saturday, Sunday, and holidays from noon to 5pm; closed January 1 and December 25. Admission is 3€ for adults, 1.50€ for children 6 to 18, and free for children under 6.

A windmill, **De Valk,** sticks up like a sore thumb on Molenwerf in the middle of town, and a 13th-century citadel, **De Burcht,** still stands on a mound of land in the center between two branches of the river Rhine, Oude and Nieuwe, providing a great view of the rooftops around.

WHERE TO DINE

Annie's Verjaardag DUTCH/CONTINENTAL   This lively restaurant at water level has vaulted cellars that are a favorite eating spot for both students and locals, who spill out onto the canalside terrace in fine weather. When the canals are frozen, the view is enchanting, as skaters practice their turns. The dinner menu is simple but wholesome and during the day you can enjoy sandwiches or tapas.

Oude Rijn 1A. ℂ **071/512-6358.** Main courses 9.50€–17€. No credit cards. Sun–Thurs 10am–1am; Fri–Sat 10am–2am.

Stadscafé van der Werff ⭐ CONTINENTAL   A relaxed cafe-restaurant in a grand 1930s villa on the edge of the old town that is popular with the town's students and ordinary citizens alike. Even if you're not having dinner, and enjoying dishes like a basic Indonesian satay, or their surf-and-turf *kalfsbiefstukje met gebakken gambas en een kreeftensaus* (beefsteak with fried prawns in a lobster sauce), you can still while away your evening just having a drink and reading a paper. The cafe is open until 1am.

Steenstraat 2. ℂ **071/513-0335.** Main courses 9.50€–39€. AE, DC, MC, V. Daily 10:30am–5pm and 6–10pm.

LAREN
26km (16 miles) SE of Amsterdam

The Dutch legacy of impressive art was not a one-shot, Golden Age phenomenon, nor were the later 19th-century contributions solely the work of Vincent van Gogh. Visit the pretty little suburban town of Laren, in the district of Het Gooi, and you discover a less well-known Dutch art center, where a number of important painters chose to live and work at the turn of the 20th century. Among the town's star residents were Anton Mauve, the Dutch Impressionist who attracted other members of The Hague School, and the American painter, William Henry Singer, Jr., who chose to live and paint in the clear light of Holland rather than follow his family's traditional path to fame and fortune via the steel mills of Pittsburgh.

Today Laren's principal attraction is Singer's former home, once called the Wild Swans, and now the **Singer Museum,** Oude Drift 1 (ℂ **035/531-5656**). It houses both the works of the former occupant and also his collection of some 500 works by American, Dutch, French, and Norwegian painters. Open Tuesday through Saturday from 11am to 5pm and Sundays and holidays from noon to 5pm (closed Jan 1, Apr 30, and Dec 25). Admission is 5€ for adults, free for children under 13.

> **Impressions**
>
> *The immigrant Puritans displayed no religious tolerance, and in fact were some of the worst fanatics from Europe.*
> —John Chuckman,
> counterpunch.org, 2002

To reach the museum from Amsterdam, take bus no. 136, which departs from Amstel Bus Station every half hour and takes you directly to the museum stop in Laren. Trains depart every hour from Amsterdam Centraal Station to Hilversum Station, from where buses go every half hour to Laren. By car from Amsterdam, take A1 (E231) east.

Appendix A:
Amsterdam in Depth

Step aboard for a cruise through the highlights of 800 years of history in this city of canals. If your knowledge of Dutch history is confined to Peter Minuit buying Manhattan Island and Peter Stuyvesant as governor of Nieuw Amsterdam, read on. A working knowledge of the history of Amsterdam adds interesting dimensions to your visit.

1 Amsterdam's Origins

Amsterdam was founded at the place where two fishermen and a seasick dog jumped ashore from a small boat to escape a storm in the Zuider Zee. The dog threw up, thereby marking the spot. Sound like a shaggy dog story? Well, the city's original coat of arms backs up the tale, and you can see representations of it on the facade of the Beurs van Berlage (Old Stock Exchange) and the Munttoren (Mint Tower), and above the Mayor's fireplace in the old Town Hall (now the Royal Palace) on the Dam.

In some ways, it's an appropriate metaphor for a city with a lifestyle that has about as many boosters and detractors as Sodom and Gomorrah likely had. Some people, visiting for the first time, want to throw up everything and live this way forever; others just want to throw up.

At any rate, it seems that fishermen, with or without a seasick dog, did play the decisive role in founding Amsterdam. Around the year 1200, some fishermen realized that the area at the mouth of the Amstel River allowed their wooden cog boats easy access to rich fishing in the IJ inlet and on the Zuider Zee beyond. They built their huts on raised mounds of earth called *terps,* examples of which still abound in coastal Friesland. The low-lying marshy terrain left these early settlers at the mercy of tides and storms, and

Dateline

- circa 1200 Fishermen establish a coastal settlement on low-lying land at the mouth of the Amstel River.
- circa 1204 Count Gijsbrecht II van Amstel builds a castle at the village.
- circa 1270 The Amstel is dammed in an effort to control periodic flooding of the land; the settlement takes the name "Amestelledamme."
- 1275 Count Floris V of Holland grants Amestelledamme freedom from tolls on travel and trade through his lands. This is the first documented reference to the settlement and the year is regarded as Amsterdam's official foundation date.
- 1300 The Bishop of Utrecht grants Amsterdam its first town charter.
- 1323 Amsterdam's importance as a trading center receives a boost when it is declared a toll center for beer.
- 1334 The Oude Kerk (Old Church) is mentioned in contemporary city records as the first parish church, though its foundation dates from around 30 years earlier.
- 1345 The "Miracle of the Host" increases the city's religious standing and attracts pilgrims from around Europe.
- 1350 Amsterdam becomes a transit point for grain, thereby gaining further status as an important trade center.
- 1400 The city's population swells to 5,000.
- 1452 Fire destroys the city's mostly timber buildings.

many must have perished or lost their homes as a result of flooding. Traders followed the fishing families, distributing the catch to the more developed surrounding towns and villages.

Archaeological remains show that by 1204, local big wheels were moving in on what the peasants had created. The lord of Amstel, Gijsbrecht II, made the first power play, building a castle at the settlement and lording it over the locals. In the 1990s, archaeologists uncovered the foundations of the castle under a tiny side street called Nieuwezijds Kolk. Gijsbrecht had to watch his back constantly, as the count of Holland was maneuvering for position, supported by the bishop of Utrecht.

Around 1270, in an effort to control water surges, the populace dammed the Amstel (they'd probably been damning it for years) at the point where today's square called the Dam stands. This is the source of the city's original name, Amestelledamme.

There are few records of Amestelledamme before 1275, when Count Floris V of Holland granted the village privileges that allowed locals to trade anywhere in the counties of Holland and Zeeland without having to pay tolls along the way. This is the settlement's first official documentary record, and the year is celebrated today as Amsterdam's foundation date. Count Gijsbrecht IV of Aemstel resented Floris's efforts to win friends and influence people on his patch, and in 1296 he murdered Floris in his castle at Muiden.

Gijsbrecht didn't have long to enjoy his victory. Two years later Floris's brother, Guy of Hainaut, defeated Gijsbrecht in battle and hauled him up in front of the bishop of Utrecht for judgment; Gijsbrecht's land was confiscated and he was imprisoned and later exiled. In 1300, the bishop granted Aemstelledamme its town

- **1489** The Habsburg Emperor Maximilian of Austria grants Amsterdam the right to use the imperial crown on its coat of arms.
- **1514** Amsterdam is the largest town in Holland, with a population of 12,000.
- **1530** Anabaptists, a radical Protestant sect, develop a significant following in the city.
- **1535** Anabaptists seize the Town Hall; the uprising fails and its leaders are executed.
- **1560** Calvinism is becoming a growing force in the city's affairs.
- **1566** Protestant services are held in public for the first time; rioters sack Catholic churches in what becomes known as the *Beeldenstorm* (Iconoclastic Fury).
- **1578** Amsterdam abandons the Spanish, and Catholic, cause; Calvinists take over in what is called the *Alteratie.*
- **1589** The first correctional facility for men opens.
- **1596** The first correctional facility for women opens.
- **1600** Amsterdam's population reaches 50,000.
- **1602** The United East India Company (V.O.C.), which is destined to become a powerful commercial and political entity, is established.
- **1609** Amsterdam Exchange Bank opens. The English navigator Henry Hudson, under contract to the United East India Company, sails from Amsterdam and "discovers" Manhattan Island and the future site of New York (the Italian explorer Giovanni da Verrazzano might have beaten him to it in 1524).
- **1611** Amsterdam Stock Exchange opens.
- **1613** Construction begins on the three concentric waterways of the *grachtengordel* (canal belt): Herengracht, Keizersgracht, and Prinsengracht.
- **1626** Peter Minuit buys Manhattan Island from the Manhattoes Indians for the equivalent of $24, "legalizing" the Nieuw Amsterdam settlement founded the previous year at the

continues

charter and in 1317 ceded the town to the counts of Holland.

INCREASING PROSPERITY

During the 14th and 15th centuries, Holland's position at the mouths of the great European rivers made it a focal point in the many shifts of feudal power. After numerous small-scale struggles for control, the House of Burgundy became the first major feudal power in the Low Countries, consolidating its hold on the region by acquiring fiefdoms one by one through the various means of marriage, inheritance, and military force. Its day soon passed, however, as the Austrian Habsburg emperor Maximilian I acquired the Low Countries from the Burgundians by much the same means.

As these political and dynastic struggles raged beyond the rim of the broad Dutch horizon, Amsterdammers were quietly making themselves wealthy.

Amsterdam began its rise to commercial prosperity in 1323, when Count Floris VI established the city as one of two toll points for the import of beer. At that time beer was essential for health. Drinking water was a risky, germ-laden activity, particularly in overcrowded towns whose rivers were both reservoir and toilet. Drinking beer, on the other hand, had no undesirable side effects—aside from an occasional headache—and cast a warm glow over what must often have been a miserable life. Later, Amsterdam was granted toll rights on exported ale. Beer thus became a major component of its prosperity, and remains important to this day, as anyone who visits the city's Heineken Reception Center will see.

Always skillful merchants, they began to establish strong guilds of craftsmen and to put ships to sea to catch North Sea herring (an industry that took a big leap forward in 1385, when Willem Beukelszoon discovered

mouth of the Hudson River, and in 1664 renamed New York by the English.

- 1632 Rembrandt, at age 25, moves to Amsterdam from his native Leiden. Athenaeum Illustre, precursor to the city's first university, opens.
- 1634 "Tulip mania" begins; the price of tulip bulbs soars to crazy levels.
- 1637 Great Tulip Crash.
- 1642 Rembrandt paints *The Night Watch*.
- 1665 Portuguese Synagogue opens.
- 1669 Building of timber houses is forbidden due to the risk of fire.
- 1697 Russia's Czar Peter the Great lodges at Zaandam, near Amsterdam, while he is working incognito at a shipyard to study Dutch shipbuilding methods.
- 1745 Schools for needy children open.
- 1784 The Society for the Welfare of the Community is established.
- 1787 Prussia occupies the Low Countries.
- 1791 The United East India Company (V.O.C.), which has been failing for decades, is liquidated.
- 1795 Velvet Revolution. French troops occupy Amsterdam and with the aid of pro-French Dutch revolutionaries establish the Batavian Republic; William V flees to England.
- 1806–10 Louis Bonaparte, Napoléon's brother, reigns as king of the Netherlands, with Amsterdam his capital and the town hall on the Dam his palace.
- 1813 The Netherlands regains independence from the French.
- 1815 Amsterdam becomes capital of the Kingdom of the Netherlands.
- 1839 Railway line opens between Amsterdam and Haarlem.
- 1854 Poor Law passed.
- 1870s The diamond industry sees continued growth.
- 1876 The North Sea Canal between Amsterdam and IJmuiden opens, improving the city's links to the sea.
- 1877 A Municipal Sanitation Department is set up.
- 1885 The Rijksmuseum opens.
- 1889 Centraal Station opens.
- 1890 The city council assumes control of privately owned utilities.

a way to cure herring at sea). They expanded into trade in salted Baltic herring, Norwegian salted or dried cod and cod-liver oil, German beer and salt, bales of linen and woolen cloth from the Low Countries and England, Russian furs and candle wax, Polish grain and flour, Swedish timber and iron. They opened up lucrative trade by both doing business with, and competing against, the powerful Baltic-based Hanseatic League.

The city's merchants, growing rich on the contents of the warehouses they built along the canals, trampled on the toes of the Hanseatic League trading towns in the competition for wealth and came out head and shoulders in front.

PILGRIM CITY

During the Middle Ages, the Netherlands was a bastion of Catholicism, with powerful bishops in the cities of Utrecht and Maastricht and a holy shrine in the upstart town of Aemstelledamme, which attracted its own share of pilgrims during the age of the Crusades. No one is sure when Amsterdam became an independent parish, but it is thought to have been around 1334, when the Oude Kerk (Old Church) is first mentioned in the city's records, though a small timber chapel on the spot dates from around 1300.

In 1342, Floris VI granted Amsterdam another charter, giving it more independence and definitive boundaries. As the town became more of a city and grew in prosperity, churches, monasteries, nunneries, and cloisters called *begijnhofs* (beguinages) began to spring up. Eventually there were 18 begijnhofs, which functioned as social welfare agencies, providing care to the sick, orphaned, or poor and hospitality to travelers and pilgrims. You can tour the main Begijnhof (see "Sights of Religious Significance," in chapter 6). The many religious institutions helped attract people to the city.

- **1897** July 21: The first automobile arrives in the city.
- **1902** For the first time, a socialist wins a seat on the city council.
- **1910** A flushable water system for the canals is introduced.
- **1917** Despite Dutch neutrality in World War I, the Netherlands suffers from severe food shortages, triggering street riots.
- **1920** Dutch airline KLM launches the world's first scheduled air service, between Amsterdam and London.
- **1928** Amsterdam Olympics.
- **1932** Enclosure Dike at the head of the Zuider Zee is completed, transforming the sea on which Amsterdam stands into the freshwater IJsselmeer lake.
- **1934** The Great Depression leads to shortages and riots; the government calls out the army to maintain public order.
- **1940** Nazi Germany invades and occupies the Netherlands.
- **1941** Dockworkers and others launch the "February Strike" against persecution and deportation of the city's Jewish community.
- **1942** Anne Frank and her family, along with other Jewish friends, go into hiding.
- **1944** The Frank family refuge is betrayed and its occupants are transported. Anne dies the following year at Bergen-Belsen concentration camp.
- **1944–45** Thousands die during the "Hunger Winter," when Nazi occupation forces blockade western Holland.
- **1945** May 7: Allied troops of the Canadian Second Army liberate the city.
- **1945** KLM inaugurates an Amsterdam–New York air service, using a 36-seat Douglas DC-4, cruising speed 320kmph (200 mph). Journey time, including stopovers in Scotland and Newfoundland: 25½ hours.
- **1947** *The Diary of Anne Frank* is published.
- **1951** *The Dockworker* statue commemorating the 1941 February Strike is unveiled.

continues

A few years later, a major event, referred to as the "Miracle of the Host," increased the city's religious standing. It is said that on the Tuesday before Palm Sunday in 1345, a dying man sent for a priest to administer last rites. He was given the Host; a few hours later he vomited on the fire, and the next day they found the unburned Host amid the embers. Soon afterward, it was placed in a shrine built to commemorate this miracle; twice it was removed and taken to another place of worship, but each time it returned itself to the original shrine.

During a procession to the Oude Kerk involving the same Host, many miracles were said to have happened. The bishop erected a chapel in place of the dying man's house. Within a few years the place came to be known as the *Heilige Stede* (Holy Place), and, though the Host disappeared during the Protestant ascendancy in Amsterdam (when Catholics were forbidden to worship openly), an annual pilgrimage, De Stille Omgang, still recalls the miracle.

The Host might not have burned, but the city did—twice. In contrast to the solid structures you see today, early canal houses were made from timber, had thatched roofs, and stood on wood pilings that reached down through the soft upper soil to a firmer layer of sand beneath. In 1421, they went up in smoke in the city's first great fire, a performance repeated in 1452. At that point the city fathers put an end to building with wood; today, only two timber houses remain in the old city: the 15th-century Het Huyten Huis in the Begijnhof and the 16th-century 't Aepje, a former seaman's hostel, at Zeedijk 1.

THE REFORMATION

The 16th century was a time when religion was often inseparable from power and politics, when kings still routinely considered themselves their

- 1952 Completion of the Amsterdam–Rhine Canal.
- 1960s The city takes on the mantle of Europe's hippie capital.
- 1966 Street protests mar Princess Beatrix's marriage to German Claus von Amsberg, a former soldier in the World War II German army.
- 1973 The Rijksmuseum Vincent van Gogh (now the Van Gogh Museum) opens.
- 1975 Amsterdam's 700th anniversary. Cannabis use is decriminalized.
- 1978 First homeless "squatters" appear on the scene and occupy the old *Handelsblad* newspaper offices.
- 1980 Sixteen people squat at (occupy) a town house at Vondelstraat 72. Violent street confrontations erupt as police remove them.
- 1986 The new combined Stadhuis (Town Hall) and Opera (Muziektheater) opens on Waterlooplein, sealing the failure of the impassioned and sometimes violent "Stop the Stopera" campaign.
- 1987 The *Homomonument,* the world's first public memorial to persecuted gays and lesbians, is unveiled.
- 1990s The city and Holland take leading roles in liberalizing laws regarding homosexuality, including sanctioning gay marriages.
- 1990 Van Gogh Centenary. A million visitors troop through the commemorative exhibit at the Van Gogh Museum.
- 1992 Amsterdammers vote to restrict vehicle use in the city center. An El Al Boeing 747 cargo plane, carrying chemical warfare agents, takes off from Schiphol Airport and crashes into apartment buildings in the Bijlmermeer housing project, killing all four crew members and 39 people on the ground.
- 1995 Amsterdam celebrates its canals, river, and harbor with the 6-month festival "City on the Water."
- 1997 The Treaty of Amsterdam confirms European Monetary Union and the euro as the future common European currency.
- 1998–99 Redevelopment of Museumplein gives the large square a landscaped garden with an ornamental

kingdom's link with the divine. This century also witnessed the Reformation, which began in 1517 with Martin Luther nailing his *Ninety-five Theses* to the door of the Catholic Church in Wittenberg, Germany, and the eventual spread of Protestantism throughout the Christian world. It was a time of tremendous religious ferment.

Nations throughout Europe wrestled with the notion of religious diversity. In Holland, the anti-Catholic, iconoclastic ideas of Protestantism took root in the Dutch psyche at the same time as the Dutch provinces officially came under the rule of Charles V, the intensely Catholic Habsburg emperor and king of Spain. Holland, and Amsterdam in particular, became a pressure point and fulcrum for the shifting political scene that the Reformation occasioned everywhere in Europe. It was the rigorous doctrines of John Calvin and his firm belief in the separation of church and state that began to take root in Amsterdam.

Among the more radical Protestant sects were the Anabaptists, some of whom had left Germany in 1530 in

pool at its heart. The Van Gogh Museum gets a new wing.

- **2000** Amsterdam co-hosts the Euro 2000 championship soccer tournament. Passenger Terminal Amsterdam opens to cruise ships.
- **2001** Schiphol Airport, one of Europe's busiest airports, with 40 million passengers passing through in a year, is rocked by two separate explosions. Both cause the passenger terminal to be evacuated. The first blast, detonated by a disturbed individual, injures three people; the second, later in the year, caused by an accident at the Burger King franchise, ignites a large fire but no one is injured.
- **2002** The world's first same-sex marriage, husband and husband, with a legal status identical to heterosexual matrimony, takes place in Amsterdam. Wedding bells peal again when Crown Prince Willem Alexander marries Argentine beauty Máxima Zorreguieta in the city's Nieuwe Kerk; the marriage stirred controversy because the bride's father, Jorge Zorreguieta, was a government official of the military junta during Argentina's 1976–83 "dirty war," in which 10,000 suspected opposition activists were tortured and killed.

hopes of finding a more tolerant climate in Amsterdam. The Anabaptists rejected the Catholic celebration of saints' days and infant baptism, favoring adult baptism instead, and did not believe in the Trinity. For the most part, they gained their following among the poor. In general, the city's Catholics tolerated the presence of Anabaptists in their midst—until 1535, when a group of them seized the Town Hall in anticipation of the Second Coming. The Anabaptists found the city unwilling to go along and the leaders of the uprising were executed.

Despite the reprisals, the Anabaptists continued their agitation. On February 11, 1535, a so-called prophet, Hendrick Hendrickszoon, was preaching to a small group of men and women when he suddenly told them that the Lord had spoken to him and that all present were damned to Hell. The congregation asked for forgiveness, which was immediately granted, but then Hendrickszoon ripped off his clothes, threw them on the fire, and bade the others to do the same—which they did. Then, they all ran naked through the city, including the landlady of the building in which they had been holding their meeting. These zealots have been referred to as the "Naked Runners"—Amsterdam's original streakers—ever since. The men were all executed and the landlady was hanged in the doorway of her building as an example to the public. In this, Amsterdam became like many communities in Europe, abandoning religious toleration in favor of religious repression.

Fun Fact **What's in a Name?**

Let's clear up some matters of nomenclature. "Dutch" is the result of a 15th-century ethnological misunderstanding on the part of the English, who couldn't distinguish too clearly between the people of the northern Low Countries and the various German peoples. So, to describe the former, they simply corrupted the German *Deutsch* to "Dutch."

The term "Holland" is a bit of a misnomer, too, because, strictly speaking, it refers only to the provinces of North Holland and South Holland and not to the whole country. The Dutch themselves call their country *Nederland* (the Netherlands) and themselves *Nederlanders*. But they recognize that "Dutch" and "Holland" are popular internationally and are here to stay, so, being a practical people, they make use of them.

Not all events had religious fanaticism as their motive force. A big step forward in our knowledge of Amsterdam at this time took place in 1538, when Cornelis Anthoniszoon created a painted woodcut map, giving a bird's-eye view of the city that clearly showed landmarks such as the Dam, the Oude Kerk and the harbor. Anthoniszoon's woodcut began a long and illustrious tradition of mapmaking in the city, and if you can find a reproduction of it you can compare both the similarities with today and the changes that almost 5 centuries have wrought.

About 20 years later a series of events changed the course of history in Holland and Amsterdam, turning the country toward a path that would make it a world-renowned symbol of religious, political, and intellectual tolerance. In 1555, Philip II, son of Charles V and a great-grandson of Emperor Maximilian I, became king of Spain. An ardent Catholic, he was determined to defeat the Reformation and set out to hunt heretics everywhere throughout his empire. The Dutch resented Philip's intrusion into their affairs and began a resistance movement. Within 10 years a League of Protestant Nobles had been formed in the Netherlands by the taciturn but tactful William of Orange, count of Holland, known also as William the Silent. Philip's response was to send the vicious duke of Alba to Holland. He was to function as an overseer, with specific instructions to establish a Council of Blood to enforce the policy of "death to heretics."

The Dutch nobles fought back, though they had no army, no money to raise one, and little support from the Dutch cities, including Catholic Amsterdam, which was interested mostly in maintaining its prosperous trade. William of Orange and his brother John of Nassau managed to wage war on Spain despite all this, their only ally a ragtag "navy" of Protestant pirates called the Sea Beggars. They were helped when Spain levied a new tax on its Dutch "colony," an action so unpopular as to rally the majority of Dutch people—Protestant and Catholic alike—to the anti-Spanish cause.

A few towns, including Amsterdam, declined to join the fight against Alba, deeming resistance bad for business. These communities were spared destruction when the Spanish invaded. The Spanish armies marched inexorably through Holland, besting the defenses of each city to which they laid siege, with few exceptions. In an ingenious if desperate move, William of Orange saved the city of Leiden by flooding the province, allowing the Sea Beggars to sail their galleons right up to the city's walls. The attack surprised the Spaniards in the middle of dinner; they were promptly routed. A stew pot left behind became a national symbol of freedom for Holland, and its contents inspired the traditional Dutch dish called *hutspot.*

This victory galvanized the Dutch in fighting for their independence. The Calvinist merchants of Amsterdam turned out their Catholic city council in 1578 in a revolution called the *Alteratie* (Changeover), and the city abandoned the pro-Catholic Spanish cause. As the Protestant Reformation took hold, the city's many Catholics were forbidden to hold public office or to worship openly, a situation that continued for more than a century.

The Dutch nobles strengthened their commitment to each other in 1579 by signing the Union of Utrecht, in which they agreed to fight together in a united front. Although the union was devised solely to prosecute the battle against Spain, consolidation inevitably occurred, and by the turn of the 17th century what had once been the Spanish Netherlands became the Seven United Provinces—North Holland, South Holland, Zeeland, Friesland, Utrecht, Gelderland, and Groningen (Overijssel). The struggle with Spain would continue through the first half of the 17th century, but Holland's strength was growing and a new, prosperous era was about to begin.

2 The Golden Age

Over the first 50 to 75 years of the 17th century, the legendary Dutch entrepreneurial gift would come into its own. These years have since become known as the Golden Age. It seemed every business venture the Dutch initiated during this time turned a profit and that each of their many expeditions to the unknown places of the world resulted in a new jewel in the Dutch trading empire. Colonies and brisk trade were established to provide the luxury-hungry merchants at home with new delights, such as fresh ginger from Java, foxtails from America, fine porcelain from China, and flower bulbs from Turkey that produced big, bright, waxy flowers and grew quite readily in Holland's sandy soil—tulips. Holland was rich and Amsterdam was growing.

Until the late 16th century Amsterdam had always lagged behind neighboring cities in economic terms, despite having extended its trade routes to Russia, Scandinavia, and the Baltic. But in 1589 Amsterdam's biggest commercial rival, the Belgian port of Antwerp, was taken over by the Spanish, prompting many industrious Protestant and Jewish craftspeople to flee to Amsterdam. Of the Jewish influx, the jurist Hugo Grotius wrote in 1614: "Plainly God desires them to live somewhere. Why not here rather than elsewhere?" These immigrants brought with them their merchant skills and their businesses, including the diamond industry, which has remained a famous and central part of the city's commerce.

Over the next 65 years Amsterdam grew into one of the world's great cities. In 1602, traders from each of the major cities in the Republic of the Seven Provinces set up the Verenigde Oostindische Compagnie (V.O.C.), the United East India Company, which was granted a monopoly on trade in the East. Printed shares in the V.O.C. were traded at the world's oldest stock exchange, founded that same year in the Oudezijds Kapel. The company's purpose was to mount safe, cost-effective, exploratory voyages and trading ventures to the East Indies. It was wildly successful and established the Dutch presence in the Spice Islands (Indonesia), Goa, South Africa, and China. The big Dutch East India Company merchant vessels could hold twice as much cargo as their English

Fun Fact **Beating the Dutch**

The 17th-century Dutch got right up the noses of the English by competing against them aggressively and successfully for maritime trade and, in 1667, by sailing boldly up the Medway near London and trashing the English fleet. So the English added verbal abuse to their counterattack arsenal. That's why we have "Dutch courage" (alcohol-induced courage); "Dutch treat" (you pay for yourself); "going Dutch" (everybody pays their share); and "double Dutch" (gibberish). Americans were kinder to their Revolutionary War supporters, speaking of "beating the Dutch" (doing something remarkable).

rivals. A full-size replica of one of these sailing ships, the *Amsterdam,* is tied up to the wharf outside the city's Netherlands Maritime Museum.

Between 1602 and its demise in 1795, the V.O.C. employed around 1,500 ships, many of them built at the Oostenburg yard in Amsterdam. No fewer than 246 were lost on the dangerous voyages to and from the East Indies to bring back pepper, cinnamon, cloves, nutmeg, coffee, tea, and textiles. Today, the site of the Oostenburg shipyard is a warren of modern apartment blocks, old warehouses, and dingy canals. Almost nothing survives of what in the 17th century was probably the world's largest industrial complex. At its height, in 1750, Oostenburg employed 350 shipwrights, 90 blacksmiths, 80 ropemakers, 28 sailmakers, 40 bargemakers, 40 blockmakers, and 18 carpenters. For processing the exotic cargoes that arrived from the East Indies, there were 80 pepper-workers and 40 spice-graders. By the end of the 18th century, the Amsterdam Chamber of the V.O.C. employed 1,500 people.

Great wealth flowed back to Amsterdam, and the merchants used it to build the canals and the impressive 17th-century architecture along the Golden Bend on the Herengracht. The merchant owners of canalside mansions liked to put up a good facade, but canal frontage was expensive and so the houses behind those elegant gables were long and narrow. Their upper floors were storerooms bulging with their owners' wares, which were hoisted up on loft-mounted rope and pulleys.

In 1613 work was begun on the three major canals (Herengracht, Keizersgracht, and Prinsengracht). City planners designed a system in which the large canals were connected by smaller transverse canals to make travel by water more convenient throughout Amsterdam. They decided that the wealthy would live facing the major canals, while the connecting canals were set aside for the middle and lower classes. Thus began the popular comparison with Venice—though Amsterdam has more canals than the Italian city—that continues to be made to this day.

The growing city bustled in many other ways: A variety of churches and other houses of worship was built during this time, traders and craftspeople of all sorts began setting up protectionist guilds, and there was an increase in interest in the arts and sciences. Artists, including Rembrandt, were working overtime, cranking out paintings commissioned by newly affluent merchants who had become obsessed with portraying themselves and surrounding themselves with beautiful images. It is thought that most affluent Dutch homes had at least four paintings in them at that time.

Golden Age Amsterdam can be compared to Renaissance Florence and Periclean Athens for the great flowering that transformed society. "There is perhaps no other example of a complete and highly original civilization springing up in so short a time in so small a territory," wrote the historian Simon Schama in *The Embarrassment of Riches* (1987). Learning flourished. Amsterdam's first school of higher education, the Athenaeum Illustre, was established in 1632. The Athenaeum Illustre was not a university, but it did raise the city's educational possibilities above the level offered before. The Guild of Surgeons began giving anatomy demonstrations to both interested doctors and laypeople. As a symbol of the city's civic pride and wealth, the new Stadhuis (Town Hall) on the Dam, completed in 1665 to replace an earlier one that was destroyed by fire, is hard to beat—so lavishly appointed was it that it was later taken over by royalty and became the Royal Palace.

Artists and architects flourished during this time, but they weren't the only ones to bask in a Golden Age glow. To help the ships of the far-ranging Dutch merchant marine and fleet to know where they were, cartographer **Willem Jansz Blaeu** (1571–1638) founded an Amsterdam company that was famous for marine publications, globes, and atlases, and for navigational and astronomical instruments. You can see examples of Blaeu's work at the Amsterdams Historisch Museum and the Netherlands Maritime Museum. Blaeu's son, Jan, published in 1663 the 11-volume *Atlas Major*.

Pieter Cornelisz Hooft (1581–1647), the leading Dutch Renaissance poet and playwright, wrote the first pastoral play in Dutch, *Granida* (1605). He later turned his hand to history, in *Nederlandsche Historien* (*Dutch History*, 1642–54), about the Dutch Revolt against Spain. Providing creative competition was the poet and playwright **Joost van den Vondel** (1587–1679), who produced such important works as *Gijsbrecht van Aemstel* and *Lucifer*. The Vondelpark is named after him.

For 45 years **Jan Pieterszoon Sweelinck** (1562–1621) was organist at the Oude Kerk. A prolific composer for organ and harpsichord, he also wrote 250 choral works. Amsterdam's music school is called the Sweelinck Conservatorium and a bust of the composer adorns the entrance to the Concertgebouw.

In the field of philosophy, **Baruch Benedictus de Spinoza** (1632–77) was a giant. Spinoza devoted his life to writing compelling and far-reaching treatises, most of which were published after his death. *Ethica,* his best-known work, attempted to prove ethical theories using mathematics. His unorthodox ideas about the Bible—he believed it should be interpreted in the light of our knowledge of the times in which it was written, rather than being considered the literal word of God—and his critique of Judaism had him expelled in 1656 from the city's Portuguese Synagogue. Spinoza's day job as a lens grinder financed his philosophizing and writing.

Another prominent scion of Amsterdam's Jewish community, **Manasseh ben Israel** (1604–57), was a rabbi at 18 and founder of the city's first Hebrew press. He counted Rembrandt among his friends and the artist sketched his portrait. Among his published works—which were popular with both Jews and Christians—are *The Hope of Israel* (1650), *Vindication of the Jews* (1656), and *Conciliador,* an attempt to reconcile contradictory biblical passages.

After 80 years, the war with Spain finally ended in 1648. By then Holland had a fleet of 2,700 trading ships. Though the Nieuw Amsterdam colony (present-day New York) in North America was lost to the English in 1664, the Dutch continued to grow wealthy from their Spice Islands holdings. The descendants of William of Orange had by then established a de facto monarchy, which was further strengthened when William III married into the English royal family. The ascension of William III and his wife, Mary, to the English throne in 1688 may have been the beginning of the end for the Dutch Republic, however. Wars, commercial failures, misguided political decisions, and low morale were the hallmarks of the next century of Dutch history, which ended with the House of Orange in exile.

DECLINE & FALL
In the final reckoning, a Golden Age is a nostalgic concept, a looking back wistfully to a "better age" that can exist only in the past. Gold is the color of a late afternoon in autumn: The light of spring may shine once again, but first must come the long night of winter. Anyone who had given the matter much thought—and there is not much sign that anyone did—might have concluded that Holland's golden moment would likely fade away gently into the mists of time. In reality, it came to an end with all the unexpected suddenness of a crash of blue-sky thunder.

The Dutch call 1672 the *Rampjaar* (Year of Disaster). France, under Louis XIV, invaded the United Provinces by land and the English attacked by sea. This war (1672–78) and the later War of the Spanish Succession (1701–13) drained the country's wealth and morale. The buccaneering, can-do, go-anywhere spirit of traders, artists, and writers began to ebb, replaced by conservatism and closed horizons.

Still, in the 1680s the Dutch merchant fleet was larger than those of England, Spain, Portugal, and France combined, and in Amsterdam the illumination from more than 2,000 whale oil–burning lamps made the nighttime streets among the safest in the world.

A long period of decline set in during the 18th century. At the Museum Willet-Holthuysen and Museum Van Loon you get an idea of the decadent, French-influenced style in which wealthy Amsterdam families lived during the Golden Age's fading afterglow. In 1748 the city's taxpayers signaled they had as much as they could stomach of watching the rich get richer, the poor get poorer, and civic leaders blatantly help themselves from the public purse, by going on a rampage. Tax collectors' houses and the fine canalside mansions of the merchants and bankers, particularly favored targets of the mob's anger, were stormed and looted. But the riot was suppressed and its ringleaders hanged.

By the second half of the century, Amsterdam was a hotbed of intrigue by pro-French, antiroyalist democrats called the Patriots, who seized control of the city on April 27, 1787. An army of Prussian troops soon came to the rescue of the House of Orange, tramping into the city on October 10 to put down the rebellion. In 1791 the United East India Company was liquidated, a key indicator of the nation's steep commercial decline.

An equally significant milestone in the downward spiral was passed when the Dutch navy, which had once been all but invincible, was captured by a company of horsemen. That happened in January 1794, when the fleet found itself stuck in the frozen waters between Den Helder and Texel Island. French cavalry simply rode out to the ships and captured them all. The humiliating defeat was quite a fall from the heights of glory the navy had known off the same coast in 1673, when Admirals de Ruyter and Tromp had led Dutch ships to victory over a combined English and French fleet.

3 The 19th Century to the Present

Revolutionary France invaded Holland in 1794, capturing Amsterdam and establishing the Batavian Republic in 1795, headed by the pro-French Dutch Patriots. Napoléon brought the short-lived republic to an end in 1806 by setting up his brother, Louis Napoléon, as king of the Netherlands, and installing him in the town hall on the Dam in Amsterdam, which was converted for the purpose to a palace. What Napoléon the emperor wanted, of course, was a fraternal puppet on the Dutch throne to do his bidding. Far from being a puppet, Louis did a such a good job of representing the interests of his new subjects—for instance, permitting them to trade surreptitiously with Britain, which was at war with Napoléon and under French blockade—that in 1810 Napoléon deposed him and brought the Netherlands formally into the empire.

The French reign was short lived, but the taste of royalty proved sweet. When the Dutch recalled the House of Orange in 1815, it was to fill the role of king in a constitutional monarchy. The monarch was yet another William of Orange; however, because his reign was to be a fresh start for the republic, the Dutch started numbering their Williams all over again (which makes for a very confusing history).

In the 1860s Amsterdam's economy grew strong again as the city worked to equip itself for modern trade. The first improvement was the building of a railway line between Haarlem and Amsterdam in 1839. The North Sea Canal, which ran from Amsterdam to IJmuiden and gave Amsterdam a better crack at German industrial trade, was built in 1876. Another major boon to the city was the building of the Suez Canal in 1869, which made travel to Asia easier.

For about 2 centuries after Amsterdam's Golden Age the city's population remained at a quarter of a million. Between 1850 and 1900, however, it jumped to half a million. As did most major cities during the Industrial Revolution, Amsterdam began to face issues of overpopulation. Housing was in short supply, the canals were increasingly befouled with sewage, and for many life in the city became increasingly nasty, brutish, and short.

THE WORLD WARS & THE GREAT DEPRESSION

Holland maintained strict neutrality during World War I, but the war still had an impact on Amsterdam. While the wealthy exploited the situation by selling arms and other supplies, the city suffered from acute food shortages, and the poor were constantly faced with starvation. In 1917 there were food riots; Amsterdam answered with soup kitchens and rationing. In the 1920s Amsterdam shared in the wealth as Europe's condition improved, but conditions were very bad during the 1930s, when the widespread unemployment brought on by the Great Depression caused the government to use the army in 1934 to control the unruly masses. During this time many poor Dutch families were forced to move to Germany, where jobs were easier to come by.

Amsterdam was just beginning to recover from the Depression when on May 10, 1940, the Germans invaded. The overmatched Dutch army resisted bravely, but with Rotterdam blitzed into ruins and a similar fate threatened for Amsterdam and other cities, the end came quickly. Queen Wilhelmina, a tiny woman whom Churchill called "the only man in the Dutch government," fled to England, where she stayed until 1945. An Austrian Nazi, Arthur Seyss-Inquart, was put in charge of the occupied Netherlands.

As he did in most other cities he conquered, Hitler managed to gain a following in Amsterdam. However, there was resistance by the citizens to Nazi treatment of Jews, Gypsies, and homosexuals. In February 1941 city workers organized a strike to protest the deportation of Jews. Today, in the Old Jewish Quarter, where many Jews lived until the war, you can see the statue *The Dockworker,* a tribute to the February Strike (Amsterdam was the first city in the world to have a memorial—the *Homomonument*—to the 250,000 gays and lesbians killed by Nazis during World War II). Unfortunately, the strike did little good; by 1942 the Nazis had forced all Dutch Jews to move to three isolated areas in Amsterdam. Between July 1942 and September 1943 most of Amsterdam's Jews were sent to death camps. Of the 60,000 Jews in Amsterdam, only 6,000 survived (the figures for the Netherlands as a whole were 140,000 and 16,000, respectively).

Among the murdered was a teenage girl who has come to symbolize the many victims of the Holocaust—Anne Frank (1929–45). Anne is famous the world over for her diary, a profoundly moving record of a Jewish teenager's struggle to cope with the horrific realities of war and the Nazi occupation. When the Germans began deporting the Jews Anne and her family went into hiding in an Amsterdam canal house, now the Anne Frankhuis. Cut off from other outlets for her energies, she began to keep a journal telling of her thoughts, feelings, and experiences. The last entry was on August 1, 1944, shortly before she and her family were discovered and deported to concentration camps. Anne and her sister were sent to Bergen-Belsen, where they died of typhus just a few days before Allied forces liberated the camp. Otto Frank, Anne's father, was the only survivor of the Frank family, and it was he who first had Anne's diary published.

By September 1944 the people of Amsterdam hoped for liberation, as the German armies were on the run after their defeat in Normandy and Allied troops had crossed into Holland from Belgium. On September 17, the greatest airborne assault in history, Operation Market Garden, was launched. Paratroops of the U.S. 101st and 82nd Airborne Divisions landed near Eindhoven and Nijmegen, and after bitter fighting, captured the cities and their river bridges. Farther north, the British 1st Airborne Division landed at Arnhem to take the vital bridge over the Rhine—the gateway to Hitler's Germany and the key to hopes of ending the war in 1944. It was, in a phrase that has gone down in history, "a bridge too far." The British division was virtually destroyed after landing virtually on top of the German 2nd SS Panzer Corps.

Amsterdam's citizens were then faced with what is known as the Hunger Winter. Food supplies were practically nonexistent, and many people were forced to steal or buy provisions on the black market. Those who ventured into the country in hopes of getting milk and eggs were in danger of not getting back to the city before curfew. On May 5, 1945, the grim ordeal came to an end, as the Dutch celebrated the Allies' liberation of the Netherlands. Canadian troops reached Amsterdam first, on May 7—a short way behind that intrepid war correspondent and later popular television news anchorman, Walter Cronkite. A few diehard Nazis opened fire on jubilant crowds at the Dam, killing 22 people.

POSTWAR TURBULENCE

With the coming of peace, Amsterdam was still a simple, homogeneous city, notable for its hundreds of arching bridges, thousands of historic gabled houses, and many canals. The city seemed to have survived intact from its moment of glory in the 17th century. It was a quiet, unhurried, provincial sort of town, and it was very, very clean. But, beginning with its recovery from World War II, Amsterdam began to grow and prosper again, and to change.

In the 1960s the city was just as much a hotbed of political and cultural radicalism as San Francisco. Hippies trailing clouds of marijuana smoke took over the Dam for their downtown *pied-à-terre* and camped out in Vondelpark and in front of Centraal Station. Radical political activity, which began with "happenings" staged by the small group known as the Provos—from *provocatie* (provocation)—continued and intensified in the 1970s. In 1966, the Provos were behind the protests that marred the wedding of Princess Beatrix to German Claus von Amsberg; smoke bombs were thrown and fighting broke out between protesters and police. The Provos formally disbanded in 1967, but much of their program was adopted by the Green Gnomes, or *Kabouters*. This group won several seats on the municipal council, but it too eventually faded.

Some radicals joined neighborhood groups to protest specific local government plans. The scheme that provoked the greatest ire was a plan to build a subway through the Nieuwmarkt area. Demonstrations to defend the housing that had been condemned to make way for the subway were launched in 1975, with the most dramatic confrontation between the police and the human barricades taking place on Blue Monday, March 24. Thirty people were wounded and 47 arrested in a battle of tear gas and water cannons against paint cans and powder bombs. Despite the protests, the subway was built and opened in 1980.

With the influx of immigrants from newly independent Surinam and other countries, the shortage of decent affordable housing continued to be a major issue; in fact, it was to spark the squatting movement that came to dominate the late 1970s and '80s. Squatting, or *kraaken* in Dutch, is the occupation by homeless people of empty or temporarily unoccupied properties. In a city with such a severe shortage of housing, it has been, and to some extent remains, a viable option, particularly for the young. The squatting movement is well organized, but its associations with anarchist, antisocial groups and its disregard for private property rights make it an unsavory phenomenon to many, though there is some public sympathy for the *squatters'* plight.

In 1978 the first squatters occupied the old *Handelsblad* newspaper office building, but it took a series of squatter initiatives to unify the squatters into a movement. The biggest confrontations came in 1980, first at the Vondelstraat squat in the heart of the museum area, where 500 police with armored vehicles evicted squatters. Riots followed, and 50 people were wounded and much damage was sustained. The second and larger disturbance occurred on Beatrix Coronation Day, when 200 buildings were occupied in 26 cities, and in Amsterdam itself protesters battled the police and totally disrupted the festivities. Other squatting incidents followed, but slowly both sides developed a more constructive dialogue that has managed to avert further violent confrontations.

Despite all the politicking, CS gas, and seeking of alternatives, the undoubted local hero of the 1970s was soccer maestro **Johann Cruyff** (b. 1947). There are many with fond memories of his supreme artistry, poetry, and skill as he captained Amsterdam's Ajax club, proponents of a highly mobile, fluent, and deadly system of play called Total Football, to three successive European Cup triumphs (1971–73) and led Holland to the World Cup final in 1974.

Protests similar to those that had been started against the subway were launched against the proposals to build a new Stadhuis (Town Hall) and Opera (Muziektheater) side by side on Waterlooplein, a complex that became known as the Stopera. Despite an energetic and at times violent campaign to "Stop the Stopera," both buildings were completed in 1986, and the Muziektheater is now a star in the city's cultural firmament.

The Provos and Green Gnomes had long advocated specific environmental programs, such as the prohibition of all motor vehicles from the city. At one point, they actually persuaded the city authorities to provide 20,000 white-painted bicycles free for citizens' use—sadly, this admirable scheme was abandoned when most of the bicycles were stolen, no doubt to reappear in freshly painted colors as "private" property. Some of their ideas came to fruition in 1992, however, when the populace voted to create a traffic-free zone in the city center.

Although the turbulent events of the 1970s and '80s seem distant today, the independent spirit and social conscience that fueled them remains, and Amsterdam is still one of the most socially advanced cities in Europe. New priorities have emerged, however, with the general aim of boosting Amsterdam's position as a global business center and the location of choice for foreign multinationals' European headquarters, and of consolidating its role as one of Europe's most important transport and distribution hubs. These aims are aided by an ongoing effort to change the city's hippie-paradise image to one more in tune with the needs of commerce.

AMSTERDAM TODAY

Amsterdam is the capital and major city of the Netherlands, a tiny country that's barely half the size of the U.S. state of Maine. Today, this sophisticated international city has a multicultural population of 725,000 (and 600,000 bikes), a busy harbor, and an abundance of industrial towers, multistory apartment communities, and elevated highways — all the hallmarks of a modern urban center. The modernization process has had its pluses and minuses. Much tranquillity has been lost along the way, although it has been replaced with an increased vibrancy. But Amsterdam still remains a kind of big village, retaining a human scale that at least affords the illusion of simplicity.

More and more people from Holland, Europe, and farther afield are making tracks toward the city. Footloose young Hollanders seem to have no other ambition than to live here — and who can blame them when you consider the "excitement" of growing up in a squeaky clean Dutch village?

Young Americans and Europeans still see Amsterdam as a kind of mecca of youth rebellion to which a pilgrimage must be made (though Prague has stolen some of Amsterdam's allure in that respect). Immigrants find social support systems and a relative absence of the discrimination they face in many other European cities, but areas like Amsterdam East and the Bijlmermeer housing project, with a high percentage of immigrants, are experiencing growing social problems.

Impressions

To understand the Dutch, you've got to start out with the word gedogen. *It basically means to permit, to live with, to be able to tolerate. A lot of what you see in terms of legislation has been subject to* gedogen *for years. By the time it's written into law, it almost doesn't make a difference.*

— K. Terry Dornbush, former U.S. ambassador
to the Netherlands (2001)

Shopkeepers still keep their portals tidy, and a few homemakers still wash their steps each morning, but graffiti, miscellaneous grime, and other problems of city life inhabit Amsterdam as much as any other urban center. (The ubiquitous mounds of dog poop on the sidewalks, for instance, have become something of a symbol of the city.)

But maybe you just want to know what to expect from the person in the street and behind the shop counter. The most honest thing to say about Amsterdammers is that they can be both the most infuriating and the most endearing people in the world.

> ### Impressions
>
> *Amsterdam will at least give one's regular habits of thought the stimulus of a little confusion.*
> — Henry James, American novelist (1875)

One minute, they treat you like a naughty child (surely you've heard the expression about someone talking to you like a Dutch uncle), and the next, they're ready for a laugh and a beer. They can be rude or cordial (it may depend on the weather), domineering, or ever ready to please (it may depend on you). In a shop, they may get annoyed with you if you don't accept what they have, or get mad at themselves if they don't have what you want.

Fortunately, it's easy to overlook all shortcomings. The historic heart of the city is still there to charm you with its tree-lined canals, gabled houses, and graceful bridges. The Dutch National Monument Care Office (Monumentenzorg) has exercised great foresight in working to preserve the feel of the 17th century along the canals. There are still traces of yesteryear in the street life, too: You see barrel organs and bicycles, antiques shops, and herring stands. In addition to the palpable sense of history a trip to Amsterdam will occasion, there are other lures — great museums, fine dining, and a diverse nightlife scene.

You'll have no problem finding the legacy of the city's Golden Age, nearly 400 years ago, in the new Amsterdam. Fuming traffic, power drills, telephone boxes, bikes, tour boats, and souvenir shops have dulled some of the luster, but a moment always arrives when a window in time opens and Amsterdam's heritage asserts itself.

Appendix B:
Useful Terms & Phrases

The Dutch people you encounter will likely speak English every bit as well as you do—some of them, annoyingly, perhaps even better. That said, no Amsterdammer will fault you for having a go at Dutch. In fact, they'll appreciate hugely any effort you make to string together words and sentences in their tongue-twister of a *taal* (language). An occasional *dank U wel* (thank you) and *alstublieft* (please) can take you a long way.

These lists of words and phrases should help you to get started—and help out in those rare situations where you are dealing with people who don't understand English. If nothing else, perusing the "Dutch Menu Savvy" section (below) will give you something to do while you wait for the waitperson to take your order.

1 Basic Vocabulary

ENGLISH & DUTCH PHRASES

English	Dutch	Pronunciation
Hello	**Dag/Hallo**	dakh/*ha*-loh
Good morning	**Goedenmorgen**	*khoo*-yuh-*mor*-khun
Good afternoon/ evening	**Goedenavond**	*khoo*-yuhn-*af*-ond
How are you?	**Hoe gaat het met U?**	hoo *khaht* et met oo
Very well	**Uitstekend**	out-*stayk*-end
Thank you	**Dank U wel**	*dahnk* oo wel
Good-bye	**Dag/Tot Ziens**	dakh/tot zeenss
Good night	**Goedenacht**	*khoo*-duh-nakht
See you later	**Tot straks**	Tot strahkss
Please	**Alstublieft**	*ahl*-stoo-bleeft
Yes	**Ja**	yah
No	**Neen**	nay
Excuse me	**Pardon**	par-*dawn*
Sorry	**Sorry**	*so*-ree
Do you speak English?	**Spreekt U Engels?**	spraykt oo *eng*-els
Can you help me?	**Kunt U mij helpen?**	koont oo *may-* ee *hel*- pen
Give me . . .	**Geeft U mij . . .**	*khayft* oo may . . .
Where is . . .?	**Waar is . . . ?**	*vahr* iz . . .
the station	**het station**	het *stah*-ssyonh
the post office	**het postkantoor**	het *post*-kan-tohr
a bank	**een bank**	ayn bank
a hotel	**een hotel**	ayn *ho*-tel
a restaurant	**een restaurant**	ayn res-to-*rahng*

English	Dutch	Pronunciation
a pharmacy/ chemist	**een apotheek**	ayn a-po-*tayk*
the toilet	**het toilet**	het *twah*-let
To the right	**Rechts**	rekhts
To the left	**Links**	links
Straight ahead	**Rechtdoor**	rekht-*doar*
I would like . . .	**Ik zou graag . . .**	ik zow khrakh . . .
to eat	**eten**	*ay*-ten
a room for	**een kamer voor**	ayn *kah*-mer voor
one night	**een nacht**	ayn nakht
How much is it?	**Hoe veel kost het?**	hoo fayl kawst het
The check	**De rekening**	duh *ray*-ken-ing
When?	**Wanneer?**	vah-*neer*
Yesterday	**Gisteren**	*khis*-ter-en
Today	**Vandaag**	van-*dahkh*
Tomorrow	**Morgen**	*mor*-khen
Breakfast	**Ontbijt**	*ohnt*-bayt
Lunch	**Lunch**	lunch
Dinner	**Diner**	*dee*-nay

USEFUL WORDS

English	Dutch	Pronunciation
Airmail	**Luchtpost**	*lookht*-post
Airport	**Luchthaven**	*lookht*-haff-uhn
Bus stop/Tram stop	**Bushalte/Tramhalte**	*boos*-haltuh/*tram*-haltuh
Cheap	**Goedkoop**	*khood*-kope
Church	**Kerk**	kerk
Cinema	**Bioskoop**	*bee*-oss-kope
Closed	**Gesloten**	*khuh*-slo-ten
Expensive	**Duur**	door
Firefighters	**Brandweer**	*brand*-vayhr
Free	**Gratis**	*khra*-tis
Hospital	**Ziekenhuis**	*zeek*-en-howss
Magazine	**Tijdschrift**	*tied*-skhrift
Newspaper	**Krant**	krant
Open	**Geopend**	*khuh*-oh-pend
Parking lot	**Parkeerplaats**	par-*kayhr*-plahtss
Police	**Politie**	po-*lee*-tsee
Registered post	**Aangetekend**	*ahn*-khu-tay-kend
Shop	**Winkel**	*vhin*-kuhl
Stamp	**Postzegel**	*post*-zay-khel
Theater	**Theater**	tay-*ah*-ter

NUMBERS

1	**een** (ayn)		8	**acht** (akht)
2	**twee** (tway)		9	**negen** (*nay*-khen)
3	**drie** (dree)		10	**tien** (teen)
4	**vier** (veer)		11	**elf** (elf)
5	**vijf** (vayf)		12	**twaalf** (tvahlf)
6	**zes** (zes)		13	**dertien** (*dayr*-teen)
7	**zeven** (*zay*-vun)		14	**veertien** (*vayr*-teen)

15	**vijftien** (*vayf*-teen)	50	**vijftig** (*vayf*-tukh)
16	**zestien** (*zes*-teen)	60	**zestig** (*zes*-tukh)
17	**zeventien** (*zay*-vun-teen)	70	**zeventig** (*zay*-vun-tukh)
18	**achtien** (*akh*-teen)	80	**tachtig** (*takh*-tukh)
19	**negentien** (*nay*-khun-teen)	90	**negentig** (*nay*-khen-tukh)
20	**twintig** (*twin*-tikh)	100	**honderd** (*hon*-dayrt)
30	**dertig** (*der*-tukh)	1,000	**duizend** (*douw*-zend)
40	**veertig** (*vayr*-tukh)		

DAYS OF THE WEEK

Monday	**Maandag** (*mahn*-dakh)
Tuesday	**Dinsdag** (*deens*-dakh)
Wednesday	**Woensdag** (*voohns*-dakh)
Thursday	**Donderdag** (*donder*-dakh)
Friday	**Vrijdag** (*vray*-dakh)
Saturday	**Zaterdag** (*zahter*-dakh)
Sunday	**Zondag** (*zohn*-dakh)

MONTHS

January	**Januari** (*yahn*-oo-aree)
February	**Februari** (*fayhb*-roo-aree)
March	**Maart** (mahrt)
April	**April** (ah-*pril*)
May	**Mai** (*mah*-eey)
June	**Juni** (yoo-*nee*)
July	**Juli** (yoo-*lee*)
August	**August** (awh-*khoost*)
September	**September** (sep-*tem*-buhr)
October	**Oktober** (oct-*oah*-buhr)
November	**November** (noa-*vem*-buhr)
December	**December** (day-*sem*-buhr)

SEASONS

Spring	**Lente** (*len*-tuh)
Summer	**Zomer** (*zoh*-muhr)
Fall/autumn	**Herfst** (herfsst)
Winter	**Winter** (*vin*-tuhr)

SIGNS

Doorgaand Verkeer	Through Traffic
Doorgaand Verkeer Gestremd	Road Closed
Geen Doorgaand Verkeer	No Through Traffic
Niet Parkeeren	No Parking
Tentoonstelling	Exhibit
Verboden Te Roken	No Smoking
Vrije Toegang	Admission Free/Allowed
Wegomlegging	Diversion

2 Dutch Menu Savvy

BASICS
ontbijt breakfast
lunch lunch
diner dinner
boter butter
boterham sandwich
brood bread
  stokbrood French bread
  voorgerechten starters
honing honey
hoofdgerechten main courses
hutspot mashed potatoes and carrots
jam jam
kaas cheese
mosterd mustard
pannekoeken pancakes
peper pepper
saus sauce
suiker sugar
zout salt

SOUPS (*SOEPEN*)
aardappelsoep potato soup
bonensoep bean soup
erwtensoep pea soup (usually includes bacon or sausage)
groentensoep vegetable soup
kippensoep chicken soup
soep soup
tomatensoep tomato soup
uiensoep onion soup

EGGS (*EIER*)
eieren eggs
hardgekookte eieren hard-boiled eggs
omelette omelette
roereieren scrambled eggs
spiegeleieren fried eggs
uitsmijter fried eggs and ham on bread
zachtgekookte eieren boiled eggs

FISH (*VIS*)
forel trout
garnalen prawns
gerookte zalm smoked salmon
haring herring
kabeljauw cod
kreeft lobster
makreel mackerel
mosselen mussels
oesters oysters
paling eel
sardienen sardines
schelvis haddock
schol plaice
tong sole
zalm salmon

MEATS (*VLEES*)
bief beef
biefstuk steak
eend duck
fricandeau roast pork
gans goose
gehakt minced meat
haasbiefstuk filet steak
ham ham
kalfsvlees veal
kalkoen turkey
kip chicken
konijn rabbit
koude schotel cold cuts
lamscotelet lamb chops
lamsvlees lamb
lever liver
ragout beef stew
rookvlees smoked meat
runder beef
spek bacon
worst sausage

VEGETABLES/SALADS (*GROENTEN/SLA*)
aardappelen potatoes
asperges asparagus
augurken pickles
bieten beets
bloemkool cauliflower
bonen beans
champignons mushrooms
erwten peas
groenten vegetables
knoflook garlic
komkommer cucumber
komkommersla cucumber salad
kool cabbage
patates frites french fries

prei leek
prinsesseboonen green beans
purée mashed potatoes
radijsen radishes
rapen turnips
rijst rice
sla lettuce, salad
spinazie spinach
tomaten tomatoes
uien onions
wortelen carrots
zuurkool sauerkraut

DESSERTS (*NAGERECHTEN*)

appelgebak apple pie
appelmoes appelpuree
cake cake
compôte stewed fruits
gebak pastry
ijs ice cream
jonge kaas young cheese (mild)
koekjes cookies
oliebollen doughnuts
oude kaas old cheese (strong)
room cream
slagroom whipped cream
smeerkaas cheese spread
speculaas spiced cookies

FRUITS (*VRUCHTEN*)

aapel apple
aardbei strawberry
ananas pineapple
citroen lemon

druiven grapes
framboos raspberry
kersen cherries
peer pear
perzik peach
pruimen plums

BEVERAGES (*DRANKEN*)

bier (or pils) beer
cognac brandy
fles bottle
glas glass
jenever gin
koffie coffee
melk milk
rode wijn red wine
thee tea
water water
　mineral water spa
witte wijn white wine

COOKING TERMS

gebakken fried
gebraden roast
gegrild grilled
gekookt boiled/cooked
gerookt smoked
geroosteerd boiled
gestoofd stewed
goed doorgebakken well done
half doorgebakken rare
koud cold
niet doorgebakken rare
warm hot

Index

See also Accommodations and Restaurant indexes, below.

Wickedly honest guides for sophisticated travelers—and those who want to be.

Irreverent Guide to Amsterdam
Irreverent Guide to Boston
Irreverent Guide to Chicago
Irreverent Guide to Las Vegas
Irreverent Guide to London
Irreverent Guide to Los Angeles
Irreverent Guide to Manhattan
Irreverent Guide to New Orleans
Irreverent Guide to Paris
Irreverent Guide to Rome
Irreverent Guide to San Francisco
Irreverent Guide to Seattle & Portland
Irreverent Guide to Vancouver
Irreverent Guide to Walt Disney World®
Irreverent Guide to Washington, D.C.

Available at bookstores everywhere.

Frommer's
Portable Guides
Complete Guides for the
Short-Term Traveler

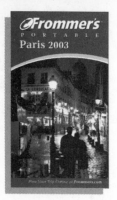

Portable Acapulco, Ixtapa & Zihuatanejo
Portable Amsterdam
Portable Aruba
Portable Australia's Great Barrier Reef
Portable Bahamas
Portable Berlin
Portable Big Island of Hawaii
Portable Boston
Portable California Wine Country
Portable Cancún
Portable Charleston & Savannah
Portable Chicago
Portable Disneyland®
Portable Dublin
Portable Florence
Portable Frankfurt
Portable Hong Kong
Portable Houston
Portable Las Vegas
Portable London
Portable Los Angeles
Portable Los Cabos & Baja

Portable Maine Coast
Portable Maui
Portable Miami
Portable New Orleans
Portable New York City
Portable Paris
Portable Phoenix & Scottsdale
Portable Portland
Portable Puerto Rico
Portable Puerto Vallarta, Manzanillo &
    Guadalajara
Portable Rio de Janeiro
Portable San Diego
Portable San Francisco
Portable Seattle
Portable Sydney
Portable Tampa & St. Petersburg
Portable Vancouver
Portable Venice
Portable Virgin Islands
Portable Washington, D.C.

Available at bookstores everywhere.

FROMMER'S® COMPLETE TRAVEL GUIDES

Alaska
Alaska Cruises & Ports of Call
Amsterdam
Argentina & Chile
Arizona
Atlanta
Australia
Austria
Bahamas
Barcelona, Madrid & Seville
Beijing
Belgium, Holland & Luxembourg
Bermuda
Boston
Brazil
British Columbia & the Canadian Rockies
Budapest & the Best of Hungary
California
Canada
Cancún, Cozumel & the Yucatán
Cape Cod, Nantucket & Martha's Vineyard
Caribbean
Caribbean Cruises & Ports of Call
Caribbean Ports of Call
Carolinas & Georgia
Chicago
China
Colorado
Costa Rica
Denmark
Denver, Boulder & Colorado Springs
England
Europe
European Cruises & Ports of Call
Florida

France
Germany
Great Britain
Greece
Greek Islands
Hawaii
Hong Kong
Honolulu, Waikiki & Oahu
Ireland
Israel
Italy
Jamaica
Japan
Las Vegas
London
Los Angeles
Maryland & Delaware
Maui
Mexico
Montana & Wyoming
Montréal & Québec City
Munich & the Bavarian Alps
Nashville & Memphis
Nepal
New England
New Mexico
New Orleans
New York City
New Zealand
Northern Italy
Nova Scotia, New Brunswick & Prince Edward Island
Oregon
Paris
Philadelphia & the Amish Country
Portugal
Prague & the Best of the Czech Republic

Provence & the Riviera
Puerto Rico
Rome
San Antonio & Austin
San Diego
San Francisco
Santa Fe, Taos & Albuquerque
Scandinavia
Scotland
Seattle & Portland
Shanghai
Singapore & Malaysia
South Africa
South America
South Florida
South Pacific
Southeast Asia
Spain
Sweden
Switzerland
Texas
Thailand
Tokyo
Toronto
Tuscany & Umbria
USA
Utah
Vancouver & Victoria
Vermont, New Hampshire & Maine
Vienna & the Danube Valley
Virgin Islands
Virginia
Walt Disney World® & Orlando
Washington, D.C.
Washington State

FROMMER'S® DOLLAR-A-DAY GUIDES

Australia from $50 a Day
California from $70 a Day
Caribbean from $70 a Day
England from $75 a Day
Europe from $70 a Day

Florida from $70 a Day
Hawaii from $80 a Day
Ireland from $60 a Day
Italy from $70 a Day
London from $85 a Day

New York from $90 a Day
Paris from $80 a Day
San Francisco from $70 a Day
Washington, D.C. from $80 a Day

FROMMER'S® PORTABLE GUIDES

Acapulco, Ixtapa & Zihuatanejo
Amsterdam
Aruba
Australia's Great Barrier Reef
Bahamas
Berlin
Big Island of Hawaii
Boston
California Wine Country
Cancún
Charleston & Savannah
Chicago
Disneyland®
Dublin
Florence

Frankfurt
Hong Kong
Houston
Las Vegas
London
Los Angeles
Los Cabos & Baja
Maine Coast
Maui
Miami
New Orleans
New York City
Paris
Phoenix & Scottsdale

Portland
Puerto Rico
Puerto Vallarta, Manzanillo & Guadalajara
Rio de Janeiro
San Diego
San Francisco
Seattle
Sydney
Tampa & St. Petersburg
Vancouver
Venice
Virgin Islands
Washington, D.C.

FROMMER'S® NATIONAL PARK GUIDES

Banff & Jasper
Family Vacations in the National Parks
Grand Canyon

National Parks of the American West
Rocky Mountain

Yellowstone & Grand Teton
Yosemite & Sequoia/ Kings Canyon
Zion & Bryce Canyon

FROMMER'S® MEMORABLE WALKS

Chicago
London

New York
Paris

San Francisco
Washington, D.C.

FROMMER'S® GREAT OUTDOOR GUIDES

Arizona & New Mexico
New England

Northern California
Southern New England

Vermont & New Hampshire

SUZY GERSHMAN'S BORN TO SHOP GUIDES

Born to Shop: France
Born to Shop: Hong Kong,
  Shanghai & Beijing

Born to Shop: Italy
Born to Shop: London

Born to Shop: New York
Born to Shop: Paris

FROMMER'S® IRREVERENT GUIDES

Amsterdam
Boston
Chicago
Las Vegas
London

Los Angeles
Manhattan
New Orleans
Paris
Rome

San Francisco
Seattle & Portland
Vancouver
Walt Disney World®
Washington, D.C.

FROMMER'S® BEST-LOVED DRIVING TOURS

Britain
California
Florida
France

Germany
Ireland
Italy
New England

Northern Italy
Scotland
Spain
Tuscany & Umbria

HANGING OUT™ GUIDES

Hanging Out in England
Hanging Out in Europe

Hanging Out in France
Hanging Out in Ireland

Hanging Out in Italy
Hanging Out in Spain

THE UNOFFICIAL GUIDES®

Bed & Breakfasts and Country
  Inns in:
  California
  Great Lakes States
  Mid-Atlantic
  New England
  Northwest
  Rockies
  Southeast
  Southwest
Best RV & Tent Campgrounds in:
  California & the West
  Florida & the Southeast
  Great Lakes States
  Mid-Atlantic
  Northeast
  Northwest & Central Plains

  Southwest & South Central
    Plains
    U.S.A.
  Beyond Disney
  Branson, Missouri
  California with Kids
  Chicago
  Cruises
  Disneyland®
  Florida with Kids
  Golf Vacations in the Eastern U.S.
  Great Smoky & Blue Ridge Region
  Inside Disney
  Hawaii
  Las Vegas
  London

Mid-Atlantic with Kids
Mini Las Vegas
Mini-Mickey
New England and New York with
  Kids
New Orleans
New York City
Paris
San Francisco
Skiing in the West
Southeast with Kids
Walt Disney World®
Walt Disney World® for Grown-ups
Walt Disney World® with Kids
Washington, D.C.
World's Best Diving Vacations

SPECIAL-INTEREST TITLES

Frommer's Adventure Guide to Australia &
  New Zealand
Frommer's Adventure Guide to Central America
Frommer's Adventure Guide to India & Pakistan
Frommer's Adventure Guide to South America
Frommer's Adventure Guide to Southeast Asia
Frommer's Adventure Guide to Southern Africa
Frommer's Britain's Best Bed & Breakfasts and
  Country Inns
Frommer's Caribbean Hideaways
Frommer's Exploring America by RV
Frommer's Fly Safe, Fly Smart
Frommer's France's Best Bed & Breakfasts and
  Country Inns
Frommer's Gay & Lesbian Europe

Frommer's Italy's Best Bed & Breakfasts and
  Country Inns
Frommer's New York City with Kids
Frommer's Ottawa with Kids
Frommer's Road Atlas Britain
Frommer's Road Atlas Europe
Frommer's Road Atlas France
Frommer's Toronto with Kids
Frommer's Vancouver with Kids
Frommer's Washington, D.C., with Kids
Israel Past & Present
The New York Times' Guide to Unforgettable
  Weekends
Places Rated Almanac
Retirement Places Rated

America Online Keyword: Travel
Booked seat 6A, open return.
Rented red 4-wheel drive.
Reserved cabin, no running water.
Discovered space.

You Need A Vacation.

700 Airlines, 50,000 Hotels, 50 Rental Car Companies, And A Million Ways To Save Money.

Travelocity.com
A Sabre Company
Go Virtually Anywhere.